Maritime Networks

Maritime transport is one of the most ancient supports to human interactions across history and it still supports more than 90 per cent of world trade volumes today. The changing connectivity of maritime networks is of crucial importance to port, transport, and economic development and planning. The way ports, terminals, but also cities, regions, and countries, are connected with each other through maritime flows is not well-known and difficult to represent and measure, even for the transport actors themselves. There is a strong, urgent need for reviewing the relevant theories, concepts, methods, and sources that can be mobilized for the analysis of maritime networks.

With contributions from reputable scholars from all over the world, this book investigates the analysis of maritime flows and networks from diverse disciplinary angles going across archaeology, history, geography, regional science, economics, mathematics, physics, and computer sciences. Based on a vast array of methods, such as Geographical Information Systems (GIS), spatial analysis, complex networks, modelling, and simulation, it addresses several crucial issues related with port hierarchy; route density; modal interdependency; network robustness and vulnerability; traffic concentration and seasonality; technological change and urban/regional economic development. This book examines new evidence about how socio-economic trends are reflected (but also influenced) by maritime flows and networks, and about the way this knowledge can support and enhance decision-making in relation to the development of ports, supply chains, and transport networks in general.

This book is an ideal companion to anyone interested in the network analysis of transport systems and economic systems in general, as well as the effective ways to analyse large datasets to answer complex issues in transportation and socio-economic development.

César Ducruet is research fellow at the French National Centre for Scientific Research (CNRS) in Paris, France.

Routledge Studies in Transport Analysis

Maritime Networks

Spatial structures and time dynamics

Edited by César Ducruet

Routledge
Taylor & Francis Group

LONDON AND NEW YORK

European Research Council
Established by the European Commission

First published 2016
by Routledge
2 Park Square, Milton Park, Abingdon, Oxon OX14 4RN

by Routledge
711 Third Avenue, New York, NY 10017

First issued in paperback 2018

Routledge is an imprint of the Taylor & Francis Group, an informa business

British Library Cataloguing in Publication Data
A catalogue record for this book is available from the British Library

Library of Congress Cataloging in Publication Data
   Maritime networks : spatial structures and time dynamics /
   edited by César Ducruet.
   1. Shipping. 2. Harbors. 3. Trade routes. I. Ducruet, César, editor.
   HE571.M3685 2015
   387.5–dc23   2015016244

ISBN 13: 978-1-138-59930-7 (pbk)
ISBN 13: 978-1-138-91125-3 (hbk)

Typeset in Times New Roman
by Sunrise Setting Ltd, Paignton, UK

To Léonard, Hong, Sophie, Michel, and Diane.

Contents

Figures

Tables

Notes on contributors

César Ducruet is Research Fellow at the French National Centre for Scientific Research (CNRS), Paris, France.

Kamel Ait-Mohand is post-doctoral Research Fellow at the French National Centre for Scientific Research (CNRS), Paris, France.

Erwan Alincourt works on maritime-related issues for the French Navy.

Marc Barthelemy is a former student of the Ecole Normale Superieure of Paris and is currently working on various aspects of the emerging science of cities.

Charles Bouveyron is Professor of Statistics and head of Department of Statistics at Université Paris Descartes, Paris, France.

Anne Bretagnolle is Professor of Geography at University Paris 1 Panthéon-Sorbonne, France.

Marie-Anne Coche has been working as research engineer in 2014 for data collection in the ERC World Seastems project team.

Sylvain Cuyala is post-doctoral Research Fellow at the French National Centre for Scientific Research (CNRS), Paris, France.

Thomas Devogele is a Professor in Computer Science at University Francois Rabelais since 2010 in Tours, France.

Laura Didier is Research Engineer at the French National Centre for Scientific Research (CNRS), Paris, France.

Ali El Hosni obtained his bachelor and master's degrees from the Transport, Logistics, Territory, Environment (TLTE) department of the Université Paris 4 Sorbonne, France. Since 2015 he is in charge of urban and maritime data collection and computing in the ERC World Seastems project team.

Laurent Etienne is an Assistant Professor at Université Francois Rabelais, Tours, France.

Tim Evans is Senior Lecturer in Theoretical Physics at the Physics Department and the Centre for Complexity and Networks at Imperial College London, UK.

Mélanie Fournier is Researcher at Dalhousie University, Canada.

Antoine Frémont is Director of Research at the IFSTTAR, the French Institute of Science and Technology for Transport, Development And Networks, Paris, France.

Michael T. Gastner is a Marie Curie Research Fellow in the Complex Systems research group at the Hungarian Academy of Sciences in Budapest, Hungary.

Claude Grasland is full Professor of Human Geography at Université Paris Diderot – Sorbonne Paris Cités, France.

David Guerrero is Researcher at the freight studies team (Ame-Splott) at the French Institute of Science and Technology for Transport, Development and Networks, Ifsttar, France.

Frédéric Guinand received his MSc degree in Computer Science in 1991, and PhD degree in Computer Science in 1995, both from the Grenoble Institute of Technology, France. From 2009 to 2015 he headed the post-graduate programme in computer science and mathematics of Le Havre University.

Ronald A. Halim is a PhD researcher of the transport and logistics group at Delft University of Technology (DUT), the Netherlands.

Sébastien Haule is Research Engineer at the French National Centre for Scientific Research (CNRS), Paris, France.

Hidekazu Itoh is Professor of Marketing with the School of Business Administration, and Adjunct Professor of Technology Management, Institute of Business and Accounting (IBA), Professional Graduate School, Kwansei Gakuin University, Japan.

Carl Knappett teaches in the Department of Art at the University of Toronto, Canada, where he holds the Walter Graham/Homer Thompson Chair in Aegean Prehistory.

Zuzanna Kosowska-Stamirowska is PhD student at the Université Paris 1 Panthéon-Sorbonne and affiliated with the UMR 8504 Géographie-cités and the French National Centre for Scientific Research (CNRS), France.

Jan H. Kwakkel is Assistant Professor at the Delft University of Technology, the Netherlands.

Pierre Latouche is Associate Professor in Applied Mathematics at the SAMM laboratory at Université Paris 1 Pantheon-Sorbonne, France.

Serge Lhomme is Assistant Professor at the University of Paris Est Créteil and Lab'URBA, France.

Igor Lugo is Research Professor at the Centro Regional de Investigaciones Multidisciplinarias-UNAM in Mexico since 2012 where he focuses on systems of cities and transportation networks.

Nora Mareï obtained her PhD from the University of Nantes, where she carried out her thesis under the direction of Pr. Jacque Guillaume in the Laboratory Géolittomer (UMR 6554 LETG).

Bruno Marnot is Professor in Late Modern History at the University of La Rochelle, France, and member of the Center for Research in International and Atlantic History. His works deal with the economic history of trading ports in the nineteenth and twentieth centuries.

Silvia Marzagalli is full-time Professor for Early Modern History at the University of Nice, and senior member of the Institut Universitaire de France.

Theo Notteboom is a Professor and High-End Foreign Expert at Dalian Maritime University in China, a part-time Professor at University of Antwerp and the Antwerp Maritime Academy in Belgium and a visiting Professor in Shanghai, Singapore and Chongqing.

Yoann Pigné is Assistant Professor of Computer Science at the University of Le Havre, France.

Peter J. Rimmer AM is an Emeritus Professor in the School of History, Culture and Language, ANU College of Asia & the Pacific, Australian National University, Canberra, Australia.

Ray Rivers is Emeritus Professor and Distinguished Research Fellow at Imperial College London, UK.

Ross Robinson is Professorial Research Fellow at the Institute for Supply Chain and Logistics, Victoria University, Melbourne, Australia.

Lóránt A. Tavasszy is Principal Scientist at the research institute TNO in Delft and Professor in Freight and Logistics at the Delft University of Technology, the Netherlands.

Liehui Wang is associate professor at the Center for Modern Chinese City Studies, East China Normal University, Shanghai, China. He obtained his PhD in historical geography from Fudan University in 2008. He is interested in port geography. He was visiting scholar at the Institute Transport and Maritime Management Antwerp (ITMMA), University of Antwerp, Belgium.

Lei Yang is lecturer at the College of History and Social Development, Shandong Normal University, Jinnan, China.

Rawya Zreik is a PhD student in Statistics at the universities Paris 1 and Paris 5, under the supervision of C. Bouveyron and P. Latouche.

Foreword

Over 50 years ago scholars were preoccupied with matching the internal workings of ports with phases in James Bird's (1963) 'Anyport' model first presented at the Liverpool meeting of the Institute of British Geographers in 1962. Consequently the model of transport development in underdeveloped countries postulated by Edward Taaffe, Richard Morrill and Peter Gould (1963) provided a welcome alternative to those researchers seeking a wider perspective. But the model was deficient in one significant respect: this prototypical representation was concerned primarily with the development of land communications and its influence on settlement. The study neglected the impact on settlement patterns stemming from the nuanced and contingent process of maritime flows and networks over time.

Attempts to remedy this deficiency over the ensuing five decades have proceeded apace with an array of empirical studies aided by an explosion in computer capacity, employment of more refined analytical techniques to undertake dynamic network analyses and, albeit at a cost, the greater availability of data for digitization. This current volume provides an exhaustive analysis of past and contemporary maritime flows and networks featuring evocative graphical representations, as well as supplying an invaluable springboard for undertaking further research into cognate areas.

A comprehensive overview provides an important multidisciplinary outline of past studies of maritime flows and networks in a bid not only to highlight the contributions of economists and econometricians, but also those of geographers, historians and political scientists. Not to be forgotten is the seminal work on emphasizing continuities in the Mediterranean and the rise of the Hanseatic port/urban networks in Northern Europe written by Henri Pirenne (1862–1935) during his First World War internment and published posthumously by his son Jacques Pirenne (1936); his great successor was Fernand Braudel (1949).

The four parts that follow are seen collectively as a much-needed contribution towards securing maritime studies a more highly regarded place within the multidisciplinary transport arena. They involve moving away from the substantial literature privileging the port city category, which Howard Dick (2002/03: 416) argues lack substance, and harnessing explorations of maritime flows to theoretical models.

The first part provides an introduction to analysing maritime flows and networks. Not only does it offer a historical framework linking maritime flows and networks to the evolution of city systems over the past seven centuries, but also injects the often overlooked organizational ingredient into the mix through an analysis of a leading shipping company's changing network over time. Then it critically reviews the notion of what constitutes a spatial network and the array of tools available to characterize its structural features.

Then the second part provides a significant input into modelling the dynamic evolution of past maritime networks from the oar and sail that characterized the proto-globalization age through Carola Hein's (2013) eras of steam, petroleum and containerization strongly linked to distinctive phases in the evolution of the capitalist system. This dredging of the past beyond the pioneering work of the coterie of maritime historians has involved data mining of hitherto untapped material on flows from searches of company histories, and shipping lists and registers. Now the quantitative material is being distilled using optical character recognition and geographical information system platforms in ingenious ways to visualize the development of maritime networks over time in order to offer an important counterpoint to classic historical studies exemplified by Anthony Reid (1993 [1988]) and Leonard Blussé (2013) in Southeast Asia.

A third part demonstrates the important progress made in expanding and sharpening the array of tools available for undertaking the spatial analysis of voluminous amounts of data derived from monitoring ship trajectories and maritime traffic. Explorations of daily shipping movements, real time positioning data, clusters, and scale-free and small-world networks have been variously and sensitively distilled under different scenarios to identify recurring patterns in liner shipping, unique shipping behaviour, port node specialization, network vulnerability, the significance of direct port calls and shifts in the port hierarchy in response to technological change.

The final part brings us full circle to make the link between maritime networks and regional socio-economic development that was deficient in the original graphic model of transport development in undeveloped countries outlined over fifty years ago. This study has remedied the situation by connecting the global and the local spheres explored by Matthew Heins (2013) through investigations of the links between maritime and land transport. Simulation, econometric methods and gravity models, network analysis and geographical information systems, singly or in combination, have been used to quantitatively assess links between maritime networks, trade and economic development, maritime regionalization within a global context, and the diverging relationship between port and urban systems over time.

Looking ahead from this benchmark volume in analysing maritime flows and networks the next challenge is to complement this focus on sea–land transport and regional development by incorporating air transport and telecommunications into the nexus. The ultimate goal is to be able to analyse the network of networks – sea–land, air and telecommunications – in an all-encompassing study of logistics systems to address the vulnerability of gateways serving multimodal corridors.

Peter J. Rimmer
Australian National University

References

Bird J. H., 1963. *The Major Seaports of the United Kingdom*. London: Hutchison.

Blussé L. 2013. 'Port cities of South East Asia: 1400–1800', in Peter Clark (ed.) *The Oxford Handbook of Cities in World History*. Oxford: Oxford University Press, pp. 345–63.

Braudel, F. 1949. *La Méditerranée et le monde méditerranéen à l'époque de Philippe II*. Paris: Armand Colin. Translated by Sian Reynolds as *The Mediterranean and the Mediterranean World in the Age of Philip II* (2 vols). London: William Collins & Sons/New York: Harper & Row, 1972 and 1973.

Dick, Howard, W. 2002. *Surabaya, City of Work: A Socioeconomic History, 1900–2000*. Athens: Ohio University Press/Singapore: Singapore University Press.

Hein, C. 2013. 'Port cities', in Peter Clark (ed.) *The Oxford Handbook of Cities in World History*. Oxford: Oxford University Press, pp. 808–27.

Heins, Matthew W. 2013. The shipping container and the globalization of American infrastructure. Unpublished PhD dissertation submitted in Architecture at the University of Michigan. Available online at http://deepblue.lib.umich.edu/bitstream/handle/2027.42/102480/mheins_1.pdf?sequence=1 [accessed 14 April 2015].

Pirenne, Henri and Pirenne, Jacques. (1936). *Histoire de l'Europe au XVIe siècle*. Paris: F. Alcan/ Bruxelles, Nouvelle Société d'éditions. Translated by Bernard Miall as *History of Europe: From the End of the Roman World in the West to the Beginnings of the Western States* (2 vols). London: Allen & Unwin, 1939.

Reid, Anthony, (1993 [1988]). *Southeast Asia in the Age of Commerce, 1450–1680*, (2 vols). New Haven: Yale University Press.

Taaffe, E. J., Morrill, R. L. and Gould, P. R. 1963. 'Transport expansion in underdeveloped countries: a comparative analysis', *Geographical Review*, 53: 503–29.

Acknowledgments

The editor would like to acknowledge funding from the European Research Council under the European Union's Seventh Framework Programme (FP/2007-2013)/ERC Grant Agreement n. [313847] 'World Seastems'.

Part I

Introduction to maritime network analysis

1 Maritime flows and networks in a multidisciplinary perspective

César Ducruet

It is almost inevitable when introducing a book about maritime networks to recall that more than 90 percent of world trade volumes are still supported by maritime transport. Seas and oceans occupy about 70 percent of the Earth's surface and coastal areas concentrated 16 and 39 percent of the world's total and urban populations respectively in the 1990s (Noin, 1999). This overwhelming importance is reflected by the great quantity of cultural, social, political, and scientific research about the sea in all its aspects. Dedicated sub-disciplines such as maritime history, geography, engineering, biology, and economics as well as institutions organize large-scale meetings to discuss the organization and evolution of the sea as an ecosystem, a natural resource, and a vector of exchanges.

But what remains striking is that maritime transport has been much less studied than any other transport mode, especially from a network perspective. Existing research remains rather fragmented and scattered across the academic spectrum, which makes it difficult to review it exhaustively and to define any possible common framework. Five main reasons contribute to explaining such a fact: the dominance of a continental culture favouring studies of populated rather than "empty" spaces (Steinberg, 1999; Lewis and Wigen, 1999); the vague geographic distribution and morphology of maritime flows due to the absence of a track infrastructure (White and Senior, 1983; Rodrigue *et al.*, 2013); the capture of most passenger and information flows by air transport and telecommunications since the second half of the twentieth century; the continuous decline of maritime transport costs compared with other logistics costs; and the reluctance of scholars and experts to access and compile costly and hard to obtain maritime traffic statistics.

The World Seastems project No. 313847, funded by the European Research Council (ERC) over the period 2013–18, is aimed primarily at compiling and analysing untapped historical records of global vessel movements over the contemporary period. Its international workshop held in June 2014 at the Paris Institute for Complex Systems (ISC-PIF), gathered many researchers with a similar focus, namely to provide a quantitative analysis of maritime networks in space and time. In so doing, the 20 chapters of the present book, written by 40 scholars from 12 countries and 10 academic backgrounds, offer a multidisciplinary perspective about one of the most vital pillars of world society.

The maritime network: late emergence of a multifaceted concept

A simple online search via *Science Direct* provided about 100 results for "maritime network" (as of 16 September 2014) compared with more than 10,000 results for road, global, or transport network, taking into account all scientific disciplines. Airline network scored 261, while trade, logistics, street, river, and railway ranged between 1,000 and 4,000 results each. Among maritime-related terms, "maritime network" scored less than maritime transport, trade, and traffic, shipping, port, or route, whereas "maritime transport" scored far below "road network," thereby illustrating the paramount importance of roads for daily commuting and trucking. Such a situation echoes the work of Danisch *et al.* (2014) who in their analysis of word co-occurrences found that "global shipping network" occupied a peculiar, peripheral situation with regard to the graph theory community. As a matter of fact, many scholarly works using the term maritime (or shipping) network make no reference to graph theory per se, in contrast to road, railway, air, and even river transport where network analysis had become a very common approach since the 1960s in the social sciences (Ducruet and Lugo, 2013).

As pointed out by Lemarchand (2000: 1–2), "the literature on networks ignores maritime places [while] port and maritime actors do not refer much to the concept of network." If the network traditionally describes technical systems made of material infrastructure, maritime routes exist on the map only so that the maritime network remains rather abstract, invisible, and decentralized, especially at the national scale where only a fragment of the network is perceived. The maritime network may refer to various realities according to different disciplines, such as trading linkages by sea organized by merchants in maritime history (Gipouloux, 2011; Tartaron, 2013), tactical or wireless communication networks between vessels in engineering, inter-firm alliances in maritime economics (Caschili *et al.*, 2014), distribution of ocean carriers' schedules, and physical flows of vessels between ports. With reference to the European Motorways of the Sea initiative, Baird (2010) even proposed to treat the floating deck of vessels just like road and rail infrastructure to favour integrated policies. In geography for instance, the maritime network had long been termed "system" (Bird, 1984: 26): "the ultimate system of maritime transportation is a true freedom of the seas whereby every port node can theoretically be linked to every other port node" (see also Slack, 1993).

The concept of "port system," suggesting linkages between ports was found in many works, but "in their preoccupation with the development of land communications (...) the authors neglected the development of maritime space" (Rimmer, 2007: 76). In addition, the port system concept was used interchangeably to describe multiple realities such as port (or maritime) range, region, façade, or seaboard, and mostly at the national scale, leading to confusion. The phased model of port system evolution proposed by Rimmer (1967) initially incorporated maritime linkages contrary to earlier models (see Figure 1.1), but without concrete empirical validation as subsequent works continued focusing on individual port traffics and port hinterlands. The classic distinction between a French school focusing on forelands and a Dutch school more interested in

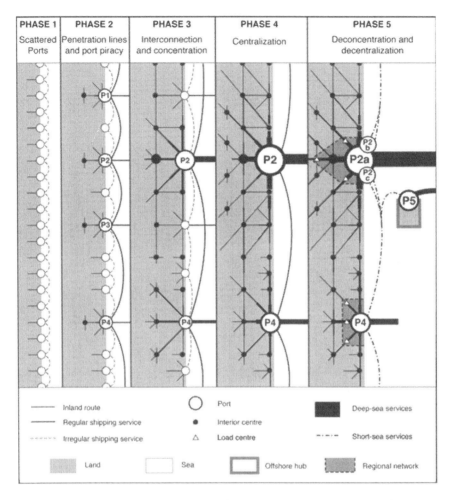

Figure 1.1 Spatial model of the evolution of a port system including maritime linkages.
Source: Rimmer (2007).

hinterlands (Weigend, 1956) led to distinct research pathways. For instance, the "port network" concept was proposed by Van Klink (1998) to describe the inland shift of port activities, but the same concept used in another context could also refer to a set of ports belonging to the portfolio of a given ocean carrier or terminal operator. When it comes to forelands, the French geographer André Vigarié (1979) proposed the concept of "port triptych" to think simultaneously the port itself, the hinterland (inland market area), and the foreland (overseas markets). Yet, out of 399 scientific articles published in major geography journals between 1950 and 2012, only seven mentioned foreland in their title, against 29 for hinterland; 12 mentioned "network" of which only five for maritime networks and seven for barge, hinterland, and other networks (Ng and Ducruet, 2014). Other concepts such as transport chain, logistics chain, commodity chain, and value chain became frequent to describe ports' place in networks with a qualitative approach (see Robinson, 2002).

The emergence of a dedicated network vocabulary for describing maritime patterns and traffic came long after using more imaginary semantics. The French geographers René Perpillou (1959) and André Vigarié (1968), for instance, mentioned the constellation of ports and compared sea lanes to urban streets delivering flows of life in a city like arteries in a biological organism, respectively. Other concepts taken from other fields were gradually applied to maritime transport, such as corridor, loop, cycle, and hub. Graph-related concepts such as centrality and intermediacy were used about ports (Fleming and Hayuth, 1994) alongside studies of site and situation, carrier choice and selection factors, and port competition to explain the emergence of hubs at certain locations, but without yet applying network analysis to maritime flows, so that "a connectivity index is used for airports (...) but does not exist for seaports" (de Langen *et al.*, 2007: 31). This deficit became a growing issue, especially given that "the structure of [maritime] networks evolves over time [and therefore] the position of ports as nodes in the network also changes over time (...) understanding these changes is crucial for analysing the competitive position and growth prospects of (...) ports" (de Langen *et al.*, 2002: 1). The conceptualization of maritime transport as a network gave birth to many discussions that did not necessarily lead to empirical analyses of actual maritime flows, such as about security issues (Kristiansen, 2004; Angeloudis *et al.*, 2007) or operations research on navigation safety, ship routing and scheduling, and optimization (Christiansen *et al.*, 2013; Windeck, 2013). Maritime economics barely refers to either graphs or networks in its central focus on management, pricing, markets, and finance, which is also true of wider transport economics (Zwier *et al.*, 1994; Brooks *et al.*, 2002; Leggate *et al.*, 2004; Stopford, 2008).

The diversity of maritime data analyses

Before analysing maritime transport as a network, graphical representations of maritime flows long remained broad estimates of amount and geographic distribution (Scarborough, 1908; Siegfried, 1943; Alexandersson and Norström, 1963; Central Intelligence Agency, 1973). Still in 2014, a geophysics paper reported "a lack of knowledge in the actual global distribution of the ships, i.e. vessel density, and its evolution over time due to economics or other causes" (Tournadre, 2014). This situation was already deplored in the 1940s when early economic geographers such as Ullman (1949) provided an innovative cartography of maritime routes connecting the United States, claiming that maritime flows were useful to "take the pulse of world trade and movement" (see also Figure 1.2). Such a call did not, however, have many followers. Foreign trade statistics served to analyze overseas connections or maritime forelands of single ports such as Toronto (Kerr and Spelt, 1956), Genoa (Rodgers, 1958), Hobart (Solomon, 1963), Victoria

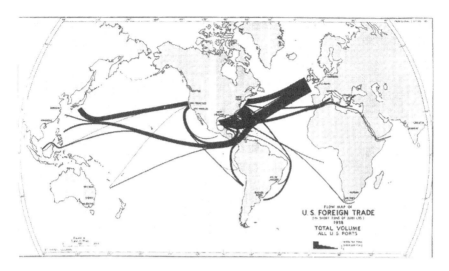

Figure 1.2 A cartography of US maritime trade, 1938.
Source: Ullman (1949).

(Britton, 1965), Clyde (De Sbarats, 1971), Halifax and Saint John (Patton, 1961), Irish Sea ports (Andrews, 1955), and ports in the countries of Norway (Sommers, 1960), England (Bird, 1969; Von Schirach-Szmigiel, 1973), and Sweden (Von Schirach-Szmigiel, 1978). Such studies grew scarce until a recent revival based on the Chinese case (Wang and Ng, 2011). Accurately calculating and representing ship traffic densities on a larger scale demanded enormous data collection and extraction from printed reports on vessel movements such as on a world square grid (McKenzie, 1975). Until the 2000s, analyses of global maritime flows were bound to diagrams and simplified maps using United Nations (van den Bremen and de Jong, 1986) or other data (Fossey and Pearson, 1983; Rodrigue, 2004). Nevertheless in the 1980s, a few works mapped the nodal hierarchy of ports based on small data samples (Marti, 1981; Marti and Krausse, 1983) using trade data to and from United States ports (see Figure 1.3).

It is only recently that scholars from various backgrounds, through interdisciplinary collaboration, have produced more elaborate representations of maritime flows on a larger scale, often from unexpected research domains. One of them is climatology, which made particular use of *log books* that reported weather conditions during ship voyages, as in the *Climatological Database for the World's Oceans* (*CLIWOC*) project for the period 1750–1850 (Herrera *et al.*, 2003), affiliated with similar projects such as ICOADS, RECLAIM, and *Old Weather* (see Figure 1.4). The same data also was used by historians to analyze technological progress in terms of sailing speed (Ronnback, 2012). The extraction of archival records provided unprecedented knowledge of transatlantic slave voyages over the period 1500–1900 (*Transatlantic Slave Voyages* project), and trade

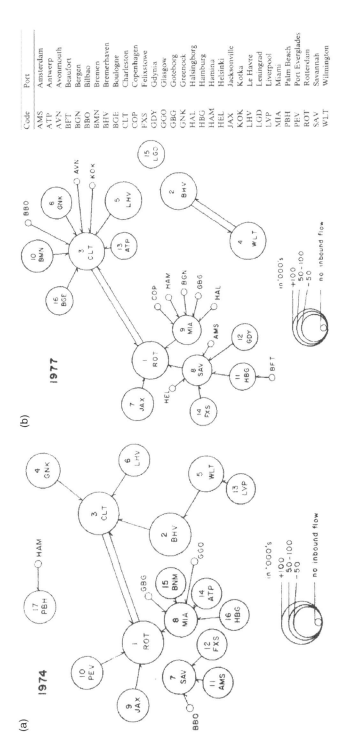

Code	Port
AMS	Amsterdam
ATP	Antwerp
AVN	Avonmouth
BFT	Beaufort
BGN	Bergen
BBO	Bilbao
BMN	Bremen
BHV	Bremerhaven
BGE	Boulogne
CLT	Charleston
COP	Copenhagen
FXS	Felixstowe
GDY	Gdynia
GGO	Glasgow
GBG	Goteborg
GNK	Greenock
HAL	Halsingborg
HBG	Hamburg
HAM	Hamina
HEL	Helsinki
JAX	Jacksonville
KOK	Kotka
LHV	Le Havre
LGD	Leningrad
LVP	Liverpool
MIA	Miami
PBH	Palm Beach
PEV	Port Everglades
ROT	Rotterdam
SAV	Savannah
WLT	Wilmington

Figure 1.3 Nodal hierarchy of US–European ports in maritime container flows, 1974 (a) and 1977 (b).

Source: Marti and Krausse (1983).

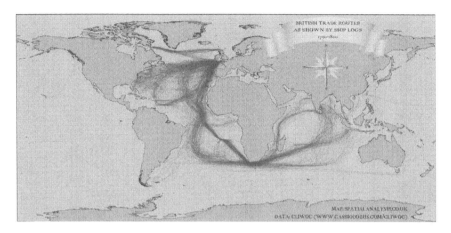

Figure 1.4 Map of British vessel flows based on log books, 1750–1800.
Source: James Cheshire (2012).

flows across the Oresund Strait for the period 1634–1857 (*Sound Toll* project).[1] In other fields such as anthropology and archaeology, the lack of knowledge on precise maritime circulations could be overcome by looking at sailing distances to explain the spread of languages in Australasia (Coupé and Hombert, 2005), demographic migrations in the Caribbean (Friedman *et al.*, 2009), the diffusion of techniques (Leidwanger, 2013), and sea–land accessibility in the Roman Mediterranean (Scheidel, 2013).

Other themes and issues included the effects of network centricity on maritime warfare based on the queuing theory (Fewell, 2003), geospatial analysis of maritime piracy (Leymarie *et al.*, 2014), modelling of optimal shipping routes to prevent collisions and oil spills (Höglund and Meier, 2012), simulation of attacks on the intermodal shipping network (Earnest *et al.*, 2012), calculation of a composite index of global urban accessibility based on raster data including maritime flows (Nelson, 2008) (see Figure 1.5), and the mapping of traffic densities based on ship detection (Tournadre, 2014), voluntary observing ships (Vettor and Guedes Soares, 2014), and Automated Identification Systems (AIS) (Le Guyader *et al.*, 2011). Measuring the environmental impacts of shipping also provided among the most detailed and aesthetically advanced maps of global maritime flows, focusing on ship emissions (Eyring *et al.*, 2010; Halpern *et al.*, 2008; Leonardi and Browne, 2010). Specific commodity flows in relation to United States ports using MARAD data were mapped also using Geographical Information Systems (GIS) methods combined with Google Earth 3D visualizations (Shen *et al.*, 2013) (see Figure 1.6). In maritime geography, scholars proposed mapping the service networks of ocean carriers based on schedule data (Robinson, 1998; Comtois and Wang, 2003; Frémont and Soppé, 2004; Rimmer and Comtois, 2005; Frémont, 2007, 2010) but still without direct engagement in network science, although some

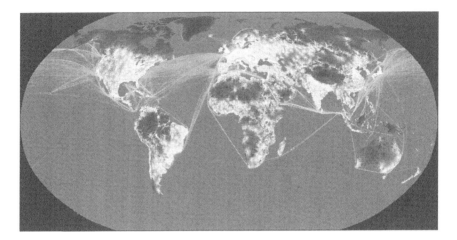

Figure 1.5 A global map of urban accessibility. Travel time to major cities (from one hour (lightest) to ten days (darkest)) and shipping lane density.

Source: Nelson (2008).

visualizations already underlined the centralization of links around certain hubs (Figure 1.7). Another example is in maritime economics where disaggregated data of shipments served to measure the effect of maritime networks, services structure, and port infrastructure variables on maritime transport costs (Martinez-Zarzoso *et al.*, 2011).

A recent surge in maritime network analysis: towards a convergence?

Maritime networks for many years did not fit well into the traditionally "planar culture" of graph theoretical approaches of the academic literature (Ducruet and Beauguitte, 2014). In the 1960s, the vast majority of network analyses focused on planar graphs (no crossing between links, or edges, without creating a node, or vertex) such as power grids, road networks, etc. The only exception was the PhD dissertation of Ross Robinson (1968), deeply rooted in graph theory, geography, and regional science, for its application to the analysis of the maritime network within Vancouver port and with other British Columbia ports (see Figure 1.8):

> it is possible to define the spatial patterns of functional relationships between ports by examining the linkages which are sustained by the inter-port shipping movements of foreign trade vessels. Such an analysis provides not only an accurate measure of the linkages themselves but also clarifies the relationships between ports, the spatial organisation of port functions and the functional status of individual ports within the total group (. . .) The system

of ports operating interdependently may now be regarded in abstract form as
a set of points or nodes in a network, a transportation network in which the
lines or links in the network are in fact 'imaginary routes'.

Robinson (1968: 95–7)

A port network development model was also proposed to depict four phases that
may apply to other regions of the world (Figure 1.8). Strangely enough, and even

(a)

(b)

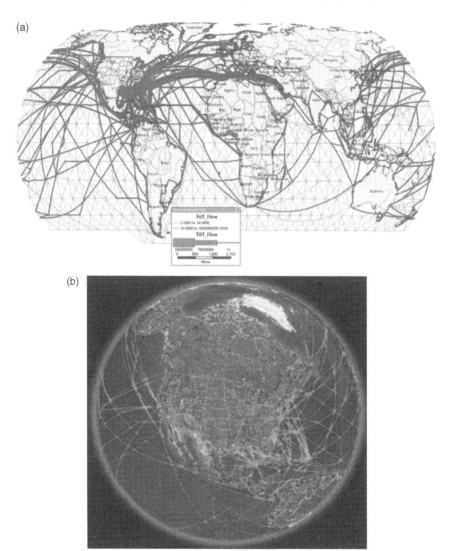

Figure 1.6 World distribution of US maritime trade in 2D and 3D, 2002.

Source: Shen *et al.* (2013).

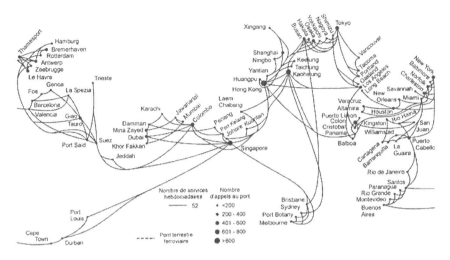

Figure 1.7 The port network of Evergreen based on schedule data, 2000.

Source: Comtois and Wang (2003).

after its partial publication in a renowned journal a few years later (Robinson, 1976), that pioneering work found no followers until the 1990s, mainly due to the wider shift from quantitative to behavioural approaches in the social sciences (Ducruet and Beauguitte, 2014; Ng and Ducruet, 2014). It was only in the 1990s that scholars began to analyze maritime flows using a dedicated network methodology, just like airline or multinational firms networks; there was another unpublished PhD dissertation, this time on the North Atlantic region based on carrier schedule data (Helmick, 1994), but with no reference to Robinson's initial breakthrough.

Starting with a simple count of vessel calls at world ports (Brocard *et al.*, 1995), and a preliminary paper on the matter (Joly, 1995), another pioneering work was the PhD dissertation of Olivier Joly (1999) who provided the first-ever network analysis of maritime container flows at the global scale, revealing the bipolar structure of the global maritime network centred upon Europe and Asia (Figure 1.9). The fast-growing field of complex networks recorded its first paper about maritime networks in 2007, which described the topological structure of container shipping networks in China (Xu *et al.*, 2007) and later on, the world (Deng *et al.*, 2009; Hu and Zhu, 2009; Doshi *et al.*, 2012); these works were based on carriers' schedules and collaborations with physicists. Most of the time such works looked at the small-world and/or scale-free network structure of container flows (see also Hu and Zong, 2013), with reference to drastically different concepts and literatures than those of scholars interested in operations research and optimization. The latter school recently provided many applications of the hub allocation model to container flows among Asian ports (Low and Tang, 2012; Asgari *et al.*, 2013; Jiang *et al.*, 2015). Research on marine bioinvasions benefitted from globally available

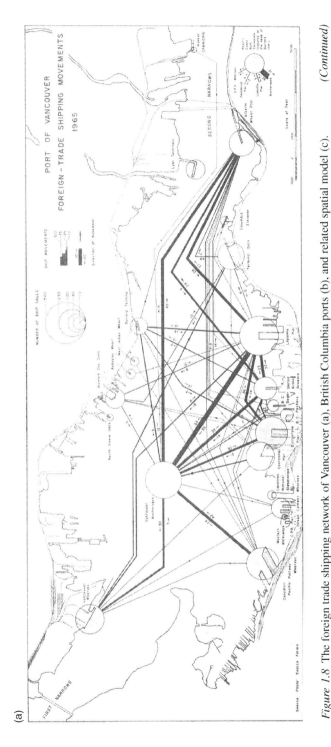

Figure 1.8 The foreign trade shipping network of Vancouver (a), British Columbia ports (b), and related spatial model (c). *(Continued)*

Source: Robinson (1968).

(b)

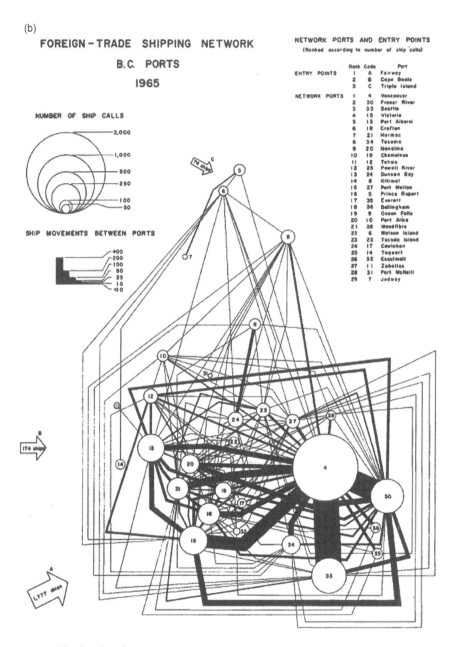

FOREIGN - TRADE SHIPPING NETWORK

B.C. PORTS

1965

NUMBER OF SHIP CALLS

SHIP MOVEMENTS BETWEEN PORTS

NETWORK PORTS AND ENTRY POINTS
(Ranked according to number of ship calls)

	Rank	Code	Port
ENTRY POINTS	1	A	Fairway
	2	B	Cape Beale
	3	C	Triple Island
NETWORK PORTS	1	4	Vancouver
	2	30	Fraser River
	3	33	Seattle
	4	15	Victoria
	5	13	Port Alberni
	6	18	Crofton
	7	21	Harmac
	8	34	Tacoma
	9	20	Nanaimo
	10	19	Chemainus
	11	12	Tahsis
	12	25	Powell River
	13	24	Duncan Bay
	14	8	Kitimat
	15	27	Port Mellon
	16	5	Prince Rupert
	17	39	Everett
	18	36	Bellingham
	19	9	Ocean Falls
	20	10	Port Alice
	21	28	Woodfibre
	22	6	Watson Island
	23	22	Tasada Island
	24	17	Cowichan
	25	14	Toquart
	26	32	Esquimalt
	27	11	Zeballos
	28	31	Port McNeill
	29	7	Jedway

Figure 1.8 (Continued)

(c)

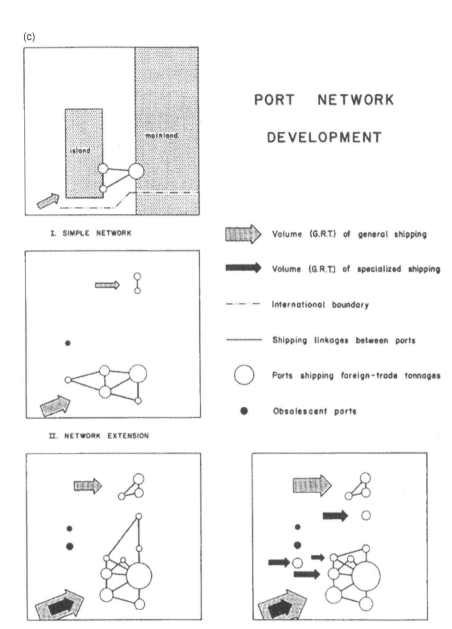

PORT NETWORK

DEVELOPMENT

I. SIMPLE NETWORK

II. NETWORK EXTENSION

III. NETWORK INTENSIFICATION

IV. NODAL CENTRALIZATION

Volume (G.R.T.) of general shipping

Volume (G.R.T.) of specialized shipping

International boundary

Shipping linkages between ports

Ports shipping foreign-trade tonnages

Obsolescent ports

Figure 1.8

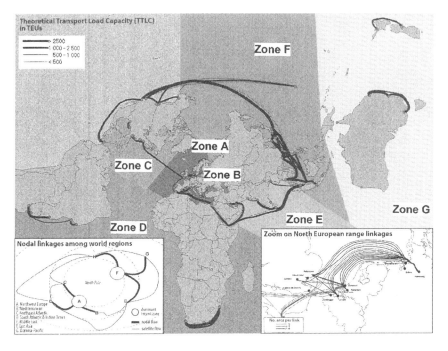

Figure 1.9 Modelling and mapping global maritime container flows on various scales, 1992.

Source: Joly (1999).

AIS data tracking the real-time position of vessels through growing collaboration between biology and physics (Kaluza *et al.*, 2010; Concepcion *et al.*, 2010; Keller *et al.*, 2011; Seebens *et al.*, 2013) (see Figure 1.10).

Geographers also provided various studies of hub-and-spokes systems in liner shipping networks at the regional level using elements of graph theory and spatial analysis, such as for the Caribbean basin (Veenstra *et al.*, 2005; McCalla, 2004), Canary Islands (Tovar*et al.*, 2015), Mediterranean basin (Cisic *et al.*, 2007), north-east Asia (Ducruet *et al.*, 2008; 2010a), and southern Africa (Fraser *et al.*, 2014). Global-level analyses also gradually became prominent about the container business to map nodal regions (Wang and Wang, 2011; Ducruet and Notteboom, 2012) and evaluate network vulnerability with reference to interoceanic canals (Ducruet, 2015), also based on multiple fleet types and the concept of multigraph or multiplex graph (Ducruet, 2013). Economists as well recently started to investigate the correlation between centrality and accessibility measures of port nodes and their broader traffic attributes (Wang and Cullinane, 2008; Lam and Yap, 2011; Li *et al.*, 2015; Xu *et al.*, 2015), such as macro-scale analyses of country pairs based on their maritime connectivity (Fugazza *et al.*, 2013). In the same vein, Ducruet *et al.* (2014a) used a multilevel analysis to show the influence of port centrality

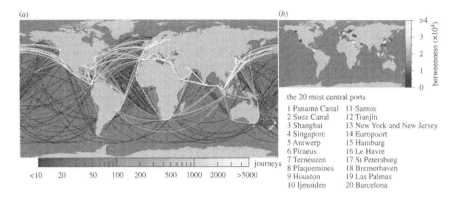

Figure 1.10 Distribution and density of world maritime flows based on AIS data, 2007.
Source: Kaluza *et al.* (2010).

on average ship turnaround times globally. In particular, degree centrality and hub position of ports (as measured by the clustering coefficient) speed up their cargo handling operations while the volume of container throughput has the opposite effect, but this is even truer in richer countries.

Another avenue of research has been to unravel the regionalism of maritime flows. A wide variety of network clustering methods has been used in various contexts, such as the Atlantic (Ducruet *et al.*, 2010b) and the world (Ducruet and Zaidi, 2012; Ducruet *et al.*, 2014b) to detect the influence of geographic proximity on the distribution of flows or the emergence of a cohesive region such as Europe. Complementary views were offered by the study of particular regions such as the Korean Peninsula (Ducruet and Roussin, 2007), the East Asian maritime corridor (Ducruet *et al.*, 2011a), the Le Havre–Hamburg range (Plasschaert *et al.*, 2011), the East–West maritime corridor (Tran and Haasis, 2014), inter-island connectivity in Greece (Tsiotas and Polyzos, 2014) and Finland (Makkonen *et al.*, 2013), and regional integration across North Africa (Mohamed-Chérif and Ducruet, 2015). Graph theoretical methods as well as social network analysis (SNA) revealed the backbone of maritime flows and emergent hub ports (Cullinane and Wang, 2012; Montes *et al.*, 2012; Gonzalez-Laxe *et al.*, 2012; Freire Seoane *et al.*, 2013; Wang and Cullinane, 2014). The global maritime network was also analyzed through its complementarity with the global airline network regarding their respective and mutual connectivities (Parshani *et al.*, 2010; Ducruet *et al.*, 2011b; Woolley-Meza *et al.*, 2011) and the spread of infectious diseases (Tatem *et al.*, 2006), and with the global road network to estimate cost effects on port and route performance (Tavasszy *et al.*, 2011; Wang *et al.*, 2012).

Perspectives and structure of the book

Although the late application of network analytical methods to maritime transport flows has been somewhat counterbalanced by a growing number of empirical studies, this book addresses several unresolved issues. First, most studies remain static, so that the dynamic properties of change in maritime network organization and spatial distribution remain unclear. Second, the majority of recent works have focused on flow patterns but without explicit reference to any theoretical model, be it spatial or statistical. Third, the maritime network is not an isolated entity floating in an abstract space or defined only by its costs or benefits. It is a component of the society we live in, and as such its analysis should consider its local and regional embedding.

This first part of the book, "Introduction to maritime network analysis," addresses the aforementioned issues in both theoretical and practical ways. Chapter 2, by Anne Bretagnolle, particularly stresses the emergence of city-systems throughout history, defined as networks of cities linked by certain transport modes, including maritime transport, although it lost its ability to move information and people in the second half of the twentieth century. Chapter 3, by Antoine Frémont, complements the previous chapter in that it concerns maritime transport actors (shipping lines) and how CMA-CGM has evolved alongside technological and managerial transformations in the container business. Chapter 4, by Marc Barthelemy, focuses on the concept of spatial network and how it is analyzed in the current transdisciplinary literature. It implicitly raises a crucial question: how can maritime networks contribute to such a fast-growing, mainstream research arena?

The second part of the book, "Modelling past maritime networks," comprises five chapters all concerned with the specific difficulties of using old data sources to map and analyze maritime networks. The lack of knowledge on actual Bronze Age maritime routes created the opportunity for Ray Rivers, Tim Evans, and Carl Knappett, to simulate the distribution of inter-island maritime links in the Aegean Sea based on archaeological records and spatial models (Chapter 5). When route data does exist, problems are all but eliminated as new ones emerge, as seen in the other contributions. This was particularly well discussed and overcome by Mélanie Fournier in the visualization experiment of Venice's maritime trade during the Middle Ages (Chapter 6); by Silvia Marzagalli when creating a new database on eighteenth-century shipping flows allowing her to map, among other things, the distribution of French seaborne trade in the world (Chapter 7); by Liehui Wang, Theo Notteboom, and Lei Yang, who show the convergence or divergence of British and Japanese maritime colonial networks in 1920s China, based on local archives (Chapter 8); and by César Ducruet, Sébastien Haule, Kamel Ait-Mohand, Bruno Marnot, Zuzanna Kosowska-Stamirowska, Laura Didier, and Marie-Anne Coche, who have extracted and mapped thousands of vessel movements from the world's biggest source of shipping information, *Lloyd's List*, to represent major shifts of maritime activity since the late nineteenth century to the present (Chapter 9).

The third part, composed of five chapters, is entitled "Topology and spatial distribution of maritime networks." These works all apply wider statistical and spatial models of networks and trajectories to massive maritime data. The analysis by Frédéric Guinand and Yoann Pigné (Chapter 10) of daily connectivity changes in the global container shipping network is a very innovative approach that sheds new light on seasonal and cyclical dynamics in liner shipping as well as on temporal graphs, a novel approach to maritime networks with huge potential to zoom in on particular events and nodes. The following chapter by Laurent Etienne, Erwan Alincourt and Thomas Devogèle (Chapter 11) provides a critical analysis of real time vessel positioning data based on radar information or AIS to identify peculiar ship behaviour within aggregated maritime trajectories, an approach which has direct implications for port and maritime security. The identification of clusters in the global maritime network by Charles Bouveyron, Pierre Latouche, Rawya Zreik, and César Ducruet (Chapter 12) allows us to better define the functional specialization of port nodes within a system of interlocked components connected by various fleet types, with cores, peripheries, and brokers. Another way to link maritime networks with mainstream network analytical research is shown by Serge Lhomme (Chapter 13) who measures the vulnerability of liner shipping networks to random or targeted failures of port nodes. This work sheds new light on the geographic dimension of network dereliction under certain attack scenarios, taking into account the weight of links and nodes as well as possible traffic shifts due to rerouting. Lastly, Michael Gastner and César Ducruet (Chapter 14) question the statistical structure of global cargo ship traffic with reference to well-known models such as scale-free and small-world networks. They also emphasize noticeable changes over time in the distribution of the port hierarchy that correspond to important technological breakthroughs in the industry.

The last part of the book, "Maritime networks and regional development," provides a closer look at the local embedding of maritime flows. Ronald Halim, Jan Kwakkel, and Lóránt Tavasszy (Chapter 15) use simulation and spatial econometric methods to show direct connections between port traffic, maritime network design, trade, and economic development by choosing different parameters and scenarios in their global network model. An exploratory analysis of Pacific Rim port regions is proposed by César Ducruet and Hidekazu Itoh (Chapter 16) to seek the local socio-economic determinants of maritime connectivity in a network composed of different fleet types. Territorial factors thus play an important role as seen with the tendency for richer, more urbanized regions specialized in the tertiary sector to be more dominant in the network and to centralize higher-valued flows. At the country level, David Guerrero, Claude Grasland, and César Ducruet (Chapter 17) revisit the gravity model by comparing trade flows to maritime container flows on country pairs. They particularly highlight the facilitation of trade by shipping frequency, especially for manufactured goods, and the geographic essence of this relationship notwithstanding a number of outliers among countries. By linking spatial economics with spatial statistics, network analysis, and GIS, Igor Lugo provides a novel approach to systems of cities (Chapter 18) based on the case of Mexico, where urban nodes as well as port locations are connected via road segments. Such a combined approach has important implications for further understanding multimodal urban centrality and accessibility. The analysis by Nora Mareï and César Ducruet (Chapter 19) of the network configuration of maritime container flows in three different regions of the world discuss the respective influences of regional integration processes and carrier/port selection and competition dynamics on port hierarchies. A new measure of intra- versus extra-regional vessel circulation allows us to detect noticeable differences in the way such basins are organized and have evolved in recent decades. The last contribution to this part and to the book by César Ducruet, Sylvain Cuyala, Ali El Hosni, and Zuzanna Kosowska-Stamirowska (Chapter 20) re-explores the long-standing port-city issue by measuring the influence of urban demographic size on the spatial pattern of global maritime flows between 1950 and 1990. Larger cities maintained their overwhelming dominance in terms of centrality, but at the same time, port hierarchy and urban hierarchy gradually became less overlapped.

Acknowledgements

The research leading to these results has received funding from the European Research Council under the European Union's Seventh Framework Programme (FP/2007-2013)/ERC Grant Agreement n. [313847] "World Seastems."

Note

1 Other sources are worth mentioning although they have not yet been studied, such as the archives of the Suez Canal Authority, where every ship reported the precise content and value of its cargoes as well as the origin and destination of its voyage (see: http://suezcanal.bibalex.org/Presentation/home/home.aspx [accessed 27 May 2015]).

References

Alexandersson G., Norström G. (1963) *World shipping: an economic geography of ports and seaborne trade*. Stockholm: Almqvist & Wiksell.

Andrews J.H. (1955) Eighteenth century port forelands in the Irish Sea. *Irish Geography*, 3(2): 114–17.

Angeloudis P., Bichou K., Bell M.G.H. (2007) Security and reliability of the liner container-shipping network: analysis of robustness using a complex network framework. In: Bichou K., Bell M.G.H., Evans A. (Eds), *Risk Management in Port Operations, Logistics and Supply Chain Security*, London: Informa, pp. 95–106.

Asgari N., Farahani R.Z., Goh M. (2013) Network design approach for hub ports-shipping companies competition and cooperation. *Transportation Research Part A*, 48: 1–18.

Baird A. (2010) Redefining maritime transport infrastructure. *Proceedings of the ICE – Civil Engineering*, 163(5): 29–33.

Bird J. (1969) Traffic flows to and from British seaports. *Geography*, 54: 284–302.

Bird J. (1984) Seaport development: Some questions of scale. In: Hoyle B.S., Hilling D. (Eds), *Seaport Systems and Spatial Change*, Chichester: Wiley, pp. 21–41.

Britton J.N.H. (1965) Coastwise external relations of the ports of Victoria. *Australian Geographer*, 9: 269–81.

Brocard M., Joly O., Steck B. (1995) Les réseaux de circulation maritime. *Mappemonde*, 1: 23–8.

Brooks M.R., Button K.J., Nijkamp P. (2002) *Maritime Transport*. Cheltenham: Edward Elgar.

Caschili S., Medda F.R., Parola F., Ferrari C. (2014) An analysis of shipping agreements: the cooperative container network. *Networks and Spatial Economics*, 14(3–4): 355–77.

Central Intelligence Agency (1973) World shipping lanes. Cited by Walbridge S. (2013) *Assessing ship movements using volunteered geographic information.* Master Thesis in Ecology, Evolution, and Marine Biology, University of California, Santa Barbara.

Cheshire, J. (2012) Mapped: British, Spanish and Dutch Shipping 1750–1800. Available online at http://spatial.ly/2012/03/mapped-british-shipping-1750-1800/ [accessed 27 May 2015].

Christiansen M., Fagerholt K., Nygreen B., Ronen D. (2013) Ship routing and scheduling in the new millennium. *European Journal of Operational Research*, 228(3): 467–83.

Cisic D., Komadina P., Hlaca B. (2007) Network analysis applied to Mediterranean liner transport system. Paper presented at the International Association of Maritime Economists Conference, Athens, Greece, 4–6 July.

Comtois C., Wang J.J. (2003) Géopolitique et transport: nouvelles perspectives stratégiques dans le détroit de Taïwan. *Etudes Stratégiques*, 34(2): 213–27.

Concepcion G.T., Kahng S.E., Crepeau M.W., Franklin E.C., Coles S.L., Toonen R.J. (2010) Resolving natural ranges and marine invasions in a globally distributed octocoral (genus Carijoa). *Marine Ecology Progress Series*, 401: 113–27.

Coupé C., Hombert J.M. (2005) Les premières traversées maritimes: une fenêtre sur les cultures et les langues dans La préhistoire. In: Hombert J.M. (Ed), *Aux Origines des Langues et du Langage*, Paris: Fayard, pp. 118–61.

Cullinane K.P.B., Wang Y. (2012) The hierarchical configuration of the container port industry: An application of multiple linkage analysis. *Maritime Policy and Management*, 39(2): 169–87.

Danisch M., Guillaume J.L., Le Grand B. (2014) Complétion de communautés par l'apprentissage d'une mesure de proximité. ALGOTEL 2014 – 16èmes Rencontres Francophones sur les Aspects Algorithmiques des Télécommunications, June, Le Bois-Plage-en-Ré, France, pp. 1–4.

De Langen P.W., Nijdam M.H., Van der Horst M.R. (2007) New indicators to measure port performance. *Journal of Maritime Research*, 4(1): 23–36.

De Langen P.W., Van der Lugt L.M., Eenhuizen J.H.A. (2002) A stylized container port hierarchy: a theoretical and empirical exploration. Paper presented at the International Association of Maritime Economists Conference, Panama, 13–15 November.

De Sbarats J.M. (1971) A geographical analysis of the Clyde's forelands. *Tijdschrift voor Economische en Sociale Geografie*, 62: 249–63.

Deng W.B., Long G., Wei L., Xu C. (2009) Worldwide marine transportation network: efficiency and container throughput. *Chinese Physics Letters*, 26(11): 118901.

Doshi D., Malhotra B., Bressan S., Lam J.S.L. (2012) Mining maritime schedules for analyzing global shipping networks. *Business Intelligence and Data Mining*, 7(3): 186–202.

Ducruet C. (2013) Network diversity and maritime flows. *Journal of Transport Geography*, 30: 77–88.

Ducruet C. (2015) The polarization of global container flows by interoceanic canals: geographic coverage and network vulnerability. *Maritime Policy and Management* (in press).

Ducruet C., Roussin S. (2007) Inter-Korean maritime linkages: economic integration vs. hub dependence, 1985–2005. 15th European Conference on Theoretical and Quantitative Geography (ECTQG), Montreux, Switzerland, IGUL-UNIL, September 7–11, pp. 133–9.

Ducruet C., Notteboom T.E. (2012) The worldwide maritime network of container shipping: spatial structure and regional dynamics. *Global Networks*, 12(3): 395–423.

Ducruet, C., Zaidi, F. (2012) Maritime constellations: a complex network approach to shipping and ports. *Maritime Policy and Management* 39(2): 151–68.

Ducruet C., Lugo I. (2013) Structure and dynamics of transportation networks: models, concepts, and applications. In: Rodrigue J.P., Notteboom T.E., Shaw J. (Eds), *The SAGE Handbook of Transport Studies*, SAGE Publications Ltd., pp. 347–64.

Ducruet C., Beauguitte L. (2014) Spatial science and network science: review and outcomes of a complex relationship. *Networks and Spatial Economics*, 14(3–4): 297–316.

Ducruet C., Gelézeau V., Roussin S. (2008) Les connexions maritimes de la Corée du Nord: recompositions territoriales dans la péninsule coréenne et nouvelles dynamiques régionales en Asie du Nord-Est. *L'Espace Géographique*, 3: 208–24.

Ducruet, C., Lee, S.W., Ng, A.K.Y. (2010a) Centrality and vulnerability in liner shipping networks: revisiting the northeast Asian port hierarchy. *Maritime Policy and Management*, 37(1): 17–36.

Ducruet C., Rozenblat C., Zaidi F. (2010b) Ports in multi-level maritime networks: evidence from the Atlantic (1996–2006). *Journal of Transport Geography*, 18(4): 508–18.

Ducruet C., Lee S.W., Ng A.K.Y. (2011a) Port competition and network polarization at the East Asian maritime corridor. *Territoire en Mouvement*, 10: 60–74.

Ducruet C., Ietri D., Rozenblat C. (2011b) Cities in worldwide air and sea flows: a multiple networks analysis. *Cybergeo: European Journal of Geography*, 528. Available online at http://cybergeo.revues.org/23603 [accessed 27 May 2015].

Ducruet C., Itoh H., Merk O. (2014a) *Time Efficiency at World Container Ports*. OECD-ITF Discussion Paper 2014-08.

Ducruet C., Joly O., Le Cam M. (2014b) Europe in global maritime flows: gateways, forelands, and subnetworks. In: Pain K., Van Hamme G. (Eds), *Changing Urban and Regional Relations in a Globalizing World. Europe as a Global Macro-Region*, Edward Elgar, pp. 164–80.

Earnest D.C., Yetiv S., Carmel S.M. (2012) Contagion in the transpacific shipping network: International networks and vulnerability interdependence. *International Interactions*, 38(5): 571–96.

Eyring V., Isaksen I.S.A., Berntsen T., Collins W.J., Corbett J.J., Endresen O., Grainger R.G., Moldanova J., Schlager H., Stevenson D.S. (2010) Transport impacts on climate and atmosphere: shipping. *Atmospheric Environment*, 44(37): 4735–71.

Fewell M.P. (2003) An approach to modelling the effects of network centricity in maritime warfare. *Proceedings of the 5th International Conference on Industrial and Applied Mathematics*, Sydney, New South Wales.

Fleming D.K., Hayuth Y. (1994) Spatial characteristics of transportation hubs: centrality and intermediacy. *Journal of Transport Geography*, 2(1): 3–18.

Fossey R., Pearson R. (1983) *World Deep-Sea Container Shipping: A Geographical Economic & Statistical Analysis*. Aldershot: Gower.

Fraser D., Notteboom T.E., Ducruet C. (2014) Peripherality in the global container shipping network: the case of the Southern African container port system. *Geojournal* (in press).

Freire Seoane M.J., Gonzalez-Laxe F., Montes C.P. (2013) Foreland determination for containership and general cargo ports in Europe (2007–2011). *Journal of Transport Geography*, 30: 56–67.

Frémont A. (2007) Global maritime networks: the case of Maersk. *Journal of Transport Geography*, 15(6): 431–42.

Frémont A. (2010) Maritime networks: a source of competitiveness for shipping lines. In: Cullinane K. (Ed), *International Handbook of Maritime Business*, Edward Elgar, pp. 150–73.

Frémont A., Soppé M. (2004) Les stratégies des armateurs de lignes régulières en matière de dessertes maritimes. *Belgeo*, 4: 391–406.

Friedman E., Look C., Perdikaris F. (2009) Using viewshed models in GIS to analyze island inter-connectivity and ancient maritime pathways of the Pre-Columbian people in the Caribbean. Working Paper. Available online at http://www.brooklyn.cuny.edu/pub/departments/bcurj/pdf/FriedmanErinART.pdf [accessed 27 May 2015].

Fugazza M., Hoffmann J., Razafinombana R. (2013) Building a dataset for bilateral maritime connectivity. United Nations Conference on Trade and Development (UNCTAD), Policy Issues in International Trade and Commodities Series No. 61. Available online at http://unctad.org/en/PublicationsLibrary/itcdtab63_en.pdf [accessed 27 May 2015].

Gipouloux F. (2011) *The Asian Mediterranean: Port Cities and Trading Networks in China, Japan and Southeast Asia, 13th–21st Century*. Cheltenham and Northampton: Edward Elgar.

Gonzalez-Laxe F., Freire Seoane M.J., Montes C.P. (2012) Maritime degree, centrality and vulnerability: port hierarchies and emerging areas in containerized transport (2008–2010). *Journal of Transport Geography*, 24: 33–44.

Halpern B.S., Walbridge S., Selkoe K.A., Kappel C.V., Micheli F., D'Agrosa C., Bruno J.F., Casey K.S., Ebert C., Fox H.E., Fujita R., Heinemann D., Lenihan H.S., Madin E.M.P., Perry M.T., Selig E.R., Spalding M., Steneck R., Watson R. (2008) A global map of human impact on marine ecosystems. *Science*, 319(5865): 948–52.

Helmick J.S. (1994) *Concentration and Connectivity in the North Atlantic Liner Port Network, 1970–1990*. Unpublished PhD Dissertation, Miami: University of Miami.

Herrera R.G., Wheeler D., Können G., Koek F., Jones P., Prieto M.R. (2003) *Climatological Database for the World's Oceans 1750–1850*. CLIWOC Final Report. Available online at http://pendientedemigracion.ucm.es/info/cliwoc/Cliwoc_final_report.pdf [accessed 5 June 2015].

Höglund A., Meier H.E.M. (2012) Environmentally safe areas and routes in the Baltic proper using Eulerian tracers. *Marine Pollution Bulletin*, 64(7): 1375–85.

Hu B., Zong G. (2013) Topology analysis of China's port shipping network. *Journal of Software*, 8(10): 2581–86.

Hu Y., Zhu D. (2009) Empirical analysis of the worldwide maritime transportation network. *Physica A*, 388(10): 2061–71.

Jiang J., Lee L.H., Chew E.P., Gan C.C. (2015) Port connectivity study: an analysis framework from a global container liner shipping network perspective. *Transportation Research Part E*, 73: 47–64.

Joly O. (1995) Structuration des lignes maritimes régulières de navires porte-conteneurs. Paper presented at the 2nd Theoquant meeting, Besançon, 4–5 October.

Joly O. (1999) *La structuration des réseaux de circulation maritime*. Unpublished PhD Dissertation in Territorial Planning, Le Havre University, CIRTAI.

Kaluza P., Kölzsch A., Gastner M.T., Blasius, B. (2010) The complex network of global cargo ship movements. *Journal of the Royal Society Interface*, 7(48): 1093–103.

Keller R.P., Drake J.M., Drew M.B., Lodge D.M. (2011) Linking environmental conditions and ship movements to estimate invasive species transport across the global shipping network. *Diversity and Distributions*, 17(1): 93–102.

Kerr D., Spelt J. (1956) Overseas trade at the port of Toronto. *The Canadian Geographer*, 2: 70–9.

Kristiansen S. (2004) *Maritime Transportation: Safety Management and Risk Analysis*, Abingdon: Routledge.

Lam J.S.L., Yap W.Y. (2011) Dynamics of liner shipping network and port connectivity in supply chain systems: analysis on East Asia. *Journal of Transport Geography*, 19(6): 1272–81.

Le Guyader D., Brosset D., Gourmelon F. (2011) Exploitation de données AIS pour la cartographie du transport maritime. *Mappemonde*, 104(4). Available online at http://mappemonde.mgm.fr/num32/articles/art11405.html [accessed 27 May 2015].

Leggate H., McConville J, Morvillo A. (2004) *International Maritime Transport: Perspectives*. Abingdon: Routledge.

Leidwanger J. (2013) Modeling distance with time in ancient Mediterranean seafaring: a GIS application for the interpretation of maritime connectivity. *Journal of Archaeological Science*, 40(8): 3302–8.

Lemarchand A. (2000) *La Dynamique des Ports: Mesures de La Valeur et des Emplois, Emplois et Valeur des Mesures.* CERENE: Le Havre University.

Leonardi J., Browne M. (2010) A method for assessing the carbon footprint of maritime freight transport: European case study and results. *International Journal of Logistics Research and Applications*, 13(5): 349–58.

Lewis M.W., Wigen K. (1999) A maritime response to the crisis in area studies. *Geographical Review*, 89(2): 161–8.

Leymarie P., Rekacewicz P., Stienne A. (2014) *UNOSAT Global Report on Maritime Piracy. A Geospatial Analysis 1995–2013.* United Nations Institute for Training and Research (UNITAR).

Li Z., Xu M., Shi Y. (2015) Centrality in global shipping network basing on worldwide shipping areas. *Geojournal*, 80(1): 47–60.

Low J.M.W., Tang L.C. (2012) Network effects in the East Asia container ports industry. *Maritime Policy and Management*, 39(4): 369–86.

McCalla R.J. (2004) Hierarchical network structure as seen in container shipping liner services in the Caribbean basin. *Belgeo*, 4: 407–17.

McKenzie F.D. (1975) *Maritime Dynamic Traffic Generator. Volume III: Density Data on World Maps.* Working Paper No. AD-A012 498, Transportation Systems Center, Cambridge, Massachusetts.

Makkonen T., Salonen M., Kajander S. (2013) Island accessibility challenges: rural transport in the Finnish archipelago. *European Journal of Transport and Infrastructure Research*, 13(4): 274–90.

Marti B.E. (1981) Patterns of United States–Canadian maritime container flows. *Maritime Policy and Management*, 8(4): 253–9.

Marti B.E., Krausse G.H. (1983) Trade route 11: methods to assess port exchanges of maritime containerized cargo flows. *Ocean Management*, 8(4): 317–33.

Martinez-Zarzoso I., Wilmsmeier G., Perez-Garcia E., Marquez-Ramos L. (2011) Maritime networks, services structure and maritime Trade. *Networks and Spatial Economics*, 11(3): 555–76.

Mohamed-Chérif F.Z., Ducruet C. (2015) Regional integration and maritime connectivity across the Maghreb seaport system. *Journal of Transport Geography* (in press).

Montes C.P., Freire Seoane M.J., Gonzalez-Laxe F. (2012) General cargo and containership emergent routes: a complex networks description. *Transport Policy*, 24: 126–40.

Nelson A. (2008) *Travel time to major cities: a global map of accessibility.* Global Environment Monitoring Unit, Joint Research Centre of the European Commission, Ispra Italy. Available online at http://bioval.jrc.ec.europa.eu/products/gam/index.htm [accessed 27 May 2015].

Ng A.K.Y., Ducruet C. (2014) The changing tides of port geography (1950–2012). *Progress in Human Geography*, 38(6): 785–823.

Noin D. (1999) La population des littoraux du monde. *L'Information Géographique*, 63(2): 65–73.

Parshani R., Rozenblat C., Ietri D., Ducruet C., Havlin S. (2010) Inter-similarity between coupled networks. *Europhysics Letters*, 92: 68002.

Patton D.J. (1961) Railroad rate structures, ocean trade routes and the hinterland relations of Halifax and Saint John. *Tijdschrift voor Economische en Sociale Geografie*, 52(1): 2–13.

Perpillou A. (1959) *Géographie de La Circulation.* Paris: Centre de Documentation Universitaire.

Plasschaert K., Derudder B., Dullaert W., Witlox F. (2011) Redefining the Hamburg–Le Havre range in maritime networks. *Proceedings of the BIVE-GIBET Transport Research Day 2011.* Zelzate University Press, pp. 240–4.

Rimmer P.J. (1967) The search for spatial regularities in the development of Australian seaports 1861–1961/2. *Geografiska Annaler*, 49B: 42–54.

Rimmer P.J. (2007) Port dynamics since 1965: past patterns, current conditions and future directions. *Journal of International Logistics and Trade*, 5(1): 75–97.

Rimmer P.J., Comtois C. (2005) China's extra and intra-Asian liner shipping connections, 1990–2000. *Journal of International Logistics and Trade*, 3: 75–97.

Robinson R. (1968) *Spatial structuring of port-linked flows: the port of Vancouver, Canada, 1965*. Unpublished PhD dissertation in Geography, Vancouver: University of British Columbia.

Robinson R. (1976) Modelling the port as an operational system: a perspective for research. *Economic Geography*, 52(1): 71–86.

Robinson R. (1998) Asian hub/feeder nets: the dynamics of restructuring. *Maritime Policy and Management*, 25(1): 21–40.

Robinson R. (2002) Ports as elements in value-driven chain systems: the new paradigm. *Maritime Policy and Management*, 29(3): 241–55.

Rodgers A.L. (1958) The port of Genova: external and internal relations. *Annals of the Association of American Geographers*, 48: 319–51.

Rodrigue J.P. (2004) Straits, passages and chokepoints: a maritime geostrategy of petroleum distribution. *Cahiers de Géographie du Québec*, 48(135): 357–74.

Rodrigue J.P., Comtois C., Slack B. (2013) *The Geography of Transport Systems*. New York: Routledge.

Ronnback K. (2012) The speed of ships and shipping productivity in the age of sail. *European Review of Economic History*, 16(4): 469–89.

Scarborough (1908) *Carte du Monde, Europe, Asie, Afrique et Océanie. Indiquant les Pays et leurs Colonies les principaux moyens de transport*. Paris: Scarborough.

Scheidel W. (2013) *The Shape of the Roman World*. Working Paper, Stanford University.

Seebens H., Gastner M.T., Blasius B. (2013) The risk of marine bioinvasion caused by global shipping. *Ecology Letters*, 16(6): 782–90.

Shen G., Wang C., Pulat P.S. (2013) An exploratory analysis and visualization of US global trade patterns through maritime freight movement between US ports and world ports: 1997–2007. Paper presented at the International Forum on Shipping, Ports and Airports (IFSPA), Hong Kong, 3–5 June.

Siegfried A. (1943) Les routes maritimes internationales. In: *L'Empire et La Mer*, Paris: Institut Maritime et Colonial, pp. 7–18.

Slack B. (1993) Pawns in the game: ports in a global transportation system. *Growth and Change*, 24(4): 579–88.

Solomon R.J. (1963) External relations of the port of Hobart 1804–1961. *Australian Geographer*, 9: 43–53.

Sommers L.M. (1960) Distribution and significance of the foreign trade ports of Norway. *Economic Geography*, 36: 306–12.

Steinberg P.E. (1999) Navigating to multiple horizons: toward a geography of ocean-space. *The Professional Geographer*, 51(3): 366–75.

Stopford M. (2008) *Maritime Economics*. Abingdon: Routledge.

Tartaron T.F. (2013) *Maritime Networks in the Mycenaean World*. Cambridge: Cambridge University Press.

Tatem A.J., Hay S.I., Rogers D.J. (2006) Global traffic and disease vector dispersal. *Proceedings of the National Academy of Sciences*, 103(16): 6242–7.

Tavasszy L., Minderhoud M., Perrin J.F., Notteboom T.E. (2011) A strategic network choice model for global container flows: specification, estimation and application. *Journal of Transport Geography*, 19(6): 1163–72.

Tournadre J. (2014) Anthropogenic pressure on the open ocean: the growth of ship traffic revealed by altimeter data analysis. *Geophysical Research Letters*, 41(22): 7924–32.

Tovar B., Hernandez R., Rodriguez-Deniz H. (2015) Container port competitiveness and connectivity: the Canary Islands main ports case. *Transport Policy*, 38: 40–51.

Tran N.K., Haasis H.D. (2014) Empirical analysis of the container liner shipping network on the East–West corridor (1995–2011). *Netnomics* (in press).

Tsiotas D., Polyzos S. (2014) Analysing the maritime transportation system in Greece: a complex network approach. *Networks and Spatial Economics*, doi: 10.1007/s11067-014-9278-y.

Ullman E.L. (1949) Mapping the world's ocean trade: a research proposal. *The Professional Geographer*, 1(2): 19–22.

Van den Bremen W.J., de Jong B. (1986) The aggregate spatial patterns of maritime transport at world scale: A macro-scale approach in transport geography. *Geojournal*, 12(3): 289–303.

Van Klink H.A. (1998) The port network as a new stage in port development: the case of Rotterdam. *Environment and Planning A*, 30(1): 143–60.

Veenstra A.W., Mulder H.M., Sels R.A. (2005) Analysing container flows in the Caribbean. *Journal of Transport Geography*, 13(4): 295–305.

Vettor R., Guedes Soares C. (2014) Detection and analysis of the main routes of voluntary observing ships in the North Atlantic. *Journal of Navigation* (in press).

Vigarié A. (1968) *Géographie de La Circulation. La Circulation Maritime*. Paris: Genin.

Vigarié A. (1979) *Ports de Commerce et Vie Littorale*. Paris: Hachette.

Von Schirach-Szmigiel C. (1973) Trading areas of the United Kingdom ports. *Geografiska Annaler B*, 55: 71–82.

Von Schirach-Szmigiel C. (1978) Competition for the general cargo transports of Sweden's foreign trade. *GeoJournal*, 2: 133–46.

Wang C., Wang J. (2011) Spatial pattern of the global shipping network and its hub-and-spoke system. *Research in Transportation Economics*, 32(1): 54–63.

Wang J., Pulat P.S., Shen G. (2012) Data mining for the development of a global port-to-port freight movement database. *International Journal of Shipping and Transport Logistics*, 4(2): 137–56.

Wang J.J., Ng A.K.Y (2011) The geographical connectedness of Chinese seaports with foreland markets: a new trend? *Tijdschrift voor Economische en Sociale Geografie*, 102: 188–204.

Wang Y., Cullinane K. (2008) Measuring container port accessibility: an application of the Principal Eigenvector Method (PEM). *Maritime Economics and Logistics*, 10: 75–89.

Wang Y., Cullinane K. (2014) Traffic consolidation in East Asian container ports: a network flow analysis. *Transportation Research Part A*, 61: 152–63.

Weigend G.G. (1956) The problem of hinterland and foreland as illustrated by the port of Hamburg. *Economic Geography*, 32(1): 1–16.

White H.P., Senior M.L., 1983. *Transport Geography*. Hong Kong: Longman House Ltd.

Windeck V. (2013) *A Liner Shipping Network Design*. Wiesbaden: Springer Gabler.

Woolley-Meza O., Thiemann C., Grady D., Lee J.J., Seebens H., Blasius B., Brockmann D. (2011) Complexity in human transportation networks: a comparative analysis of worldwide air transportation and global cargo-ship movements. *The European Physical Journal B*, 84: 589–600.

Xu M., Li Z., Shi Y., Zhang X., Jiang S. (2015) Evolution of regional inequality in the global shipping network. *Journal of Transport Geography*, 44: 1–12.

Xu X., Hu J., Liu F. (2007) Empirical analysis of the ship-transport network of China. *Chaos*, 17(2): 023129.

Zwier R., Hiemstra F., Nijkamp P., Van Monfort K. (1994) Connectivity and isolation in transport networks: a policy scenario experiment for the Greek island economy. Working Paper, Vrije Universiteit Amsterdam, Faculteit der Economische Wetenschappen en Econometrie.

2 City-systems and maritime transport in the long term

Anne Bretagnolle

The notion of city-systems relates to a complex geographical object, which has been mainly defined by Brian Berry (1964), Allan Pred (1973) and Brian Robson (1973). It refers to a set of cities which strongly interact and are interdependent at the regional, national, or international scale. Railways of the nineteenth century played a major role by structuring national city-systems, for instance in Western Europe and in the United States. According to McKenzie (1933: 6), railways "brought the entire settlement of the United States into a single economic unity integrated through a system of gateway cities of varying importance." Gateway cities are of particular importance, as city-systems are open and need to exchange with environments, particularly with other city-systems. Since the Middle Ages, seaport gateways were developed "in the contact zones between areas of differing intensities or types of production" (Burghardt, 1971: 270), long before the emergence of airport gateways (Bird, 1983). As city-systems are interlocked (one city belonging simultaneously to regional, national, and macro-regional systems), their precise delineation and contents are difficult to define, especially as they are evolving through time due to increasingly fast communications. The purpose of this chapter is to point to the particular role of maritime inter-urban links and their long-term evolution. The scale under study is international as it is at this level that maritime transport has long been much more cost efficient than others. International scale does not necessarily mean the whole globe, but rather the world economy, that emerged for the first time in the European Middle Ages.

Three different periods are distinguished and constitute the time frame of the chapter. A first stage (thirteenth to eighteenth centuries) was characterized by weak inter-urban links but strong maritime transport, representing a key factor for urban development. City-systems existed, for instance in Europe, but were characterized by indirect links between large cities, with successive stops in-between, using mainly water transportation. A second stage (nineteenth to the first half of the twentieth century) was characterized by strong links between cities; these were technical and long-standing transportation infrastructures, with maritime transport being articulated with canals and railroads. A positive feedback process between accessibility and centrality led to the emergence and growth of world metropolises. The third and current stage (second half of the twentieth century and after) is characterized by a weak relationship between maritime transport and world cities.

Because of cheap cost-distances, maritime transport still plays a huge role in the globalization of exchange for bulky and low-value merchandise but is much less determinant than air transport, rapid trains, and information technology in the selection process of world cities, based on time–distance parameters.

City-systems and water links

Maritime transport played a major role in the first globalization phase of the fourteenth and fifteenth centuries. For Fernand Braudel (1979a), this period underwent a "transport revolution" based both on improvements in ships (stern rudder, strake hull) and in navigation systems (maritime astrolabe and maritime compass). These developments laid the foundation for the first world economy, with the opening of trans-oceanic exchanges. Merchants entrepreneurship benefited in Europe from a relative independence from rulers. This situation created a sort of political polycentrism that favoured emulation between cities and led to the first world economy (Grataloup, 2007). In China, characterized by more efficient boats, centralized political power permitted the construction of a maritime empire based on Zeng He's explorations (1405–33). This empire collapsed shortly thereafter when forces were concentrated toward the inland military defence of the Ming Empire (Gipouloux, 2011).

The city-system that emerged in Europe was based on weak interdependencies, i.e. indirect links from one large city to another passing through a series of small outposts and trading centres one day apart along the long-distance itineraries (Reclus, 1895; Bretagnolle *et al.*, 1998). These links were established from the twelfth century and the renewal of long-distance trade and were mainly based on inexpensive water transportation. Maritime and river roads fed European centres of gravity (Braudel, 1979b), first located in northern Italy (e.g. Genoa and Venice) and then in Hanseatic cities (e.g. Ghent, Antwerp, and Bruges), complementing continental roads passing through Switzerland and Germany after the opening of Italian mountain passes.

These water links propelled urban growth for the few cities that developed long-distance trade. Indeed, maritime trade can be considered as an economic innovation cycle, just as manufacturing coal and steel in the nineteenth century, manufacturing, electricity, and automobile at the turn of the nineteenth and twentieth centuries, new technologies of information and communication in the 1950s–1970s, and nanotechnology biology information and communication since the 1990s–2000s (Pumain, 2008). The maritime trade cycle was not only based on new navigation technologies but also on innovative financial and management systems like holding companies and bills of exchange. When following the demographic trajectory of selected centres of gravity (Figure 2.1), one can see the impacts of maritime innovations. Each curve represents the evolution of the share of the city population in the total population of all European cities. Venice, which represents the ancient Mediterranean world, is constantly declining, whereas Antwerp, as a centre of the new Atlantic world, grew from the fifteenth to the seventeenth century, then declined with the shift of trade toward

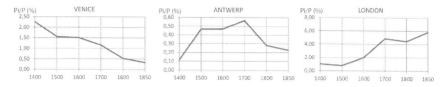

Figure 2.1 Individual trajectories of selected cities in the European urban system, 1400–1850.

Source: Bairoch *et al.* (1988).

Note: Pi/P (%) is the population of the city divided by the total population of European cities.

the Netherlands and Great Britain, especially London, which was not only an important port but also a continental centre for proto-industry.

City-systems and steam transportation

A second stage in the relationship between maritime transport and city-systems began with the industrial revolution of the nineteenth century. As with the first stage, technological progress in communication technologies played a key role and the British geographer Halford Mackinder (1902) suggested a maritime "transport revolution" allowing the world to become equivalent to the surface of the globe, especially because of the construction of canals that brought together the different oceans. With the Suez (1869) and Panama (1914) canals, the total length of the maritime road from Singapore to London was reduced from 16,000 to 10,000 kilometers, and from New York to Los Angeles from 21,000 to 8,000 kilometers (Rodrigue *et al.*, 2013). Crossing the Atlantic (New York–London) required 42 days at the end of the eighteenth century and only five days in 1920 (Berger, 2003), and ticket prices (New York–Le Havre) were reduced ninefold between 1850 and 1913 (Grataloup, 2007). Progress was also significant in terms of regularity of transportation; due to mechanical energy, ships could travel in every season of the year and in every direction, regardless of wind patterns.

Relations between city-systems and transport networks were deeply trans-formed. Accessibility that now mattered was based on multimodal transport (railroad, canals, rivers, and maritime ports) and on long-term static infrastruc-ture (steel and major projects like canals and modern ports). As pointed at by the French geographer Paul Vidal de la Blache (1922), the world metropolises (called "world emporia") were natural junction points in the "world network of communications," like New York or London. Edward Glaeser (2011) observed that in 1900, the top 20 US cities were all located on water links, and Roder-ick McKenzie (1933) highlighted a major specificity of US cities compared to European ones: due to the immensity of the country, the opening of the Panama Canal led to a booming development of many additional ocean gateways, such as Gulf and Pacific seaports, as "it is now possible to ship by water from Philadelphia or other North Atlantic ports to the Pacific coast as cheaply as by rail from points west to Denver" (p. 155). As the adoption of steel hull corresponded to the birth of industrial shipping, the new articulation of steel production, manufacturing and ports meant that maritime empires were no longer situated in forest-rich regions but in "coal and iron regions" (Vallaux, 1908: 276).

From this first industrial revolution, differences in accessibility patterns between "connected" and "not connected cities" dramatically increased. The limited capacity of the wooden hull (70 meters maximum according to Camille Vallaux, 1908) was now replaced by the "quite unlimited capacity" of the steel hull, and ports had to reinvest constantly in new equipment in order to adapt to the new technologies (Marnot, 2005). The increasing size of boats led to "a reduction of their number" (Vallaux, 1908: 278) and a selection of ports that were able to accommodate these sea giants. Between 1860 and 1914, £153 million (at 1900 prices) was invested in docks and harbours in England and Wales, and development costs were considerably higher at the end of this period than before (Konvitz, 1994: 300). Similarly, the ten largest ports along Europe's northwestern façade handled 3.9 million tons in the middle of the nineteenth century and 44.6 million tons in 1914 (ibid.: 303). Another source of differential accessibility consisted in a constant search for increasing speed, leading to a reduction of the number of entry points in order to "eliminate breaks in movements between points of origin and destination" (McKenzie, 1968b). This process of short-circuiting was well established for railways: "The improvement of communication tends everywhere to eliminate the trade of the smaller middlemen" (Mackinder, 1902: 338). In maritime transport, the reduction of the number of ports of call due to increasing speed was also observed, especially in Mediterranean and Baltic countries, by the French geographer Camille Vallaux (1908: 300): "with steam, ancient stages are short-circuited in the same way as small localities with express trains on land. Each acceleration in transportation, according to Ratzel, renders intermediate locations unnecessary."

Increasing speed and fleet capacity led to a "geographical selection" process (Mackinder, 1902), resulting in declining port capacities and elimination of a few ports (Figure 2.2). Between 1890 and 1925, the total number of ports was reduced by 8 percent and the average growth rate of calls dramatically decreased in some regions, for instance in the Mediterranean and Atlantic parts of Europe (Ducruet, 2012; Ducruet and Marnot, 2015).

This selection process can be summarized as positive feedback between multimodal accessibility and centrality (Figure 2.3). With increasing speed and handling capacity, the level of centrality of the well-connected railroad and port cities was growing in tandem with economic concentration factors based on economies of scale which also benefited from this higher accessibility (Bird, 1977). Centrality refers not only to the central place theory developed by Walter Christaller in 1933 (urban functions dedicated to serving the local and surrounding population in goods and services) but also to specialized functions like long-distance trade or manufacturing, described for instance in Vance (1970) and Bird (1977). Cities that loose in accessibility and centrality are polarized by the connected ones and generally register a relative decline, a process that helps explain the empirical

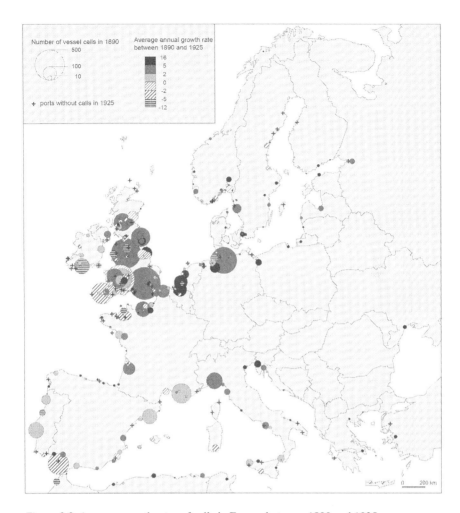

Figure 2.2 Average growth rates of calls in Europe between 1890 and 1925.

Source: own realization based on *Lloyd's Shipping Index.*

observations of more unequal distributions of city sizes (Bretagnolle, 2009). The well-connected cities increase their range of polarization and attraction, and finally their wealth. They can, in return, invest in new equipment to increase their accessibility potential, both at the local level (for instance improving access for the largest boats) and at the global level (number and quality of routes converging on the port or station). McKenzie describes this interaction loop in very clear terms (1968c: 125–6):

> As the power-driven factory displaced handicraft production and the steamboat and railway became the leading agencies of transportation, a new

basis for a geographic division of labour was introduced. The process was cumulative, advancing with accelerated speed throughout the nineteenth century. Industrial cities sprang into existence, first in England, then in surrounding European countries and in the United States.

Maritime transport and the feedback process in the current globalization

The third and current globalization phase began at the end of the Second World War, and can be partly explained by progress in communication technologies that allowed a spatial extension of exchange at a world scale (Figure 2.4). Due to containerization, maritime transport became the "backbone of globalisation" (Frémont and Soppé, 2005). Since the invention of the first shipping container in 1956, freight capacity and speed have doubled, and energy consumption has been reduced by 90 percent (Bavoux *et al.*, 2005). Around 90 percent of world trade volume is currently carried by maritime transport. Alongside deregulation, containerization was responsible for "the acceleration of the globalisation of the world economy since 1960" (Bernhofen *et al.*, 2013: 1). Moreover, hub-and-spokes organization reinforced the port hierarchization process with the emergence of a global system based on large and multi-functional redistribution platforms (Ducruet, 2014).

This period is also characterized by a decreasing role of maritime transport in the competition between world cities. This transport mode is no longer useful for transmitting information, as it was in the first globalization phase. Indeed, "electrical mechanisms of communication annihilated space in the transmission of intelligence" (McKenzie, 1968a: 136). Similarly, it is of little use for transporting passengers, and tourists and business people use airplanes or high-speed trains for international travel. Maritime transport is mainly used for transporting low-value goods and energy products, due to the differential in cost-distance between land and water. Articulated with manufacturing activities near the main ports, it is responsible for the dynamics of some coastal

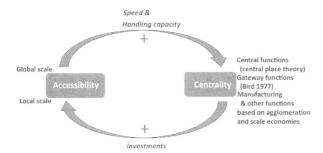

Figure 2.3 A positive feedback between accessibility and centrality.

Source: own realization.

Figure 2.4 Main interregional maritime flows and port hierarchy in the world in 2008.
Source: modified after Ducruet (2014).

regions. But when considering time-distance, competition with airplanes and trains gives the advantage to the latter. As McKenzie observed as early as 1929:

> The real revolution in land-time distance has been brought by the motor car and the airplane. The former has introduced a new scale of distance for local travel, the latter for travel between more distant points (. . .) Symbiotically the coast regions of the world are being drawn closer together due to the cost differential in water transportation, whereas sociologically the peoples on the continuous land masses are intermingling more and more freely as a result of new facilities of transport."
>
> McKenzie (1968b: 223–4)

Maritime functions are no longer considered by researchers who establish rankings of world cities competing for the control and domination of the world economy (Sassen, 1994; Derudder *et al.*, 2010).

Nevertheless, the stakes remain high and explain why world cities continue to develop strategies to keep their position in maritime networks, for instance through major investments in port infrastructure (recently in Singapore, Shanghai, Rotterdam, Antwerp, and Hamburg). This maintains the physical flows that remain necessary to a considerable amount of population and enterprises of the world cities and their surroundings, and it also preserves a key position in terms of logistics and hierarchy inside the global hub and spokes organization.

Conclusion

Maritime transport was a major actor in the structuring and dynamics of city-systems until the second half of the twentieth century. During the mercantile capitalism phase (fourteenth to eighteenth centuries), maritime transport gave rise to the first world-economy, in Europe, and one of the most sound hypotheses for explaining the shift from northern Italy to northwest Europe was the scarcity of wood, a necessary resource for the construction of boats (Carmelo Trasselli, quoted in Braudel, 1979a). During the industrial capitalism phase (nineteenth century to the first half of the twentieth century), maritime and railroad transport were closely related with the world metropolis selection processes through a feedback loop between accessibility and centrality. The huge growth of world metropoles can be explained not only by economies of scale but also by the relative position of cities in trade networks. During the third and current stage (the second half of the twentieth century to twenty-first century), I argue, following Roderick McKenzie, that maritime transport was decoupled from this feedback process and lost its structuring role in the competition between world metropoles (see Chapter 20 by Ducruet *et al.* for a global quantitative analysis of port-city relations between 1950 and 1990). However, due to cumulative processes and path dependence, the world cities of todays are still located near major seaports and river ports. Keeping a competitive position in the maritime network seems to be wise and highly recommended, especially in a context of uncertainty regarding energy resources and ongoing settlement concentration in coastal regions.

References

Bairoch P., Batou J., Chèvre P. (1988), *La population des villes européennes. Banque de données et analyse sommaire des résultats: 800–1850*. Centre d'Histoire économique International de l'Université de Genève, p. 339.

Bavoux J.J., Beaucire F., Chapelon L., Zembri P. (2005) *Géographie des Transports*. Paris: Armand Colin.

Berger S. (2003) *Notre Première Mondialization. Leçons d'un échec Oublié*. Paris: Seuil.

Bernhofen D.M., El-Sahli Z., Kneller R. (2013) *Estimating the effects of the container revolution on world trade*. Lund University Working Paper 2013:4, Department of Economics, School of Economics and Management.

Berry B. (1964) Cities as systems within systems of cities. *Papers of the Regional Science Association*, 13: 147–63.

Bird J. (1977) *Centrality and Cities*. London: Routledge & Kegan Paul.

Bird J. (1983) Gateways: slow recognition but irresistible rise. *Tijdschrift Voor Economic en Sociale Geografie*, 74(3): 196–202.

Braudel F. (1979a) *La Méditerranée et le Monde Méditerranéen à l'Epoque de Philippe II*. Paris: Armand Colin.

Braudel F. (1979b) *Civilisation Matérielle, Economie et Capitalisme, 15ème–18ème Siècles*. Paris: Armand Colin.

Bretagnolle A. (2009) *Villes et Réseaux de Transport: des Interactions dans La Longue Durée (France, Europe, Etats-Unis)*. Habilitation à Diriger des Recherches, Paris: Université Paris 1 Panthéon-Sorbonne. Available online at https://tel.archives-ouvertes.fr/tel-00459720/ [accessed 27 May 2015].

Bretagnolle A., Pumain D., Rozenblat C. (1998) Space-time contraction and the dynamics of urban systems. *Cybergeo: European Journal of Geography*, 61. Available online at http://cybergeo.revues.org/373 [accessed 27 May 2015].

Burghardt A.F. (1971) A hypothesis about gateway cities. *Annals of the Association of American Geographers*, 61(2): 269–85.

Christaller W. (1933) *Die zentralen Orte in Süddeutschland*, Jena, Fischer, translated in 1966 by Baskin C. W., Central Places in Southern Germany, Englewood Cliffs, New Jersey: Prentice Hall.

Derudder B., Taylor P., Ni P., De Vos A., Hoyler M., Hanssens H., Bassens D., Huang J., Witlox F., Shen W., Yang X. (2010) Pathways of change: shifting connectivities in the world city network, 2000–2008. *Urban Studies*, 47(9): 1861–77.

Ducruet C. (2012) Ports et routes maritimes dans le monde (1890–1925). *Mappemonde*, 106. Available online at http://mappemonde.mgm.fr/num34/lieux/lieux12201.html [accessed 27 May 2015].

Ducruet C. (2014) Réseau maritime mondial et hiérarchie portuaire. *Questions Internationales*, 70: 21–9.

Ducruet C., Marnot B. (2015) Analyser les trafics portuaires mondiaux en 1890 et 1925 à partir des registres du Lloyd's. GIS d'Histoire Maritime.

Frémont A., Soppé M. (2005) Transport maritime conteneurisé et mondialisation. *Annales de Géographie*, 114(642): 187–200.

Gipouloux F. (2011) *The Asian Mediterranean: Port Cities and Trading Networks in China, Japan and Southeast Asia, 13th–21st Century*. Cheltenham and Northampton: Edward Elgar.

Glaeser E. (2011) *Triumph of the City*. New York: Penguin Press.

Grataloup C. (2007) *Géohistoire de La mondialisation. Le temps long du monde*. Paris: Armand Colin.

Konvitz J.W. (1994) The crisis of Atlantic port cities, 1880 to 1920. *Comparative Studies in Society and History*, 36(2): 293–318.

McKenzie Roderick D. (1968a) Movements and the ability to live. In: Amos Henry Hawley (Ed.): *Roderick MacKenzie: On Human Ecology: Selected Writings*, Chicago: University of Chicago Press.

McKenzie Roderick D. (1968b) Spatial distances. In: Amos Henry Hawley (Ed.): *Roderick MacKenzie: On Human Ecology: Selected Writings*, Chicago: University of Chicago Press.

McKenzie Roderick D. (1968c) Industrial expansion and the interrelations of people. In: Amos Henry Hawley (Ed.): *Roderick MacKenzie: On Human Ecology: Selected Writings*, Chicago: University of Chicago Press.

McKenzie Roderick D. (1933), *The Metropolitan Community*. New York: Russell & Russell.

Mackinder H (1902) *Britain and the British Seas*. London: William Heinemann.

Marnot B. (2005) Interconnexion et reclassements: l'insertion des ports français dans La chaîne multimodale au XIXe siècle. *Flux*, 59(1): 10–21.

Pred A. (1973) The growth and development of systems of cities in advanced economies. In: Pred A., Törnqvist G. (Eds), *Systems of Cities and Information Flows, Two Essays*. Lund: The Royal University of Lund.

Pumain D. (2008) The socio-spatial dynamics of systems of cities and innovation processes: a multi-level model. In: Albeverio S., Andrey D., Giordano P., Vancheri A. (Eds), *The Dynamics of Complex Urban Systems. An Interdisciplinary Approach*. Berlin: Physica Verlag, Springer, pp. 373–89.

Reclus E. (1895) The evolution of cities. *The Contemporary Review*, 67(2): 246–64.

Robson B.T. (1973) *Urban Growth: An Approach*. London: Methuen and Co.

Rodrigue J.P., Comtois C., Slack B. (2013) *The Geography of Transport Systems*. New York: Routledge.

Sassen S. (1994) *Cities in a World Economy*. Thousand Oaks, CA: Pine Forge Press.

Vallaux C. (1908) *La Mer: Géographie Sociale. Populations Maritimes, Migrations, Pêche, Commerce, Domination de La Mer*. Paris: Octave Doin.

Vance J.E. (1970) *The Merchant's World: The Geography of Wholesaling*. Englewood Cliffs, NJ: Prentice Hall.

Vidal de La Blache P. (1922) *Principes de Géographie Humaine*. Paris: Armand Colin.

3 A geo-history of maritime networks since 1945

The case of the Compagnie Générale Transatlantique's transformation into CMA-CGM

Antoine Frémont

Since 1945, the maritime networks of liner shipping companies have profoundly changed. It is possible to interpret their evolution as a direct adaptation to the world's new geo-economical configurations. Maritime transport is a service which, in the first place, makes it possible for global trade flows to exist. In return, it contributes to shape the world and the exchanges between places. The evolution of maritime networks and their configuration explains globalization as much as the latter influences the former. This systemic interaction has been much empowered thanks to containerization (Frémont, 2007b). Since the mid-1960s, containerization on an international scale allowed reliable transport of immense quantities of finished and semi-finished goods at low prices, a privilege that previously only applied to bulk products carried by giant tankers and ore carriers (Levinson, 2006).

The goal of this chapter is to envisage the evolution of maritime networks since the end of the Second World War in a geo-historical perspective. These networks participate in the overall interconnection of the world. But this interconnection occurs in a long-term period. Networks hesitate in their evolution. A simple replication of the present or the past cannot foster new spatial dynamics such as globalization. Conversely, more or less radical innovations contribute to the transformation of the world and of the links connecting places.

We then take as a hypothesis that liner shipping networks are designed in a relatively autonomous manner with regard to international trade flows (demand). Such autonomy is explained by a specific internal organization of the industry. Competition between shipping lines is a powerful motivation to reduce transport costs. Shipping lines seek to meet shippers' needs, for example by proposing regular destinations based on a given network. They offer a service. But at the same time, shipping lines constantly search for productivity gains bearing in mind that the mobilized capital (ships) are considerable. Servicing international trade, maritime transport also functions like an industry. The growing size of vessels, notably with containerization, is the industry's most frequent response to such challenges. Our second hypothesis is that the configuration of maritime networks allows shipping companies to be more or less in line with the market and as such to be more or less competitive.

These hypotheses can be tested through the example of the company CMA-CGM, which is today the world's third largest company for the maritime transport of containers. It has reached a global dimension by expanding not only its transport capacity but also the geographic coverage of the markets it offers to shippers. This company's roots go back to the Compagnie Générale Transatlantique (CGT), founded in 1861 by the Pereire brothers. The CGT, having become a mixed company in 1933, in 1976 merged with the Messageries Maritimes, a national company, to become the Compagnie Générale Maritime (CGM). In 1996, CGM was privatized, acquired by the CMA (Compagnie Maritime d'Affrètement), which gave birth to the CMA-CGM group. These multiple rebirths are perfect markers of the progressive adaptation of this company to world transformations, specifically the maritime world, which evolves while transforming the world. From the Compagnie Générale Transatlantique to the CMA-CGM, this chapter is about a geo-history of maritime networks.

1945–1962: The network of the Compagnie Générale Transatlantique and the world order

The segmented maritime space of the 1950s

During the 1950s, the North Atlantic region constituted the centre of the global maritime space. This was the route that saw the greatest traffic of passengers, bulk, and break-bulk goods. There was fierce competition between European and American shipping lines. International competition also took place along the two other east–west segments, namely trans-Pacific and Europe–Far East. These two segments can barely be compared with the powerful North Atlantic route, although Japan was rising from the ashes. Commercial and maritime relations were mostly bilateral, from one country to the other, and were organized under the umbrella of maritime conferences, which tended to limit excessive competition. Elsewhere, dominant maritime linkages mainly connected the British, French, and Dutch to their respective empires, such markets being mutually closed. The world maritime space of the 1950s was relatively comparable to the pre-war period. It was characterized by the segmentation of different maritime routes dedicated to different markets (Figure 3.1).

Following lengthy post-war reconstruction, the CGT reached its peak activity in 1962 when launching the ocean liner *France* (Frémont, 1998). The company's existence and prosperity expressed the logic of world maritime space. State support and maritime conferences allowed its durable presence on the North Atlantic among similarly large international companies. Servicing a vast national maritime space guaranteed its activity, protected from any competition.

The CGT on competing routes

For the *Transat* (a nickname for the CGT), the most competitive route was the North Atlantic (Barbance, 1955). To cope with competition, the strategy was to participate in maritime conferences: "Our Company's rule has always been to be

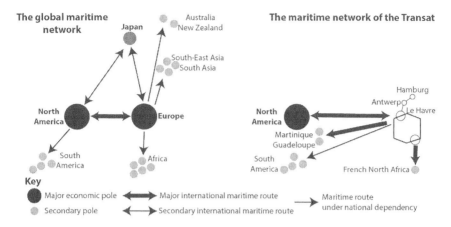

Figure 3.1 The global maritime network and the maritime network of the Transat during the 1950s.

associated with all the conferences covering the traffic served by its lines. We are founding members of many of the oldest ones. This policy remains our rule."[1] Maritime conferences are primarily "clubs of liner shipping operators, 'gentlemen's agreements' initiated by Great Britain" (Bauchet, 1991). The first one was born in 1875. Their main objective was to organize the transport supply, both in terms of traffic and tariffs, because

> the importance of fixed costs in liner shipping had always pushed shipowners during crises to deliver their services at prices that only covered marginal costs, thereby constraining the regularity of the lines due to excessive competition. This corresponds to the typical example of the cartel, or inter-firm agreement destined to organise competition.
>
> Bauchet (1991)

Thanks to conferences, the Transat and then the CGM could count on relatively stable tariffs, protected from high market fluctuations. The French shipping line, which was structurally expensive, could not ensure profitable management of its fleet in the advent of shrinking tariffs. Conferences also allowed fighting against outsiders by proposing short-term tariffs to eliminate them. For the ocean liners, notably the most prestigious ones working in the North Atlantic, state subsidies supporting postal services palliated the structural deficit of such services.

A national maritime network

The Transat based its activity on tight relations with the national market and the port of Le Havre. Until decolonization, it serviced a national maritime space, fully protected from foreign competition. In the 1950s, France's commercial relations remained centred on its empire. As during the interwar period, trade with over-seas possessions represented between one-third and one-half of French exports and imports. This trade was a French flag monopoly either through law, such as between France and Algeria, for banana trade since 1935, or through practice.

Freed from foreign competition, French shipowners, large and small, defended their protected and precious market shares, even minimal, which ensured the via-bility of their activities. This explains chronic problems in fixing freight rates and the recurrent internal tensions which evoked, to quote President Lanier during the 1964 general assembly, "rivalries of small lords in feudal times."

The Transat depended on this national maritime space. Servicing the French Antilles and North Africa surpassed the international activity of the company, both for passengers and freight. The Antilles provides a typical example of this fully protected activity. With more than 30 percent of transported passengers being pub-lic officials, the line was doubly subsidized: first through a financial contribution to run the contractual lines, and second by the presence of captive clients whose fares were already covered in part.

1962–1980: CGM and the internationalization of maritime space

The internationalized maritime space of the 1970s

From the 1960s, maritime space internationalized through trade growth, reori-entation following the dismantling of colonial empires and the emergence of new commercial powers and maritime nations, and technical innovation, namely containerization. This internationalization forced shipping lines to ally within international consortia, no longer based on a country-to-country logic but on rela-tions across wider markets, between entire maritime seaboards. The demise of ocean liners on the North Atlantic and the emergence of Japan as the world's second-largest economic power mitigated the overwhelming dominance of the North Atlantic route to the advantage of the two other east–west segments. The three main economic powers of the northern hemisphere (i.e. the "Triad" com-posed of Europe, North America, and East Asia) emerged but the three main maritime routes still operated independently from each other (Figure 3.2).

The creation of the CGM in 1973 followed the bankruptcy of the Transat and of the Messageries Maritimes, which could not resist the end of ocean liners and the downfall of protected national maritime space. There was a difficult adaptation to the internationalized maritime space thanks to a modernized fleet, but this was financed only by loans and through participation in powerful consortia. The CGM in 1979 ranked among the world's top ten shipping lines.

The adaptation of the CGM to containerization

Containerization won out in the North Atlantic in 1966 and then progressively on the other main maritime routes. To cope with the considerable investments, the Transat participated in international groups of shipping lines, or consortia,

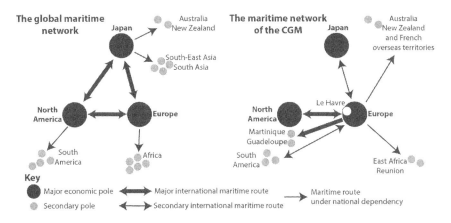

Figure 3.2 The global maritime network and the maritime network of the Transat at the end of the 1970s.

which regrouped the resources of several shipping lines over one service, offering quality service to shippers, such as weekly frequency. In 1966, the Transat integrated the Atlantic Container Line (ACL)[2] consortium on the North Atlantic. Never had shipping lines cooperated so far without merging. The capital of the society was spread up to 20 percent among each partner and each shipping line ensured the commercial representation of ACL in its national territory. Each year, financial profits were split among associates proportionate to their participation in the group, all gains and expenses having been previously put in common. ACL is the first consortium in merchant marine history. The CGM also pursued such a policy: ScanDutch for Far East trades, Europacific for the US West Coast, ANZECS for Australia and New Zealand, and SAECS for southern Africa. These consortia dominated their maritime segments. Coupled with companies' participation in maritime conferences, they allowed market regulation.

Dependence upon national maritime space

Decolonization meant that the Transat's and the Messageries Maritimes' relationships with their formerly dominated countries shrank. However, the network of the new CGM continued to serve mainly French overseas territories. In order to balance its traffic between the Antilles and metropolitan France, from 1979 CGM used four multipurpose refrigerated containerships (*porte-conteneurs réfrigérés polyvalents*, PCRP) to transport bananas from the Antilles to France and manufactured products on the return trip. This high technology service granted relative supremacy to CGM while making profits. Thanks to its overseas territories, France reached every part of the world. CGM eventually took over the lines ensured by the Messageries Maritimes.

The port of Le Havre constituted the second national anchor. There, the presence of the Transat was linked to the development of transatlantic passenger traffic. The port always evolved alongside the needs of the company: the launch of the vessel *Normandie* in 1935 required deepening the Théophile Ducrocq dock, thereby increasing by 40 percent the total water surface area of the port. In 1971, the first crane of the Terminal de l'Atlantique was dedicated to the roll-on/roll-off containerships of the ACL consortium. Since 1972 the Terminal de l'Europe was entirely dedicated to the container business of CGM.

Among European ports, Le Havre concentrated the most important traffic of the Transat and then of CGM. In 1958, Le Havre's share of total port activity was 28 percent against 18 percent for Antwerp. Other French ports occupied a secondary rank since the Transat systematically favoured Le Havre for concentrating its services there and to realize important economies of scale. In 1979, all the consortia in which the CGM participates have included Le Havre in the European calls of their services. In 1960, the share of the Transat in the total tonnage of the port reaches over 17 percent. Twenty years later, the CGM controls nearly 30 ercent of Le Havre's total container throughput, with 180,000 TEUs[3] handled. The Transat-CGM cannot ignore Le Havre which in turn cannot ignore the company. Their destinies are linked.

Since the 1980s: globalized maritime space and the growth of the CMA-CGM

From the 1980s onwards, east Asia emerged on the international economic scene. Maritime transport played a vital role in such unprecedented growth. These structural evolutions led to the globalization of maritime space which meant the end of the old CGM. The end of the 1990s witnessed the growth of three European companies of a new kind: Maersk, MSC, and CMA-CGM, whose networks perfectly matched the new world order.

Globalized maritime space

Since the mid-1980s, east Asia has lain at the heart of the world containerized transport system. The two largest transoceanic routes, trans-Pacific and Europe–Asia, start there. North Atlantic traffic remained limited but complemented the circumterrestrial freight circulation artery that links the three major poles of the world economy. North–south and south–south linkages accounted for only about 20 percent of total traffic, but did not cease growing in absolute terms. Traffic disequilibria over each of these routes only reflected those of international trade.

Already in the early 2000s, maritime space was globalized. Figure 3.3 was built based on the weekly services offered by the top 26 shipping lines. The system is global for three reasons: it has worldwide coverage, with actors operating at this scale and with regions interconnected by these services (Frémont and Soppé, 2004). It is towards Asia that containerized routes concentrating the largest traffic volumes are directed. The transformation of hierarchies is maximal. Since the nineteenth century, the North Atlantic was naturally seen as the only

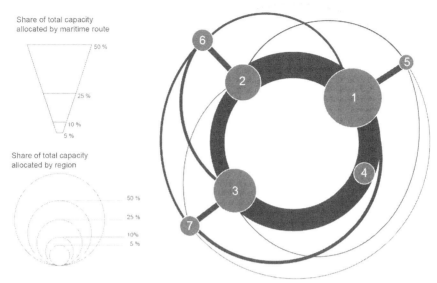

Share of total capacity
allocated by maritime route

Share of total capacity
allocated by region

1- East Asia, 2 - North America, 3 - Europe, 4 South Asia, 5 - Australia/New Zealand, 6 - South America, 7 - Africa

Figure 3.3 The global maritime network during the 2000s. Percentage of the total transport
capacity of the top 26 carriers.

major transoceanic route for passengers and goods and for competing shipping
lines. From the mid-1980s, the trans-Pacific route (US–Asia) reached the first
rank until the Europe–Asia route became even more important from the 2000s.
Progressively, the trans-Atlantic route became almost secondary (Figure 3.3).

Competition from Asian shipping lines and disappearance of the CGM

The expansion of Asian traffic has been reinforced since the 1970s by the
emergence of the newly industrialized countries there. Like Japanese maritime
companies created during the Meiji era, the new companies were a supplementary
tool within a production process entirely focusing on exports. From the 1980s,
Asian shipping lines gradually challenged the domination of European and American shipping lines, profiting from exponential growth of national markets but also
by adopting systematically an outsider strategy (Ryoo and Thanapoulou, 1999).
They remained outside the old system of maritime conferences and participated
only marginally into consortia which still structured intercontinental maritime
flows. With low market entry costs, notably due to the success of South Korean
shipyards and the low cost of their flag, they embarked on a systematic race for
overcapacity. Competition was fierce. From being outsiders, Asian shipping lines
gradually grew dominant within a market where the pole had shifted from the
Atlantic to the Pacific.

Table 3.1 Major maritime routes provided by the CGM

	Percentage of total capacity in TEUs	
	1979	*1989*
North America	16.1	21.8
East Asia	14.4	8.3
South Pacific	29.6	13.0
Martinique/Guadeloupe	23.7	23.7
Africa	3.1	8.1
Australia/New Zealand	7.7	7.6
South Asia	9.8	3.6
Indian Ocean	0.0	6.0
Total	100.0	100.0

Source: own calculation from data provided by the shipping line.

The CGM could not resist this Asian trend. As a national company it was chronically indebted since its creation and gradually lost state support. The successive restructuring plans of the 1980s reduced the labour force as well as the fleet, which decreased from 62 vessels in 1979 to 30 in 1989. Structurally weak, the CGM belonged to consortia whose market shares continually diminished due to Asian competition. And the very lucrative transport of French Antilles bananas alone could no longer compensate for the accumulated losses on the major east–west routes. At the end of the 1980s, the maritime network of the CGM had become split amongst many routes (see Table 3.1). One could have the illusion of a truly global presence, as the company operated on all the world's routes. But in fact it was structurally weak and fragile on the most crucial east–west segments. In 1993, the government of Edouard Balladur decided to privatize the CGM to get rid of a *canard boiteux* which had been wasting state money for too long.

CMA-CGM: The new paradigm of the European "carrier" shipping lines

In 1996, the CGM was sold to the CMA for 20 million francs, although it had just been recapitalized at around 1.3 billion francs by the state. The conditions of this privatization are morally difficult to accept, but one must acknowledge that the return on investment was very positive only a few years later, given the impressive growth of the CMA-CGM.

CMA-CGM is very similar to two other European shipping lines: Maersk and MSC. All three underwent enormous growth during the 1990s and the 2000s and became global. They have been the top three leading carriers since the middle of the 2000s. They are characterized by family management (Slack and Frémont, 2009). They refuse to take part in global alliances.

But above all, they operate very innovative maritime networks. Maersk was a forerunner in the creation of hub-and-spokes networks, using the port of Algeciras (Spain) in particular. From its hubs, it gradually deployed a network of North–South lines (Frémont, 2007a). In 1994, the maritime networks of MSC and CMA were very limited, but completely dissimilar from those of their competitors. Since it was set up in 1970, MSC has had a preference for routes between Northern Europe and Africa, particularly South Africa and the east coast of Africa.

In 1994, all CMA's activities were focused on a single line between Europe and East Asia. CMA was one of the first shipping lines to target the Chinese market. In 1993–4, it was one of the very first to serve Chinese ports from Hong Kong using feeder vessels from the Chinese shipping line Cosco, which at the time was the only shipping line with authorization to call at Chinese ports. CMA opened its first agency in Shanghai in 1992. It forged early links with the Chinese shipping agents Sinotrans and Penavico, a subsidiary of Cosco, which at the time were the only agents authorized to pack freight and produce documentation (Neumeister, 1994). By establishing itself early on in a market which grew from a niche position to become the largest market in the world, CMA experienced exceptional growth which paralleled that of the Chinese market.

By the middle of the 2000s, the CMA maritime networks had become genuinely global by offering full coverage of all markets, both principal and secondary (Figure 3.4). These markets tended to become similar to Maersk's. CMA diversified its network; in 2005 it purchased the shipping line Delmas, which historically operated routes between Europe and the west coast of Africa. The result is that the maritime network of CMA-CGM, like those of Maersk and MSC, is much more balanced between the different regions of the world than the networks of Asian shipping lines. Due to their size and the enormous capacities of their vessels, their market shares for the major regions of the world are equal to those of the East Asian alliances. But their market shares are very much greater in the other markets, particularly the secondary ones.

Finally, unlike the Asian shipping lines, Maersk, MSC, and CMA are dependent neither on the country where their head office is located nor on any other country. For example, they do not possess a home hub. In this respect, maritime networks serve international trade as a whole, independently of their nationality, which contrasts with Asian shipping lines that primarily serve their country's external trade. This is why these three European shipping lines could be described as "carrier" shipping lines.

CMA-CGM: a global carrier in the 2008 financial crisis

How to remain a global carrier while preserving the independence of the family group? This was the question posed by the 2008 crisis to the CMA group and to the Saadé family. The year 2008 was the eve of a period of uncertainty for containerized transport in contrast with previously high and uninterrupted growth. In 2015, uncertainty still affects the evolution of freight rates.

The year 2008 put CMA-CGM in a very difficult situation. Its profits shrank because of an acquisition programme for new ships and the development of its intermodal activities (stevedoring and rail services) to compete with other global carriers such as Maersk, MSC, and Asian companies. In 2009–10, CMA could not pay its dues but several actions saved the company. The debt was restructured with

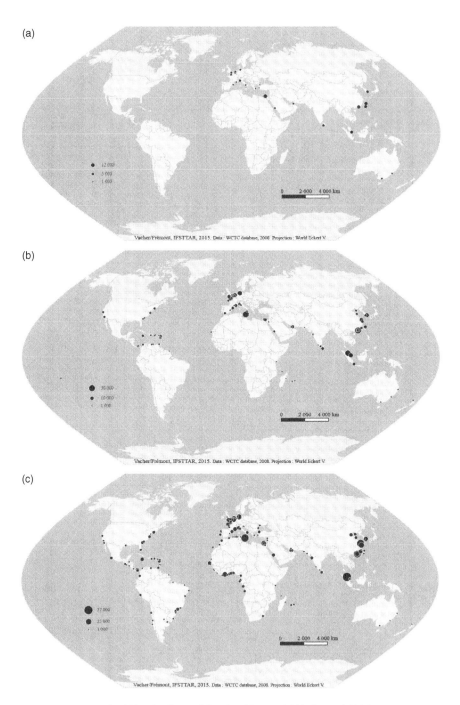

(a)

(b)

(c)

Figure 3.4 Ports of call by the CMA-CGM in 1994 (a), 2002 (b), and 2006 (c).

Note: Circles are proportional to the weekly capacity (TEUs) provided by the CMA-CGM.

the agreement of banks. CMA sold shares in stevedoring and delayed its new ship orders. In 2011, the Turkish group Yildirim brought in capital. The French state also brought in strategic investment funds. Nevertheless, the Saadé family kept control of the group.

To confront the crisis, and an increasingly uncertain container business, the world's biggest shipping lines embarked upon a global alliance strategy. This was rather new for MSC and CMA-CGM, which only participated sporadically in such alliances. Several internal causes pushed them to do so. First, global carriers ordered very large vessels or ultra large container carriers (ULCCs) of about 20,000 TEUs, maintaining overcapacity over main trading routes. These vessels are judged necessary to reduce transport costs and cope with competition. Filling these vessels requires the rationalization of services on the main routes and therefore the sharing of physical means, i.e. the ships.

In the 1990s, Asian shipping lines launched such alliances on the main east–west routes. Only two mega-alliances exist today: G6 and CKYHE. To confront them, Maersk, MSC, and CMA-CGM launched the P3 Network in 2013. This "armada," which would have accumulated 225 vessels and 2.6 M TEU capacity deployed over 29 routes, at the behest of the Chinese Ministry of Commerce, faced the veto of China's antitrust authority in June 2014. China objected to such an alliance, which concentrated almost 47 percent capacity of the Europe–Asia route. Plans were then reoriented. In August 2014, the ten year, 2M alliance between Maersk and MSC was signed (see Table 3.2). In September, CMA-CGM joined

Table 3.2 The four major alliances of the east–west trades in 2015

Alliance	*Carriers*	*Country*	*Market share of the Asia–North Europe trade (%)*
G6	American President Line Hapag Lloyd Hyundai Merchant Marine Mtsui OSK Line NYK Line Orient Overseas Container Line	Singapore Germany South Korea Japan Japan Hong Kong	24
CKYHE	COSCO K Line Yang Ming Hanjin Shipping Evergreen	China Japan Taiwan South Korea Taiwan	24
2M	Maersk MSC	Denmark Switzerland	31
Ocean Three	CMA-CGM China shipping (CSCL) UASC	France China Qatar	21

Source: own realization based on Drewry data.

the Ocean Three alliance with two other shipping lines that had never been part of an alliance: China Shipping and United Arab Shipping Company (UASC, Qatar).

Conclusion

From the Transat to the CMA-CGM, from 1945 to present, the maritime space has been reshaped dramatically by geo-economic changes. Containerization was one of the key factors of this turmoil. The segmented maritime network which was characterized by protected markets and dominated by national interests has been replaced by a globalized maritime network. Container carriers are now operating global networks. The core of their networks is shaped by the two major east–west routes connecting East Asia with Europe and North America.

The carrier CMA was one of the key players of these tremendous changes. Its geo-history breaks up the geo-history of the CGM, ex-Transat. These shipping lines belonged to the past because their national maritime network had not matched the development of the world. Furthermore, due to the lack of capital which was not provided by their shareholder, the state, they were not able to deal with new emerging markets.

The CMA-CGM is an innovative carrier. Prior to its competitors, it became a key player in the booming Chinese market. But it was also able to diversify its network through secondary but very lucrative markets as, for example, the West African range. From that perspective, it is clear that CMA-CGM is very similar with two other European carriers, Maersk Line and MSC. They have freed themselves from their national markets to become global carriers. At the same time, Asian carriers have remained dependent on their national market.

For containerization, the crisis is perhaps the beginning of a new era of maturity after three decades of tremendous growth. After being managed as a start-up, the CMA-CGM has become a major worldwide group. To cope with the lack of new markets, the group developed a classic strategy based on alliances in order to strengthen its existing position. Innovation through the network should be only possible during a period of economic growth, while conversely crisis times should be periods for consolidating market positions acquired by various competitors.

Notes

1 Bulletin d'informations commerciales, 15 January 1957.
2 ACL comprised the Dutch shipping line Holland Amerika Lijn, the Swedish Wallenius, the Swedish America Line and Swedish Transatlantic Line, the British Cunard and CGT.
3 Twenty-foot equivalent units.

References

Barbance M. (1955) *Histoire de La Compagnie Générale Transatlantique*. Paris: Arts et Métiers Graphiques.
Bauchet P. (1991) *Le Transport International dans l'économie Mondiale*. Paris: Economica.
Frémont A. (1998) *La French Line face à La mondialisation de l'espace maritime*. Paris: Anthropos.

Frémont A. (2007a) Global maritime networks: the case of Maersk. *Journal of Transport Geography*, 15(6): 431–42.

Frémont A. (2007b) *Le Monde en Boîtes. Conteneurisation et Mondialisation.* Paris: INRETS.

Frémont A., Soppé M. (2004) Les stratégies des armateurs de lignes régulières en matière de dessertes maritimes. *Belgeo*, 4: 391–406.

Levinson M. (2006) *The Box. How the Shipping Container made the World Smaller and the World Economy Bigger.* Princeton and Oxford: Princeton University Press.

Neumeister M. (1994) CMA: le bouillonnement. *Journal de La Marine Marchande*, 1323.

Ryoo D.K., Thanapoulou H.A. (1999) Liner alliances in the globalization era: a strategic tool for Asian container carriers. *Maritime Policy and Management*, 26(4): 349–67.

Slack B., Frémont A. (2009) Fifty years of organizational change in container shipping: regional shifts and the role of family firms. *Geojournal*, 74(1): 23–34.

4 Spatial networks

Tools and perspectives

Marc Barthelemy

Complex and spatial networks

There has been intense research activity these last ten years on complex networks (Albert and Barabási, 2002; Barrat *et al.*, 2008; Dorogovtsev and Mendes, 2013) with many new empirical results and models that are impossible to review thoroughly in this chapter. In particular, it is now clear that there are essentially two classes of random networks according to the statistical abundance of hubs (Amaral *et al.*, 2000). The presence of hubs strongly affects the structure of networks and their dynamics. These effects can be found in many books and articles (Dorogovtsev, 2003; Barrat *et al.*, 2008; Caldarelli, 2007; Newman, 2010; Cohen and Havlin, 2010), which usually discuss the spatial dimension of networks only very briefly. However, for many infrastructures, communication or biological networks, space is relevant, their nodes and edges are constrained by some geometry and are usually embedded in a two- or three-dimensional space. For example, power grids and transportation networks depend obviously on distance, many communication network devices have short radio range, the length of axons in a brain has a cost, and the spread of contagious diseases is not uniform across territories.

For most practical applications, the space is the two-dimensional space and the metric is the usual Euclidean distance, and we need both the topological information about the graph (given by the adjacency matrix) and the spatial information about the nodes (given by the position of the nodes). Spatial constraints have important effects on the topological properties of networks and consequently on the processes at stake (Barthelemy, 2011). If there is a cost associated to the edge length, regions that are spatially closer have usually a larger probability of being connected than remote regions, as longer links are more costly in terms of material and energy. Longer links must be compensated for by some advantage, such as being connected to a well-connected node – that is, a hub. For spatial networks such as roads and streets, the link length distribution is peaked while in other networks such as the Internet or the airline network, the distribution can be broader. The topological aspects of the network are then correlated to spatial aspects such as the location of the nodes and the length of edges.

All planar graphs (Clark and Holton, 1991) can be embedded in a two-dimensional space and can be represented as spatial networks but the converse is not necessarily true: there are some spatial and non-planar graphs. In general, however, most spatial networks are, to a good approximation, planar graphs such as road or railway networks. But there are some important exceptions such as maritime networks (Ducruet and Notteboom, 2012), or the airline network (Barrat *et al.*, 2004). For many infrastructure networks, however, planarity is unavoidable. Power grids, roads, rail and other transportation networks are good approximation planar networks. For many applications, planar spatial networks are the most important and most studies have focused on these examples.

Spatial networks were actually the subject, a long time ago, of many studies in quantitative geography. Objects of studies in geography are locations, activities, flows of individuals and goods, and already in the 1970s scientists working in quantitative geography focused on networks evolving in time and space. One can, for example, consult books such as the remarkably modern *Network Analysis in Geography* by Haggett and Chorley (1969) to realize that many modern questions in the complex system field are actually almost 50 years old. In these books, authors discuss the importance of space in the formation and evolution of networks. They develop tools to characterize spatial networks and discuss possible models. Maybe what was lacking at that time were datasets of large networks and larger computer capabilities, but a lot of interesting thoughts can be found in these early studies.

Tools for characterizing spatial networks

A graph is usually characterized by its adjacency matrix which completely characterizes its topology and is enough for most applications. This is, however, not the case for spatial networks where the spatial information is contained in the location of nodes. Two topologically identical graphs can then have completely different spatial properties and this is at the heart of the richness and complexity of spatial networks. In this section we will discuss some tools which can be helpful to characterize some aspects of spatial networks and how we can distinguish them from generic, 'non-spatial' complex networks.

The 'standard' measures: degree distribution, clustering and average shortest path length

In complex networks, the degree distribution, the clustering spectrum and the average shortest distance are of utmost importance (Albert and Barabási, 2002). Knowledge of these already gives a useful picture of the graph under study. This is, however, not the case for spatial networks where these quantities mostly inform about constraints and not really about interesting features.

Degree distribution

In very heterogeneous networks, the degree distribution is very broad and behaves often as a power law with exponent γ usually in the range [2, 3]. This form which contains no intrinsic scale (hence the name of scale-free networks) implies that the variance is very large and the average degree has no meaning: some nodes have very large degrees and are known as hubs. The existence of such hubs has important consequences on many processes taking place on networks, such as epidemic spread or synchronization, etc. In contrast with most complex networks, the physical constraints existing in spatial networks determine some of their properties (Mossa *et al.*, 2002). In particular, there is usually a sharp cut-off on the degree distribution and it is peaked around its average (Amaral *et al.*, 2000). This is true for most spatial and planar networks such as power grids or transportation networks, for example. For a spatial, non-planar network such as the airline network, the cut-off can be large enough and the degree distribution could be characterized as broad. In general, however, the range of values of the degree is very limited and we cannot observe scale-free features in spatial networks.

Clustering coefficient

The clustering coefficient of a node counts how its neighbours are connected with each other. For spatial networks, the dominant mechanism is usually to minimize a cost associated with length, and nodes have a tendency to connect to their nearest neighbours, independently from their degree. This in general implies that the clustering spectrum $C(k)$ is relatively flat for spatial networks. The same argument can be used to show that the assortativity 'spectrum' defined as the function $k_{nn}(k)$ is also approximately constant in general when spatial constraints are very strong (see Barthelemy (2011) for more details).

Average shortest path

Usually, there are many paths between two nodes in a connected network and the shortest one defines a distance on the network

$$l(i, j) = \min_{paths(i \to j)} |path|$$

where its length $|path|$ is defined as its number of edges. This quantity is infinite when there are no paths between the nodes and is equal to one for the complete graph. In most complex networks, one observes a small-world behaviour (Watts and Strogatz, 1998) where the average shortest path behaves as

$$\langle l \rangle \sim \log N$$

where N is the number of nodes in the network. Even for large N, we still have a very small average shortest path (of order 6 for N of order a million), which justifies the name of small-world network. In contrast, for a real-world spatial network embedded in a d-dimensional space, we usually observe the very different behaviour

$$\langle l \rangle \sim N^{1/d}$$

where d is the dimension of the embedding space ($d = 2$ for most cases). This result also means that to go from one node to another one, one has to cross a path of length of the order the diameter (which is not the case when shortcuts exist, such as in small-world networks). The measure of the average shortest path length could thus be a first indication whether a network is spatial and close to a lattice or if long-range links are important.

Betweenness centrality

There are many different centrality indicators characterizing the importance of a node, such as the degree, the closeness, etc., but we will focus here on the betweenness centrality (BC) $g(i)$ which is defined as (Freeman, 1977)

$$g(i) = \sum_{s \neq t} \frac{\sigma_{s,t}(i)}{\sigma_{s,t}}$$

where $\sigma_{s,t}$ is the number of shortest paths going from s to t and $\sigma_{s,t}(i)$ is the number of shortest paths going from s to t through the node i (the BC for a link is defined in a similar way). This quantity $g(i)$ thus characterizes the importance of the node i in the shortest path flow in this network and is determined by its ability to provide a path between separated regions of the network. Hubs are natural crossroads for paths and it is natural to observe a marked correlation between large values of the degree k of a node and its BC. We expect this correlation to be altered when spatial constraints become important and in order to understand this effect we consider a one-dimensional lattice which is the simplest case of a spatially ordered network. For this lattice the shortest path between two nodes is simply the Euclidean geodesic and for two points lying far from each other, the probability that the shortest path passes near the barycentre of the network is very large. In other words, the barycentre (and its neighbours) will have a large centrality as illustrated in Figure 4.1a.

In contrast, in a purely topological network with no underlying geography, this consideration does not apply anymore and if we rewire many links (as illustrated in Figure 4.1b) we observe a progressive decorrelation of centrality and space while

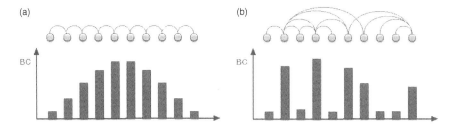

Figure 4.1 Betweenness centrality for the (one-dimensional) lattice case. The central nodes are close to the barycentre (a). For a general graph, the central nodes are usually the ones with large degree (b).

the correlation with degree increases. In a lattice, it is easy to show that the BC depends on space and is maximal at the barycenter, while in a network the BC of a node depends essentially on its degree. When the network is constituted of long links superimposed on a lattice, we then expect the appearance of 'anomalies' characterized by small degree and large BC (or conversely). Correlations between spatial position and centrality thus compete with the usual correlations between degree and centrality, leading to large fluctuations of centrality at fixed degree.

The spatial distribution of the BC thus contains a lot of information about the global structure of the network. We illustrate this on the evolution of the street network of Paris over more than 200 years with a particular focus on the nineteenth century, a period when Paris experienced large transformations under the guidance of Baron Haussmann (see Jordan, 1995 and references therein). By digitizing historical maps, we reconstructed the detailed road system (including minor streets) at six different moments in time: 1789, 1826, 1836, 1888, 1999 and 2010. We thus have snapshots of the street network before Haussmann's works (1789–1836) and after (1888–2010) which allows us to study quantitatively the effect of such central planning. Surprisingly enough, most quantitative measures on these networks reveal nothing but a natural evolution of the network. The average degree is roughly constant and the total length of the network scales as any almost regular lattice (Barthelemy *et al.*, 2013). In sharp contrast, the spatial distribution of the BC reveals the important structural changes, as shown in Figure 4.2. In particular, we observe a very important redistribution of centrality during the Haussmann period with the appearance of a reticulated structure on the 1888 map. This example illustrates well the fact that interesting information lies in the interplay between space and topology of the network and that this can be revealed by mapping the BC.

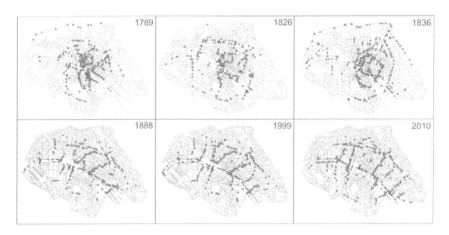

Figure 4.2 Spatial distribution of the most central nodes (with centrality g such that $g > \max\{g\}/10$).

Source: Barthelemy *et al.* (2013).

Mixing space and topology

All previous indicators describe essentially the topology of the network but are not specifically designed to characterize spatial networks. We will here briefly review other, mostly recent, indicators which provide useful information about the spatial structure of networks (for a longer discussion and references about other indices see, for example, Barthelemy, 2011).

Cell area and shape

For planar spatial networks, we have faces (or cells, or blocks for road networks) which have a certain area and shape. In order to characterize statistically these shapes, various indicators were developed some time ago (see Haggett and Chorley, 1969, for a list of these indicators). The first, simple important information is the distribution of the area $P(A)$ which in many cases follows a power law (Lammer *et al.*, 2006; Barthelemy, 2011)

$$P(A) \sim A^{-\tau}$$

where $\tau \cong 2$. We note here that a simple argument on node density fluctuation leads indeed to this value $\tau = 2$ and further empirical analysis is needed to test the universality of this result. In addition to the cell area, its shape also contains a large part of the information about the structure of the network, and can be simply characterized with the form factor ϕ. If we denote by L the major axis of the cell, the shape ratio is defined as A/L^2. In the paper, by Lammer *et al.* (2006), on the road network structure, another definition is used

$$\phi = \frac{4A}{\pi D^2}$$

where πD^2 is the area of the circumscribed circle. If this ratio is small, the cell is very anisotropic, and if ϕ is closer to one, the corresponding cell is almost circular. In many cases where rectangles and squares predominate (Lammer *et al.*, 2006; Strano *et al.*, 2012), we have $\phi \cong 0.5 - 0.6$. More recently (Louf and Barthelemy, 2014), it has been shown that an interesting characterization of the street network can be obtained with the distribution of factor ϕ given its area A: $P(\phi \mid A)$. This quantity allows to compare various planar networks and to propose a classification of street patterns (Louf and Barthelemy, 2014).

Detour index

In spatial networks, we can define at least two distances between pairs of nodes. There is the natural Euclidean distance $d_E(i, j)$ which can also be seen as the 'as crow flies' distance, and the total 'route' distance $d_R(i, j)$ from i to j by computing the sum of the length of segments that belong to the shortest path between i and j. The detour index – also called the route factor – for this pair of nodes

(i, j) is then given by

$$Q(i, j) = \frac{d_R(i, j)}{d_E(i, j)}$$

This ratio is always larger than one and the closer to one, the more efficient the network. The statistics of $Q(i, j)$ contain a lot of information about the spatial network under consideration and, for example, one can define the interesting quantity (Aldous and Shun, 2010).

$$\rho(d) = \frac{1}{N_d} \sum_{ij/d_E(i,j)=d} Q(i, j)$$

where N_d is the number of nodes such that $d_E(i, j) = d$. The shape of this function results from the combination of spatial and topological properties and can thus provide an interesting characterization of the network. This profile tells us, for various classes of Euclidean distances, how efficient the network is.

Cost and efficiency

The minimum number of links to connect N nodes is $E = N - 1$ and the corresponding network is then a tree. We can look for the tree which minimizes the total length given by the sum of the lengths of all links

$$l_T = \sum_{e \in E} d_E(e)$$

where $d_E(e)$ denotes the length of the link e. This procedure leads to the minimum spanning tree (MST) which has a total length $l_{T MST}$ (see, for example, Clark and Holton, 1991), and which can serve as a useful benchmark: it is the graph which connects all the nodes with a minimal cost. Obviously the tree is not a very efficient network from the point of view of transportation for example, and more edges are usually added to the network, leading to an increase of accessibility but also of l_T. A natural measure of the 'cost' of the network is then given by

$$C = \frac{l_T}{l_{T MST}}$$

Another measure of efficiency was also proposed in Latora and Marchiori (2001) and is defined as

$$E = \frac{1}{N(N-1)} \sum_{i \neq j} \frac{1}{l(i, j)}$$

where $l(i, j)$ is the shortest path distance from i to j. Combination of these different indicators and comparisons with the MST or the maximal planar network can be constructed in order to characterize various aspects of the networks under consideration (see, for example, Buhl *et al.*, 2006).

Simplicity

Shortest paths are not always simple and in planar networks, they can be very different from those with the smallest number of turns – the simplest paths. The statistical comparison of the lengths of the shortest and simplest paths provides non-trivial and non-local information about the spatial organization of these graphs. It tells us how the straight lines are organized in the system and in the case of time evolving networks, is able to reveal important structural changes during their evolution.

To identify the simplest path (if there is more than one such path we choose the shortest one), we first convert the graph from the primal to the dual representation, where each node corresponds to a straight line in the primal graph. These straight lines are determined by a continuity negotiation-like algorithm (Porta *et al.*, 2006). Edges in dual space, in turn, represent the intersection of straight lines in the primal graph. We denote by $l(i, j)$ the total length of the shortest path from i to j and by $l^*(i, j)$ the total length of the simplest path. The ratio $l^*(i, j)/l(i, j)$ is always larger than one and it is natural to introduce the simplicity index S as the average (Viana *et al.*, 2013)

$$S = \frac{1}{N(N-1)} \sum_{i \neq j} \frac{l^*(i, j)}{l(i, j)}$$

The simplicity index is larger than one and exactly equal to one for a regular square lattice and any tree-like network, for example. Large values of S indicate that the simplest paths are on average much longer than the shortest ones, and that the network is not easily navigable. This metric is a first indication about the spatial structure of simplest paths but mixes various scales, and in order to obtain more detailed information, we can use the simplicity profile

$$S(d) = \frac{1}{N(d)} \sum_{i, j/d_E(i, j)=d} \frac{l^*(i, j)}{l(i, j)}$$

where $N(d)$ is the number of pairs of nodes at Euclidean distance d. This quantity $S(d)$ is larger than one and its variation informs us about the large scale structure of these graphs. We can draw a generic shape of this profile: for small d, at the scale of nearest neighbours, there is a large probability that the simplest and shortest paths have the same length, yielding $S(d \to 0) \cong 1$, and increases then for small d. For very large d, it is almost always beneficial to take long straight lines when they exist, and we expect then $S(d)$ to decrease when $d \to d_{\max}$ (a similar behaviour is observed for the route-length efficiency, Aldous and Shun, 2010).

The simplicity profile will then display, in genera, *l* at least one maximum at an intermediate scale d^* for which the length differences between the shortest and the simplest path is maximum. The length d^* represents the typical size of domains not crossed by long straight lines. At this intermediate scale, the detour needed to find long straight lines for the simplest paths is very large.

These measures applied to various systems enable us to track structural changes (such as central planning operations, for example, Barthelemy *et al.*, 2013) and also to distinguish networks with different functions such as navigation (as in a street network) or distribution such as veins in leaves or in insect wings (Viana *et al.*, 2013).

Detecting communities

Community detection is an important topic in complex network studies (see the review by Fortunato, 2010). Loosely speaking, a community (or a 'module') is a set of nodes which have more connections among them than with the rest of the nodes. One of the first and simplest methods to detect these modules consists in maximizing the quantity called modularity defined in Newman and Girvan (2004), and which essentially compares the actual network with a random null model. The comparison with the null model represented by the randomized network is, however, misleading and is not well adapted to spatial networks in particular when the node attribute of interest is correlated with space (Cerina *et al.*, 2012).

Community detection was applied to many transportation networks such as cargo movements (Kaluza *et al.*, 2010), and to the worldwide air transportation network (Guimera *et al.*, 2005). In this latter case, most nodes in a community are actually determined by geographical factors and this is not very informative: the most important flows are among nodes in the same geographical regions and communities will then naturally correspond to spatial delimitation or barriers (De Montis *et al.*, 2013). More interesting are the spatial 'anomalies' which are nodes that belong to a community but which are in a disconnected geographical region. For example, in the airline network, the community of Western Europe also contains airports from Asian Russia which reveals information that goes beyond simple spatial proximity.

More generally, it is clear that in the case of spatial networks, community detection offers a visual representation of large exchange zones. It also allows the identification of inter-community links which probably play a very important role in many processes, such as trading for example.

Discussion and outlook

More historical data is always being digitized and network science appears as an important tool for analysing them. When the data are georeferenced, the networks which appear are spatial networks, for which space is a very important component. Nodes such as homes, individuals, settlements, have a particular location in space and the relation between them implies the notion of distance: individuals are connected to their neighbours, and villages and cities develop because of proximity reasons. Roughly speaking, as soon as distance plays a role in the formation of links in a network, one has to be careful with its analysis. The spatial aspect determines the way we characterize these networks and how we extract useful information. For spatial networks, most of the richness and complexity actually comes from space, and the interplay between the topology and the spatial distribution of nodes is at the heart of the structure of these networks.

For these spatial networks, it is important to distinguish the 'pure' spatial part which could have been expected for purely spatial reasons, from other reasons which may contain more interesting information (social, economic, etc.). Social networks, for example, are mostly spatials, and the probability that two individuals are connected usually decreases with distance. The study of spatial features of relations in a social network thus allows us to identify 'anomalous' relations whose probability – based on space only – is very small, but which nevertheless are observed in real situations. Such 'unexpected' links might play an important role in many phenomena such as migrations or relations between villages. Communities in networks will also contain a trivial spatial component and nodes which belong to a certain community without being in its neighborhood, are 'anomalies' which contain interesting information (Barthelemy, 2011). The importance of these meaningful links and nodes goes beyond social networks and could actually be very relevant in other, more abstract networks made of object, texts or places.

One of the main goals of spatial network analysis, beyond characterizing their structure, is to disentangle the various effects in the formation and evolution of a network and to identify the hierarchy of mechanisms. This hierarchy, in turn, will then be helpful in constructing a model based on a minimal number of parameters and assumptions.

Obviously, the list of tools presented here is not exhaustive, but more crucially it is important to keep in mind that in many situations one has to create new tools or to adapt existing ones to the questions asked and to the dataset studied.

References

Albert R., Barabási A.L. (2002) Statistical mechanics of complex networks. *Rev. Mod. Phys.*, 74: 47–97.

Aldous D.J., Shun J. (2010) Connected spatial networks over random points and a route-length statistic. *Statistical Science*, 25: 275–88.

Amaral L.A.N., Scala A., Barthelemy M., Stanley H.E. (2000) Classes of small-world networks. *Proceedings of the National Academy of Sciences*, 97(21): 11149–52.

Barrat A., Barthelemy M., Vespignani A. (2008) *Dynamical Processes in Complex Networks*. Cambridge: Cambridge University Press.

Barrat A., Barthelemy M., Pastor-Satorras R., Vespignani A. (2004) The architecture of complex weighted networks. *Proc. Natl. Acad. Sci. USA*, 101: 3747.

Barthelemy M. (2011) Spatial Networks. *Physics Reports*, 499: 1–101.

Barthelemy M., Bordin P., Berestycki H., Gribaudi M. (2013) Self-organization versus top-down planning in the evolution of a city. *Nature Scientific Reports*, 3: 2153.

Buhl J., Gautrais J., Reeves N., Solé R.V., Valverde S., Kuntz P., Theraulaz G. (2006) Topological patterns in street networks of self-organized urban settlements. *The European Physical Journal B*, 49(4): 513–22.

Caldarelli G. (2007) *Scale-free Networks: A Textbook for Graduate Students*. Oxford: Oxford University Press.

Cerina F., De Leo V., Barthelemy M., Chessa A. (2012) Spatial correlations in attribute communities. *PloS One*, 7(5): e37507.

Clark J., Holton D.A. (1991) *A First Look at Graph Theory*. Singapore: World Scientific.

Cohen R., Havlin S. (2010) *Complex Networks: Structure, Robustness and Function*. Cambridge: Cambridge University Press.

De Montis, A., Caschili S., Chessa A. (2013) Commuter networks and community detection: a method for planning sub regional areas. *The European Physical Journal Special Topics*, 215(1): 75–91.

Dorogovtsev S.N. (2003) Renormalization group for evolving networks. *Physical Review E*, 67: 045102.

Dorogovtsev S.N., Mendes J.F. (2013) *Evolution of Networks: From Biological Nets to the Internet and WWW*. Oxford: Oxford University Press.

Ducruet C., Notteboom T.E. (2012) The worldwide maritime network of container shipping: spatial structure and regional dynamics. *Global Networks*, 12(3): 395–423.

Fortunato S. (2010) Community detection in graphs. *Physics Reports*, 486(3): 75–174.

Freeman L.C. (1977) A set of measures of centrality based on betweenness. *Sociometry*, 40(1): 35–41.

Guimera R., Mossa S., Turtschi A., Amaral L.A.N. (2005) The worldwide air transportation network: Anomalous centrality, community structure, and cities' global roles. *Proceedings of the National Academy of Sciences*, 102(22): 7794–9.

Haggett P., Chorley R.J. (1969) *Network Analysis in Geography*. London: Edward Arnold.

Jordan D. (1995) *Transforming Paris: The Life and Labors of Baron Haussmann*. Chicago: University of Chicago Press.

Kaluza P., Kölzsch A., Gastner M.T., Blasius, B. (2010) The complex network of global cargo ship movements. *Journal of the Royal Society Interface*, 7(48): 1093–103.

Lammer S., Gehlsen B., Helbing D. (2006) Scaling laws in the spatial structure of urban road networks. *Physica A*, 363(1): 89–95.

Latora V., Marchiori M. (2001) Efficient behavior of small-world networks. *Physical Review Letters*, 87: 198701.

Louf R., Barthelemy M. (2014) A typology of street patterns. *Journal of The Royal Society Interface*, 11(101): 20140924.

Mossa S., Barthelemy M., Stanley H.E., Amaral L.A.N. (2002) Truncation of power law behavior in 'scale-free' network models due to information filtering. *Physical Review Letters*, 88 (13): 138701.

Newman M.E.J. (2010) *Networks: An Introduction*. Oxford: Oxford University Press.

Newman M.E.J., Girvan M. (2004) Finding and evaluating community structure in networks. *Physical Review E*, 69(2): 026113.

Porta S., Crucitti P., Latora V. (2006) The network analysis of urban streets: a primal approach. *Environment and Planning B*, 33(5): 705–25.

Strano E., Nicosia V., Latora V., Porta S., Barthelemy M. (2012) Elementary processes governing the evolution of road networks. *Nature Scientific Reports*, 2: 296.

Viana M.P., Strano E., Bordin P., Barthelemy M. (2013) The simplicity of planar networks. *Nature Scientific Reports*, 3: 3495.

Watts D.J., Strogatz S.H. (1998) Collective dynamics of 'small-world' networks. *Nature*, 393(6684): 440–2.

Part II

Modelling past maritime networks

5 From oar to sail

The role of technology and geography in the evolution of Bronze Age Mediterranean networks

Ray Rivers, Tim Evans, Carl Knappett

Overview

As evidenced by island and other archaeological records, it is hard not to be impressed by the ability of individuals in early prehistoric periods to travel long distances over water despite the simple nature of the prevailing marine technology. However, the difficulty of making such journeys and the relatively low levels of long-distance exchange has meant that such early attenuated, and often fragmented, links do not constitute substantive networks. In this chapter we chart ways in which, from such small beginnings, sea-based exchange has evolved to a point that is recognizable in sea travel of much more recent history.

Networks for sea travel do not come fully formed. There is a symbiosis between technological improvements in vessel production to make travel more reliable and straightforward and the growth of exchange that exploits this ability to travel longer distances. Moreover, the difficulty of land travel in these periods is such as to enhance the virtues of travel by water to the extent that coastal communities can often be treated as islands for the purposes of communication. Here we explore the relationship between technology and network breadth in the Mediterranean Bronze Age. Conveniently for our purposes, the Mediterranean Bronze Age has its 'dark ages' reflecting dislocation arising from the collapse of the local prevailing culture and its replacement, after some hiatus, by one with improved vessels and maritime skills. For the purpose of our premise we shall discuss the emergence of exchange networks in three distinct chronological phases; the Early Bronze Age (EBA) Cyclades, the later Middle Bronze Age (MBA) south Aegean and the Late Bronze Age (LBA) east Mediterranean. The increasing scale of the networks with the passage of time is very clear in the subsequent figures. In each case we have shown an exemplary network, discussed in more detail in the text.

In all our work we are beholden to Cyprian Broodbank whose two texts, on the EBA Cyclades (Broodbank, 2000) and the historic Mediterranean as a whole (Broodbank, 2013), are truly inspirational. For the MBA south Aegean we call heavily on our own work (Evans *et al.*, 2009; 2012: Knappett *et al.*, 2008, 2011; Rivers, 2015b). We begin with a brief resumé, to be explored in more detail later.

Geographically the Cyclades constitute a roughly homogeneous set of islands in the centre of the Aegean which, in the EBA had a common cultural identity.

Despite the need for tin, not available in the Cyclades themselves, it is argued that in the EBA prior to 2000 BC they constitute a largely self-contained inter-island network only weakly linked to the mainlands (Broodbank, 2000).

The Aegean networks of the late MBA/early LBA incorporate the Cyclades, but are now centred on north Crete, not a major part of the EBA Cycladic culture. By this time (1700–1450 BC) Minoan culture has largely replaced the original Cycladic culture and has spread through the Cyclades to the Greek and Anatolian mainlands, with which it is strongly linked.

By the LBA (1400–1100 BC) the Minoan culture has to some extent been superseded by Mycenaean culture and the range of exchange has expanded out of the south Aegean to the east Mediterranean from Egypt to Italy, encompassing several states all participating in a strong maritime network.

What is very clear is how the huge expansion of network scale from EBA to LBA is related to improvements in maritime technology. In the EBA, vessels are rowed, from dugout canoes to elite longboats with multiple rowers (Broodbank, 2000). However, it is not just technological advance that matters, but its (partial) democratization beyond elite hands. By the MBA, there are rigged sails in general use, permitting substantial cargoes and enabling much longer distance to be covered. By the time of the LBA rigging has improved further, together with the construction of larger vessels. Change in network scale and technology goes hand in hand with change in the nature of exchange. Initially we anticipate more social storage, affiliation through soft and hard power, latterly more trade.

We shall argue later that these maritime networks are conditioned by the prevailing geographic settings in which these exchanges were implemented. In particular, geography and technology come together in determining the ease with which links arise. To be acceptable, our models need to do more than provide a plausible snapshot of a network at a particular time. For example, although the EBA Cyclades remains agriculturally marginal with small populations, population does grow over the period and the network is obliged to change to take new sites into account. For the MBA Aegean, the Minoan culture centred on Knossos endures the local catastrophe of the eruption of Thera, from which it bounces back before succumbing later to Mycenaean influence. By the LBA the Mycenaean south Aegean culture is one of several in the east Mediterranean which, although they may individually wax and wane, remain part of a strong mercantile network (Broodbank, 2013).

Networks are graphs in which nodes/vertices are connected by links/edges. Our nodes are island settlements and not individuals or households. At their smallest in the EBA they are settlements within islands, of the order of 50–100 individuals. By the MBA and LBA these settlements can often be aggregated into whole-island communities, each represented by a single node, or coastal communities behaving with some sense of isolation, because of the difficulties of land travel, with a single identity. Links between islands can be aggregated similarly (Evans *et al.*, 2009). Even when we have ignored the less quantifiable connections of affiliation, 'exchange' is multivariate, incorporating migration, cultural transfer as well as the more obvious barter and trade. As to what constitutes quantifiable 'exchange' we have to fall back upon the artefact record, mainly ceramic, which even in the context of 'stuff' is limited e.g. omitting wood, slaves, animals. In our models we conflate all these components of exchange into a single numerical label, the values of which are meaningless in themselves except that, when small, they denote little connection between sites and, when large, strong connection. Similarly, the labelling of the sites is simplified, at most labelled by carrying capacities/resources and population/resource usage. Nonetheless, even if the detail is lacking, we can address broader issues concerning the success and failure of the enterprise that a network constitutes.

Models

Network modelling comes in many guises. When the data is good, network analysis provides a framework for modelling this data from which we tease out the structures within society which enable it to function and how they do so. The first problem is that Bronze Age data is very poor in comparison to that of more recent historical exchange networks. Our approach here is thus one of 'theory modelling' rather than 'data modelling' in which we turn the question around by asking to what 'agency' the networks of the different periods subscribe, if any. By definition, the networks of which we had a record did something 'well' for the periods that they existed. Can we understand what this is, and if so are there any lessons that we can carry over to other historical networks?

With poor data, it is pointless using a model that is more sophisticated than the data itself. This would lead to curve-fitting of the most banal kind. This matching of model to data is a delicate exercise. Even the most sophisticated models will do little more than give us insights in how things worked, with some similarities and some differences in detail from the archaeological record, with luck more of the former than the latter. However, the poverty of the data will leave much of the detail of their outputs unsubstantiated. We need to coarse-grain the data to the best shape that the model can address, which may also require that we coarse-grain the model. The models that we shall discuss have very few variable parameters. This is not because we have withheld parameters or fixed them arbitrarily but because many model types are naturally constrained, and there is no simple way to go beyond them without seeming arbitrary. There is a strength in using null models and otherwise restricted models in that their failure, when it occurs, tells us something about how society does not work or, more subtly, about the importance of contingency (Rivers and Evans, 2014; Rivers, 2015a). This is unlike the case in agent-based models with high dimensional parameter spaces (Premo, 2010), which we shall not consider here. When there is a wide parameter choice it is not clear whether we can always confirm our prejudices to justify them post hoc (Rivers, 2015b).

At the risk of creating a false dichotomy, it is often tactically convenient to divide our theory models into the manifestly epistemic, those models which make best use of our limited knowledge of the system, and the manifestly ontic, which make explicit assumptions about how societies behave.

The former are informed by Jaynes' principle of 'maximum ignorance' – that we should not use any information that is not given in the statement of the problem (Jaynes, 1973). That is, if we list the ways a network can occur that comply with the totality of our knowledge (and therefore we have no reason to believe that one way will occur preferentially compared to another, since that would have meant withholding information), the network will be equally likely to have occurred in any of these ways. The resulting compilation of networks will include some types that occur with greater frequency than others. We adopt the viewpoint that the networks which have occurred in the past are these 'most likely' ones. What makes this a practical way to proceed is that the 'most likely' networks are those with maximum entropy (Jaynes, 1957). Entropy is colloquially understood in terms of the disorder of a system – but can also be understood in terms of the information we possess about it. Specifically, the entropy is directly related to the number of questions we need to ask about a system to get complete understanding of it, hence the equivalence. Since we have not used any information that is not given in the statement of the problem, this maximal network does not have to be understood through a historical or social narrative beyond our initial assumptions about social behaviour. Such models include 'gravity' and 'generalized gravity' models, including the 'retail' gravity model of Wilson (e.g. see Rihll and Wilson, 1987; Davis *et al.*, 2014). What makes a gravity model 'generalized' is that, unlike for simple gravity models, the whole is no longer the sum of the parts, which is one definition of a network!

Such an epistemic approach looks passive in that it requires us to make best use of our knowledge although, even then, it is often possible to rephrase generalized gravity models in terms of social behaviour (Wilson, 2010). This is not the only approach. We shall also consider a manifestly ontic approach which assumes that the inhabitants/participants of the network are active in attempting to create the 'best' network possible, although 'best' can be moderated into something which is 'good enough' (Simon, 1957). The antecedents of this modelling lie in socioeconomics (Jackson, 2008) as cost–benefit models. Many different cost–benefit models can be constructed, although they will have important features in common. Tactically cost–benefit models allow new options in their formulation, in particular the inclusion of exploitable local resources, difficult to implement in entropy modelling. If circumstances for exchange collapse, a community now has the option of living on its own resources if it can. An example of such 'bounded rationality' is given by our cost–benefit model, termed 'ariadne', created by Tim Evans and developed by us (Evans *et al.*, 2009) to encode the costs of sustaining the populace and maintaining the network and the benefits from exchange and, as just mentioned, the use of local resources.

A willingness to accept the 'good enough' can be reformulated in terms of 'stochastic' behaviour. The idea is straightforward. Because it requires global knowledge a network does not arrive fully formed and best able to minimize 'costs' and maximize 'benefits'. It achieves the best outcome through a series of local adjustments which tend to make it 'better' step by step. These adjustments can be thought of as taking place within a 'landscape' of networks, in which each point of this landscape is a network, and where the lowest point of this landscape corresponds to the 'best' network. These sequential local adjustments do not guarantee to achieve the 'best' result, since local communities do not have access to all the information. Nonetheless, if we think of this 'landscape' as a space of hills and valleys the effect of these adjustments is, in general, to drive us 'downhill'. We may not be driven to the lowest of all valleys, but it is enough to be sufficiently downhill. That is, the resulting network may not be the 'best', but hopefully it is 'good enough'. In consequence identical initial conditions can lead to different outcomes for the same model parameters, each of which is 'good enough' without being best. This is our stochastic behaviour, which we might wish to think of in terms of contingency. It is important that this contingency is small since, otherwise, slightly different decisions made by communities in the earlier stages of adjusting to changing circumstances will lead to very different, and unpredictable, outcomes. This is unlike models like proximal point and gravity models, whose outcomes are unique, as formulated. Although they encode Poisson-like fluctuations (Leung and Yan, 1997) these do not easily lend themselves to an interpretation in terms of contingent behaviour.

This leads to an interesting question. Just as a social network has to work out its 'best' configuration through trial and error, knowing when to proceed and when to back off, so does a computer trying to find the 'best' network. We adopt such a computational scheme, the Monte Carlo algorithm, in our applications. The question is whether we should interpret 'machine time', the time steps through which the computer hunts for an optimal solution, as in any way analogous to 'historical time'. That is, might the social network have evolved in the same way, from a non-optimal beginning? Wilson (Rihll and Wilson, 1987, 1991) has argued that this is the case for the (very different) maximum entropy simulations, but the principle is the same for cost–benefit models. This has implications for how we understand evolution that we shall pursue elsewhere. It is not an issue in what follows.

There is a third class of models which we might construe as the 'easiest' networks for communities to implement, by beginning with local links which are used to leapfrog across the whole region. They can often belong to either or both of our categories with judicious redefinition although sometimes this redefinition is a little tortured (Wilson, 2010). In particular, they include the familiar proximal point analysis (PPA) which assumes that each site is only capable of interacting with a limited number k (typically $k = 3, 4$) nearest sites, a generalized Dunbar number for communities rather than individuals (Dunbar, 1992). However, as posed, each community is obliged to interact with its neighbours. It cannot withdraw from the social compact as is permitted with cost–benefit analysis. This is tempered in more general intervening opportunity models (IOMs) which, most simply, assume that the likelihood of exchange between sites is diminished the more opportunities for exchange there are between them (Stouffer, 1940; Schneider, 1959). Rather than the brutal cut-off in connections after the first few sites of PPA, IOMs smooth the diminution of interest (e.g. exponential fall-off) and, with variable strength interactions, permit relative withdrawal. In fact, there are good empirical reasons as to the importance of weak links (Granovetter, 1973), in particular that they add stability to networks (Csermely, 2004).

As a more sophisticated example of an IOM we choose the recent 'radiation' model of Simini *et al.* (2012), developed to describe commuting/employment patterns. It is stochastic, in that whether a transaction is completed after a particular journey or not is determined by whether an acceptable offer is made by merchants whose willingness to pay is taken from an arbitrary (but uniformly applied) distribution. In its original form the transaction was a job offer; in our usage it is 'payment' for a cargo. In its simplest form there are no free parameters (Simini *et al.*, 2012).

Whereas gravity and cost–benefit models measure site separation by path length, effort and time, IOMs measure it relatively; nearest neighbour, next-nearest neighbour, etc. Of course, we need the former 'geographic' results to determine the ranking. In what follows we shall be as simple as possible. For sea journeys we take the distance d_{ij} between two sites labelled i and j to be the geographic distance (in km) once headlands have been negotiated. If, on occasion, part of the journey requires land passage we introduce a frictional multiplier (greater than unity) that reflects the relative difficulty of land travel. We have taken it to be three but the outcome is insensitive to this value. We ignore winds (and tides). We know how to introduce winds at a simple level (northerly/southerly) but have yet to understand the consequences of this.

Maritime networks differ from land-based networks in that you cannot cross the sea until you have the requisite vessel that enables the journey to be made with reasonable ease. This can be understood in terms of the distance scale d, the site 'geography' scale built from the local separations d_{ij} of those sites which are necessary for the network to be connected, and the distance scale D which characterizes the distance that can be covered in a single journey ('maritime technology'). Their relative magnitude informs our choice of model. Crudely, as we shall discuss below, the EBA, MBA and LBA are characterized by $D \leq d$, $D \approx d$ and $D > d$ respectively. We stress that D is not the maximum distance that can be accomplished in a single journey, but distances beyond it are increasingly difficult.

The distance scale D can arise both explicitly and implicitly. For IOMs where sites are ranked by relative separation it is assumed that D is sufficiently large that journeys of this length enable some sort of network to appear, even if it doesn't encompass the totality of sites completely. This is somewhat less demanding than $D \geq d$, but depends on the nature of the distribution of sites. For entropy/generalized gravity models and cost-benefit models D enters explicitly through an 'ease-of-travel' or, equivalently, 'deterrence' function $V(d_{ij}/D)$ for exchange between sites i and j. We give two common examples in Figure 5.1.

The dashed line corresponds to equal 'costs' per equal 'distance' as used by Rihll and Wilson (1987) and Davis *et al.* (2014) for land-based travel. The continuous line is the profile adopted by us for the south Aegean (Evans *et al.*, 2009) and subsequent papers. The 'shoulder' accommodates the 'cost' of embarking and disembarking and handling cargo.

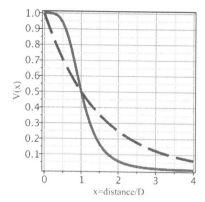

Figure 5.1 The deterrence function for relative distance $x = d/D$.

Note: The dashed line corresponds to equal 'cost' for equal 'distance' whereas the continuous curve has a shoulder that makes relatively short trip distances equally easy.

We shall introduce models as we need. One thing that is clear is that these models are socially 'neutral', whose success and failure is couched in the network terminology of rank, centrality, betweenness, etc. (Newman, 2010). They eschew narratives of civil strife, alliances, drought, etc. Insofar as they work, they reflect the 'ordinariness' of collective maritime behaviour, the 'obvious' response to population pressure, resource use and the ability to connect. We shall proceed chronologically.

Early Bronze Age Cyclades (2800–2200 BC)

The EBA Cyclades (Figure 5.2) arguably constitute a socially coherent archipelago that, for the period of interest, is largely self-contained (Broodbank, 2000). In a society of marginal agriculture, communities are small and increasing population is reflected by more, rather than larger, settlements. This leads to a problem. New sites appear in tandem with the repositioning of earlier sites, which makes it difficult to compare the Early, Middle and Late EBA. The pattern is complicated and poorly understood. Moreover, with so few communities on a typical island we cannot use standard missing data methods. For the sake of argument we adopt Broodbank's simple algorithm for positioning sites (Broodbank, 2000). Essentially, as a first guess, we keep sites as far removed from one another as possible (see Figure 5.2).

In this period exchange is bimodal. On the one hand, there are elite vessels capable of journeys of $D \approx 40$–50 km whereas local exchange is conducted via canoes of small carrying capacity, capable of journeys of $D \approx 20$ km (Broodbank (2000)). What matters is that the typical distance d that needs to be traversed to permit the Cyclades to be connected is $d \approx 40$–50 km. That is, for long distance travel the longboat technology permits single journeys just long enough to make

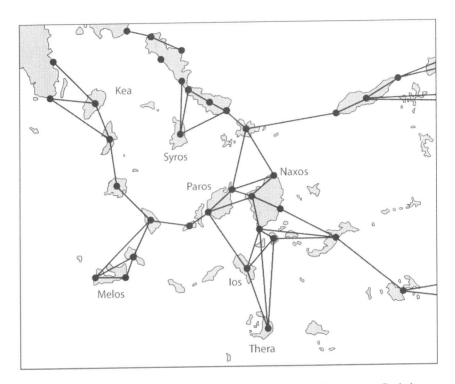

Figure 5.2 Exemplary network (PPA) for exchange in the Early Bronze Age Cyclades.

Note: Site positions are constructed from Broodbank's (2000) algorithm. The more significant sites (with larger numbers of links) are only in accord with the record at slightly better than average. See text for more details.

a functioning network across the whole Cyclades. However, travel by canoe with $D \approx 20$ km is enough for connection to local sites, which form a roughly linear U-shaped connected section (centre-west with a NNE axis). This makes access from Kea to Naxos, for example, difficult but not impossible if individuals are willing to go the long way round.

We are not looking for a single model to accommodate these different technologies. Local and global exchange has different agency and we adopt different models for each. For local exchange the inability to make long single journeys invalidates models such as proximal point analysis and intervening opportunity models which are predicated on relative separation (nearest neighbour, next-nearest neighbour, etc.) of sites when those distances are longer than the relevant D. All other models, with the exception of the retail model, give a stepping stone pattern of links along the lines above with disconnected parts where distances are too large. That is, the influence of the network as a whole on individual sites is small. This is plausible but not easily testable.

Key sites in this period lie in Greater Paros, Naxos, Melos, Keros, Ios, Syros and Kea (see Broodbank, 2000). A successful model should highlight some or more of these sites for large D. The situation is quite complicated. Some models such as the inflexible radiation model manifestly fail, as does the retail model, which fails at all distance scales. The best models, PPA (with all its faults) and ariadne give comparable results at the level of identifying plausible areas favourable to longboat activity, for instance, but only identify key sites at slightly better than chance. The main discriminant between ariadne and IOMs, in general, is that, as the number of sites on an island increases with time to reflect the increase in population, there are more island-based opportunities with IOMs. The outcome is that islands become more self-contained, with less need to look elsewhere for exchange. This can only be partly true and is not the case for gravity models and cost–benefit models, for which inter-island exchange always has advantages. In the absence of any compelling outcomes we show the PPA network in Figure 5.2. It could be argued that our poor understanding of the location of EBA sites inevitably makes the models unreliable but we would argue that what the models show is that site geography and site propinquity is not enough to determine the network. The availability of key resources, obsidian and metals, that network models of this type omit, provide social forces that skew the picture.

Middle Bronze Age south Aegean (1700–1450 BC)

Modelling comes to its fore for the pivotal case of the MBA south Aegean of Figure 5.3 in which we have displayed some of the most significant sites (named in Table 5.1). As anticipated, we have assumed the aggregation of individual sites within an island into collective sites without loss of information at the level of coarse-graining at which we are working (Evans *et al.*, 2009). Increased population is now understood as leading to a stronger island-labelled basis for exchange.

At that time the south Aegean was the scene of a thriving maritime exchange network based on the Minoan culture of north Crete, centred on Knossos (site 1). There is evidence for intensive regional trade, for example, within Crete itself, and within the Dodecanese/coastal Anatolia area, and also for important links between the regions, particularly from north Crete through Thera (site 10) and the Cylades and onwards to the two mainlands (e.g. see Knappett and Nikolakopoulou, 2005). We find that $d \approx 100$ km is the critical distance that holds the regions together. By coincidence, the Cyclades are roughly equidistant from Crete and the two mainlands at this separation.

It is this identity of distance scales across the whole south Aegean that makes network formation so special since, for sailing vessels of this period $D \approx 100$ km is also the reach of a single journey. It is no surprise that a flourishing exchange network comes into existence in the south Aegean as soon as non-elite vessels, now able to travel the necessary distance for all the components of the network to form, become readily available.

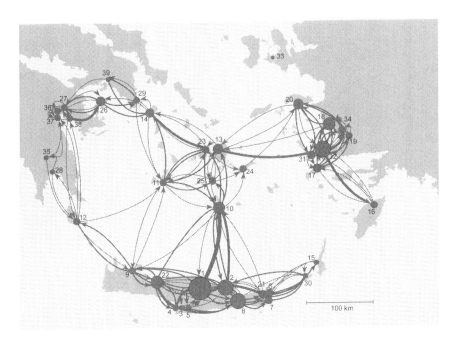

Figure 5.3 Exemplary network (ariadne) for the middle Bronze Age south Aegean.

Note: The importance of north Crete (in particular, Knossos, site 1) and its connection to the Cyclades through the Cycladic island of Thera (site 10). Site sizes represent rank and link thicknesses, flow.

Table 5.1 The sites enumerated in the MBA south Aegean of Figure 5.3 and the size of their local resource base/carrying capacity, with (S), (M), (L) denoting 'small', 'medium' or 'large' respectively *(input)*. This is to be distinguished from their 'populations', which are *outputs*

1. Knossos (L)	14. Kea (M)	27. Mycenae (L)
2. Malia (L)	15. Karpathos (S)	28. Ayios Stephanos (L)
3. Phaistos (L)	16. Rhodes (L)	29. Lavrion (M)
4. Kommos (M)	17. Kos (M)	30. Kasos (S)
5. Ayia Triadha (L)	18. Miletus (L)	31. Kalymnos (S)
6. Palaikastro (L)	19. Iasos (M)	32. Myndus (M)
7. Zakros (M)	20. Samos (M)	33. Cesme (M)
8. Gournia (L)	21. Petras (L)	34. Akbuk (M)
9. Chania (L)	22. Rethymnon (L)	35. Menelaion (S)
10. Thera (M)	23. Paroikia (M)	36. Argos (M)
11. Phylakopi (M)	24. Amorgos (S)	37. Lerna (M)
12. Kastri (M)	25. Ios (S)	38. Asine (S)
13. Naxos (L)	26. Aegina (M)	39. Eleusis (M)

Our network models need to take this confluence of geography and technology into account. We have discussed this in some detail elsewhere (Evans *et al.*, 2012; Rivers, 2015b). The models most sensitive to geography are the simple gravity and cost–benefit models. In particular, inter-regional links vary from strong to weak and the other models either do not show that pattern or, if they do, do not show the importance of north Crete and its northern links. The best of the rest is the 'radiation' model. However, neither this nor the gravity model can accommodate the shift in exchange patterns after the eruption of Thera (Knappett *et al.*, 2011; Rivers, 2015b). An example of our cost–benefit model, termed ariadne (Evans *et al.*, 2009), is displayed in Figure 5.3. The network shows the importance of north Crete and the strong connections between north Crete and the Cyclades through Thera. More details are given elsewhere (Evans *et al.*, 2012).

Although, again, ariadne stresses the importance of geography, it also stresses the importance of balancing the benefits of local resources against those of exchange and the costs of sustaining the network. Although we did not discuss this for the EBA there are, in addition to the deterrence function, two parameters that characterize the model; the relative benefits of exchange to local resources and the relative costs of sustaining the population and the network to either. When the benefits of exchange are costs of sustaining the network are relatively strong we find ourselves in a Goldilocks situation, in which being 'just right' between boom and bust restricts our options strongly, which is what we need for postdictive power (Knappett *et al.*, 2008). Moreover, our stochastic ambiguity, or contingency, is low for this scenario. Further, ariadne not only takes us through the eruption with an explanation of the necessary shifts in exchange patterns but also provides a plausible scenario for the demise of Minoan culture, in an environment in which increasing costs makes contingency high (Knappett *et al.*, 2011).

Late Bronze Age east Mediterranean (1400–1100 BC)

A major characteristic of LBA maritime exchange is the presence of large sailing vessels, such as that of the well-documented wreck of the Uluburun ship of about 1300 BC (Pulak, 1998), capable of carrying heavy cargoes, tramping the Mediterranean coast. For the EBA and the MBA the journeys that we have in mind are typically journées, those that can be accomplished in a day, 100 km or so, at best (MBA). For the sites displayed in Figure 5.4, named in Table 5.2, it needs journeys of 175 km to connect the south Aegean to include Rhodes and, separately, to link the Anatolian coast to Cyprus. Journeys of 300 km link Egypt to Anatolia but it needs journeys of 400 km to link Rhodes to Cyprus.

Models sensitive to these large distances between ports, such as the simple gravity model and ariadne, are ill-equipped to deal with the multi-day journeys which are necessary in the LBA. For example, they find it very difficult to connect the more far-flung sites like Sicily. For long links to be made possible in these models, short links have to be overwhelmingly strong. Constraining the gravity models leads to little improvement. In situations like this, intervening opportunity models would seem to have the advantage in connectivity, where site ranking leads to

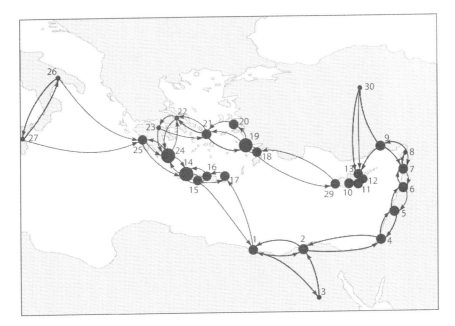

Figure 5.4 Exemplary network (radiation intermediate opportunity model) for the Late
Bronze Age east Mediterranean.

Note: Site sizes represent total inflows, link thicknesses flows. For clarity there has been some
simplification with less relevant small links omitted.

Table 5.2 The sites enumerated in the LBA east Mediterranean of Figure 5.4, taken to have
the same local resource base

1. Marsa Matruh	11. Hala Sultan Tekke	21. Grotta-Aplomata
2. Alexandria	12. Enkomi	22. Athens
3. Amarna	13. Kazaphani	23. Mycenae
4. Tel el-Ajjul	14. Chania	24. Kythera
5. Tel Abu Hawam	15. Kommos	25. Pylos
6. Byblos	16. Knossos	26. Scoglio Del Tonno
7. Ugarit	17. Palaikastro	27. Thapsos
8. Alalakh	18. Rhodes	28. Antinori (off Figure)
9. Tarsus	19. Kos	29. Kouklia
10. Maroni	20. Miletus	30. Hattusa

a natural progression of linked sites, as most likely happened with the voyage of
the Uluburun vessel (Figure 5.3). However, the sensitivity of IOMs as to which
sites have been included nullifies their advantage to some extent. We have already
seen this with the EBA Cyclades for which the more island sites there are, there
is less need for islands to interact. There is a tendency for the same effect here,
because of the large number of sites on or near Cyprus and on Crete and the nearby

south Aegean. We also have the additional problem that dropping anchor off an inhospitable coast to enable a longer journey to be made effectively constitutes an additional site with zero attributes. Since its only role is to let a single journey pass through it, the effect can be a shuffling of ranked distance. We adopt this once for the east Mediterranean where we halve the long link between Rhodes and Cyprus (e.g. Kouklia) to make the journey happen once it has begun. Otherwise the two halves of the network do not connect. We show the network following from the resulting radiation model in Figure 5.3. We see a network of coastal links from north Africa and Egypt to the Levant, with strong sea links between the Levant and Cyprus. The south Aegean (of our MBA analysis) and the Greek and Anatolian coasts form an interstitial role in this wider network in which Crete still plays an important role. However, while there are weak links between Crete and north Africa/Egypt there are none from Crete to Cyprus. Cyprus connects (after our tweaking) to this Mycenaean network through Rhodes. In turn, the Mycenaean network connects to Italy and Sicily from the west. Although many of the features seem correct (Broodbank, 2013) we are not yet in a position to say to what extent this overall pattern agrees with the mercantile networks of the time since we have taken the simplest case of equal state carrying capacities and we have not properly explored the sensitivity to sites that we have not included. We postpone this to future work.

Summary

There is continual feedback between maritime geography and technology. New maritime networks come into existence as soon as the improvements in vessels permit but the agency changes most simply according as the relative distance scale D/d for ease of travel (D) and geographic connectivity (d) increases. This is reflected in our models which, beginning with simple models for the EBA in which PPA works as well as anything, to highly distance sensitive cost–benefit models in the MBA, to intervening opportunity models to accommodate tramping in the LBA. We should not ask too much of our models, particularly given the poverty of the data (reflected in the very small number of sites). At best they help our understanding of how the 'real world' works rather than demonstrate what happens in detailed reality. However, by the LBA we are seeing maritime networks of a type that survive for centuries. The new age has begun.

References

Broodbank C. (2000) *An Island Archaeology of the Early Cyclades*. Cambridge: Cambridge University Press.

Broodbank C. (2013) *The Making of the Middle Sea*. London: Thames and Hudson.

Csermely P. (2004) Strong links are important, but weak links stabilize them. *Trends in Biochemical Science*, 29: 331–4.

Davis T., Fry H.,Wilson A., Palmisano A., Altaweel M., Radner K. (2014) Application of an energy maximizing and dynamics model for understanding settlement structure: the Khabur Triangle in the Middle Bronze and Iron Ages. *Journ. Arch. Sci.*, 43: 143–54.

Dunbar R.I.M. (1992) Neocortex size as a constraint on group size in primates. *Journal of Human Evolution*, 22: 469–93.

Evans T., Knappett C., Rivers R. (2009) Using statistical physics to understand relational space: a case study from Mediterranean prehistory. In: Lane D., Pumain D., Van der Leeuw S., West G. (Eds), *Complexity Perspectives in Innovation and Social Change*, Berlin: Springer Methodos Series, pp. 451–79.

Evans T., Rivers R., Knappett C. (2012) Interactions in space for archaeological models. *Advances in Complex Systems*, 15: 1150009.

Granovetter M.S. (1973) The strength of weak ties. *American Journal of Sociology*, 78(6): 1360–80.

Jackson, M.O. (2008) *Social and Economic Networks*. Princeton, NJ: Princeton University Press.

Jaynes E.T. (1957) Information theory and statistical mechanics. *Physical Review*, 106(4): 620–30.

Jaynes E.T. (1973) The well-posed problem. *Foundations of Physics*, 3: 477–93.

Knappett C., Nikolakopoulou I. (2005) Exchange and affiliation networks in the MBA southern Aegean: Crete, Akrotiri and Miletus. In: Laffineur R., Greco E. (Eds), *Emporia: Aegeans in East and West Mediterranean*, Liège: Aegaeum 25, pp. 175–84.

Knappett C., Evans T., Rivers R. (2008) Modelling maritime interaction in the Aegean Bronze Age. *Antiquity*, 82: 1009–24.

Knappett C., Evans T., Rivers R. (2011) Modelling maritime interaction in the Aegean Bronze Age, II: the eruption of Thera and the burning of the palaces. *Antiquity*, 85: 1008–23.

Leung Y., Yan J. (1997) A note on the fluctuation of flows under the entropy principle. *Transportation Research Part B*, 31: 417–23.

Newman M.E.J. (2010) *Networks: An Introduction*. Oxford: Oxford University Press.

Premo, L.S. (2010) Equifinality and explanation: the role of agent-modelling in post-positivist archaeology. In: Costopoulos A., Lake M. (Eds), *Simulating Change. Archaeology into the Twenty-First Century. Foundations of Archaeological Inquiry*, Salt Lake City: The University of Utah Press, pp. 28–37.

Pulak, C. (1998) The Uluburun Shipwreck: An Overview. *International Journal of Nautical Archaeology*, 27: 188–224.

Rihll T.E., Wilson, A.G. (1987) Spatial interaction and structural models in historical analysis: some possibilities and an example. *Histoire & Mesure*, 2: 5–32.

Rihll T.E., Wilson A.G. (1991) Modelling settlement structures in Ancient Greece: new approaches to the Polis. In: Rich, J., Wallace-Hadrill, A. (Eds), *City and Country in the Ancient World*, London: Routledge, pp. 59–95.

Rivers R. (2015a) Can archaeological models always fulfil our prejudices? In: Collar A., Coward F., Brughmans T. (Eds), *The Connected Past*, Oxford: Oxford University Press (in press) .

Rivers R.J. (2015b) New approaches to the Theran eruption. In: Knappett. C., Leidwanger J. (Eds), *Networks of Maritime Connectivity in the Ancient Mediterranean: Structure, Continuity, and Change over the Longue Durée*, Oxford: Oxford University Press (in press).

Rivers, R., Evans, T. (2014) New approaches to Archaic Greek settlement structure, *Les Nouvelles de l'archéologie*, 135: 21–7.

Schneider M. (1959) Gravity models and trip distribution theory. *Papers of the Regional Science Association*, 5: 51–8.

Simini F., González M.C., Maritan A., Barabási A.L. (2012) A universal model for mobility and migration patterns. *Nature*, 484: 10856.

Simon H. (1957) *Models of Man: Social and Rational*. New York: John Wiley and Sons.

Stouffer S.A. (1940) Intervening opportunities: A theory relating mobility and distance. *American Sociology Review*, 5: 845–67.

Wilson A. (2010) Entropy in urban and regional modelling: retrospect and prospect. *Geographic Analysis*, 42: 364–94.

6 Venetian maritime supremacy through time

A visualization experiment

Mélanie Fournier

Venice is not only one of the most beautiful cities in the world, but also was once a powerful colonial empire (Thiriet, 1976: 37). The Republic of Venice was born both on shore and at sea. The Venetians always knew how to take advantage of the sea—the Doge symbolically married the Republic with the sea every year. It is almost a cliché to think about Venice and its churches, canals, gondolas, architecture, and paintings. But Venice was, first and foremost, a maritime Republic; master in the art of navigation and trade (Luzzatto, 1961; Lane, 1985; Costantini, 2005; Judde de Larivière, 2008).

At the end of the thirteenth century, the Venetian Senate began to use its galleys, or warships, for commercial navigation under a state regime. After a series of tests, the Senate in 1315 established a system of auctioning galleys for individual trading voyages, called the *Incanto*. Within this system, the Senate would decide before departure all the conditions of navigation such as the calls, duration of the stopovers for loading and unloading, departure date, price of the space (*carats*) for the merchandise, and the degree of discretion the commander might be authorized to exercise.

Between 1315 and 1462, the galleys, on eight regular shipping lanes,[1] served not only the Venetian colonies all around the Mediterranean Sea but also great trade and exchange posts like Antwerp, Bruges, London, Aigues-Mortes, Seville, Lisbon, Constantinople, Beirut, Damascus, Tana, and Heraklion. As it was necessary to make profitable use of the warships during peacetime, those shipping lanes were dedicated to high-value merchandise such as silk, gold, and spices.

Frederic Lane described the Venetian maritime trading system as complex and polymorphic (Lane, 1985). There were several systems for maritime trade. We have chosen to focus on the *Incanto* because it would be pretentious of us to try to visualize the Venetian navigation system all at once. Following the example of Braudel, for whom there was not a single Mediterranean Sea, but rather several seas participating in a global and complex system (Braudel, 1949), no single visualization can adequately describe the complexity of maritime routes and exchanges. Our discussion of Venetian maritime trade, within the *Incanto* system, via the Mediterranean Sea, the Black Sea, and the Atlantic coast, from Portugal to Belgium, is only a representation of the maritime space dominated by the Venetians, such as it was reported in official sources.

We divided our work into three phases. The first was dedicated to identifying the sources and their location, digitizing documents and then processing them. Our sources are diverse: the classic histories of Venice, the medieval economy, comprehensive studies of the Venetian economy, studies of the Venetian ships, etc. Having analyzed the secondary sources we then addressed the original documents. The archives of the *Incanti*[2] are available at the Archivio di Stato in Venice and start officially in 1329–30. Within the set of previous studies of the *Incanto*, two published works caught our attention: "Le film d'un grand système de navigation: les galères vénitiennes, XIVe-XVIe siècles," written in 1961 by Tenenti and Vivanti, and *Le Système de l'Incanto des Galées du Marché à Venise (Fin XIIIe-Milieu XV siècles)*, a dissertation defended in 1992 and published in 1995 by Doris Stöckly.

As our second step, we extracted geographical information from our sources and determined the nodes and segments, respectively the ports and landmarks, as well as the routes. A crucial step during this phase was to disambiguate different names appearing for the same location and anachronic names (e.g. French colonial names in north Africa). For that purpose, we used existing databases such as those from the *Pleiades* project[3] and the *Digital Atlas of Roman and Medieval Civilizations* (de Graauw, 2013),[4] developed and maintained by Harvard University. Unfortunately, several sites could not be idenfitied so they remained without location.

Finally, we compiled the results of these two phases into our own database, storing, analysing and visualizing our collection of information. We dedicated this third and final phase to the visualization processes and to the possibilities for refining the ships' trajectories and navigation patterns, including seasonal variations, winds, currents, technical developments, geopolitics, and dangers. We limited ourselves to the 170 years of Stöckly's study (1283–1453). We then focused our efforts on a visualization of the past using geographic information systems (GIS) and mathematical modeling. Until now representations of the *Incanto* were restricted to tabular and narrative formats, but today GIS and the more recent use of algorithms improve the way we practice history.

Sources

An endless framework

The Venetian maritime world has been much studied, as have maritime routes in general (Robinson and Wilson, 2011; Arnaud, 2005), the establishment of important flows on long distances since antiquity and before (see Chapter 5 on Bronze Age Mediterranean networks), and appreciation of time, distance and environmental considerations (Arnaud, 1993). We also have good knowledge, at a very fine level of granularity, of the structure of the Venetian system of trade, which was built on economic and political monopolies, even leading to the economic asphyxia of competing islands on its own lagoon (Crouzet-Pavan, 1995).

Several authors have analyzed the *Incanto* system (Doumerc, 1991; Hocquet, 2006; Lane, 1985; Luzzatto, 1941; Tenenti and Vivanti, 1961; Thiriet, 1962), with differences in beginning and end dates. For example, Vivanti and Tenenti only refer to the documents within the *Senato Misti, Senato Mar*, and *Incanti di galere* series, from 1332 to 1508. As for Hocquet, he made the transfer of galleys by auction start in 1325–29, on the basis of a 1962 study by F. Thiriet (Hocquet, 2006: 94, 108). But none of these studies made modeling and visualization a priority, with one exception: Tenenti and Vivanti focused on the cartographic representation of voyages between 1332 and 1534. They studied the *Incanto* system on the basis of documents found in the official source, the Senate's registers. For each year, Jacques Bertin,[5] who worked with Tenenti and Vivanti, mapped the shipping lanes as they were described in the archives. In his visualization, the thumbnails are put end to end, providing a "film sequence" (see Figure 6.1). Although it is excellent and original cartographic work, the article is limited in terms of the data described.

Even if authors such as Lane or Tenenti and Vivanti made an effort at cartographic representation always keeping in mind the idea that history has two eyes—geography and chronology—later studies still demonstrate a lack of modeling and visualization of the data, overwhelming the reader with dense details and information. For example, Massimo Costantini in *Una Repubblica nata sul mare*, published in 2005, presents ten years of research on navigation and trade in Venice with only one tiny and unreadable map that cannot help the reader understand the two possible itineraries used by the Venetians from Negroponte (Eubea) to Constantinople (Istanbul) (Costantini, 2005: 18).

An exhaustive analysis of primary sources and cross-referenced information

For our model, we used Stöckly's work, in which the accent is clearly put on an exhaustive compilation of geographical and economic information, including indicators of information availability in the raw documents of several archival collections (see Figure 6.2) from 1283 until 1453. Her research led her to consider the start of the embryonic auctioning system in around 1283, and to choose not to describe the eighth and last lane, called *Trafego* (set up in 1460), justifying this because of a decline of the auctioning system after 1453 (the fall of Constantinople) and the general maritime decline of Venice after 1424.

In spite of impressive use of databases and cross-referenced information, the lack of visualization and more systematic modeling of the data she extracted and translated led to inconsistencies and contradictions from one chapter to another, making understanding of the phenomena (the *Incanti*, maritime traffic, etc.) sometimes difficult. One of the best examples is the reference to Candia. Candia was the Venetian name of the island of Crete, but also of the capital (today Heraklion). In the appendices, Stöckly uses the Latin name Creta to refer to the island, whereas Candia referred to the port, which is not clear and not followed scrupulously in the chapters.

The idea of modeling the past faces some difficulties and constraints that have been defined and studied since the end of the 1990s and the beginning of the 2000s (Plewe, 2002; Knowles, 2002; Gregory and Healey, 2007; Hillier and Knowles,

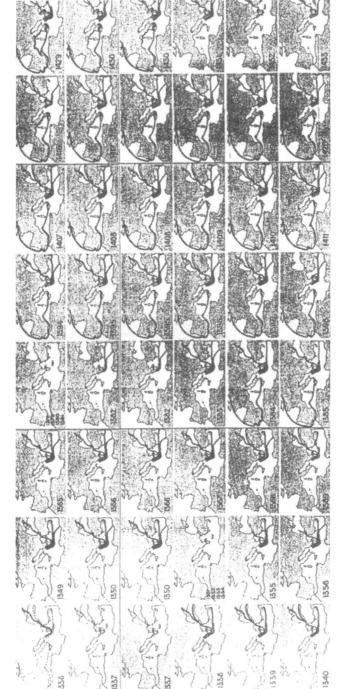

Figure 6.1 Example of the maps of the *Incanto* according to Tenenti and Vivanti, in *les Annales*, 1961.

Note: Cartography by Jacques Bertin.

Figure 6.2 Example of the appendix of D. Stöckly's thesis (1992) prepared for optical character recognition.

2008; Grossner, 2010), notably because of the growing interest of historians for geographical information systems. In spite of the large volume of publications on Venetian maritime navigation, modeling and visualization of the data are rarely the central points of the studies.

Methodology

Our workflow has consisted of selecting information from Stöckly's work traceable to the original documents. Then we applied optical character recognition (OCR) software, and transformed the data into a graphic maritime network under a GIS format.

How to deal with the navigation routes and their obstacles?

Pascal Arnaud defines navigation routes as the planned itineraries for a journey which were actually used to go from a port of origin to a destination port (Arnaud, 2005). We define obstacles as the parameters limiting or slowing down the design of the maritime routes as described and reported in the documents for the researchers now, mariners then. They are divided into two categories. In the first, we find, among others, lack of information, misinterpretation of the documents, or inconsistencies between primary and secondary sources. The second category deals with the physical (winds, climate, piracy), economic (veto from the Pope, rise and fall of prices), and political (rebellion, war, diplomatic issue) obstacles which would cause a ship to follow a route other than the ordinary one and ports of call imposed in the Senate's instructions.

At the same time, we studied routes and ports with a morphological and functional approach, essentially for the disambiguation of names. Several publications deal with parameters in order to take into account elements such as different types of journeys, in particular the differentiation between the overseas connection and coastal short-range connections.

Optical character recognition (OCR)

In order to have access to the records from the *Incanto* auctions, we scanned 37 pages from the original document of Stöckly (see Chapter 9 by Ducruet et al. for another example of OCR application). The auctions are represented in tables, where each line corresponds to one vessel with convoys grouped together. We decided to set aside information like the name of the captain or the date of departure, and focused in particular on each final destination, as well as on all the intermediate stopovers. In many cases, the tables mention the number of days spent in a harbour, or the number of ships that were still present at that port. Because the original format of the document was obsolete (*dBase III+*), we had to use OCR software on the paper version (see Figure 6.2). This process allowed us to extract the data, store it in an appropriately formatted database, and manipulate the entries efficiently, for example when disambiguating place names and extracting the number of maximum days allowed in a port.

From OCR to GIS and networks

The resulting database includes the year, the name of the shipping lane, and, when available, names of intermediary harbours, indications of the number of ships, or the number of days spent in a city, among other things. We decided to transform these data into a GIS; a map web app; and a geospatial network (with the collaboration of Dr. Karl Grossner from Stanford University Libraries).[6]

> **GIS:** We created our own gazetteer with the names extracted from Stöckly that we compared with other sources and existing databases such as *DARMC* and *Pleiades*. We indicated the variants of the names, if possible, the sources, and an image when it was available. Then we created two layers of vectors in shapefile format. The first shapefile contains the ports and the average number of days spent in stopover for our period (1283–1453), when the information was available. The layer is of course incomplete, as we have not been able to identify all the sites listed in the archives. In the second shapefile we drew, per date, the segments that the convoys were required to make by order of the Senate (see Figure 6.3). Between 1294 and 1453, 278 ships left Venice for Cyprus and Armenia with a regular call in Crete and sometimes going on to Syria (Stockly, 1995: 119). Finally, we used one of the story map templates developed by ESRI[7] to make documents easily "digestible," visible, and dynamic when they are difficult to access and/or read. The reader can

compare Figure 6.3 with the tabular format created by Stöckly and displayed in Figure 6.2.

Map web app (Fournier, 2013): We created eight maps (displayed in the center of the screen), one for each line and a final summary displaying all the lines (see Figure 6.4). By clicking on the black points, a pop-up window displays information about the port, as well as an engraving where it has been possible to find one. The size of the points is based on the average number of days authorized in a port. The left panel of the screen contains information necessary to understand the functioning of the lines and their phases of implementation, development, and decline, as well as period of use, number of ships identified, and interruptions. The user can scroll up and down, choose the line, and create customized map. Finally, in the upper right corner, a legend appears and disappears by clicking. It explains information layers previously presented as well as the territories dominated by the Venetians in 1200, 1300, and 1400. Data have been created by Euratlas,[8] a Swiss-based company providing historical digital data representing the geopolitical situation at the end of each century. The recourse to these vectors is a temporary solution. In the course of the readings, we extracted in parallel the territories (*Stato da Mar*) acquired and lost over time by the Venetians or in their name during the centuries along with temporal indications.[9] Currently the interface exists only in French but there are plans to publish an English version, implement a more complete and accurate layer of Venetian possessions, and transform the actual tool into not only a spatial, but also a temporal navigator, allowing the user to imagine the movement of lines over time as the breath of Venice.

Geospatial network: Data for the 1283–1453 period was shared with a group from Stanford University Libraries who developed and implemented ORBIS.[10] Each ship entry was divided into segments, one for each leg of a maritime route, as it was followed by ships and reported in secondary sources. The model consists of 570 distinct segments linking 114 sites. Figure 6.5 represents route density by the number of ships, with line thickness corresponding to several ranges of weights. Sites are sized according to the total number of ships that stopped there. For all place pairs the shortest paths have been calculated using the Mediterranean Sea grid of ORBIS. The sharp route edges reflect the 0.10 degree spacing of that grid. The thickness of the segments shows perfectly the importance of the connections between Venice and the oriental Mediterranean basin and the Black Sea.

Visualizing the maritime deployment of Venice

From book to GIS

GIS allows us to decrypt what books cannot show. The added-value is spatial reasoning along with the ability to make observations based on variations of temporal granularity, and thus to cross-check sources. For example, Stöckly, when we

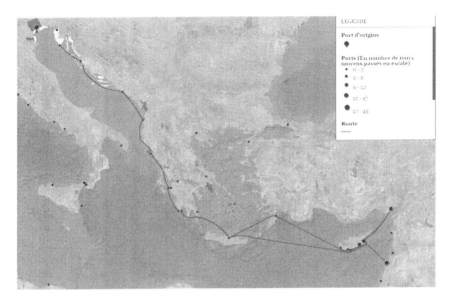

Figure 6.3 The Cyprus–Armenia line (1294–1453).

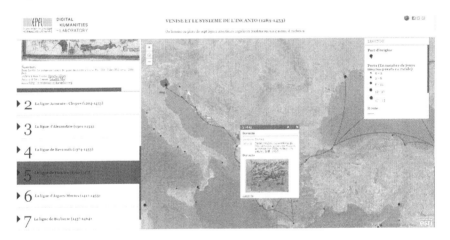

Figure 6.4 The *Incanto* system as we represented it in our GIS (http://incanti.dhlab.ch/).

met her, had identified the diaries of pilgrims, travellers, and surgeons as valuable sources of information. In Marino Sanudo, *I diarii,* we found the story of a voyage that took place in October 1498. The vessel left Cadiz on 21 October 1498, passed the Finisterra on 24 October 1498 and was in Southampton on 30 October 1498. Those types of sources helped us, among others, to validate that navigation between the Strait of Gibraltar and the English Channel had no calls, or that some of the journeys between Pula and England took 42 days without any stops.

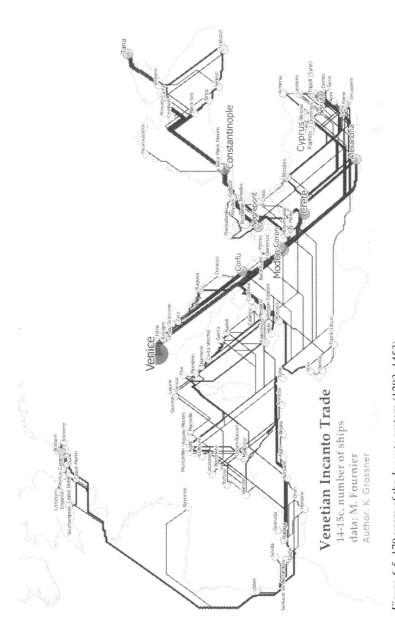

Figure 6.5 170 years of the *Incanto* system (1283–1453).

Note: The position of nodes are based on actual coordinates, with slight modifications for readability. The size of a node depends logarithmically on its degree (max = 35, min = 1). An arc shows the direction of the corresponding route.

What have we learned from using a GIS platform? In our non-probabilistic hypothesis, we chose to represent only the more credible and plausible segments described in the primary sources and re-transcribed by Stöckly in the appendices of her thesis (see Figure 6.3). Unlike some historians (Costantini, 2005) who assume that the non-written calls in the Adriatic are familiar and used for each journey, we decided not to represent any segment that had not been verified or reported by any primary source in our possession.

This first visualization is obviously simplified and truncated, as it represents only the major segments for which we have information. However, it provides us with a basis on which we can calibrate the model step by step, adding the parameters which constrain potential sea routes.

In this work, only the voyages from Venice are represented. It is very rare in the documents to find references to calls on the way back to Venice, but we know the return itineraries were generally different than the outbound route (Stöckly, 1992; Janni, 1984). Because of the dynamic nature of traffic patterns, by applying motion to the visualization, the user can better understand how communication axes set the pace of life around the Mediterranean Sea (Doumerc, 2012).

The same logic has been applied for the ports, anchorages, and landmarks transcribed in the secondary sources that we located based on cross-referencing with projects like *Pleiades* and the *DARMC*, or collections of studies such as *Ports and navigation in the Mediterranean Sea during the Middle Age* (Fabre *et al.*, 2004), in which we identified some of the sites mentioned in the *Incanti* documents, especially in the western basin (Gulf of Lion and along the west coast of Italy, and for Cyprus). When it was impossible to identify the site, the name, or even an approximate location, we decided not to represent them. However, we kept those names for the mathematical modeling (see next sub-section). We represented the port of origin, ports of call, and arrival port, which, in the case of the *Incanti* was the destination of the shipping lane as designated in the Senate documents. Some of those ports were used as hubs, i.e. as platforms used for the redistribution of goods for local and regional markets (e.g. Negroponte). Those platforms were also an interesting and valuable gate to more distant markets such as Tana on the Black Sea, which opened the way to China (Cathay).

Counting active nodes and links to show the vitality of the system

Other ways to visualize and analyze the system based on the extraction and counting of nodes and segments include complex networks, port centrality, and shortest paths calculation. Of course, the recourse to graphs to show the evolution of a phenomenon over time or to measure the vitality of a port is not new. However, the counting of active links and nodes has not been done in an extensive manner in the case of Venice; growth and decline of its system were demonstrated either in a very general way and confounded with the Venetian maritime activity in general, or by each shipping line (Karpov, 1991; Stockly, 1995; Thiriet, 1979).

The graph shown in Figure 6.6 is composed of three lines representing, from 1283 until 1453, the number of nodes, the number of segments linking sites, and

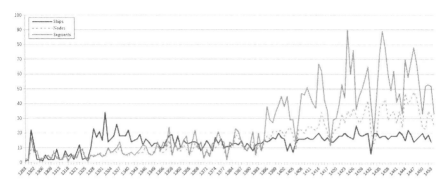

Figure 6.6 The evolution of the *Incanto* system based on the comparison between the number of nodes, segments, and ships for the 1283–1453 period.

Note: Graph by Ducruet, ships' data by Fournier, segments and nodes data by Rochat.

the number of ships recorded according to the figures extracted from secondary sources. It is important to note that we only took into account the total number of ships per year and not the number of convoys. Four periods appear clearly in the graph. Except from a peak in 1301, the evolution of ports and routes used from 1283 until 1327 follows the number of ships sent from Venice to Cyprus, Armenia, Romania, the Black Sea, Alexandria, and Flanders. The 1301 peak can be explained by a lack of information about the number of ships in the convoys as recorded by Stöckly (1302–27), interruptions, and because this period is a test phase for the Senate (Stockly, 1995: 104–5).

The period from 1327 to 1349 is a very active one; the graph shows an increase of the number of ships sent overseas. This rise is due to activity growth in the Black Sea, the development of exchanges with Armenia via Cyprus, and the lift of the papal interdiction to trade with Egypt and Syria in 1344. Ports such as La Tana and Trabzon became regular calls, and a truce signed in 1332 facilitated exchange between Venice and the Black Sea, which explains the higher number of active nodes and segments. From 1343, even if more than ten ships left Venice every year, the situation in the Black Sea deteriorated (Lane, 1978) concluding in an interdiction of navigation for the galleys in 1347. This can explain the decrease of nodes and segments used until 1350. During the war with Genoa (1351–4), the state requisitioned the galleys. However, this total absence of convoys did not mean a total interruption of the trade for the Venetians as the private navigation continued.

Besides a new war with Genoa (1378–81), the period from 1355 to 1395 is unstable, but the diversification in terms of ports touched and navigation segments is higher. The sawtooth-like evolution can be partly explained by the difficult political context around the Black Sea, and also shows the adaptation capacities in this context: when the usual ports cannot be reached, new ones appear. This is the case, for example with the Cyprus line that is replaced by the Beirut line between 1372 and 1438.

The last period (1395–1453) shows a boost in the relations, either by a greater ship density on established segments or by the implementation of new ones. This growth is linked to the increase of new active nodes, especially when there is a new site acquired by Venice. Although itineraries and number of ships per convoy are relatively stable during this period, we can see three distinct and important drops in the number of active nodes and segments: 1406, 1418, and 1433. The decrease can be explained by the recourse to a double convoy generally used by the Venetians when a dangerous situation is known to be at the destination port. For example, instead of sending a convoy to Beirut and another one to Alexandria they group the two. The diminution can also be related to the lack of interest of the Venetian merchants for some traditional destinations. The drops in the number of ships per year are, to a certain extent, less visible, with the exception of 1403, 1405, and especially 1432.

More can be done and more explanations, node by node and segment after segment, can be given. This is why the recourse to complex networks, as it opens new opportunities of work, deserves to be pushed[11] as it can bring clarifications on the functioning of these commercial activities, and a new way to visualize the data.

Conclusions and perspectives

Traditionally, people have relied on narrative formats to deal with history. But history cannot be dissociated from geography and visualization. Even in recent work, the lack of digital literacy and understanding of the capabilities of modern tools remains. Readers still have to deal with too many details, and therefore the risk of confusion is high, and the sheer volume of information in tables like Stöckly's obscures important patterns. The value of digital formats is that they enable us to go beyond narration by analyzing and documenting the processes behind the construction of history and its representation (Nuessli and Kaplan, 2014).

The goal of our work is to set up a temporal navigator with which we can visualize not only a particular geographic area but also changes through time and how those changes have been interpreted, documented, and reported. It also allows us to build the different realities of that space through time. Like (Braudel, 1949) and his concept of multiple Mediterranean seas, we consider that there is not a single Venice, but multiple Venices. Only a digital format and an algorithmic approach can help historians to visualize the diverse situations, and deal, in a dynamic way, with the richness of geographic and temporal data.

The non-probabilistic hypothesis

Ancient geographers used averages and simplifications to draw their maps. We used the same logic in our first phase of research and attempt at visualization as we represented only the segments described in the *Incanti* documents. We thus arrived, by a systematic process, at a representation which is reasonable but incomplete. Even if we represented phenomena at a fine temporal granularity (the original GIS can be displayed in motion), that poses problems in terms of the representation of uncertainty. Now that we have a solid foundation, we need to add to our next analysis the incompleteness of the data, forgery, the uncertainty of the event itself, and variable parameters such as winds, currents, speed, route, etc. How do we deal with this situation? We use an algorithm, a simulation. What is very interesting here is that the visualization shows, in the same interface, the results of what the sources say and the hypotheses.

The probabilistic hypothesis

What also led us to a probabilistic approach is the fact that the Adriatic calls that are not recorded as mandatory are implied. Between 1257 and 1422, Venice increased its territorial waters from an area located between Ravenna and Pula, in the northern Adriatic, to an area from Ancona (in the middle of the western Italian shore) to Segna (on the upper Adriatic coast of Croatia). Even if the Adriatic was policed and had been used by Venice as a maritime playground, many cities had been far from docile during this period (e.g. Zara), and Uskok, Catalan, and Barbary piracy was an important factor to make the navigation difficult. The idea is to run a multi-criteria analysis to determine: where did they go? Where can or can't they go?

Looking for a representation of several realities

Cartographers for centuries have been obsessively attempting to represent the reality of the world as they saw it, or as it was reported to them, weighing information with their critical senses. But imagination and legend were, and still are, never very far away. During the seventeenth century, a cartographer, Fra Mauro received merchants, legates, missionaries, ambassadors, travellers, and scholars who had heard about his enterprise to design an exhaustive world map; however, the map could never be completed, it was always being updated, always outmoded. Four centuries later, we are encountering the same difficulties: uncertainty, mistakes, misinterpretations, and forgery. However, the theory and practice of using GIS to deal with uncertainty continues evolving rapidly. Coupled with the use of algorithms in history, we know how to present not only one reality, but several.

Acknowledgements

The authors would like to thank: Dr. Andrea Mazzei (DHLAB/EPFL) for the help with the OCR and processing; Dr. Isabelle Vonèche-Cardia and David N. Griffiths for their valuable comments and feedback, and Dr. Karl Grossner from Stanford University Libraries.

Notes

1 The last line, called Trafego, is not taken into account here. It linked Venice, the Maghreb, and the Mamluk ports.
2 We use *Incanto* for the system and *Incanti* when we make a reference to the official source, the Senate registers.
3 See Pleiades: a community-built gazetteer and graph of ancient places. Available online at http://pleiades.stoa.org/ [accessed 1 June 2015].

4 See *DARMC*. Available online at http://medievalmap.harvard.edu/icb/icb.do [accessed 1 June 2015].
5 Jacques Bertin in 1961 was director of the Cartographic Service at the Ecole Pratique des Hautes Etudes. He did the cartography for Tenenti and Vivanti.
6 Available online at http://kgeographer.com/wp/ [accessed 1 June 2015].
7 Available online at http://storymaps.arcgis.com/en/ [accessed 1 June 2015].
8 © 2010 Christos Nuessli. Available online at www euratlas.net [accessed 1 June 2015].
9 Students from the EPFL worked on a timeline associating historical events and boundaries evolution. See The Venice Atlas. Available online at http://veniceatlas.epfl.ch/atlas/timelines/dominio-da-mar/ [accessed 1 June 2015].
10 ORBIS is available online at http://orbis.stanford.edu/. Open the Geospatial tab and check the paragraph *The Sea Model* [accessed 1 June 2015].
11 A first attempt to use the betweeness centrality and networks for the *Incanto* system has been presented by M. Fournier and Y. Rochat at the DH2014 in Lausanne and at the Renaissance Society of America annual conference in Berlin in March 2015 (available online at http://www.slideshare.net/yrochat/dh-2014-42306102 [accessed 1 June 2015]).

References

Arnaud P. (1993) De La durée à La distance: l'évaluation des distances maritimes chez les géographes anciens. *Histoire et Mesure*, 8(3–4):225–247.
Arnaud P. (2005) *Les Routes de La Navigation Antique. Itinéraires en Méditerranée*. Paris: Errances.
Braudel F. (1949) *La Méditerranée et le monde méditerranéen à l'époque de Philippe II*. Paris: Armand Colin.
Costantini M. (2005) *Una Repubblica nata sul mare: navigazione e commercio a Venezia*. Saggi: Marsilio editori.
Crouzet-Pavan E. (1995) *La mort lente de Torcello: histoire d'une cité disparue*. Paris: Fayard.
de Graauw A. (2013) Geodatabase of Ancient Ports and Harbors. DARMC Scholarly Data Series, Data Contribution Series # 2013-2. DARMC, Center for Geographic Analysis, Harvard University, Cambridge MA 02138.
Doumerc B. (1991) Le galere da mercato. In: Tenenti A., Tucci U. (Eds), *Storia di Venezia. Dalle origini alla caduta della Serenissima, Temi, Il mare*, Rome, pp. 357–395.
Doumerc B. (2012) *Venise et son Empire en Méditerranée. IX-XVème Siècle*. Paris: Ellipses.
Fabre G., Le Blévec D., Menjot D. (2004) *Les Ports et La Navigation en Méditerranée au Moyen Age*. Actes du colloque de Lattes, November 12–14, Musée Archéologique Henri Prades.
Fournier M. (2013) Venise et le système de l'Incanto (1283–1453) ou la mise en place de sept lignes maritimes régulières fondées sur un système d'enchères, Digital Humanities Lab, EPFL, Lausanne, http://www.sitweb.ch/Incanti/
Gregory I., Healey R. (2007) Historical GIS: Structuring, mapping and analysing geographies of the past. *Progress in Human Geography*, 31(5): 638–653.
Grossner K. (2010) *Representing Historical Knowledge in Geographic Information Systems*. University of California.
Hillier A., Knowles A.K. (2008) *Placing History: How Maps, Spatial Data, and GIS are Changing Historical Scholarship*, ESRI, Inc.
Hocquet J.C. (2006) *Venise et La mer XIIème-XVIIIème siècle*. Paris: Fayard.
Janni P. (1984) *La mappa e il periplo: cartografia antica e spazio odologico*. Bretschneider.
Judde de Larivière C. (2008) *Naviguer, commercer, gouverner: économie maritime et pouvoirs à Venise (XVe-XVIe siècles)*. Brill.

Karpov S. (1991) Les routes des galères de lignes en Mer Noire. In: *Byzance, mer Noire, paix slave*, Moscou, pp. 82–97.

Knowles A.K. (2002) *Past Time, Past Place: Gis for History*. ESRI, Inc.

Lane F.C. (1978) *The Venetian Galleys to Alexandria, 1344*. Wirtschaftskräfte und Wirtschaftswege: Festschrift für H. Kellenbenz, Stuttgart, pp. 431–440.

Lane F.C. (1985) *Venise: Une République Maritime*. Paris: Flammarion.

Luzzatto G. (1941) *Navigazione di linea e navigazione libera nelle grandi città marinare del Medio Evo*. Popoli A.I. (under the pseudonym of G. Padovan), Milano.

Luzzatto G. (1961) *Storia economica di Venezia dall'XI al XVI secolo*, Venezia, Centro internazionale delle arti e del costume, 298p.

Nuessli M.A., Kaplan F. (2014) *Encoding metaknowledge for historical databases*. Digital Humanities 2014, Lausanne, Switzerland, July 7–12, 2014, http://www.bar. admin.ch/themen/01555/01809/01907/index.html?lang=fr

Plewe B. (2002) The nature of uncertainty in historical geographic information. *Transactions in GIS*, 6(4): 431–456.

Robinson D., Wilson A. (2011) *Maritime Archaeology and Ancient Trade in the Mediterranean*. Oxford: Oxford Centre for Maritime Archaeology.

Stöckly D. (1992) *Le Système de l'Incanto des Galées du Marché à Venise (Fin XIIIe-Milieu XV siècles)*, PhD Dissertation, Université Paris-I Sorbonne.

Stöckly D. (1992) *Le Système de l'Incanto des Galées du Marché à Venise (Fin XIIIe-Milieu XV siècles), The Medieval Mediterranean, Vol. 5*. Leiden: E.J. Brill.

Tenenti R., Vivanti C. (1961) Le film d'un grand système de navigation: les galères vénitiennes, XIVe-XVIe siècles. *Annales Economie, Sociétés, Civilisations*, 16(1): 83–86.

Thiriet F. (1962) Quelques observations sur le trafic des galées vénitiennes d'après les chiffres des incants (XIV-XVe siècles). In: Guiffré A. (Ed), *Studi in onore di Amintore Fanfani*, Milano, pp. 459–522.

Thiriet F. (1976) *Histoire de Venise*. Paris: Presses Universitaires de France.

Thiriet F. (1979) Les Vénitiens en mer Noire – Organisation et trafics (XIIIe-XVe siècle). *Archeion Pontou*, 35: 38–53.

7 Navigocorpus database and eighteenth-century French world maritime networks

Silvia Marzagalli

From a European point of view, early modern history is characterized by three major phenomena which dramatically changed the nature of societies and led to the world we live in: the emergence of modern states, the rupture of confessional uniformity, and the worldwide expansion of trade. The latter phenomenon, which some historians have labelled as the "first globalization," increased interconnections among cities and hinterlands, both within Europe and with the Americas, Africa, and Asia (on this process, see Pomeranz and Topik, 2006; see also O'Rourke and Williamson, 1999; de Vries, 2010). As most commodities travelled by sea, while focusing on European commercial growth scholars have highlighted the central role port cities played in structuring trade and markets, and they have pointed to shifts over time—Venice and Antwerp giving way to Amsterdam, Cadiz, or London as major trade centers in this globalizing world (Braudel, 1979). They researched the political and economic factors leading to such changes and linked maritime trade expansion to imperial and commercial policies as well as to merchants' entrepreneurial initiative and their self-organized networks. In France, historians have devoted great attention to measure shipping and trade in major ports, and have stressed the importance of merchants' business connections and migration in structuring them. Such analyses have been based on aggregated data of ship entrances and clearances for specific ports (Dardel, 1963; Meyer, 1999; Butel, 1974; Carrière, 1973) or trades (Mettas and Daget, 1984; Tarrade, 1972), and some of them have sketched the geography of trade of a given port. But although it provides precious insights, the nature of such research does not make it possible to focus on the way ports were connected with each other and built a network, nor to question the organization of shipping services as a global system and their evolution over time.

The main obstacle to a network approach is not conceptual but rather is linked to the state of the sources. Data on early modern and modern shipping and trade flows are scattered, non-standardized,[1] and incomplete. Collecting, processing, and matching a significant amount of them, therefore, is extremely time-consuming and exceeds by far individual capacities.[2] Generally speaking, scholars have been gathering data on shipping and maritime trade for the purpose of their specific research and have then organized them in non-standardized databases which are unavailable to a wider audience and disconnected to data produced by other scholars. Under these circumstances, a global understanding of interconnections among ports and markets is hardly possible.

In order to promote a network approach of past maritime trade and shipping, we run a research program called Navigocorpus, which was financed in 2007–11 by the French Agence Nationale de la Recherche. Its purpose was to create a common database structure, preserving individual efforts and producing an online tool for scholarly use. We wanted the database to be able to cope with a variety of sources, produced in different languages and containing all sorts of information on ships and their movements in time and space.[3]

The methodological challenge was complex, but we believe that the results are encouraging and that Navigocorpus has the capacity to sustain innovative research on maritime networks, if the scholarly community recognizes its utility and implements it systematically within a collaborative project. In order to illustrate the potentialities of the database and to test it, we have inserted all available data on shipping in French ports in 1787, i.e. approximately 35,000 records (for more details, see Dedieu *et al.*, 2012).[4] After presenting the aim and the methodological choices we faced, this chapter presents some of the results on French maritime networks on the eve of the French Revolution.

On the complexity of dealing with early modern sources to reconstruct maritime networks: a short introduction to the database

Contrary to other database projects on shipping—such as Slavevoyages website, which inspired us, and STR online or World Seastems,[5] which were conceived almost simultaneously—Navigocorpus does not rely on a standardized single source or on a pre-determined (however important) amount of ships and data, nor on a predefined set of scientific questions which might help to structure the database. We therefore had to cope with an unlimited open database and to configure information so that researchers could retrieve it efficiently, while preserving at the same time the complexity of information provided by the sources.[6]

Creating the database has been a complex task because of the composite nature of sources early modern historians have to deal with when trying to reconstruct the puzzle of maritime trade and shipping. Originally, our intent was to backup existing databases created by colleagues, pour them into a common database, and put them online. We quickly realized, however, that databases created to answer specific scientific questions did not always organize the information to efficiently support historical queries on different topics. We aimed, on the contrary, at creating a database which structures data to reflect all information provided by original sources, without predetermining the kind of queries researchers might have in the future.

This issue posed three major methodological challenges. First, we needed to fully understand the nature of the information provided by the sources and to input it even when it was implicit. Consular registers, for instance, omit mentioning the ships' flag simply because all records pertain to vessels registered in the state the consul represents. More complex, the status of information provided by the sources varies according to their nature: a register of arrivals tells us about past actions, a register of clearances tells about future intentionality. We cannot essentialize the reality of a voyage which was situated in the future of the past: the ship might have been shipwrecked, captured, or never even arrived at its destination. We therefore had to introduce specific fields specifying the status of the information.

Second, we had to conceive an open database able to cope with the integration of new sources which might possibly provide additional information on ship voyages already recorded in the database. The structure we chose reflects the open and potentially endless nature of the information we collect. The main table of the database records the points touched by a ship, which are subsequently reordered chronologically as the database expands (on the technical aspects of the database structure see Dedieu *et al.*, 2011). A point is defined by its geo-localization, a date, and an event which occurs in it. Unlike scholars processing a single source, we confront multiple information on the same voyage provided by different sources produced in different places or by different institutions. Just to take an example, a ship coming from Riga and bound for Bordeaux was recorded in Riga, at Helsingør when it passed the Sound, in Bordeaux, and eventually at a call in Dunkirk. None of the sources provides complete information, so that we need to exploit their complementarities. The Sound toll registers do not record the ship's name, for instance, but provide full details concerning the cargo, whereas the clearance register in Dunkirk does not state the cargo but provides the ship's name, its tonnage, and the date of departure. An American ship entering Leghorn was recorded both by the consul and by the health office. Whereas the United States consul stated the name and residence of ship- and cargo-owners and the value of the cargo, the health office was more accurate in listing the quantity of each cargo item, the encounters at sea, and the ports where the ship stopped on her way. As we do not know in advance which sources will be poured into Navigocorpus, we structured the database so as to collect all possible information but also to avoid a situation in which a researcher might run the risk of adding redundant information from different sources and come to false results. We dealt with this aspect by structuring the database on geographical points (defined as a place through which a ship sailed, characterized by a date and an action: clearance, arrival, passage, capture, loss, etc.) rather than on ships or entries, as with most existing databases. An entry (which we call a "documentary unit," i.e. a single entry in a given source) of the health office in Marseille mentioning a ship arriving at Marseille from Smyrna and calling at Genoa will thus produce three points, to which all other information are related. Navigocorpus today (March 2015) contains information on a total of 184,000 points which correspond to 75,000 different documentary units, the bulk of them ranging from 1750 to 1850.

The kind of data we are dealing with—implying overlapping information on ship voyages—meant we had to identify ships and captains. This is one of the most original features of Navigocorpus, which is much more than the digitalized online transcription of sources. Once we provide ships with an identifier, points can be ordered chronologically to reconstruct the itinerary of ships over time, regardless of the number of sources providing information. If new data are poured into the database, we do not need to change the structure of the records in order to cope with new information, but only to order the points chronologically and to correct the neat-markers accordingly.[7] When the amount of data is dense enough, we can track small boats like Jean Esnol's *Bonne Aventure*, 9 *tonneaux*[8] clearing 26 times between Port Bail and Saint Malo between January and December 1787, or larger ships like the *Femme et enfants* of Riga, 180 *tonneaux*, clearing in February 1787 from Dunkirk to Bordeaux, and sailing twice thereafter from Bordeaux to Riga before the end of the year.

The identification of ships and captains is by far the most delicate and time-consuming task when adding new data to Navigocorpus. The decision is taken manually, ship by ship and captain by captain, after taking into account the ship class, its tonnage, its flag and port of register, the consistency of the itinerary and dates, and the information on the ship name or captain name. Generally speaking, none of the sources provides the integrality of these pieces of information, and spellings of names (person, places, and ships) rarely match entirely in different early modern and modern sources.[9] The identification of ships makes it possible to add missing information to other records pertaining to the same ship, notably on flag, tonnage, and registered port. Navigocorpus adds this information automatically to ships with the same identifier after putting them in brackets so that researchers know the information does not come from the source used to produce the documentary unit (Dedieu *et al.*, 2012). At a time where many institutions did not record tonnages, this is useful to reconstruct total outward or inward tonnages and flows.

Besides identification, Navigocorpus offers a series of other tools to researchers. Among others, it provides all places with a code. The codes are linked to a 3.8 million-point geo-referenced database, which is available online. This geo-general database provides some additional functions, such as administrative maps for a quick check in case of homonyms. We also facilitated the possibility for researchers to create a rough working map to visualize their results.[10]

In order to deal with information on cargoes, we created a cargo table in the database, and inserted cargo items as individual records linked to the point where information was produced: a cargo entering the port of Marseille on a ship coming from Smyrna is attached to Marseille.[11] In constructing the cargo table, we adopted the terminology provided by the sources without trying to introduce any imposed notion of commodity. As a general rule, while constructing Navigocorpus, we deliberately chose not to impose any pre-conceptualized categories other than those of the sources. However, we do not leave researchers alone with the task of dealing with thousands of different item names. One of the most evident problems in such a database as Navigocorpus comes from the variety of languages and spellings to designate products. There was an obvious need to help users wishing to locate an item whatever the language of the sources and the spelling. Navigocorpus handled this aspect by introducing a field in which cargo items are standardized in contemporary English. In order to allow flexibility to the user, we also introduced the possibility of classifying on-the-way or on-the-run, that is, that we created a field in which researchers can add a term or a string of terms which correspond to the categories of classification they wish to adopt. Finally, we added a third level of codification, through permanent coding, designed to provide an identifier in the form of a string of characters based on the three possible criteria used to classify goods: raw material, elaboration process, and standard use of the product (for more details on the way Navigocorpus deals with cargoes, see Dedieu and Marzagalli, 2015).

From the database to results: French maritime networks on the eve of the French Revolution

One of the problems we faced while creating Navigocorpus was that, contrary to other databases on shipping, ours was conceived as a tool, and not as a response to specific research goals. Whereas researchers can find, for instance, all known slave voyages on slavevoyages.org, or all ships crossing the Danish Sound on the STR online, they will find no complete, homogeneous set of data in Navigocorpus. We became aware that Navigocorpus could become a common tool among researchers only if the cost of entering it—in terms of the time needed to learn how to use a complex database—was compensated for by the benefit of accessing a rich collection of data and refined query tools. Within the frame of our four-year project, we decided to collect a homogeneous set of data which could serve as an example to validate the potential of our database. We therefore input all available *congés* for 1787. *Congés* are clearance permits that eighteenth-century vessels, including small boats, had to obtain when sailing from a French port. Their delivery was subject to the payment of a duty, called *droit de congé*, to the Admiralty of France.[12] The duties were collected in the admiralty head offices and in secondary posts. By the end of the Old Regime, there were 37 head offices on the French Atlantic coast, 13 along the Mediterranean coast, and two in Corsica.[13] A total of approximately 160 ports in France delivered *congés* in the eighteenth century and produced records, both for their own accounts and for central authorities.

Most *congés* were delivered at each clearance, but a few exceptions existed. Coastal fishermen could apply for a three-, six-, or twelve-month *congé* depending on where they lived, whereas *caravane* traders in the Mediterranean obtained a two-year *congé* which allowed them to travel freely back and forth.[14] In some provinces, moreover, such as in Brittany, Corsica, and Bayonne, it was possible to apply for a six- or twelve-month *congé* for coastal trade within the province, for an unlimited number of voyages. Finally, a ship making a direct return journey within the jurisdiction of the same admiralty head office needed to apply for a *congé* when departing, but not for the return journey.[15] To put it shortly, the number of *congés* does not correspond to the number of total real clearances, but, with the major exception of the Levant trade, all international, colonial, and national voyages beyond the province of departure are systematically recorded.

The French Admiralty, moreover, produced aggregated data which make it possible to assess the extent of surviving detailed data on individual clearances.

According to the summary surveys ("*comptes rendus*"), a total of 44,537 *congés* were delivered in 1787 in 148 French ports (colonies excluded). Surveys for 1787 are missing for a few ports only, most notably Caen, where 506 *congés* were delivered in 1786.[16] The number of *congés* issued shows a strong concentration in 11 ports—which delivered almost half of them—and a large dispersion of a few clearances in a large number of minor ports—over three-quarters of them totaling less than one-quarter of total *congés*.[17]

If aggregated data of the *comptes rendus* provide an overview of the relative importance of shipping in different French ports, the information concerning individual clearances we were able to process thanks to the *congés* registers presents the possibility of much deeper historical analysis. Out of a total of 34,208 *congés* delivered in the French Atlantic ports, we have detailed information for 88.5 percent. No major port is missing. The most notable register loss concerns Libourne, issuing 650 *congés* according to the *compte rendu*. Many registers of ports in Brittany are lost as well, none of which, however, delivered more than 300 *congés,* Douarnenez excepted (338). Even these ports, however, show up in other registers as intended destinations, so that it is possible to reconstruct at least part of their traffic even when the registers of clearances no longer exist: Pierrick Pourchasse was, for instance, able to identify 142 ships out of the 207 which cleared in Vannes (Dedieu *et al.*, 2012: 340–3). The situation is much less favorable for the 10,329 *congés* delivered in the French Mediterranean ports—4,557 of which were in Marseille—as we retrieved registers for less than 20 percent of them. If we added to the database information on more than 3,000 entrances in Marseille in 1787 from the health office, the following analysis will focus exclusively on French Atlantic shipping and trade, for which data are fairly exhaustive.[18]

These data, once processed through Navigocorpus, make it possible to get a clear global picture of French maritime traffic and networks on the eve of the French Revolution. At a time where there was no cheap alternative to maritime trade for transport, notably for bulky goods, global trade was the result of the interplay of local, regional, national, international, and transcontinental flows. Looking at how ports and littoral societies responded to demand in transport services and how increasing interconnections among ports sustained global trade growth is a key element for understanding a globalizing world on the road to industrialization. While markets expanded, shipping was crucial in structuring links among them. Competition among carriers reduced costs, while integration and demand growth offered increasing possibilities of employing ships intensively. According to Richard Unger (2011), shipping was the decisive factor of European growth.

For the first time, we are able to quantify the number and the tonnage of national and foreign ships clearing French Atlantic ports, and to establish which of them were connected to foreign ports.[19] We can, for instance, measure the huge amount of smuggling across the Channel. If historians have so far paid attention mainly to French colonial and slave trades, we can now map the geography and the intensity of the links French ports had among themselves and with other European, American, African, and Asian ports. In focusing on ships' registered ports—a piece of information which Western French Atlantic ports systematically recorded—we produced a graph of the transport services provided by the ports in the Charente for the trades of Nantes, Bordeaux, and La Rochelle, showing the different opportunities minor ports enjoyed in this region (Marzagalli and Pfister-Langanay, 2016). What follows provides some examples of the kinds of analysis of maritime networks which data presently in Navigocorpus can sustain.

To begin with, the sources we processed provide a global picture of the relative importance of French ports in 1787. As average tonnage differed greatly from port to port—from 122 *tonneaux* in Bordeaux to 49 *tonneaux* in Dunkirk or La Rochelle among the top nine ports in terms of total cleared tonnage, but 12 *tonneaux* only in Boulogne-sur-Mer despite it being the fifth most important French Atlantic port in terms of number of clearances—the relative importance of shipping and trade is best evaluated by looking at total tonnage rather than at the sheer number of *congés*. Dunkirk, Rouen, Le Havre, Nantes, and Bordeaux totaled over 100,000 *tonneaux* each, while four other ports ranked between 50,000 and 100,000 *tonneaux*. Figure 7.1 shows the corresponding data.

The share of international shipping and trade in French Atlantic ports—which is assessed here by looking at flags and destinations respectively—differs just as greatly. Thirty-eight of the 87 recorded French Atlantic ports were not frequented by any foreign vessel or small boat at any moment of the year. Out of the remaining 49 ports, in only 22 did foreign shipping represent more than a quarter of total cleared tonnage—an element pointing to their strong internationalization. In some instances, however, shipping was extremely low altogether; in other instances, strong links with international markets were the result of their geographical proximity to national frontiers. Figure 7.2 represents those French Atlantic ports where total clearances were higher than 15,000 *tonneaux*, and the share of foreign shipping. As the map shows, dependency on foreign shipping varied greatly from port to port. Among the five French Atlantic ports in which total foreign tonnage was higher than 20,000 *tonneaux*, only in Bordeaux, Dunkirk, and Calais did it account for more than national shipping. Whereas in Bordeaux this reflected connections to worldwide markets, the strong presence of foreign ships in Dunkirk and Calais was linked to trade to England: one-third and two-thirds respectively of the two ports' total shipping was British-flagged.

In the eighteenth century, recourse to a given flag was not the result of the undisturbed play of supply and demand in transport services but was strongly affected by mercantilist regulations. The analysis of the destinations and flags of the *congés* delivered in French Atlantic ports in 1787 (Table 7.1) clearly shows that specific international markets were dominated by specific flags. In particular, shipping to colonial and Asian markets, where European countries imposed monopolies, was overwhelmingly French-flagged. Foreigners sailing to Atlantic fisheries made a call in French ports to load salt, but returns were seldom to France, where differential duties encouraged national fisheries. Foreigners sailing between two French ports did so, in general, to find a return cargo, as coastal shipping between French ports was reserved for national shipping. France, however, did not regulate shipping to European markets, and French shipping in this area was thus exposed to open international competition. Whereas the French controlled the

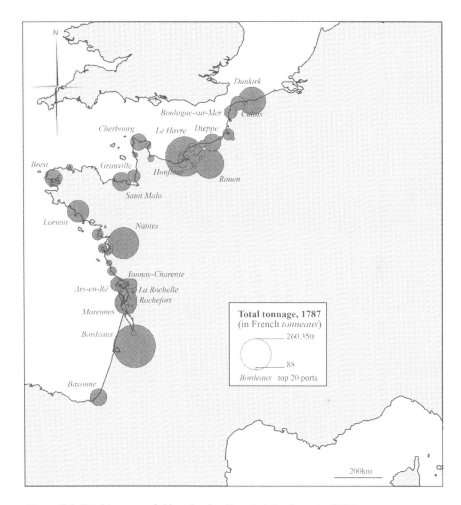

Figure 7.1 Total tonnage of ships clearing French Atlantic ports, 1787.

majority of transport to the Iberian Peninsula and the Mediterranean, 10 percent of tonnages were Iberian, and possibly twice as much were Scandinavian.[20] As Leos Müller demonstrated, about a third of the late eighteenth-century Swedish merchant fleet was engaged in southern European trades and tramping (Müller, 2004); our data show that one Swedish ship out of ten bound southward made a call in a French port.

Colonial trade was notoriously one of the most dynamic branches of eighteenth-century French shipping and trade (Figure 7.3). Previously we had global overviews based on the statistics of the Ministry of the Navy and Trade—Jean Tarrade published data for 1773 and 1788 (Tarrade, 1972: 730–4)—and data on some individual ports, but no possibility to appreciate, among other things, the

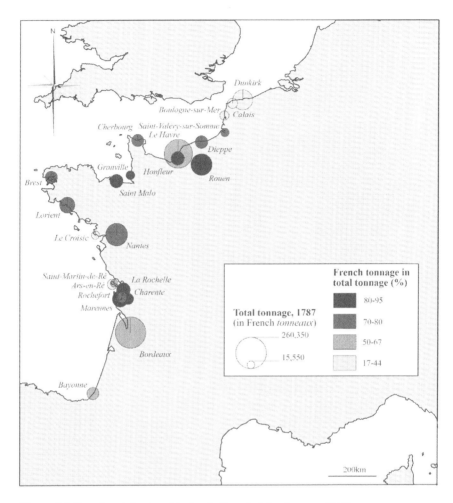

Figure 7.2 French and foreign shipping in French Atlantic ports, 1787.

relative importance of the different ports in Saint-Domingue or the extremely large variety of tonnages of ships sailing to the French West Indies, ranging from 43 *tonneaux* for the *Petite Nancy*, to 700 *tonneaux* for the *Nathalie*, both from Bordeaux. Despite such great variability, colonial shipping was clearly employing the overwhelming part of France's biggest ships. A comparison between colonial shipping versus total shipping clearing from French Atlantic ports shows that, whereas 43 percent of clearances to the West Indies and Guyana pertained to vessels of 300 *tonneaux* or more, this was the case for only 1.5 percent of total clearances. The West Indies represented the destination of 60 percent of French-flagged ships over 300 *tonneaux*, and Africa an additional 12 percent. Market connections were the result of an extremely wide range of sizes of carriers.

Table 7.1 French versus foreign shipping to different areas, 1787

Destination	Foreign tonnage	French tonnage	French tonnage %
	In French tonneaux		
Asia: beyond the Cape of Good Hope	288	16,150	98.25
West Indies and Africa	200	162,431	99.88
North America	23,157	1,498	6.08
French Atlantic ports	70,772	839,733	92.23
Atlantic fisheries	7,907	45,678	85.24
Iberian peninsula and Mediterranean	28,276	58,352	67.36
Northern Europe and Baltic	389,318	23,276	5.64
Unidentified/not stated*	6,810	46,401	87.20
Total	**526,728**	**1,193,519**	**69.38**

Note: *This category includes an overwhelming majority of coastal fishing-boats and local coastal traders.

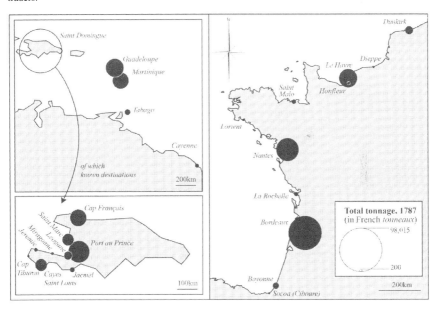

Figure 7.3 French Atlantic shipping to the West Indies, 1787. Ports of departure and declared destinations.

One ship out of five among those clearing to the West Indies before the end of April managed to sail there again before the end of the year. Departures from France were partly affected by the hurricane season in the Caribbean, with four clearances out of ten taking place in the last four months of the year.

If we focus on those foreign destinations (French colonies, Newfoundland fisheries, and slave trade excepted) which were more attractive for ships clearing

French Atlantic ports, there is no clear sign of a strong concentration: only six of them total more than 2 percent (17,000 *tonneaux*) of the total. London, Amsterdam, Hamburg, and Rotterdam are quite expected destinations, as they were among the main European ports at that time, whereas Newcastle and Dover are a possibly more surprising result. Dover, in fact, was the declared destination of an extremely active smuggling trade across the Channel which concerned Guernsey and Jersey as well, but also the generic destination "England".[21] The total tonnage engaged in smuggling was more relevant than tonnage shipped to London *and* Newcastle. Cadiz and Lisbon came far behind, totalizing approximately 10,000 tons.

Figure 7.4 represents the 32 French Atlantic ports which were connected to at least one of these six top European destinations and the overall importance of

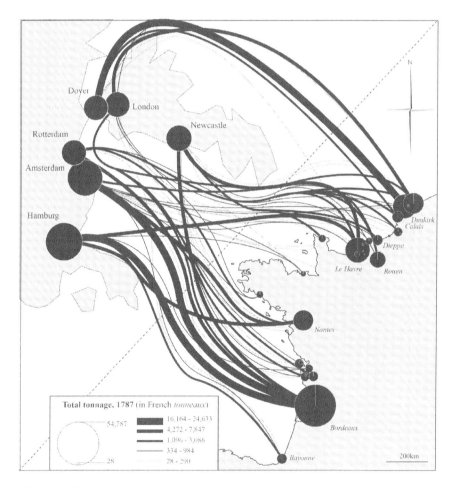

Figure 7.4 Total tonnage from French Atlantic ports to their main European destinations, 1787.

tonnage clearing to them. Bordeaux, Calais, Dunkirk, Le Havre, and Rouen totaled more than 10,000 *tonneaux* to these six destinations. Some of them were strongly dependent on a single market. Dover attracted 94 percent of Calais' tonnage clearing to these top six destinations, whereas over half of Dunkirk's expeditions were bound for London. Bordeaux and Nantes, which re-exported the bulk of West Indian goods abroad, were strongly connected to Hamburg and Amsterdam.

The analysis of the number of clearances and total tonnage provides an indication of shipping flows but cannot be considered as an equivalent to trade flows: ships might—and in fact did—travel also on ballast. The quantification of actual trade flows in early modern and modern times is an extremely delicate task for historians. Even when states started generalizing data collection of foreign trade values and volumes in the eighteenth century, the use of the statistics they

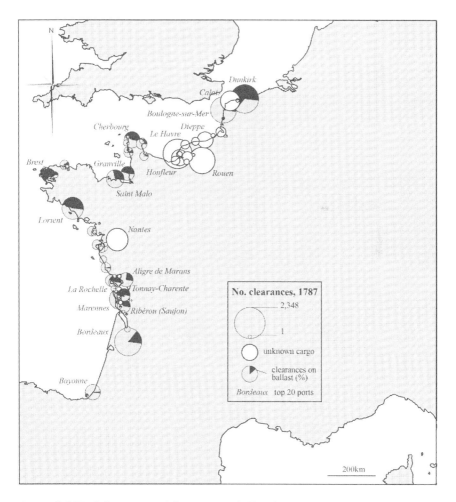

Figure 7.5 Total clearances and departures on ballast from French Atlantic ports, 1787.

produced is highly problematic.[22] Recourse to data on shipping possibly represents the best alternative, provided that we are able to get some information on cargoes. The registers of *congés* were established to record the perception of a duty, which depended on the ship's flag and eventually on her tonnage. Authorities were not interested in the nature of the cargo as such, but some admiralty offices systematically noted one or two main cargo items, whereas others did so occasionally. We therefore have some information on the nature of the outward cargo for slightly less than two-thirds of clearances. Figure 7.5 shows the number of *congés* per port of clearance and, for those where half of the *congés* at least mention the outward cargo, the percentage of clearances on ballast on total known clearances. The total share of departures on ballast was relatively high (27 percent of total clearances and 15 percent of total tonnage[23]), and it would be extremely

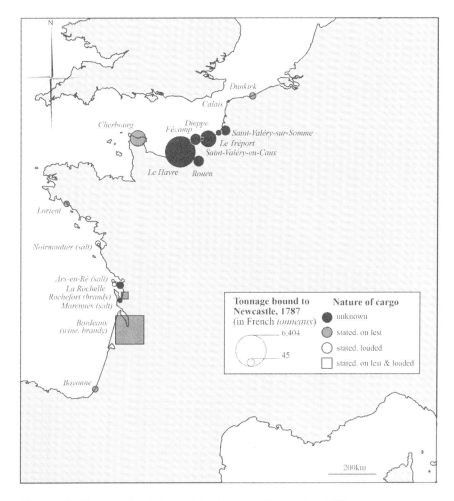

Figure 7.6 Ship cargo from French Atlantic ports to Newcastle, 1787.

interesting to analyze its evolution over time. The discrepancy between these two figures, however, clearly reveals that smaller ships were employed in those trades which were more likely to imply either the outward or the return voyage on ballast.

In some instances, notably in the French Navy dockyards of Brest and Rochefort, and the East Indian Company dockyard in Lorient, the strong percentage of departures on ballast (respectively 68 percent, 46 percent, and 59 percent) is clearly linked to the fact that vessels came in to provision the dockyards, where they could hardly charge a return load (an impressive study of the needs in Lorient is in Le Bouëdec, 1982). In some instances, however, the return on ballast was linked to the original port of departure when bound for France, rather than to the peculiar nature of the French port of departure. Newcastle, for instance, exported coal to France, but homeward voyages were overwhelmingly on ballast (Figure 7.6).

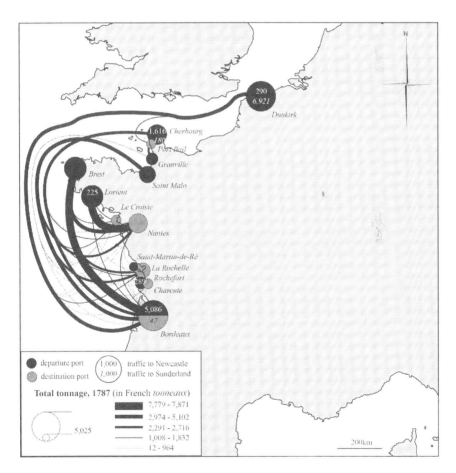

Figure 7.7 Main destinations and main ports of departure of ships on ballast clearing from the French Atlantic ports, 1787.

The registers of *congés* make it possible to analyze structural imbalances of volumes of trade and demand in maritime carrying services. Figure 7.7 represents the top nine French Atlantic ports (in terms of tonnage) from whence ships cleared on ballast and shows the top eight destinations to which ships clearing from Atlantic ports sailed on ballast, when sources provide this information. In both instances, we restricted the analysis to ports where the total tonnage on ballast was higher than 5,000 *tonneaux*. The correlation is strong: the nine departure ports accounted for more than 84 percent of total shipping on ballast bound to the top eight destinations. However, ships departed on ballast from these ports bound for many other destinations as well. Bordeaux represents a most interesting case: the main French Atlantic port was both the destination and the port of departure of a considerable amount of ships on ballast (25,531 and 26,942 *tonneaux*, respectively)—a clear sign of the simultaneous presence of different, non-integrated trades and markets. Coastal ships in particularly came empty to Bordeaux in order to load wine, such as the *Marquis de l'Aigle* of Landernau, 60 tons, which sailed three times in 1787 to Bordeaux on ballast from Boulogne-sur-Mer, Cherbourg, or Isigny, and each time left Bordeaux or Blaye (down the Garonne river) loaded with wine for Cherbourg or Lannion. As a major producer of wine and salt, the western coast of France was, generally speaking, more likely to provide cargoes than the northern ports of France. The incompleteness

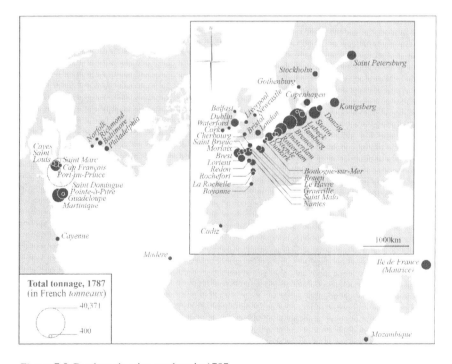

Figure 7.8 Bordeaux's wine markets in 1787.

of information on cargoes makes any further analysis difficult. For those ports for which cargoes are systematically stated by the registers of *congés*, however, we can measure the extent of markets for the main products. Bordeaux's wine markets, for instance, ranged worldwide, from the West Indies to the Indian Ocean (Figure 7.8).[24]

Conclusion

This analysis of French maritime networks on the eve of the French Revolution was based on French clearances in 1787. The nature of the data we collected can sustain a detailed study of both maritime flows among French ports and international and colonial outward connections. The data on tonnages and flags we produced are entirely new, and they are helpful for formulating a future research agenda. We could highlight the major destinations and distinguish the respective importance of national and foreign flags in different markets, but the significant difference in the recourse to French vessels in the Iberian trade versus the North Sea and Baltic trades calls for further enquiry. Answers are probably a complex mixture of institutional factors with the interplay of supply and demand both of transport services and goods in different and complementary market segments. The fact that direct shipping from French Atlantic ports to the Mediterranean is not significant does not mean that the two areas were not interconnected: Newfoundland ships from northern France regularly sold cod to Marseille before sailing back to their home port—a phenomenon which clearance registers in French Atlantic ports cannot reveal (Brière, 1990; Pfister-Langanay, 2011).

If we conceive of globalization as a process in which markets integrated and prices converged, the question of transport costs, linked to the optimization of ships' employment, is crucial. We still need to better understand how contemporary actors decided on the size of ships and the flags they employed, and whether some ports and routes made it possible to recoup costs more than others. As shipowners were merchants—and for smaller crafts, masters—it would be complicated to separate transport from commercial benefits or capital from labor, even if we had systematic information on freight costs and shipowners' account books. Looking at maritime flows is possibly an indirect means to capture actors' underlying logics. If clearances in French Atlantic ports do not provide information on shipowners, Navigocorpus integrates the possibility of network analysis based on actors.[25] In exploiting consular records providing entrances and clearances of US ships in Bordeaux at the end of the eighteenth century and at the beginning of the nineteenth century, I have been able to reconstruct, for instance, the highly intensive use that Stephen Jumel, a former refugee of Saint-Domingue who settled in New York as merchant and shipowner, made of his ships (Marzagalli, 2015b: 413–9).

The present analysis is based on a single year, on clearances only, and on the ports of just one country, so it offers only a partial view of much wider networks. The bulk of eighteenth-century ships did not travel on predetermined routes and schedules, although we could point at some differentiation in average tonnage depending on destinations. If we are able to reconstruct fairly well the itineraries of ships sailing between French ports, we cannot at this point calculate the time they were employed at sea versus the time they spent in ports. Our understanding of international shipping and trade to France would clearly be improved through the integration of entrances, notably for the study of shipping on ballast. Navigocorpus can support original research and help make a bold step forward in our understanding of past maritime networks. It will only do so, however, in the context of an intensive collaborative project to implement the database with massive data.

Acknowledgements

The author would like to thank Liliane Lizzi and César Ducruet for their help on cartography, and Jean-Pierre Dedieu for this comments.

Notes

1 Sources were produced by a set of different institutions for different purposes, and therefore contain different kinds of information, which partially overlap. The main institutions collecting records on individual ship's voyages were port authorities, health offices, toll administration, and consuls. Whereas the health offices recorded entrances only, other institutions were interested in clearances, or both. According to their scope, the sources they produced contain (or not) information on ships (name, tonnage, type, flag, etc.), captains, cargoes, itineraries, events, actors involved in shipping and trade (shipowners, brokers, cargo owners), taxes, etc.

2 Early modern maritime trade included an important share of tramping, which was tied to local demand for transport services. Moreover, ships sailed frequently on ballast. Adding entrances and clearances is clearly inadequate for understanding maritime networks and the economic and entrepreneurial logic which sustained trade in the pre-liners era. It seems more appropriate, instead, to collect as much information as possible on each ship voyage. This entails identifying actors (ships and captains) which appear in different sources and reconstructing individual itineraries.

3 Navigocorpus (Corpus des itinéraires des navires de commerce, XVIIe–XIXe siècles or the Database on the Itineraries of Merchant Ships, seventeenth–nineteenth centuries), is a research program sponsored by the French Agence Nationale de la Recherche (ANR-07-CORP-028) and coordinated by Silvia Marzagalli (Centre de la Méditerranée Moderne et Contemporaine, Nice) in collaboration with Jean-Pierre Dedieu (at that time, Laboratoire de Recherche Historique Rhône-Alpes, Lyon), who conceived the database structure, and Pierrick Pourchasse (Centre de Recherche Bretonne et Celtique, Brest). Navigocorpus was created using FileMaker, which supports online queries. Records can be exported to spreadsheets and then elaborated to produce statistics, maps, or network analyses. The Navigocorpus database is accessible online for all those who have a FileMaker 13 license. Other scholars have access to a simplified version at http://navigocorpus.org/ [accessed 2 June 2015]. The project description is available online at http://navigocorpus.hypotheses.org/ [accessed 2 June 2015].

4 In 1787, out of the 35,000 records concerning French ports, 5,000 concern Mediterranean ports. Unless otherwise stated, data concerns clearances and were collected at the French National Archives (henceforth ANF), sub-series G5. Data from Lorient in Archives départementales du Morbihan, 10B19; data for Saint Tropez, gathered by Gilbert Buti, in Archives départementales du Var, 7B 10. For Marseille, we collected data produced by the health office: Archives départementales des Bouches-du-Rhône, 200E 543.

5 Available online at Slavevoyages.org, http://www.soundtoll.nl, and http://www.world-seastems.cnrs.fr respectively [accessed 2 June 2015].

6 Sources told, for instance, about encounters at sea, convoying, and captures at sea by privateers in times of war with consequent changes of captain and flag in the course of the voyages: information had to be "atomised" and inserted into distinct fields.

7 A neat-marker is a one-digit letter which marks those points that occur twice so that the researcher can eliminate double information if he or she wishes to. A documentary unit produced in Bordeaux on a ship sailing to Lorient and another documentary unit produced in Lorient pertaining to the same ship sailing three weeks later to Dunkirk produce four points in the database: Bordeaux, Lorient (as a destination), Lorient (as point of departure), and Dunkirk. The neat-marker enables Navigocorpus users to see on the screen the actual itinerary only (Bordeaux–Lorient–Dunkirk).

8 The French ordinance of 1681 made the *tonneau de mer* a unit equivalent to 1.44 cubic meters.

9 Just to take a simple example, a British ship called *Two Brothers* is recorded as *Les deux frères* when clearing a French port.

10 In order to do so, the researcher selects the data in the database, exports the pertinent fields into a spreadsheet, and uses it as a table to create a map with Cartes & Données, a software we chose because of its intuitive simplicity and because a non-professional version of it is available for free.

11 We define as "item" a product stated by the source and expressed with the same unit of conditioning, weight, or price. A cargo of a ship originates therefore as many records as the combination of items/units of measure. The 57 bundles and 280 bales of nankeens entering Bordeaux on 28 September 1805 on the ship *Charlotte* from Providence generate two entries in the cargo table (nankeens, 57 bundles and nankeens, 280 bales), both of them being attached to the point Bordeaux, characterized by the date of entry and the action ("IN", as the ship is entering the point Bordeaux).

12 We chose 1787 for Navigocorpus because the number of existing registers of *congés* for this year is higher than for any other year in the 1780s. Copies of the registers of duties issued in the 1780s were sent to Versailles for control. They are presently held at the ANF, sub-series G5. A new detailed finding aid for this sub-series G5 (Amirauté de France et Conseil des Prises) had been compiled by Christian Pfister-Langanay: http:// navigocorpus.hypotheses.org/inventaire-anf-sous-serie-g5 [accessed 2 June 2015]. The *Ordonnance* of 1681 stated "Aucun vaisseau ne sortira des ports de notre Royaume pour aller en mer sans congé de l'Amiral enregistré au Greffe de l'Amirauté du lieu de son départ, à peine de confiscation." The *Ordonnance* in fact systematized older practices, duties and rights; see René-Josué Valin, *Nouveau commentaire sur l'ordonnance de la Marine du mois d'août 1681* (La Rochelle, 1766): livre I, titre X: "Des congés et rapports." On the *congés*, see Marzagalli and Pfister-Langanay, 2014.

13 The number of admiralty head offices evolved over time. These data are based on Chardon's survey in 1781–5 (French National Archives, Marine, C^4 174 to 176). On the French Admiralty, see Schnakenbourg, 1975.

14 On the bias of *congés,* notably for *caravane* trades, see Buti (2006).

15 Valin, *Nouveau commentaire*, titre X: "Des congés et des rapports."

16 *Comptes rendus* for 1787 are missing for only 15 French ports mentioned at least once in the 1780s. However, none of them delivered more than 100 *congés* in the last known year before 1787, with the major exception of Caen (506 *congés* in 1786).

17 For an analysis of polarization, see Marzagalli and Pfister-Langanay (2016). The top 11 ports delivered more than 900 *congés* each, whereas 114 ports delivered fewer than 300 *congés* (76 of them fewer than 100).

18 Sources are even more deceiving for colonial ports. There are *congés* registers for Saint-Pierre-et-Miquelon and Cayenne only. Summary surveys of the total number of *congés* exist for Guadeloupe and Martinique as well. Neither Saint-Domingue, which at that time concentrated three quarters of colonial trade, nor the colonies in the Indian Ocean,

are recorded in ANF, subseries G5. On the latter, shipping data can however be found in Toussaint, 1967.

19 Tonnage is almost always stated in the *congés*. The major exception is Saint-Jean-de-Luz. When information is missing, we were generally able to retrieve it through the identification of the same ship clearing at another port or another date. Tonnage is still missing for less than 1 percent of entries.

20 Eight percent of tonnages clearing from French Atlantic ports to the Iberian Peninsula and the Mediterranean were Swedish or Danish, but most of the 9.3 percent of non-French flags which could not be identified have captains with Scandinavian names.

21 *Congés* in Dunkirk contain over 950 clearances to Lisbonne of British boats of 12 *tonneaux* or less, crossing the Channel on a regular basis. We have obviously coded these ships as sailing to England.

22 For a summary on the reasons for such reticence, see Tarrade (1972: 713–30). My main concern with such data, however, is that they conceive trade as a bilateral country-to-country relationship, whereas connections ought to be conceived as a system (see Marzagalli, 2015a).

23 These percentages have been calculated on those clearances where the cargo is stated.

24 Sources do not provide quantities of items exported, so we can only add tonnages of ships loaded with wine, without knowing which part of the cargo consisted of wine.

25 The structure of Navigocorpus includes Fichoz, a database created by Jean-Pierre Dedieu to study Iberian elites which has evolved to benefit to other scientific projects (see Dedieu, 2005).

References

Braudel F. (1979) *Civilisation matérielle, économie et capitalisme, 15ème–18ème siècles.* Paris: Armand Colin.

Brière J.F. (1990) *La pêche française en Amérique du Nord au XVIIIe siècle.* Montreal: Fides.

Butel P. (1974) *Les négociants bordelais, l'Europe et les Iles au XVIIIᵉ siècle.* Paris: Aubier-Montaigne.

Buti G. (2006) Entre échanges de proximité et trafics lointains: le cabotage en Méditerranée aux XVIIᵉ et XVIIIᵉ siècles. In: Cavaciocchi S. (Ed), *Ricchezza del mare, Ricchezza dal mare, secc. XIII – XVIII*, Florence: Le Monnier, pp. 287–316.

Carrière C. (1973) *Négociants marseillais au XVIIIe siècle. Contribution à l'étude des économies maritimes*, Marseille: Institut Historique de Provence.

Dardel P. (1963) *Navires et marchandises dans les ports de Rouen et du Havre au XVIIIᵉ siècle.* Paris: SEVPEN.

de Vries J. (2010) The limits of globalization in the early modern world. *The Economic History Review*, 63(3): 710–33.

Dedieu J.P. (2005) Les grandes bases de données. Une nouvelle approche de l'histoire sociale. Le système Fichoz. *Revista da Faculdade de Letras História*, 3(5): 99–112.

Dedieu J.P., Marzagalli S. (2015) Dealing with commodities in Navigocorpus. Offering tools and flexibility. *Revue de l'observatoire Français des conjonctures economiques* (in press). Available online at http://www.ofce.sciences-po.fr/publications/revue140.php.

Dedieu J.P., Marzagalli S., Pourchasse P., Scheltjens W. (2011) Navigocorpus, a database for shipping information. A methodological and technical introduction. *International Journal of Maritime History*, 23(2): 241–62.

Dedieu J.P., Marzagalli S., Pourchasse P., Scheltjens W. (2012) Navigocorpus at work: a brief overview of the potentialities of a data-base. *International Journal of Maritime History*, 24(1): 331–59.

Le Bouëdec G. (1982) La compagnie des Indes (1737–1770). *Histoire, Economie, Société*, 3: 377–412.

Marzagalli S. (2015a) Was warfare necessary to the functioning eighteenth-century colonial systems? Some reflections on the necessity of cross-imperial and foreign trade in the French case. In: Antunes C., Polónia A. (Eds), *Beyond Empires: Self-Organizing Cross-Imperial Economic Networks versus Institutional Empires, 1500–1800*. Leyden: Brill (in press).

Marzagalli S. (2015b) *Bordeaux et les États-Unis, 1776–1815: politique et stratégies négociantes dans la genèse d'un réseau commercial*. Genève: Droz.

Marzagalli S., Pfister-Langanay C. (2014) Les pratiques administratives des amirautés du XVIIIe siècle: entre spécificité locale et uniformisation. L'exemple de La gestion des congés. *Revue d'Histoire Maritime*, 19: 259–80.

Marzagalli S., Pfister-Langanay C. (2016) Port hierarchy and polarization of shipping in France on the eve of the French Revolution: a plea for a systemic approach. *Research in Maritime History* (in press).

Mettas J., Daget S. (1984) *Répertoire des expéditions négrières françaises au XVIIIe siècle*. Paris: Société Française d'Histoire d'Outre-Mer.

Meyer J. (1999) *L'armement nantais dans la deuxième moitié du* XVIIIe *siècle*. Paris: EHESS.

Müller L. (2004) *Consuls, Corsairs, and Commerce. The Swedish Consular Service and Long-distance Shipping, 1720–1815*. Uppsala: Uppsala Universitet.

O'Rourke K.H., Williamson J.G. (1999) *Globalization and History. The Evolution of a Nineteenth Century Atlantic Economy*. London and Cambridge: MIT Press.

Pfister-Langanay C. (2011) De la Manche à la Méditerranée: la navigation du royaume de France (1781–1791). *Revue d'Histoire Maritime*, 13: 101–17.

Pomeranz K., Topik S. (2006) *The World That Trade Created: Society, Culture, and the World Economy, 1400–the Present*. Armonk, NY: M.E. Sharpe.

Schnakenbourg C. (1975) *L'Amirauté de France à l'époque de la monarchie administrative, 1669-1792*. PhD Dissertation, Paris: Université de Paris-II.

Tarrade J. (1972) *Le commerce colonial de la France à la fin de l'Ancien Régime*. Paris: Presses Universitaires de France.

Toussaint A. (1967) *La Route des îles: Contribution à l'histoire maritime des Mascareignes*. Paris: SEVPEN.

Unger R. (2011) *Shipping and Economic Growth 1350–1850*. Leyden: Brill.

8 British and Japanese maritime networks in China in the 1920s

Liehui Wang, Theo Notteboom, Lei Yang

The global maritime network and the more regional subsystems of shipping services are key enablers and facilitators of global and regional trade flows. The application of complex network methods has advanced the geographical analysis of maritime networks in recent years. Ducruet and Notteboom (2012) and Ducruet (2013) have analysed the structure and characteristics of the global maritime network in container shipping. Chinese scholars also have examined the structure and characteristics of the global maritime network (Tian *et al.*, 2007; Wang, 2008; Xiong, 2009; Lv and Zhang, 2012).

While recent dynamics in liner shipping networks are well documented in the academic literature, the history of maritime networks based on complex network theory and methods has received far less attention. This chapter analyses the maritime networks of British and Japanese companies in China in the 1920s using social network analysis software GEPHI and GIS software ARCGIS. To our knowledge, there are no comparative studies dealing with the maritime networks of the two countries. After the first Opium War in 1842, China began to open up, and trade with foreign nations started to develop. At that time, the British maritime industry was strongly represented in China. After the Sino-Japanese War of 1894–5, the Japanese maritime network in China developed quickly. By the 1920s, the British and Japanese maritime networks occupied the top two positions in China. Intense competition existed between British and Japanese maritime companies and business interests. This competitive environment and the dynamics in the economic environment led to fluctuations in ship movements and tonnages of the two countries. Many of the shipping services were subsidized by governments.

The following section provides an overview of the history of maritime companies in China. The discussion is segmented into three time periods between 1842 and 1930. Then, we present the methodology and data used to analyse maritime networks. The next section provides the empirical results of the complex network analysis of the British and Japanese maritime networks in China in the 1920s. The results cover a range of dimensions and perspectives including network coverage, the position of seaports in the network and on specific routes within the network, and the existence of communities of seaports. The last part before the conclusion discusses the main factors that have an influence on maritime network structure and reach.

A review of the history of foreign ship companies in China

The study of the development of foreign maritime companies in China dates back to the Republican period. Examples include the studies of Guo Shousheng (1930), Zhang Xincheng (1930). These authors paid particular attention to the fluctuation in countries' share of total shipments with China. The work of Kwang-Ching Liu (1959, 1962, 1964) looked into the competition between British, American and Chinese shipping companies. These studies covered the period from the 1860s to the 1880s. Fan Baichuan (2007) studied the rise of China's shipping industry, the development history of foreign ship companies in China and their impact on the Chinese shipping industry. Zhu Yingui (2008) examined the development of foreign shipping companies in China after the First World War, with a particular focus on the causes behind and the characteristics of the rivalry between the British and Japanese shipping communities.

With the development of the Japanese maritime industry, some of the main shipping companies started to research their own development history. Important research sources on development strategy, routes, and shipping data include some of the works of Osaka Shosen Kaisha (1934) and Nippon Yusen Kaisha (NYK) (1956, 1988). Another noteworthy publication by Kokaze (1995), studied the relationship between the Japanese government and the modernization of the Japanese maritime industry and also explored the routes between Korea, Taiwan and the Yangtze River.

Katayama (1996) deals with the ocean routes of Osaka Shosen Kaisha in the Meiji period and the routes in relation to Taiwan. More recently, 'The Study of the Shipping Routes between Japan and Taiwan in Modern Times' (Matsuura, 2005) and 'Maritime transport in East Asia in Modern Times' (Matsuura, 2013) were published. The former studies the routes between China and Japan. The latter book discusses the routes operated by Japanese, Chinese, and Korean shipping companies at the end of the Qing Dynasty. Neither includes the position of British shipping companies in the twentieth century.

In the following sub-sections, we discuss the main historical facts and developments related to foreign shipping companies in China by distinguishing three periods: 1842–95, 1895–1914, and 1914–30.

1842–95: Monopoly by a single clique

The Qing dynasty was defeated in the first Opium War in 1842 and signed the Nanking Treaty with Britain. Britain got the privilege of shipping activities along the coastline of China. From then on, involvement of foreign shipping companies in the provision of maritime services along the coast and on the inland waterways of China was based on a large number of treaties. In September 1845, Lady Mary Wood of the Peninsular and Oriental Company set up operations in the port of Hong Kong and started a monthly service between Southampton and Hong Kong. It was the first fixed ocean route between Europe and China. From the 1860s, merchants from the United States and Great Britain founded shipping companies in China such as the Shanghai Union Steam Navigation Company, which was founded by an American firm in 1861; Wheelock & Co., started up by a British firm in 1863; the Shanghai Tug & Lighter Co., Ltd in 1863, also originating from a British firm, and the Taku Tug & Lighter Co., were also founded by a British firm in 1864.

Until the Sino-Japanese War of 1895, Great Britain was the dominant country in China's maritime transport. The shipping tonnage of Great Britain accounted for 85 per cent of the total shipping tonnage in China, a figure that far exceeded the shares of Germany, Norway and France. British shipping companies were not only dominant when it came to the ocean routes, they also dominated coastal routes and inland waterway shipments in China. The companies Butterfield and Swire, and Jardine Matheson and Co. for a long time occupied a very strong position on the Yangtze River and in Chinese coastal shipping. The Douglas Steamship Co. was the leading company on the route between Hong Kong and Taiwan. The Hong Kong, Canton and Macau Steamboat Co. had a strong presence on the shipping scene of Hong Kong, Canton and Macau. Only the route between Qiongzhou, Beihai, to Haiphong in Vietnam was serviced by two smaller companies from Germany and France. Some American and German shipping companies shared the shipping market along the coast of China, but they could not compete with British firms. Seven British companies controlled the ocean routes between Europe and Asia. The ships of three British companies shuttled between China and India. Canadian Pacific Ocean Services, Co. Ltd dominated the market between China and Canada. Only the route between China and Japan was occupied by Nippon Yusen Kaisha. In summary, British shipping firms dominated the shipping market in China during the period under examination.

1895–1914: The rise of Japanese shipping companies

After the Sino-Japanese War of 1895, Japanese companies entered the shipping market of the Yangtze River, north China and southeast China. Nippon Yusen Kaisha and Osaka Shosen Kaisha were the main players. After getting the lease of the Liaodong Peninsula, the Japanese increased their influence in the south of the three northeastern provinces of China. Japanese shipping services soon became more important than British shipping services in calling at northern Chinese ports. One of the Japanese firms, Nisshin Kisen Kaisha, entered the Yangtze River basin, which led to increased competition between Japan and Great Britain on the Yangtze River. British shipping companies remained strong on the routes between north China and Shanghai. Some companies such as Butterfield and Swire and Jardine Matheson and Co. started to develop shipping routes between Shanghai and northern China. Russian ships soon appeared on the Songhua River and the northern Chinese coast, thereby strengthening the bonds between the Liaodong Peninsula and Russia (see also Chapter 9 by Ducruet *et al.* from a global perspective). After obtaining the lease of the Jiaozhou Bay in Shandong province, Germany established a fixed route from Shanghai to Tianjin via Qingdao and Yantai. The Germans also enlarged their market share in the Yangtze River and in Chinese coastal and deep-sea shipping. France got the lease of Guangzhou and enlarged its market share in the west of northern China. French shipping companies also emerged on the Yangtze River and the West River. All these developments eroded the dominance of Great Britain. The share of British ships of total tonnage decreased from 85.26 per cent in 1895 to 54.57 per cent in 1914. Japanese ships' share increased from 0.51 per cent in 1895 to 33.35 per cent in 1914. At the same time, the German, French and Russian shipping presence in China developed in varying degrees.

1914–30: Rising competition between Japanese and British shipping

During the First World War, the shipping firms of Great Britain and Japan got a chance to further develop in China. British shipping companies soon covered the markets which Germany and the Austro-Hungarian Empire withdrew from. Meanwhile they reached the Chuan River at the upper Yangtze River basin. The Japanese shipping sector increased its influence in northern, northeast and southern China, which resulted in more direct competition between British and Japanese firms. Great Britain's share continued to fall while Japanese shipping firms saw a growing presence in China. The gap between the two countries' respective shares evolved from 21.22 per cent in 1914 to only 9.7 per cent in 1930.

Data and methodology

In this section we present the methodology and data used to analyse the British and Japanese maritime networks in China in the 1920s.

A first dataset was obtained from China customs statistics and includes ship movements in and out of the entire Chinese seaport system after the first Opium War in 1840. However, the dataset does not give any information on ships calling at individual seaports in China, making unfeasible to reconstruct the entire maritime network. Information on individual shipping services is presented in Zhang Xincheng's (1930) book, containing data on all maritime services supplied by foreign shipping companies in 1927, which is essential to build the maritime network. Unfortunately, some records in the database are not very detailed. For example, some records do not clearly mention an individual port (e.g. service between Shanghai, Qingdao and Japan without specifying the port of call in Japan). In such cases we traced the exact name of the port of call by using the 'History of Maritime Transport' and the shipping schedules described in Shun Pao in 1927. The data collection process resulted in the identification of 66 maritime services operated by British companies of which 85 per cent could be used for further analysis (the other 15 per cent contained data flaws). Of a total of 97 services offered by Japanese firms, 11 showed data flaws, leaving 88 per cent of the total number of services ready for further analysis.

The compiled dataset of Chinese shipping services supplied by Japanese and British companies was input using Gephi and Arcgis software for further analysis and mapping. Several measures of network analysis are used to describe the properties and structure of the shipping networks of Japanese and British firms in China and are defined next.

Degree. Degree is one of the fundamental parameters of the characteristics of a network. The degree k_i of a node i in the network is equal to the number of direct links to node i. The degree k_i can be defined by the matrix $A = (a_{ij}) :\in R^{N \times N}$:

$$k_i = \sum_{j \in N} a_{ij}$$

If node i is connected to node j, $a_{ij} = 1$. On the contrary, if node i is not connected to node j, $a_{ij} = 0$. So in a sense, the degree represents the power and importance of the node. The higher the degree of a node, the more impact the node has in the whole network, and vice versa.

Average degree. The average degree k refers to the average number of nodes that link with node i. The higher the average degree, the more dense the network is:

$$K = \frac{\sum_i k_i}{N}$$

Betweenness centrality. Betweenness centrality is a measure of a node's centrality in a network. It is equal to the number of shortest paths from all vertices to all others that pass through that node. This concept measures the extent to which a particular point lies 'between' the various other points in the graph: a point of relatively low degree may play an important 'intermediary' role and so be very central to the network (Freeman, 1979). Generally speaking, if the node's betweenness centrality is high, the node is acting as a hub in the transport network (Xiong, 2009). Betweenness centrality of a node i is given by the expression:

$$B_i = \sum_{k, j} \frac{\sum_{l \in S_{kj}} \delta_j^i}{|S_{kj}|}$$

where S_{kj} is the total number of shortest paths from node k to node j and δ_j^i is the number of those paths that pass through i.

Average path length. The average path length is defined as the average number of steps along the shortest paths for all possible pairs of network nodes. It is a measure of the efficiency of information or mass transport on a network. The mathematical expression is:

$$L = \frac{2}{N(N-1)} \sum_{i \geq j} d_{ij}$$

where N is the total number of the nodes in the network and d_{ij} is the distance between node i and j. The average path length in a maritime network context refers to the average number of intermediate ports that need to be passed if goods are shipped from one port to another.

Community. A network can consist of many communities so that the nodes in the network can be subdivided into many groups (Girvan and Newman, 2002). The two obvious characteristics of the community are that the links among the nodes in the same group are dense, but the links between different groups are sparse. Because of the existence of communities, networks can take the form of complicated structures. There are also some communities in the maritime network. Some ports in the same community connect closely to each other, and the other ports in different communities connect loosely.

Empirical results on British and Japanese maritime networks in China

Network coverage

The network includes 66 nodes (ports) in the British maritime network in China and 66 nodes in the Japanese maritime network (Table 8.1). After deducting the ports in Japan, Europe and America, we are left with 45 Chinese ports in the British maritime network and only 30 Chinese ports in the Japanese maritime network. Because of Japan's location close to China, Japanese ports show strong links with Chinese ports. No fewer than ten Japanese ports show strong links with the Chinese maritime network.

The network consists of 113 and 130 edges in the British and Japanese maritime networks, respectively. The average degree is 1.97 in the Japanese maritime network and 1.712 in the British maritime network. Thus, the maritime network of Japan has a much greater density than the British network. The average distance in the Japanese maritime network is 3.675, which means that cargo using the network can move from any port to any other port in the network by transferring at three ports on average. The average distance in the British maritime network equals 5.132.

The maritime network is composed of ports and routes. The amount of navigable ports is an important indicator of the coverage of the maritime network. We will use the degree of ports as a measure for the coverage of the British and Japanese maritime networks. The higher the degree, the more routes connect to the port. Overall, Japanese shipping firms are well connected with the ports along the northern Chinese coast. British shipping firms show better connectivity with the ports in southeastern China. In the Yangtze River basin, the fleets of both countries serve the upstream city of Chongqing. However, British shipping firms have a dominant position on the middle and upper reaches of the

Table 8.1 Characteristics of the British and Japanese maritime networks in China

	Nodes	Edges	Average degree	Average distance
Britain	66	113	1.712	5.132
Japan	66	130	1.970	3.675

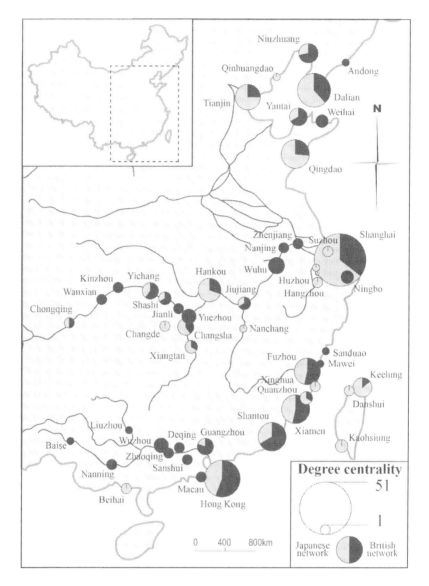

Figure 8.1 The shipping service coverage of the two countries measured by degree.

Yangtze River while Japanese firms have a stronger presence on the lower Yangtze River. British shipping firms are also dominant in the Pearl River basin. After 1895, Japan occupied Taiwan and then developed a strong maritime network with Taiwan and Japan. So, Japanese shipping firms were very visible in Taiwanese ports (Figure 8.1).

The position of seaports in the maritime network

The two maritime networks show a specific port hierarchy. Many of the routes are directed towards a few ports and most of the ports are served by only a small number of routes. Still, the two maritime networks have a different structure. The British maritime network is characterized by two dominant nodes: Shanghai, with a maritime degree value of 18, and Hong Kong, with a degree of 14. The routes radiate from Shanghai and Hong Kong into the Far East. Hong Kong, as one of the biggest trading centres in the world, and Shanghai, as one of the main shipping centres, were both well connected to maritime routes in relation to Europe, North America, Australia and the South Seas (Zhang, 1933). The Japanese maritime network was heavily centred around Shanghai (degree of 31). Dalian and Osaka came second with a degree of 13. Given these differences in maritime degree the Japanese maritime network can be described as a single-nucleus network both in terms of deep-sea and coastal flows (Zhang, 1933).

Hub-feeder structures emerged in both networks. The ocean routes of Great Britain connected with Shanghai, Hong Kong, Shantou, Xiamen, Dalian and Keelung. The ocean routes of Japan served Shanghai, Hong Kong, Dalian, Qing-dao and Tianjin. The other 15 seaports and 31 inland waterway ports in China relied on feeder connections with the aforementioned hub ports in order to secure connectivity to seaports in foreign countries. Both the British and Japanese ocean routes connect with Hong Kong, Shanghai and Dalian. At the time, these three ports were the most important seaports in shipping routes to China. The British ocean routes also connect to Shantou, Xiamen and Keelung, which are all located in south China and also are close to the (then) British colony of Hong Kong. Japanese ocean routes link strongly Qingdao and Tianjin, which are both situated in north China closer to Japan (Figure 8.3).

The position of seaports according to the type of maritime routes

The routes are divided into three types: ocean or deep-sea routes, coastal or near-sea routes, and inland waterway routes. In this section we analyse the position of Chinese ports for the different types of routes.

British ocean routes included eight shipping companies offering 24 ocean routes from China to India, Europe, America, Australia, Canada and southeast Asia. In the ocean route network, the betweenness centrality of Shanghai amounts to 314.5. Singapore, Hong Kong and Kobe follow, with a betweenness centrality of 252.5, 200 and 160 respectively. The British ocean routes radiate from Shanghai and Hong Kong into China. They connect with Japan and America via Kobe and link to Europe and Southeast Asia via Singapore (Figure 8.2).

The Japanese ocean routes were mainly in the hands of Nippon Yusen Kaisha and Osaka Shosen Kaisha. Showa Line Ltd and Mitsui & Co. Ltd also built up some ocean routes. There were 24 ocean routes overall to Europe, America, Australia, South America and India. Hong Kong's betweenness centrality in the ocean route network amounts to 165.5. Shanghai, Kobe and Singapore show values of 123, 122 and 110 respectively. Hong Kong (177), Shanghai (171.5), Colombo

(a)

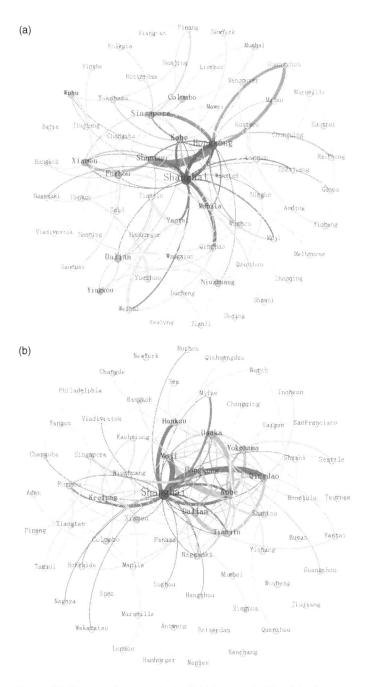

(b)

Figure 8.2 Degree of seaports in the British network (a) and the Japanese network (b).

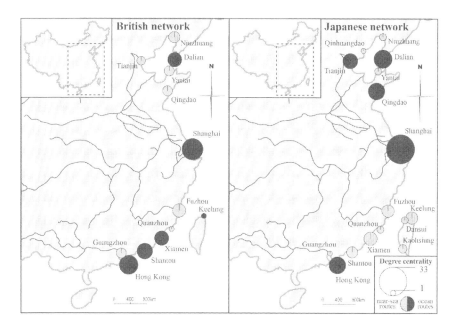

Figure 8.3 Hub-and-spokes structures in the British and Japanese maritime networks based on degree.

(170), Kobe (152) and Singapore (104) are the top five ports in the Japanese ocean route network (Figure 8.4).

The British near-sea or coastal routes were strongly centred on Hong Kong, with a betweenness centrality of 175.67. Shantou (145), Wuzhou (124), and Ducheng (105) in south China were other main nodes in the coastal route network. Shanghai only ranks eighth with a betweenness centrality of 50. Many routes radiated out of Hong Kong to other ports in south China. Before the First World War, a German shipping company controlled the route from Hong Kong to Haiphong via Haikou and Beihai. After the First World War, two British shipping companies, Butterfield and Swire and Jardine Matheson and Co., got a strong foothold on this route. Douglas Steamship Co. had a longstanding monopoly on the route from Hong Kong to Shantou. Japan even allowed British shipping firms to operate the fixed route between Fuzhou and Hong Kong (Fan, 2007).

The Japanese near-sea route network shows a strong position of Shanghai with a betweenness centrality of 395.5 followed by Osaka (239.7), Hong Kong (195), Shantou (144), Xiamen (135.5), Dalian (123.5), Qingdao (87.3), Moji (75.5) and Keelung (66.6). The Japanese near-sea routes in China relied heavily on connections from Shanghai to north and south China (Figure 8.5). Keelung is the ninth port of the 34 ports considered. After Japan occupied Taiwan in 1895, the position of Keelung rose sharply. In 1896, Osaka Shosen Kaisha began to develop a route between Japan and Taiwan. In 1897, Nippon Yusen Kaisha set up a route linking

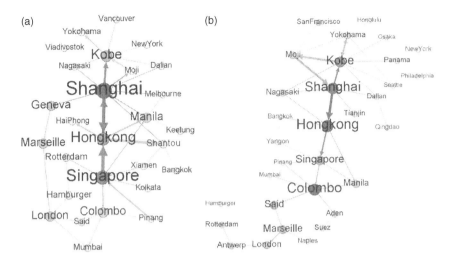

Figure 8.4 The position of ports in the British (a) and Japanese (b) ocean route networks, based on betweenness centrality.

Figure 8.5 The position of ports in the British (a) and Japanese (b) near-sea route networks, based on betweenness centrality.

Hong Kong, Shanghai, north China, Korea, Nagasaki and Keelung. The latter port soon became the largest port in Taiwan (Mao, 2005).

The Yangtze River was one of the most prominent inland waterway routes served by British shipping companies. The inland port of Hankou served as a hub for British inland shipping. From the 1880s, Butterfield and Swire and Jardine Matheson and Co. developed a strong monopoly on the Yangtze River. After 1895, the Japanese firm Nisshin Kisen Kaisha entered the Yangtze River market and started to compete with British shipping firms. Until 1911, British and Japanese firms competed heavily to gain dominance on the Yangtze River route. Shanghai, Hankou and Yicang were the main nodes for British shipping firms. They also linked with some small ports such as Shashi and Jianli, situated between Hankou and Chongqing. The British inland waterway interests also focused on Hunan, Fujian, Guangdong and Guangxi provinces. Fuzhou, Guangzhou and Wuzhou acted as the secondary hubs in these provinces.

Japanese inland waterway transport companies also had a keen interest in the Yangtze River basin (Figure 8.6). For the Japanese, Shanghai was the undisputed hub for the Yangtze River, while Hankou and Yicang were used as secondary centres. A number of direct sea–river routes were developed linking the Japanese port system with Hankou, for example the Kobe-Shashi service or the Osaka-Hankou service, which were operated by Nippon Yusen Kaisha and Nisshin Kisen Kaisha. Chongqing, a major city on the upper reach of the Yangtze River, was also served by Japanese shipping firms. Similar to the British inland waterway routes, the Japanese inland shipping routes connected important ports in the middle and lower reaches of the Yangtze River and the upper Yangtze River. However, the Japanese network covered fewer inland ports than the British network. The Japanese inland waterway network mainly focused on the Yangtze River Delta in eastern China with ports such as Suzhou, Hangzhou and Huzhou. Next to the Yangtze River, the British inland waterway network also developed strongly in the Pearl River Delta, in southern China.

The route-network analysis demonstrates that Japanese and British shipping companies competed in quite a few Chinese regions. The most important ports in the British and Japanese ocean routes were the same: Shanghai, Hong Kong,

Figure 8.6 The position of ports in the British (a) and Japanese (b) inland waterway route network, based on betweenness centrality.

Singapore and Kobe. However, the order of importance differs, as Shanghai is the top port in the British ocean route network while Hong Kong proved to be the most important port for the Japanese ocean routes. In the British near-sea route network, Hong Kong played a key role while Shanghai was only ranked eighth. The latter port was the most important node in the Japanese near-sea routes, with Hong Kong ranking third. On the Yangtze River, Hankou and Shanghai acted as the hubs in the British and Japanese inland waterway networks, respectively. The British inland waterway network mainly focused on the Pearl River Delta in the south of China while the Japanese inland waterway routes were directed to the Yangtze River Delta in the eastern part of China. In the 1920s, most of the important ports were covered by British and Japanese shipping interests, but the network structure and the port hierarchy differed.

Inter-port connections

An analysis of the connections between ports can reveal more details on the main direction of flows and regions in the two maritime networks considered (see Table 8.2).

The route between Hong Kong and Shantou is the densest in the British maritime network. Six of the ten densest routes are from or to Hong Kong. The routes from or to Shanghai and Shantou are also quite dense. Most of the dense routes concentrate in southern China. Only two routes including Yantai to Tianjin and Shanghai to Qingdao connect the ports in the north and northeast of China.

The routes Shanghai to Qingdao and Kobe to Moji are the densest in the Japanese maritime network. There are five routes from or to Shanghai in the top ten densest routes. The connections with north and northeast China and the inland route between Shanghai to Hankou are very prominent in the network. After the First World War, Japan tried to enlarge its share in the Chinese shipping market

Table 8.2 Top ten routes in the British and Japanese maritime networks

British			Japanese		
Origin	*Destination*	*Weight*	*Origin*	*Destination*	*Weight*
Hong Kong	Shantou	11	Shanghai	Qingdao	8
Yantai	Tianjin	6	Kobe	Moji	8
Singapore	Hong Kong	5	Moji	Shanghai	7
Shanghai	Hong Kong	5	Osaka	Kobe	6
Shanghai	Qingdao	5	Shanghai	Hong Kong	5
Guangzhou	Hong Kong	5	Shanghai	Hankou	5
Hong Kong	Shanghai	4	Tianjin	Dalian	5
Hong Kong	Guangzhou	4	Yokohama	Kobe	4
Shantou	Xiamen	4	Kobe	Shanghai	4
Shantou	Shanghai	4	Qingdao	Tianjin	4

with two specific objectives in mind: first to maintain and enlarge the control of the routes in northern China; and second to strengthen the ability for Japanese shipping companies to compete in southern China. In 1915, more than half of the total number of ships and the total tonnage in or out of northern China belonged to Japan. Japan did not succeed in obtaining a significant share of the shipping market in southern China.

Communities of ports in the networks

The 66 ports in the British maritime network can be divided into seven communities. The biggest community consists of 14 ports and the smallest one of five ports. There are three communities along the coast of China. Ten ports north of Ningbo form a community. Six ports in southern China and eight ports in Southeast Asia each form a community. Five ports between Ningbo and Xiamen are grouped into a small community. There are two communities in the inland waterway part of the network. One community is formed by all ports along the Yangtze River. Another is formed by all ports in the Pearl River basin. The remaining two communities include 11 ports in Europe and seven ports in Japan and North America (Figure 8.7). There are 66 ports in the Japanese maritime network, which can be divided into seven communities as well. However, the largest community counts 20 ports while there are three in the smallest. The ports in the Yangtze River basin, Fujian province and Taiwan, and some ports in Japan which link to ports in the Yangtze River directly form a large community. The ports in the northern part of China and Korea form a community. The ports in southern China and the ports in Southeast Asia form another community. Ports in the west to India including all ports in Europe form a community. Six ports in Japan and the ports along the west coast of the United States form a community. There are two small communities with only three ports: one in Jiangxi province and the other comprises Panama, New York and Philadelphia (Figure 8.8).

When comparing the communities of the two maritime networks, similarities and differences become visible. The ports in the ocean route networks can be divided into three communities. The first is composed of the ports in southern China and Southeast Asia. The second consists of ports in Japan and along the west coast of the United States. The third includes European ports. The three communities are independent in the two maritime networks. There are some differences in the communities for the near-sea routes and inland routes. The Yangtze River ports form an independent community in the British network. However, in the Japanese maritime network, the ports in the Yangtze River, Fujian province and Taiwan and some ports in Japan belong to the same community. There is a river–sea direct route between Japan and Hankou and triangular trade between Japan, Shanghai and Taiwan. The communities in the Japanese network linked more ports than in the British network. In the latter, Shanghai, Ningbo and the ports in northern China form a community. In the Japanese network, the ports in northern China and Korea are part of the same community.

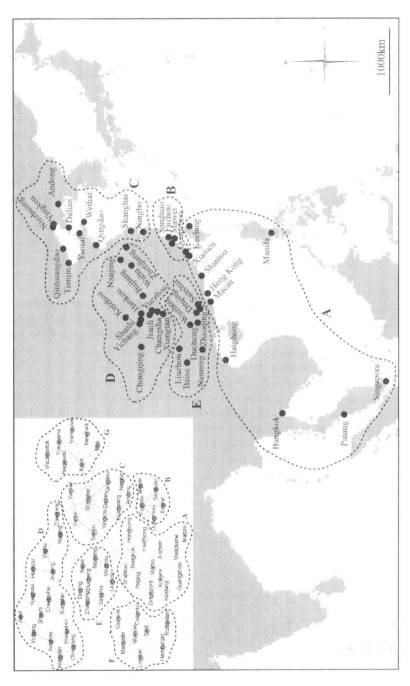

Figure 8.7 Communities in the British maritime network.

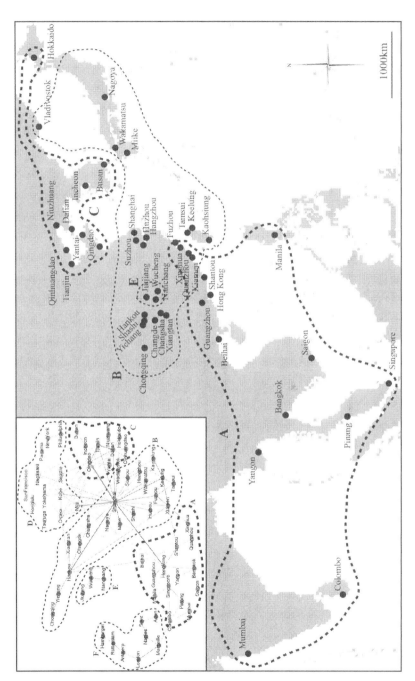

Figure 8.8 Communities in the Japanese maritime network.

Factors influencing maritime network properties in China

Geographical factors

Some geographical factors, especially the location of the country, colony or sphere of influence, affect the direction of the routes and the structure of the maritime network. North China is close to Japan and offers the lush fields and rich cities that Japan sought. The Japanese shipping firms extended their network there, and those routes are the densest. In 1913, Japan had established total supremacy over all its rivals in Andong, Dalian and Niuzhuang port (Table 8.3). Great Britain had the upper hand in Tianjin, Yantai and Qingdao. The two countries were equally strong in Qinghuangdao port. During the First World War and in 1927, the British share declined in all ports apart from Yantai. Especially in Dalian and Qingdao, the two most important ports in northern China, Japan had an advantage over its opponents, as the two cities belonged to its sphere of influence. Before the Sino-Japanese War in 1894, there were few ocean routes to Taiwan. Most goods were transported in and out of Taiwan via Xiamen. Taiwan was occupied by Japan in 1895. Nine routes were developed before 1900 including four routes to Kobe, four routes around Taiwan, and one route to Hong Kong (Mao, 2005). After a price war with a Japanese firm, the Douglas Steamship Company of Great Britain had to withdraw from the route between Taiwan and Hong Kong, which it had dominated for many years.

Hong Kong became a colony of Britain after the First Opium War. Hong Kong acted as a base camp for Great Britain to develop its interests in China. Initially routes radiated from Hong Kong to southern China. The Yangtze River basin was also in the sphere of influence of Great Britain (Wu, 1995). Although the Japanese proportion in northern China and Taiwan increased quickly, Great Britain also dominated the markets in southern China and the Yangtze River.

Competitive forces

After 1840, Britain dominated the shipping market in China. Only after 1895 did British shipping firms face increasing competition from Japanese firms. Still, the market share of Great Britain in China remained high in the 1920s. After the 1880s, Butterfield Swire and the Jardine Matheson Company began to dominate transport on the Yangtze River. In the end, competition took place among four big companies: two British, one Japanese and one Chinese. The share of the Japanese shipping company was higher than that of the other three for most of the time between 1901 and 1928. But if we add up the tonnage of the two British companies, their proportion was higher than that of the Japanese company (Table 8.4).

Japan was one of the few countries which reaped gains during the First World War. During and after the war, more and more ships were built and bought. Supported by the government's campaign to create what it called Commanding Sea-Routes, Nippon Yusen Kaisha, Osaka Shosen Kaisha and Nisshin Kisen Kaisha continued their rapid expansion in ocean, coastal and inland routes (Zhu, 2008). Japan succeeded in solidifying its dominance in northern China and Taiwan

Table 8.3 The shares of Japanese and British tonnage in the ports of North China in the period 1913–27

Year	Country	Andong	Dalian	Niuzhuang	Qinhuangdao	Tianjin	Longkou	Yantai	Qingdao	Total
1913	Japan	68.4	77.5	49.8	37.1	29.7	0.0	31.3	17.5	44.8
	Britain	14.6	11.1	29.1	35.4	36.3	0.0	34.1	31.0	26.5
	Other	17.0	11.4	21.1	27.5	34.0	0.0	34.6	51.5	28.7
1915–19	Japan	56.8	83.7	46.3	54.7	39.1	51.9	11.5	74.2	56.8
	Britain	13.8	7.1	25.1	21.1	37.7	10.2	40.8	17.3	22.9
	Other	29.4	9.2	28.6	24.2	23.2	37.9	47.7	8.5	20.3
1921–5	Japan	34.2	67.4	27.1	38.0	33.0	21.3	11.5	53.0	45.7
	Britain	20.5	8.7	28.7	20.0	29.3	11.5	40.8	19.7	20.4
	Other	45.3	23.9	44.2	42.0	37.7	67.2	47.7	27.3	33.9
1927	Japan	26.5	68.5	27.4	27.3	39.3	32.3	19.9	53.9	48.9
	Britain	7.7	7.7	15.5	12.2	26.0	5.9	35.7	18.2	16.3
	Other	65.8	23.8	57.1	60.5	34.7	61.8	44.4	27.9	34.8

Table 8.4 Tonnage controlled by Swire, Jardine Matheson, Nissei-Line and China Merchants on the Yangtze River, 1901–28

Year	Swire			Jardine Matheson			Nissei Line			China Merchants		
	Ship	Tonnage		Ship	Tonnage		Ship	Tonnage		Ship	Tonnage	
		Tonnage	%		Tonnage	%		Tonnage	%		Tonnage	%
1901	5	6550	17.5	5	7000	18.7	5	11100	29.7	10	12800	34.2
1903	4	6757	23.8	5	7236	25.5	5	6727	23.09	6	7688	27
1911	9	9863	17.9	6	10648	19.3	12	25678	46.6	7	8864	16.2
1914	9	17250	21.5	7	19172	23.8	12	25260	31.4	8	18704	23.3
1916	10	22833	24.8	8	20637	22.4	13	29237	31.7	8	19425	21.1
1918	9	19436	21.4	8	19787	21.8	14	32104	35.3	8	19025	21.5
1924	15	20744	26	11	18302	23	16	21486	27	13	19145	24
1928	20	22343	26.4	14	20766	24.6	18	22003	26	12	19425	23

Source: The data of shipping history of modern China, 1895–1927, vol. 1, 478.

and competed fiercely with Great Britain in southern China and on the Yangtze River. In 1920, Nisshin Kisen Kaisha established a route between Shanghai and Guangdong via Shantou and Hong Kong. Due to its status of Commanding Sea-Route, Japanese shipping firms could enter into the shipping market of southern China, which for a long time had been dominated by Great Britain.

The role of government

Partly as a result of support from the Japanese government, Japanese shipping firms developed strongly after 1895. Enlarging the maritime network was part of the plans of the Japanese government (Table 8.5) to extend its influence in Asia (Zhu, 2008). Commanding Sea-Routes were launched by the Japanese government. Shipping companies received subsidies and the routes were somewhat divided between the shipping firms. With the support of Commanding Sea-Routes, Nippon Yusen Kaisha and Osaka Shosen Kaisha focused on ocean routes and controlled the routes between Japan and China. Osaka Shosen Kaisha, Dairen Koshin Ginko and Nisshin Kisen Kaisha were mainly in charge of the coastal routes in China. Toyo Kisen Kaisha specialized in the route between China and the United States. Nisshin Kisen Kaisha was active on the Yangtze River. All the Commanding Sea-Routes which connected most of the main ports in China acted as the backbone of the Japanese maritime network (Fan, 2007).

The routes in the British maritime network were not arranged by the government. The large British shipping firms gradually implemented initiatives to create some division of labour and to enhance coordination among the companies. The route from London to China and Japan was operated by Peninsular and Oriental Steam Navigation Co., which also controlled the route between China and Australia. The route from Liverpool and Glasgow to China and Japan was operated by Alfred Holt and Company. The company also specialized in the route between

Table 8.5 Commanding routes of Japan in 1927

Line	Ports	Shipping Firm
Yokohama–London	Yokohama, Kobe, Shanghai, Hong Kong, Singapore, Colombo, Siad, Marseille, London	Nippon Yusen Kaisha
Kobe–Seattle	Kobe, Yokohama, Vancouver, Seattle	Nippon Yusen Kaisha
Yokohama–Melbourne	Yokohama, Kobe, Nagasaki, Hong Kong, Manila, Davao, Thursday Island, Townsville, Brisbane, Sydney, Melbourne	Nippon Yusen Kaisha
Kobe–Durban	Outbound: Kobe, Moji, Hong Kong, Singapore, Colombo, Mombasa, Zanzibar, Dar es Salaam, Peila, Durban Inbound: Durban, Mombasa, Singapore, Moji, Kobe	Osaka Shosen Kaisha
Kobe–Surabaya	Outbound: Kobe, Moji, Hong Kong, Batavia, Cheribon, Samaran, Surabaya Inbound: Surabaya, Balikpapan, Hong Kong, Moji, Kobe	Nannyou kisen Kaisha
Shanghai–Guangzhou	Shanghai, Shantou, Hongkong, Guangzhou	Nisshin Kisen Kaisha
Shanghai–Tianjin	Shanghai, Qingdao, Tianjin	Nisshin Kisen Kaisha
Shanghai–Hankou	Shanghai, Zhenjiang, Nanjing, Wuhu, Jiujiang, Hankou	Nisshin Kisen Kaisha
Hankou–Yichang	Hankou, Shashi, Yichang	Nisshin Kisen Kaisha
Hankou–Xiangtan	Hankou, Nagasaki, Xiangtan	Nisshin Kisen Kaisha
Hankou–Changde	Hankou, Changde	Nisshin Kisen Kaisha
Yichang–Chongqing	Yichang, Wanxian, Chongqing	Nisshin Kisen Kaisha
Kobe–Dianlian	Kobe, Dalian	Osaka Shosen Kaisha
Nagasaki–Shanghai	Nagasaki, Shanghai	Nippon Yusen Kaisha
Kobe–Shanghai	Kobe, Shanghai	Nippon Yusen Kaisha
Yokohama–Shanghai	Outbound: Yokohama, Nagoya or Yokkaichi, Osaka or Kobe, Moji Inbound: Nagoya or Yokkaichi, Shanghai	Nippon Yusen Kaisha
Kobe–Tianjin	Kobe, Moji, Tianjin or Dagu	Kinkai kisen Kaisha
Yokohama–Niuzhuang	Outbound: Yokohama, Nagoya or Yokkaichi, Osaka, Dalian, Tianjin or Dagu, Niuzhuang; Inbound: Niuzhuang, Dalian, Yokohama	Kinkai kisen Kaisha
Kobe–Qingdao	Outbound: Kobe, Moji, Qingdao Inbound: Qingdao, Moji, Ujina, Kobe	Nippon Yusen Kaisha, Osaka Shosen Kaisha, Harada Kisen Kaisha

China and the United States. By avoiding direct fierce competition between the companies, room was created for inter-firm cooperation (Fan, 2007).

Conclusion

This chapter has analysed the maritime networks of British and Japanese companies in China in the period 1842–1930. Three stages can be distinguished in the development of foreign shipping firms in China. From 1842 to 1894, British shipping firms dominated the maritime market in China. From 1895 to 1914, Japanese, German, American and French shipping companies competed with British firms. After the First World War, Japanese firms expanded their influence in ocean, near-sea and inland routes. In the 1920s, there was a nearly equal number of ports in the two networks. But there were more Chinese ports in the British network compared with the Japanese network.

In terms of network coverage, Great Britain had a strong presence in ports in southern China while Japan had strong links with ports in northern China. Companies of both countries were present on the Yangtze River up to Chongqing. However, the British maritime network counted more ports on the Yangtze River than did the Japanese network. The inland waterway services of British companies mainly focused on the Pearl River Delta in southern China. Japan had strong inland waterway interests in the Yangtze River Delta in eastern China.

Shanghai and Hong Kong were important hubs in the British maritime network. Japanese shipping firms relied more on a single-nucleus network centred around Shanghai. Most of the important ports in the ocean, near-sea and inland routes were served by Britain as well as Japan. However, most of the top ten densest routes in the British maritime network concentrated on southern China, while the Japanese network focused much more on northern China and the Japanese port system. The analysis of communities of ports in the maritime networks provides further insight into port structure and hierarchy. The structure and characteristics of the British and Japanese maritime networks were mainly affected by three factors: geography, competitive forces and the role of government.

Acknowledgements

The authors would like to thank César Ducruet for the help on cartography.

References

Ducruet C. (2013) Network diversity and maritime flows. *Journal of Transport Geography*, 30: 77–88.
Ducruet C., Notteboom T.E. (2012) The worldwide maritime network of container shipping: spatial structure and regional dynamics. *Global Networks*, 12(3): 395–423.
Fan B.C. (2007) *The Rise of China's Shipping Industry*. China Social Sciences Press.
Freeman L.C. (1979) Centrality in social networks: conceptual clarification. *Social Networks*, 1: 215–39
Girvan M., Newman M.E.J. (2002) Community structure in social and biological networks. *Proceedings of the National Academy of Sciences*, 99(12): 7821–6.

Guo Z.S. (1930) *National Shipping Policy and Navigation Rights*. Shanghai Huatong Press.

Japan Economic History Research Institute (1956) *A Seventy Years' History of the Ships of Nippon Yusen Kaisha*. Tokyo: Nippon Yusen Kaisha.

Japan Economic History Research Institute (1988) *A Hundred Years' History of the Ships of Nippon Yusen Kaisha*. Tokyo: Nippon Yusen Kaisha.

Katayama K. (1996) *Modern Japan's shipping and Asia*. Otyanomizu Shobou.

Kokaze H. (1995) *Japanese Maritime under Imperialism: International Competition and External Independence*. Yamakawa Shuppannsha.

Liu K.C. (1959) Steamship enterprise in nineteenth-century China. *The Journal of Asia Studies*, 18(4): 435–55

Liu K.C. (1962) *Anglo-American Steamship Rivalry in China*, 1862–1874. Cambridge MA: Harvard University Press.

Liu K.C. (1964) British-Chinese Steamship Rivalry 1873-1875. In: C. D. Cowan (ed.), *The Economic Development of China and Japan*. London: George Allen & Unwin, pp. 49–78.

Lv K.J., Zhang R.R. (2012) On the structure and characteristics of international shipping center based on complex network theory. *Journal of Systems and Management*, 21(1): 87–92.

Mao L.K. (2005) Evolution of the shipping lines and the harbor potential of the southeastern treaty ports in the late Qing period. *Journal of Historical Science*, 12: 36–42.

Matsuura A. (2005) *The Study on Shipping Routes among Modern Japan, China and Taiwan*. Tokyo: Seibundou Shuppann Kabushikigaisha.

Matsuura A. (2013) *The Shipping Time in Modern East Asian Sea*. Tokyo: Seibundou Shuppann Kabushikigaisha.

Osaka Shosen Kaisha (1934) *A Fifty Years' History of the Ships of Osaka Shosen Kaisha*.

Shun Pao (1927) Ship import and export schedule. June 3 and 10.

Tian W., Deng G.S., Wu P.J., Che W.J. (2007) Analysis of complexity in global shipping network. *Journal of Dalian University of Technology*, 47(4): 605–9.

Wang C. (2008) Spatial organization networks of world marine container transportation. *Geographical Research*, 27(3): 636–48.

Wu C.M. (1995) *Imperialist States' Investment in Modern China*. People Press.

Xiong W.H. (2009) *The Structure Properties and Evolving Mechanism of the Global Maritime Shipping System*. Qingdao University doctoral dissertation.

Zhang B. (1933) *The Japanese Invasion in China Traffic*. The Commercial Press.

Zhang Xincheng (1930) *The Development History of the Imperialists' Ship Industry in China*. Shanghai: Rixin Yudi Press.

Zhu Y.G. (2008) *The Study of Ship Industry in Modern China*. China Social Sciences Press.

9 Maritime shifts in the contemporary world economy

Evidence from the *Lloyd's List* corpus, eighteenth to twenty-first centuries

César Ducruet, Sébastien Haule,
Kamel Ait-Mohand, Bruno Marnot,
Zuzanna Kosowska-Stamirowska,
Laura Didier, Marie-Anne Coche

The *Lloyd's List* records on vessel movements are certainly the only possible source for mapping and analysing the global evolution of ports and maritime networks over the last 120 years. However, very rare reference to *Lloyd's List* is made in the literature. The first ever analysis we found dates back to the mid-1950s. Motivated by the pedagogical potential of the source for port study in schools, the geographer Henry Rees (1955) proposed a few maps of vessel movements that took place between the terminals of selected British ports. Much later, another geographer having worked 15 years in the shipping industry underlined in a footnote that "a very useful source (. . .) might be *Lloyd's Shipping Index*" (Fleming, 1968: 35) but without using it. In the second half of the 1970s, two reports proposed to map ship traffic densities at world scale using the latter source, based on a square grid and the extraction and computation of vessel movements from the *Lloyd's Shipping Index* (McKenzie, 1975; Solomon *et al.*, 1978). A few years later, the Australian Bureau of Transportation Economics published a report using vessel movement data from *Lloyd's Voyage Record* to measure the impact of introducing fully cellular container ships on Australian ports (BTE, 1982), but it is only 20 years later that this source was used to analyse the distribution of ship calls in the Baltic region (Swedish Maritime Administration, 2000).

Most of the time, *Lloyd's List* is used for genealogic investigations, for instance to retrieve a given ship or voyage based on someone's memoirs, for underwater archaeology, such as to inventory the exact location of ships sunk in Irish waters over the period 1741–1945 (Brady, 2008), or to analyse the activity of one given port on the basis of vessel calls, such as Whitby over the period 1700–1914 (Jones, 1982). Several other usages could have been reported, but they differ drastically in their objective and scope: the calculation of time difference evolution between sailing date and publication date to study the changing speed of information transmission in modern times (Kaukiainen, 2001); or in 1918 the spread of Spanish flu, through shipping, on the island of Newfoundland (Palmer *et al.*, 2007). As mentioned in the introductory chapter, it is only in the very late 1990s that a systematic analysis of containership movements listed in *Lloyd's Voyage Record* was proposed at the global scale to reveal the macro-structure of the maritime network based on graph theory (Joly, 1999). Later on, more regional analyses were proposed using digital records provided by *Lloyd's Marine Intelligence Unit* to analyze the Caribbean basin (Veenstra *et al.*, 2005) and inter-Korean maritime flows (Ducruet *et al.*, 2008); it later was expanded to analyze the long-term evolution of port hierarchies and network topologies on a larger scale (Ducruet, 2013a).

Several fundamental questions remain unanswered, such as why has *Lloyd's List* data been mentioned or analyzed so late, given its long-term existence and its uniqueness in terms of publication frequency (daily vessel movements) and geographic coverage? Lloyd's has long been the largest classification society, with a market share of around 42 percent of the world fleet throughout the period 1910–22 (Richardson and Hurd, 1923), and about 80 percent nowadays. One reason given by historians is the traditionally qualitative character of maritime history and hence, its reluctance to compile large datasets. This cannot suffice to explain why other researchers underused this source over the last century, given the early quantitative analyses of maritime flows by geographers based on other sources (see a review in Chapter 1 by Ducruet). The limited diffusion of technical reports on ship densities, data cost restricted access—Lloyd's publications were primarily targeting the shipping industry—are also not obvious factors since British libraries have been holding such documents for decades: any scholar could have extracted the data manually to undertake the analysis of even a small region.

After reviewing the contents of this corpus since its first publication in 1696, we introduce the methodology used to extract shipping information from printed documents. The core of the analysis focuses on regional shifts in the geographic distribution of maritime routes and port hierarchies over the period 1890–2008. This chapter particularly discusses the uneven diffusion and impact of technological innovation (e.g. sail, steam, combustion, mega-carriers), the long-term evolution mechanisms of ports, port systems and maritime networks, the disaggregated distribution of global trade in relation with wider economic and (geo)political changes, refining previous attempts on the matter (Ducruet and Marnot, 2015; Ducruet, 2015).

The *Lloyd's List* corpus on global vessel movements

The "List": a short historical survey

> He's lost, gentlemen, [. . .] he's lost a hundred times over! As you know, the *China* arrived yesterday—the only steamship from New York that he could have caught to Liverpool. Now here is a list of passengers published by the *Shipping Gazette*, and Phileas Fogg's name is not on it.
>
> Jules Verne (1995[1873])[1]

These words had been pronounced by Andrew Stuart, a member of the Reform Club and a character of the famous adventure novel by the French writer Jules Verne, published in 1873, *Around the World in Eighty Days*. Stuart came to this conclusion thanks to information from a newspaper which really did exist, entitled the *Shipping Gazette*. The *Shipping and Mercantile Gazette* was a competitor since 1836 of the famous *Lloyd's List* in the field of shipping and maritime intelligence. By 1890 already, Lloyd's publications even included the daily movements of ships insured by its own competitors, such as Bureau Veritas and all other major insurance registers of the world.

Lloyd's List belongs from the beginning to Marine lists, a publication reporting overseas trade and shipping. Even if the first issue of *Lloyd's List* had been printed in 1735, historical research show that its origins date back to the late seventeenth century,[2] with the creation by Edward Lloyd (*c*.1648–1713), founding proprietor of the famous eponymous coffee house, of a newspaper entitled *SHIPS Arrived at, and Departed from several Ports of England, as I have Account of them in London [. . .] An account of what English Shipping and Foreign Ships for England, I hear of in Foreign ports* (McCusker and Gravesteijn, 1991; McCusker, 1991, 1997, 2005).

The later history of *Lloyd's List*, which is descended from Edward Lloyd's newspaper, is better known. The original newspaper died out *c*.1772 with the founding in 1769 of a New Lloyd's Coffee House by a dissident group of marine insurers and the publication of *New Lloyd's List*, which was shortened to *Lloyd's List* in 1789. Publication under this title continued to 1871, when the newspaper was renamed *Lloyd's List and Commercial Daily Chronicle*. From June 1884 to July 1914, *Lloyd's List* is amalgamated with the *Shipping and Mercantile Gazette* and published as *Shipping and Mercantile Gazette & Lloyd's List* (Fayle and Wright, 1928; Barriskill, 1994; Hailey and Landon, 2009). Printed under its original title after 1914, the newspaper was renamed between 1922 and 1969 and issued as *Lloyd's List and Shipping Gazette*. Renamed again *Lloyd's List*, one of the oldest newspaper in England is published till December 20, 2013 and then replaced by digital format.[3]

The strength of *Lloyd's List* lies, since its origin, in that it provides a constantly updated shipping and maritime intelligence. As early as Edward Lloyd's time, collection of shipping information was made possible thanks to a network of correspondents, organized later into agencies and sub-agencies, with appointed staff since 1811 (Fayle and Wright, 1928). Henry Fry (1826–96), President of the Dominion Board of Trade of Canada in 1873, wrote that Lloyd's agents, whose principal task was to supply regular shipping intelligence "[. . .] are found at nearly every seaport in the world, and exercise a sort of control over the wreck of every British ship, whilst more marine insurance is effected at the head office than in any similar institution known" (Fry, 1895).[4] Fry was himself appointed Lloyd's agent at Quebec in 1856. Between the 1820s and 1920s, the number of Lloyd's agencies and sub-agencies increased by five and a half times.[5]

Transmission of collected shipping and maritime information to London was improved since Lloyd's early existence thanks to particular arrangements and regular innovations. The early one was a special agreement with the Post Office—probably since Edward Lloyd's time—which gave a preferential priority treatment to dispatch letters from Lloyd's correspondents to London (McCusker, 1991). In the second half of the nineteenth century, on Lloyd's own initiative, a network of signal stations was deployed,[6] thereby increasing accuracy of shipping movement information. Lloyd's introduction of technical progress, like wireless telegraphy or use of night signal flashing lamp aboard, contributed to set up a "world wide net" (Fayle and Wright, 1928), but also increased amount and quality of collected shipping and maritime data. Even if other factors had to be taken into consideration, and particularly a global improvement in the speed of information transmission, Lloyd's Corporation adapted its practice, taking part in the shrinking world of the second half of nineteenth century.[7]

The first Lloyd's Act passed in Parliament in 1871, besides the fact that it laid the legal foundations of Lloyd's Corporation, specified the collection, publication and diffusion of intelligence and information as one of the objects of the Corporation. It was confirmed by the Lloyd's Act of 1911[8] It is no coincidence that at the time Lloyd's Corporation began to increase the number of reference books and periodical publications in the field of shipping and maritime intelligence.

Lloyd's periodicals, a Sargasso Sea for researchers

Despite the publishing of several research guides—and particularly the various editions of Barriskill's dedicated to Lloyd's marine collection held by Guildhall Library—it is not an easy thing to navigate through Lloyd's publications.

First, each type of publication was distilled from specific data among shipping and maritime information collected by Lloyd's agents and correspondents. An advertising insert published in 1923 edition of *Brassey's Naval and Shipping Annual* put forward no less than seven publications: *Lloyd's List and Shipping Gazette*, described as the "leading daily shipping newspaper," providing readers with complete shipping intelligence; *Lloyd's Daily Index*, the "only complete publication of its kind," dealing with vessel movements engaged on oversea trade; *Lloyd's Loading List*, "a complete list of Vessels loading for Coastwise and Foreign Ports"; *Lloyd's Weekly Casualty Reports*, providing "a complete list of Marine Casualties, Missing and Overdue Vessels"; *Lloyd's List Weekly Summary*, giving a résumé of shipping news with an "exclusive list of Vessels Outward and Homeward bound"; *Lloyd's List Law Reports*, treating of maritime and commercial law cases reported in *Lloyd's List*, with verbatim reports of judgments; and *Lloyd's Calendar*, an annual seamen's almanac with "information of value to all connected with Shipping" (Richardson and Hurd, 1923).[9]

Additional confusion stemmed from title variability for periodicals, periodicity fluctuation, multiple editions, and changes in issue numbering. The aforementioned *Lloyd's List* is not the only case. For example, *Lloyd's Loading List* is a weekly periodical published by Lloyd's, with its first issue in 1920 under this title. However, *Lloyd's Loading List* absorbed an older periodical, *The General Weekly Shipping List and Postal and Mercantile Directory*, published in London since 1853. Using the *Lloyd's Loading List* corpus is complicated due to numerous editions: the original UK and, since 1978, a continental edition, renamed the European edition in 1980. Another issue is editing discontinuation, such as for *Lloyd's List Weekly Shipping Summary*, the last issue of which appeared in August 1934. Finally, among Lloyd's publications, we have noticed a kind of "ghost" periodical, the *Voyage Tables of Steamers*, a half-yearly table was published from the end of 1883, providing the number of voyages made by any steamer during the previous twelve months. This periodical, mentioned in the 1885 edition of *Hints to Captains of the Mercantile Marine* (Hozier and Watson, 1885), is nowhere to be found.[10] Voyage Record Cards replacing the *Annual Index* were handwritten between 1927 and 1945 and printed up to 1975.

For researchers, a final difficulty concerns the sensitive nature of shipping and maritime information—especially data about shipping movements—provided in Lloyd's publication. It is no accident that it was decided to extract shipping movements and casualties from *Lloyd's List* between January 1917 and November 1918, the information was separately printed as a restricted publication (Barriskill, 1994). In the same period, publication of *Lloyd's Weekly Index* was suspended[11] This was due to the risk of providing strategic information about shipping movements to the Imperial German Navy, after Germany's resumption of unrestricted U-boat warfare in 1917.[12] Since "loose lips might sink ships," the same sort of security measures were taken during the Second World War. Between August 1939 and September 1945, *Lloyd's List* shipping movements were printed separately as a restricted publication under the title *Confidential Movements* (Barriskill, 1994); *Lloyd's Shipping Index*—formerly *Lloyd's Weekly Index*, during the First World War—was also a restricted publication between September 1940 and September 1945.[13] Except for war periods, special instructions were printed on periodicals which provided very specialized and sensitive information, as *Lloyd's Shipping Index*, *Voyage Supplement*, or *Lloyd's Voyage Record*, restricting their use to subscribers only, requesting the destruction of issues when no longer required. For researchers, the consequence is that hardly any library—except for in the UK and Commonwealth—held issues of these Lloyd's periodical publications.[14]

Maritime network analysis based on Lloyd's publications

Among the huge corpus of Lloyd's publications, two periodicals are of greatest significance for studying global vessel movements: *Lloyd's Shipping Index* and *Lloyd's Voyage Record*, which are two complementary sources. Tables 9.1 and 9.2 provide information about title variability, periodicity fluctuation, and numbering change for these periodicals.

Lloyd's Shipping Index was published for the first time in January 1880 under the title *The Weekly Shipping Record*. From the very beginning, the aim of *Lloyd's Shipping Index* was to provide a list of shipping movements of all merchant

Table 9.1 Evolution of the *Lloyd's Shipping Index*, 1880–2009

Years	Title	Issues	Period
1880	*The Weekly Shipping Record*	1	1 Jan. 1880
1880–1914	*Lloyd's Weekly Shipping Index*	2–1880	9 Jan. 1880–25 June 1914
1914–1917	*Lloyd's Weekly Index*	1801–1947	3 July 1914–19 April 1917
1917–1918	Not published between 19 April 1917 and 2 Dec. 1918		
1918–1932	*Lloyd's Daily Index*	1948–6014	2 Dec. 1918–13 May 1932
1932–1936	*Lloyd's Daily Shipping Index*	6015–7142	17 May 1932–1 Feb. 1936
1936–1940	*Lloyd's Shipping Index*	7143–8560	3 Feb. 1936–30 Sept. 1940
1940–1945	*Lloyd's Shipping Index*	8561–10103	Restricted publication between 30 Sept. 1940 and 17 Sept. 1945
1945–2009	*Lloyd's Shipping Index*	10104– ?	17 Sept. 1945–December 2009?

Table 9.2 *Lloyd's Voyage Record*, 1946–2009

Years	Title	Issues	Period
1946–1972	*Lloyd's Shipping Index – Voyage Supplement*	Numbering identical to LSI; only date of publication last years	Nov 1946–April 1972
1972–2009	*Lloyd's Voyage Record*	1–?	April 1972–May 2009?

vessels, except Western Europe inshore and seagoing navigation (Hozier and Watson, 1885). This periodical has been set practically in the same way since the 1880s. Shipping movements are indexed by vessel names in alphabetical order, with several fields of information about vessels (name, type, owner, flag, and tonnage), departing port with date, arriving port with expected date, and latest report, with geographic position and sometimes casualties. In great detail, many subfields of information evolved alongside the merchant navy's progress. For example, before the Second World War, sailing vessel movements were indexed apart from those of steamers. The index is completed with the list of owners mentioned in the issue. Physical description varied over the years, with changes affecting size, and number of pages,[15] such an evolution being closely linked to shipping growth.

Lloyd's Voyage Record was created in 1946 under the title *Lloyd's Shipping Index: Voyage Supplement*. The aim of *Lloyd's Voyage Record* was to provide a list of ports of call of all merchant vessels, with some exceptions. As *Voyage Supplement*, the list concerned round voyages of vessels included in the *Lloyd's Shipping Index*. Ports of call are listed by vessel name in alphabetical order. For each vessel, the last ports of call are provided with corresponding dates. Physical description also varied over the years, with changes being linked to the evolution of a vessel's movements[16] Originally a weekly publication, *Lloyd's Voyage Record* has been published monthly since 1997.

For both collections, the last printed publication was in 2009 before they were replaced by digital format. These two periodicals constitute a great source of raw data to study global vessel movements over a long period of time and at different geographical scales. Nevertheless, specific tools are required to extract and organize such raw data into a usable database.

Data extraction methodology: designing a custom optical character recognition (OCR) system

We have tens of thousands of document images derived from the digitization of hundreds of copies of *Lloyd's Shipping Index* (LSI) and *Lloyd's Voyage Record* (LVR). This set of images is an excellent source for studying world maritime trade from the late nineteenth century until today.

To effectively use these images, we must extract the textual content of each one in a machine-readable form (ASCII, Unicode, etc.) for use with statistical analysis software such as Excel. This text extraction process can be done manually, by human operators, which has the advantage of being reliable but it is expensive, given the amount of data to be processed. A less expensive solution is to use a computer program to "read" the textual content of the document images and transcribe it into a digital format. This automated reading process is called OCR (optical character recognition).

OCR is a rather complex technology that includes several successive and complementary modules: an image preprocessing module, a structure analysis module, and a recognition module (Figure 9.1). An OCR system takes as input an image file, usually a grayscale image, which is a matrix of pixels whose values range between 0 (black) and 255 (white). At first, the preprocessing module improves the "quality" of the input image using image processing techniques such as noise reduction and contrast enhancement. This module will then make a binarization of the image, which consists of separating the pixels belonging to the foreground (characters, separators, illustrations) from those belonging to the background. In the resulting binarized image, pixels have only two possible values: 1 (foreground) and 0 (background).

Then the structure analysis module will determine the positions of the various blocks of textual content, separate them from illustrations, and segment them to

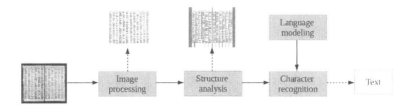

Figure 9.1 Illustration of the processing chain of an OCR system.

their different physical components: headers, columns, paragraphs, etc. Each text component is then segmented to extract its different lines. Finally, the recognition module will proceed to the "reading" of the text contained in each of these text line images thanks to the combination of a recognition engine (that uses pattern recognition techniques to discriminate among the different character shapes) with a language modeling system, which models the language constraints (using a list of possible words and a statistical model of possible sequences of words). The accuracy of each of these modules affects the success of the next ones.

Because of the great diversity in the documents' characteristics (layout, fonts, etc.), it is difficult to design systems that are generic enough to perform well on all types of documents. Accordingly, "general public" OCR software is designed to perform well on the widest possible variety of documents but its performance varies and can be very low on some atypical documents.

The tests we conducted with commercial OCR software on some samples from the Lloyd's corpus confirmed this observation. The text transcribed by this OCR system contained many errors and was not usable for reliable data analysis. It took us a long time to manually check and correct these errors before being able to use the resulting data.

In order to get better results, we decided to design a custom OCR software and to adapt it to the characteristics of our corpus to obtain the most efficient recognition and to minimize the number of errors. As a first step, we implemented a set of preprocessing operations designed to maximize recognition results on the Lloyd's images. In particular, we created two different layout analysis modules for each of the LVR and LSI documents. Each module was adapted to the specificities of the document. We also implemented a specific dewarping algorithm that corrects the distortion of the curvature of text lines that we often found on LSI documents (Figure 9.2) and a novel smearing-based text-line segmentation algorithm.

Next, we created a "recognition engine" adapted to our documents. We used an artificial neural network (ANN) to model the shapes of the characters (Shi *et al.*, 2009). ANN requires prior learning on a database of image samples: a set of text-line images associated with their "ground truth" text. These samples are extracted from a small subset of images randomly selected from our corpus so as to be representative of the textual content of LVR and LSI documents. Once its training is complete, the ANN is able to provide, for each line image, the most likely sequence of characters that it contains.

The last part of our work concerns language modeling, which consists first of identifying the different fields in each line (ports of departure and arrival, dates, name of vessel, type of vessel, tonnage, etc.) and then of identifying the words likely to appear in each field (Figure 9.3). Word lists thus created are used to constrain the recognition in each field: the recognition engine will only output words that appear on the list related to the current field.

This "custom" OCR system is currently still under development. Preliminary results are promising and outperform the results previously generated using a general usage OCR. We are currently improving the different components of the system so as to achieve the best possible results on our document images corpus.

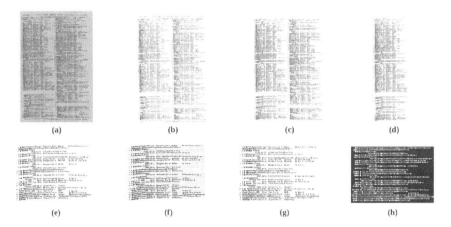

Figure 9.2 Illustration of the processing steps on a sample of the LSI dataset *Original grayscale image (a). Binarized image (b). Header and footer removal (c). Segmentation in columns (d) (left column). Part of the left column (e). Lines curvature estimation (f). Correction of lines curvature (dewarping) (g). Detection of text-line borders (h).*

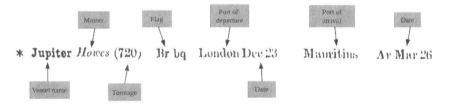

Figure 9.3 Constitutive fields of a text line from a LSI document.

The performance of the final system is essential to ensure the quality of statistical analysis to be performed on the data resulting from the OCR process.

Regional shifts in the global maritime network

Constructing the network

The LSI was used over the period 1890–2008 based on one entire publication every five years or so.[17] Global snapshots of global maritime flows only retained ports of departure and arrival as well as the number of vessel calls to construct the network where ports are nodes (vertices) and flows between them are links (edges), among other information available: dates of calls, date of construction, flag, operator, insurance registry, and gross and net tonnage. Each weekly (or daily) publication of LSI documents the last-known voyage of each vessel between two or more ports, so that it represented only 0.49 percent and

0.66 percent of the respective yearly number of vessel calls for Shanghai and Rotterdam in 2008. The number of vessel calls remains a partial view of port and shipping activity, as it does not take into account the size of vessels and the value of cargo, but still, it is a good indicator of the frequency of seaborne movements. These drawbacks are compensated for by a careful selection of each LSI around the same publication period, around late April, but further research is planned to make use of at least one publication every month to better avoid seasonal effects. In total, we counted 10,253 place names, of which 8,681 (85 percent) could have been retrieved directly or through intensive searches in older versions of the *Lloyd's Maritime Atlas* and online, taking into account historical changes of port names.[18] The remaining places were excluded, along with a number of passage points such as canals, straits, and channels.[19] Other place names such as continents, countries, seas, ranges, coasts, and regions were removed for port-level analyses but included at continent-level analyses. Vessel types were ignored in this analysis, although we calculated that steamers represented no less than 38 and 96 percent of the world fleet in 1890 and 1925, respectively (see also Ducruet, 2012).

A comparison of vessel calls with other data sources allowed us to confirm the accuracy of the Lloyd's data despite differences in collection methods and data units (Figure 9.4). Over the entire period 1890–2008, the correlation with Chinese port tonnage is over 88 percent.[20] This means that Lloyd's managed to capture the evolution trend of Chinese ports even though a closer look at fluctuations indicates certain discrepancies, especially for the two world war periods and the political changes of the late 1940s. However, correlation with international seaborne trade volumes[21] is much less significant, mostly due to the non-inclusion of vessel capacity in the calculation of vessel traffic and the fact that vessels have increased in size while reducing their number of port calls. Nevertheless, the LSI is useful for looking at particular developments and at macro-structures of maritime flows, bearing in mind that vessel capacity should be extracted in future research.

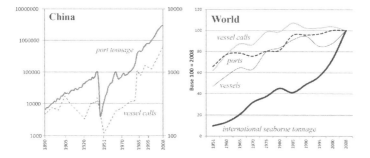

Figure 9.4 Comparing traffic evolution from diverse sources.

Source: own realization based on *Lloyd's Shipping Index*, UNCTAD, and World Bank.

The changing topological structure of the global maritime network raises important issues in terms of its underlying geography and spatial-industrial organization (see Appendix 9.1). While the number of ports and vessels has regularly increased over time, the number of links (edges) and vessel calls has shrunk rapidly since 1990, partly because non-port locations and self-loops were excluded. But certain trends are caused by real-world phenomena. For instance, the reducing average clustering coefficient since 1946 suggests that the network has become more and more centralized; containerization, which appeared in the late 1950s in the United States and spread globally much later, has prolonged rather than altered ongoing evolutions. A similar evolution is found with the *Gamma* index (proportion of actual links in the total maximum possible number of links) from 1920 and with the rich-club coefficient (*Gamma* index among ports with higher degree than world average divided by *Gamma* index among all ports) since 1946. The diameter and the average shortest path length have fluctuated until a rapid increase in 2000 and 2008, while eccentricity did not show any particular trend. One very interesting result is the disassortativity of the network (negative correlation between node degrees at each pair of nodes) and its decline over time, which suggests that on average, ports of dissimilar size were more connected in the past (i.e. larger to smaller), but this has faded away until present. All indicates a growing hierarchy of flows fostered by fleet modernization and trade growth, which favoured port selection and traffic polarization. The years 1940 and 1946 are marked by important changes, which call for further investigation into the impact of conflicts on node and network evolution in terms of route reconfiguration, network disruption, and port resilience.

Regional distribution of maritime flows

One first result is the growing share of intra- versus inter-continental maritime flows over time, from 44 percent in 1890 to 77 percent in 2008 (Figure 9.5). Such a trend based on the number of vessel calls and on large world regions, means that globalization and the expansion of trade went along with a regionalization of exchange. The fading out of mercantilism and colonial empires implied a reorganization of shipping patterns, from core–periphery to a more polycentric structure between and within regionally integrated blocs. In parallel, technological evolution in the shipping and port industries provoked a concentration of flows at a smaller number of large, multifunctional port hubs and gateways, for intraregional cargo distribution, as underlined by Marnot (2005: 10) already in the context of the 1850s: "Ports had to cope with fierce competition to capture traffic that the globalising economy always made more slippery. In such a perspective, the need to provide optimal logistics [...] became the absolute rule." The growing centralization of the network on hub ports created an artificially high frequency of vessel trips between hub ports and feeder ports within certain regions, such as the Caribbean, the Mediterranean, and Asia. Europe and Asia stand out by their impressively higher share of intra-continental flows, which reached 84 and 86 percent, respectively, in 2008.

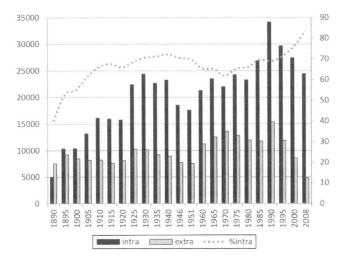

Figure 9.5 Total versus intra-continental vessel flows, 1890–2008.

Source: own realization based on *Lloyd's Shipping Index*, various issues.

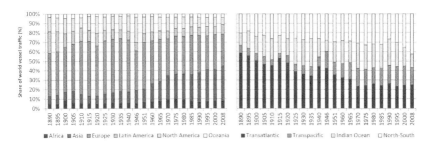

Figure 9.6 Regional distribution of world maritime flows, 1890–2008.

Source: own realization based on *Lloyd's Shipping Index*, various issues.

One second approach is to observe the changing geographic distribution of maritime flows (Figure 9.6). Europe has always been by far the world's busiest maritime region, except in 1946 and 2008, when the leaders were North America and Asia, respectively. Such importance largely contributes to the world trend observed in the previous figure, with a sharp decline during the Second World War and during the 1970s, and peaks of maritime activity in 1965 and 1990. Despite such fluctuations, Europe in 2008 maintained its world share at around 36 percent (compared with 31 percent in 1890) whereas North America declined from 31 percent in 1890 to 7 percent in 2008, slightly below Africa. Latin America fell from 24 percent to 9 percent between 1890 and 1920, with subsequent stabilization at around 7 percent. Asia as a whole went through the fastest growth, from 5 percent to 41 percent over the period.

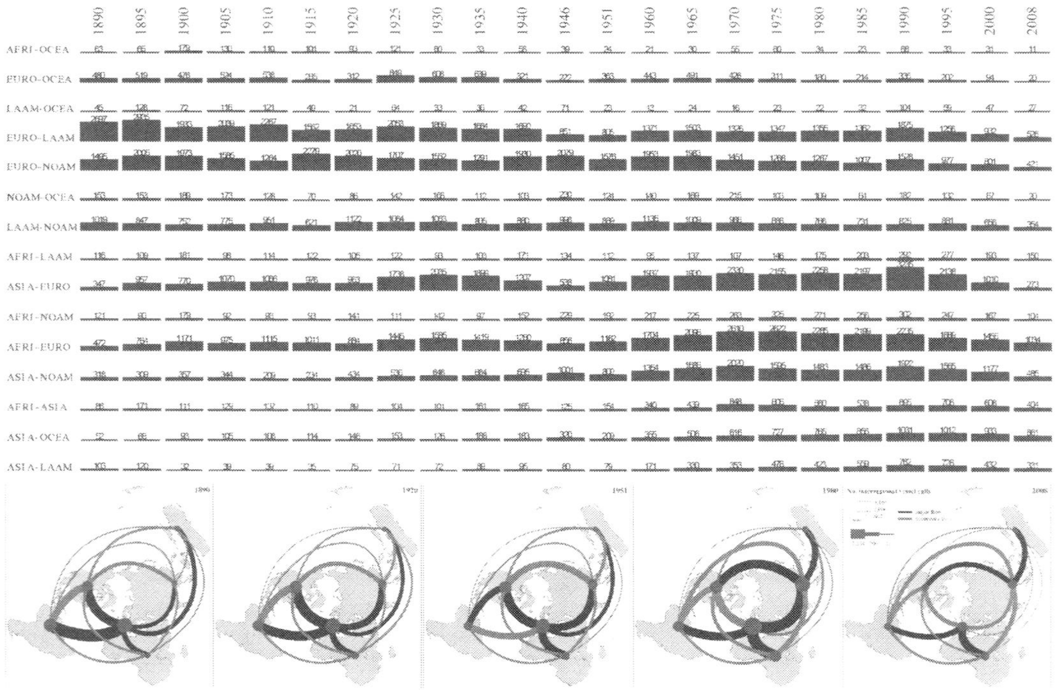

Figure 9.7 Inter-continental maritime flows, 1890–2008.

Source: own realization based on *Lloyd's Shipping Index*, various issues.

The distribution of intercontinental flows is analyzed based on a synthetic diagram and maps for selected years (Figure 9.7). The evolution towards an ever more multilateral trading system can already be observed between 1890 and 1925. Trade patterns inherited from the nineteenth-century globalization that ends with the First World War are prolonged afterwards, as seen with the explosion of inter-continental traffic (Marnot, 2012). Transatlantic exchanges reached a peak of intensity in 1890, as seen with the triangle Europe–North America–Latin America (O'Rourke and Williamson, 1999). The bipolar link between Europe and North America underwent continuous growth since the eighteenth century (Guillaume, 1998), backed by strong ties between England and its former colony (Saul, 1960; Starkey, 1999). Trade between northwestern Europe and the United States represented no less than two-thirds of international exchanges in the late nineteenth century. While before 1890 Europe exchanged manufactured goods for US raw materials (e.g. cotton, grain, ores, fuels), the United States rapidly become the world's leading industrial country and a powerful exporter of manufactured goods to Europe, notwithstanding growing migratory flows between the two economies (Konvitz, 1994).

Yet, it was the flow between Europe and Latin America that dominated the early period, partly the result of close commercial relations between England and this part of the New World. Since the early nineteenth century, Latin America represented a vital provider of raw materials for the United Kingdom, which in exchange shipped manufactured goods such as cotton textiles made in Manchester, to such an extent that Latin America was often coined the informal British empire. Many countries around 1913 had high internationalization, such as Argentina, Uruguay, Chile, Peru, Brazil, Mexico, and Venezuela (Cardoso and Pérez Brignoli, 1987). Argentina and Brazil even started to industrialize rapidly before the crisis of the 1930s.[22] The flow between North and South America followed a similar logic, revealing the imperialist ambitions of the United States over its backyard as seen with Theodore Roosevelt's policies, growing interest in the Panama Canal, and intervention in Cuba in 1898. Other main flows were clearly centred upon Europe throughout almost the entire period (Miller, 2012), such as with Asia and Africa, which provided mineral resources and food products and acquired manufactured goods. In particular, the Europe–Asia maritime route, which benefitted from declining transport costs during 1770–1830 (Solar, 2013), grew rapidly between 1890 and 1925 in the context of the British presence in the East Indies and the opening of the Far East between 1840 and 1860 and of the Suez Canal in 1869. Many Indian and Chinese ports, but also some in New Zealand and Australia, were under British rule at the time and had quasi-exclusive ties with England (Crouzet, 1964).

The rest of the period was marked by regular growth of Asia and the Pacific area as a whole at the expense of the Atlantic. This is reflected in the map by the increasing width of the Europe–Asia and Asia–North America routes. But since the 1960s, poles of the southern hemisphere have become increasingly connected to Asia as well. Europe remains the biggest region by the number of vessel calls and for Africa and Latin America, the latter being connected to Europe via intense and frequent vessel movements through the Mediterranean basin.

Port growth trajectories and resilience

Changing port hierarchies

Before describing the types of trajectories, it is important to highlight major shifts of port and maritime activity across the globe (Figure 9.8). The early period confirms the overwhelming dominance of two major seaboards of the industrial world: northwest Europe and the North American east coast. In particular the so-called northern range, from Le Havre to Hamburg, clearly emerges as a vital gateway for the whole continent (Vigarié, 1964; 1998) between 1890 and 1920 at the expense of British ports, whose growth rates fell behind those of Antwerp and Rotterdam. Germany, with its main ports of Bremen and Hamburg, was then becoming the world's second-largest industrial power and an important gateway between eastern Europe and the United States for immigration which, in turn, positively influenced rapid port growth in the Benelux for transit trade. This shift of Europe's centre of gravity was also influenced by a strong pound sterling during the 1920s, which hampered British industries. Another significant change was the emergence of the Soviet Union and the rapid growth of Baltic and Black Sea ports. A similar trend occurred along the northeastern seaboard of the United States, the megalopolis in the making (Gottmann, 1961), where New York was the core gateway of US external trade and the world's premier port for European immigrants, but whose supremacy was challenged by Boston and Baltimore in the late 1890s (Heffer, 1986).

One unexpected giant in the global port hierarchy was Buenos Aires, followed by other River Plate ports such as Montevideo and Rosario. By the number of vessel calls, Buenos Aires was the world's largest port in 1890, the main port of Latin America's most dynamic port region at the time (Barjot, 2006). Rio de Janeiro also exhibited rapid growth as it was fully modernized already in 1904. On the Pacific coast of Latin America, however, Valparaiso (Chile) and Callao (Peru), once large exporters of raw materials (copper, nitrates, guano) and intermediate hub ports between North and South America, lost ground, in part because of the opening of the Panama Canal in 1914. Elsewhere, the most impressive growth was in the Asia–Pacific region, as seen with the extremely high growth rates of certain Japanese and Australian ports, while Chinese ports suffered from internal wars and political and economic tensions (see also Figure 9.4). By contrast, Japan's growth illustrates its successful entry into the small group of world industrial powers. It sustained strong ties with North America's west coast, as the United States ensured more than 40 percent of Japan's external trade in the mid-1920s. To be noted is the shift from San Francisco to Los Angeles and Seattle–Vancouver. Other factors include Japan's imperialist strategy over the entire Asia–Pacific rim, which gave a boost to certain ports such as Vladivostok in Russia and Dalian in China. Asia as a whole benefitted from the acceleration of maritime trade through the Suez Canal, where steamers concentrated their activity (Piquet, 2009). But sailing vessels maintained an important share along certain routes for technical and economic reasons, such as across the Pacific Ocean with the windjammers, the last

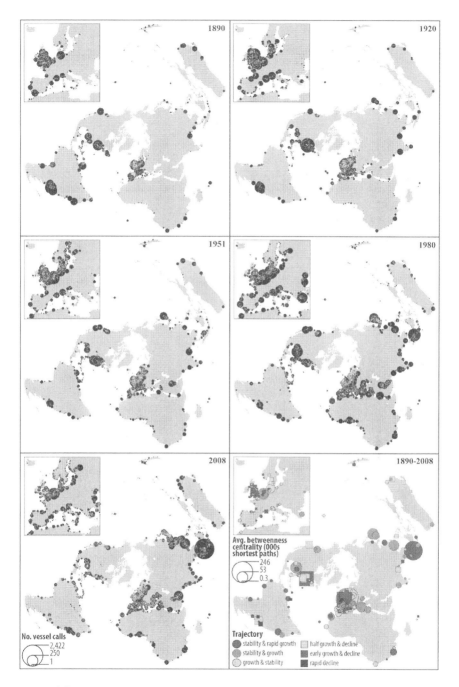

Figure 9.8 Port hierarchy evolution and typology of port betweenness trajectory, 1890–2008.

Source: own realization based on *Lloyd's Shipping Index*, various issues.

generation of clippers, which specialized in bulk cargoes (Fletcher, 1958; Lehnof, 2007).

The rest of the period was marked by a continuous concentration of vessel traffic within Asia around the large hub ports of Hong Kong and Singapore, which captured most transhipment activities at the expense of Japan (Lee and Ducruet, 2009). The demise of the British Empire caused the decline of Calcutta and Mumbai, once Asia's largest ports, while Hong Kong and Singapore, together with Taiwan and South Korea, have emerged as newly industrialized countries since the 1960s. The spread of this export-oriented development strategy to Southeast Asia and China as well as the rise of new container hubs along the Europe–Asia maritime route, such as Dubai and Colombo, occurred in parallel with the slowdown of many other traditional Asian port cities (Ducruet, 2015). Singapore is now the world's largest port by the number of vessel calls, and the second largest after Shanghai. Yet, as seen in Appendix 9.2, Shanghai's growth over the period had been anything but linear, as it had difficulty restarting its activity after the radical political changes of the late 1940s. London, Buenos Aires, and New York showed continual decline. With the exception of the 1946 peak due to the postwar revival, most leading ports went through rather complex traffic fluctuations based on a mixture of local and global factors.

A typology of port growth trajectories

In order to highlight growth similarities over space and time, a correspondence analysis was applied to the distribution of betweenness centrality among 169 ports which recorded uninterrupted activity over the period under study. One main hypothesis of this work is the influence of geographic proximity, in addition to other proximities (cultural, logistical, and political) on the nature and spatial distribution of the obtained clusters. The coordinates of ports on the orthogonal components and their weight allowed us to generate a matrix of traffic discrepancies (measured using a chi-squared (χ^2) distance). A hierarchical cluster analysis was applied to this matrix using the Ward method, which minimizes intra-class variance and maximizes inter-class variance. This method, using Trajpop freeware,[23] was recently applied to urban population time series in various economies (Pumain *et al.*, 2015), and closely echoes work by Guerrero and Rodrigue, 2014 based on port container throughputs in 1970–2010. The latter work identified five diffusion waves of containerization and their representative ports, from the pioneers of the Triade to the niche ports. Compared with these works, one major innovation of our research is to use a network centrality measure rather than traffic volume. Betweenness centrality being a fundamental indicator of global accessibility, it carries crucial information about nodes' ability to be situated on shortest paths all over the network, and to act as bridges (or hubs) between the different regions of the network. Because the number of occurrences on shortest paths depends on the size of the graph, it was decided to transform, for each port, each yearly score into a percentage of the maximum value of the period.

Six clusters were found to have a relatively balanced number of ports. Three are marked by overall decline and the three others by overall growth. The first cluster is marked by rapid decline and intense fluctuation of formerly dominant ports but without recovery afterwards: Montevideo, Rosario, Bridgetown, and St Thomas in Latin America; Cadiz, Falmouth, and Plymouth in Europe; and Port Elizabeth and Port Louis in southern Africa. Once well inserted into important Atlantic trading routes, these ports were not able to sustain their position in the network. The second cluster went through a similar evolution but with a decline from the 1950s onwards following a peak of centrality in the 1920s. Interestingly, the vast majority of these ports are located in the North Atlantic region; they include New York and Boston in North America; most British ports (Glasgow, Leith, Tyne, Hull, Liverpool, London, Swansea, Cardiff, and Newport), and Marseilles, Bordeaux, and Bergen in Europe. The two exceptions of Oran (Algeria) and Yangon (Myanmar) can be explained by the colonial factor, as their centrality closely overlapped with those of their European counterparts. The third cluster, whose ports have declined in centrality less rapidly than the two former clusters, is more widespread geographically. It is concentrated mainly in Scandinavia (Copenhagen, Gothenburg, Oslo, Kristiansand, Stockholm, Helsinki), the United Kingdom (Grangemouth, Bristol, Grimsby, Goole), North America (Halifax, Philadelphia, Baltimore, Hampton Roads, San Francisco, Houston), Latin America (Recife, Buenos Aires, Talcahuano), and the Asia–Pacific (Calcutta, Manila, Sydney, Melbourne, Adelaide). The progressive shift from the Atlantic to the Pacific, the end of colonial rule, and the centralization of maritime flows in large hub ports tended to push these ports from the network's centre of gravity.

The other three clusters had different ways of increasing their centrality over time, though they shared certain similarities. The fourth cluster tended to lose centrality up to the 1950s, followed by recovery and stabilization until the mid-1990s. In Europe this was the case of Antwerp, Rotterdam, Bilbao, Las Palmas, Piraeus, and Odessa. Elsewhere, Alexandria, Vancouver, New Orleans, Rio de Janeiro, Mumbai, Perth, Jakarta, Bangkok, Hong Kong, Kobe, and Yokohama are still important ports today, but they are challenged by competition from close neighbours. The fifth cluster has in common with the former that it ceased to grow in centrality during the late period, but showed continuous improvement until then. Most of these ports are European (Le Havre, Rouen, Bremen, Hamburg, Szczecin, Gdansk, Genoa, Trieste, Naples, Leixoes, Lisbon) or African (Algiers, Casablanca, Tunis, Dakar, Cape Town, Maputo), plus Havana (Cuba) and Brisbane (Australia). Finally, the last cluster exhibited stability until the 1950s and rapid growth since then, with Shanghai and Singapore as the top central ports on average, followed by Durban, Santos, Barcelona, Valencia, Port of Spain, Willemstad, Callao, and Valparaiso. This cluster has shifted its centrality from the bottom to the top over the period, reflecting the dynamism of their host economies (BRICS countries), the impact of port reform (Spain), and the development of hub functions (Caribbean).

Impacts of crises and shocks on port traffic and network topology

Since a maritime link is defined by the flow of goods, and given the trade importance of shipping (see Chapter 17 by Guerrero *et al.* on global trade and shipping) it is subject to changing economic and political conditions. Supply and demand, in addition to geographic and cost factors (e.g. fuel prices), combine with specific events or shocks such as financial crisis, wars, and embargo to modify the intensity and spatial structure of maritime flows. In a historical perspective, how does the topology of maritime networks respond to such shocks? Do shocks of similar nature have comparable effects on port nodes and network topology?

Further research is needed to classify shocks by their nature and scope in order to ensure some measure of comparability: economic, political, geographic, and technological. The first two cathegories are self-explanatory. The latter two may refer to natural disasters or to the opening and closure of critical choke points. Opening (or expanding) an inter-oceanic canal shortens nautical distance between certain ports, which in turn may reduce average transport costs, while its closure has opposite effects at various levels. For instance, the closure of the Suez Canal in 1967 (the Six-Day War) modified the European port hierarchy due to an increase in ship size but at the same time it favoured economies of scale on the Europe–Asia route around the Cape of Good Hope (Cullinane and Khanna, 2000). Shocks related to innovation and technological change directly impact transport costs by making ships or cargo handling more reliable, efficient, and faster (Rodrigue, 2013; Bernhofen *et al.*, 2013). The case of the Suez Canal closure was geographic, political, and local in scope as it directly affected only one node. Its opening was a mixture of geographic and technological elements in terms of rerouting and nodality. One may distinguish among local shocks, which directly affect one or few nodes, regional shocks, which are greater in scope, and symmetric shocks, which hit distant nodes simultaneously, such as in the case of an oil price shock, especially for oil tanker movements. Though data extraction from *Lloyd's List* is still in its infant stage, Appendix 9.2 already points at interesting similarities among world ports in terms of the traffic impact of war destruction (Hamburg, Rotterdam, Tokyo) and political revolution (Shanghai) for instance. A thinner-time granularity is needed to zoom on specific events, however (see Chapter 10 by Guinand and Pigné on dynamic graphs). This would allow, among other cases, to compare, for instance, the impacts of the 2008 ficial crisis (De Monie *et al.*, 2011) with the ones of the 1929 Black Friday.

Yet, related literature remains limited when it comes to measuring the impact of shocks on maritime networks. International organizations and maritime industries devoted much attention to security issues agaits terrorist attacks on ships and ports (Bichou, 2008; Ciotti Galletti, 2012). Some studies quantified the costs of a shock mainly for ports being directly affected and not for others. Rosoff and von Winterfeldt (2007) estimated that a terrorist attack on the largest US ports (Los Angeles and Long Beach) would lead to a 120 to 365-day port shutdown and would roughly cost US$30–100 billion in port, evacuation, property value, and decontamination costs. A similar study by Booz Allen Hamilton Consulting proposed a port security disaster war game to assess network impacts of a terrorist attack on a US port, resulting in a 12-day closure of the US ports and borders, US$58 billion of economic losses, and a 3-month backlog to clear (Gerencser *et al.*, 2003). Paul and Maloni (2010) adopted a more theoretical approach about the effects of US port lockout due to different types of shocks (strikes, hurricanes). Their model about the dynamic ship rerouting helped to minimize congestion and economic losses in North America.

While most of the existing literature focuses on estimating losses for the local economy or on a theoretical situation, the World Seastems project aims to study changes in global network topology resulting from historical shocks. These studies will be complemented by analyses of shock propagation mechanisms and long-term effects of the shocks in question. As discussed in Chapter 13, several possible approaches and methodological frameworks exist in graph theory and complexity science, such as the model of cascading failures. Given the specific character of different fleets, a multilayer perspective seems necessary (De Domenico *et al.*, 2013; Ducruet, 2013b), to reveal heterogeneity in responses to shocks of different subnetworks built by types of ships.

Conclusion

This first-ever systematic analysis of the *Lloyd's List* corpus over nearly 120 years provides novel evidence about the macro-level organization of global maritime flows and their local dynamics. It has confirmed drastic shifts of maritime activity from the Atlantic to the Pacific reflected in the changing pattern of both inter-continental flows and port hierarchies. One innovation was to identify Buenos Aires as the world's largest port by the number of calls in 1890 surpassing London and New York. Yet, port growth trajectories are very diverse and marked by short-term events. In terms of network structure and evolution, this chapter also contributes to the reflection on graph dynamics by highlighting long-term trends and questioning the role of technological progress. Although it would be necessary to decouple the database and compare network topologies for different fleet types, our results show that network centralization started long before the age of containers, in line with Marnot (2005) about nineteenth century port competition. Much more has to be done in several directions: extraction of more data to fully cover the period on a weekly or monthly basis, in-depth analysis of local and global shocks and crises, and retro-simulation of past network structures to allow forecasting.

Acknowledgements

The research leading to these results has received funding from the European Research Council under the European Union's Seventh Framework Programme (FP/2007-2013)/ERC Grant Agreement n. [313847] 'World Seastems'.

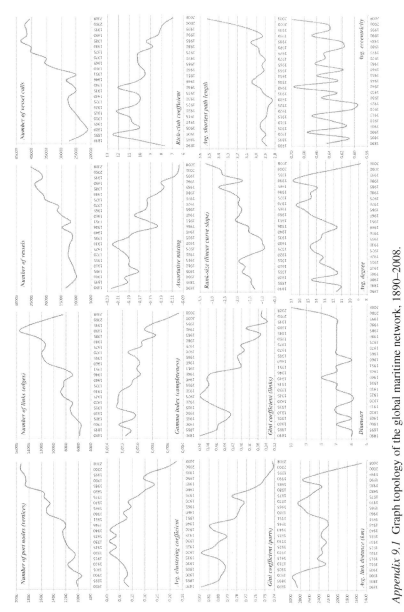

Appendix 9.1 Graph topology of the global maritime network, 1890–2008.

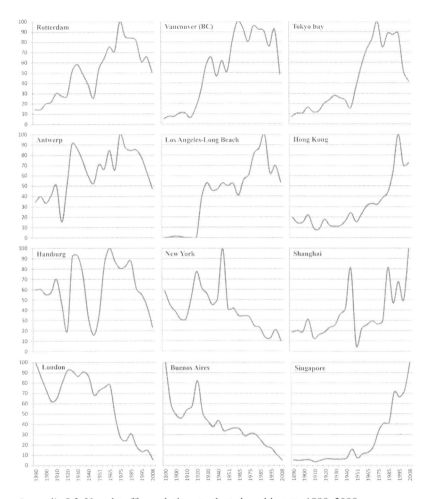

Appendix 9.2 Vessel traffic evolution at selected world ports, 1890–2008.

Source: own realization based on Lloyd's Shipping Index, various issues.

Note: Base 100 for the maximum value of vessel calls.

Notes

1 This edition of *Around the World in Eighty Days* had been translated with an introduction and notes by William Butcher. According to him, the *Shipping Gazette* is the
   Shipping Gazette & Lloyd's List Weekly Summary, published in London between 1856
   and 1909. In fact, the *Shipping and Mercantile Gazette* had been combined with *Lloyd's
   List* between 1884 and 1914 under the title *Shipping and Mercantile Gazette & Lloyd's
   List* (Barriskill, 1994).
2 Thomas Jemson (Master of Lloyd's Coffee House from 1728 to 1734) is regarded by
   most historians as the planner of the paper, and Richard Baker (Master of Lloyd's Coffee House from 1738 to 1748), as *Lloyd's List* first editor and publisher (Fayle and

Wright, 1928; Hailey and Landon, 2009; Lloyd's Register Foundation, Infosheet No. 16, 2014), while Edward Lloyd is considered as founder of the one and only *Lloyd's News*, a general political newspaper, with shipping intelligence from the ports but no regular lists. Recent evidence produced by John McCusker shows that Edward Lloyd founded a second newspaper which became *Lloyd's List* in 1735.

3   The evolution of Lloyd's periodical publications is reported by several info sheets and guides (Lloyd's Register Foundation, 2014; Merseyside Maritime Museum, 2004a, 2004b; National Maritime Museum, 2006a, 2006b, 2009), online libraries catalogues—i.e. British Library and Copac (available online at http://copac.ac.uk/ [accessed 4 June 2015])—and original issues from *World Seastems Project* collections. It seems that no exhaustive historical study had been made about the whole Lloyd's publication corpus. Only a few short studies are available online (Barnet, 2014; Palmer, 1999).

4   This booklet is available online at https://archive.org/details/cihm_91606 [accessed 4 June 2015]. For more biographical information, see Marcil E. (1990).

5   In 1820, the total number of Lloyd's agencies and sub-agencies was 274. In 1928, it was 1,500 (Fayle and Wright, 1928).

6   The first Lloyd's signal station was established in 1869. In 1884, 17 signal stations in the UK and six abroad were at Lloyd's disposal. In 1891, the number of Lloyd's signal stations was 40 in the UK and 118 overseas. In 1928, it was 28 in the UK and 134 abroad (Fayle and Wright, 1928).

7   About information revolution in nineteenth century, see Kaukiainen (2001). Kaukiainen based his research about improvements in information transmission based on material extracted from *Lloyd's List*.

8   Lloyd's Acts of 1871 and 1911 are available online at http://www.lloyds.com [accessed 4 June 2015].

9   The aforementioned advertising insert is entitled "Lloyd's shipping publications" and is placed page XVII. The list drawn up is not complete: this advertising insert does not mention other Lloyd's publications, like the famous Lloyd's *Register of Shipping*, an annual list of vessels published since the mid-eighteenth century.

10   This kind of almanac was printed for the Corporation of Lloyd's. The authors were respectively Secretary of Lloyd's and a member of his office. The *Voyages Tables of Steamers* is mentioned on p. 128.

11   See 1918 edition of *The Newspaper Press Directory*, London: C. Mitchell and Co. Available online at https://archive.org/details/73rdnewspaperpre00londuoft [accessed 4 June 2015]. A note about Lloyd's Weekly Index appears on p. 89: "This paper is suspended during the war."

12   A sequence of 1917 German propaganda film *The Enchanted Circle* (*Der magische Gürtel*) give an interesting example of Lloyd's publications use by the German Imperial Navy. This sequence shows Kapitänleutnant Lothar von Arnauld de la Perière (1886–1941), captain of U-35, examining Lloyd's Register and writing out on it torpedoed vessels. This propaganda film, a record of a voyage by the U-35 from March to May 1917 in the Mediterranean and Eastern Atlantic, is available online at http://www.iwm.org.uk/collections/item/object/1060008290 [accessed 4 June 2015].

13   A copy of Lloyd's Shipping Index issue no. 9928, dated 21 February 1945, is held by the University of Melbourne, Baillieu Library, Australia. This copy was originally registered under the no. 633, inscribed for the personal use of "Military Branch 56.S.B. 2, Admiralty, SW1." In 1994 edition of Barriskill's guide, there is reference to separate indexes of the movements of Vessels on Government Service, "[. . .] bound similarly to Lloyd's Shipping Index" (Barriskill, 1994: 17). In the British Library Catalogue, *Lloyd's Shipping Index* is described as not published between 30 September 1940 and 17 September 1945, with a gap in the numbering of issues: the last 1940s issue was no. 8560 and the first published in 1945 was no. 10104. A strange fact for a suspended publication!

14 In France, according to SUDOC online catalogue (available online at http://www.sudoc. abes.fr [accessed 4 June 2015]), issues of *Lloyd's Shipping Index* should be held only by the library of Ministère de la Mer. In fact, this collection had been probably pulped.

15 The number of pages varied between 64, for an issue printed in April 1890, to 200 in the 2000s. Periodicity fluctuated over time, *Lloyd's Shipping Index* being a weekly or daily publication. Each issue provides several thousands of ship movements.

16 A weekly issue printed in December 1946 has 96 pages whereas a monthly issue in the 2000s often contained about 300.

17 It must be acknowledged that the LSI excludes the movements of coasters, yachts, whalers, fishing vessels, and European vessels moving on the White Sea–Tarifa, UK–Cape Finisterre, and UK–Tarifa routes, and French and south European vessels on the way between Dunkirk, Mediterranean, and Black Sea ports.

18 Between 1890 and 2008, numerous ports changed names due to the political evolution of their host territory, such as Port Swettenham in Malaysia becoming Kelang or Port Klang. Different names may refer to the same port, such as Europoort (Rotterdam) or Tanjung Priok (Jakarta).

19 We calculated that the share of excluded movements oscillated between 15 and 20 percent until the 1970s, but increased since then up to 30–40 percent. There has been an increasing number of movements reporting only one port or linking a port with a non-port location in the more recent period.

20 Chinese traffic accounts for international trade measured in Hong Kong taels for the period 1868–1928 and total port tonnage measured in metric tons for the period 1932–2010. The whole period was harmonized by Wang and Ducruet (2013) in their study of the long-term evolution of the Chinese port system.

21 Data was obtained from the United Nations Conference on Trade and Development (UNCTAD) for the period 1970–2008 and was completed for the 1955–69 period thanks to Rodrigue (2013).

22 Argentina, Brazil, Chile, and Uruguay altogether concentrated 42.5 percent of coal shipping exports from main UK base ports to outside Europe in 1913, against 13.2 percent in 1920, with Argentina alone representing 20.5 percent and 7.1 percent, according to complementary data (Richardson and Hurd, 1923).

23 Available online at http://trajpop.parisgeo.cnrs.fr/ [accessed 4 June 2015].

References

Barnet L. (2014) *Lloyd's of London*. Available online at: http://www.barnettmaritime. co.uk/lloyds.htm [accessed 17 June 2014].

Barriskill D.T. (1994) *A Guide to the Lloyd's Marine Collection and Related Marine Sources at Guildhall Library*. London: Guildhall Library, second (revised) edition.

Barjot D. (2006) *La Grande Entreprise Française de Travaux Publics, 1883–1974*. Paris: Economica.

Bernhofen D.M., El-Sahli Z., Kneller R. (2013) *Estimating the Effects of the Container Revolution on World Trade*. Lund University Working Paper 2013:4, Department of Economics, School of Economics and Management.

Bichou K. (2008) *Security and Risk-Based Models in Shipping and Ports: Review and Critical Analysis*. Paris: OECD Publishing.

Brady K. (2008) *Shipwreck Inventory of Ireland: Louth, Meath, Dublin and Wicklow*. Dublin: Stationery Office of Ireland.

BTE (1982) *Cargo Centralization in the Overseas Liner Trade*. Canberra: Bureau of Transport Economics.

Cardoso C.F.S., Pérez Brignoli H. (1987) *Historia Económica de America Latina*. Editorial Critica, Vol. II, pp. 140–1.

Ciotti Galletti S. (2012) *Piracy and Maritime Terrorism: Logistics, Strategies, Scenarios*. NATO Science for Peace and Security Series E: Human and Societal Dynamics, Vol. 95.

Crouzet F. (1964) Commerce et empire: l'expérience britannique du libre-échange à La Première Guerre mondiale. *Annales ESC*, 2: 281–310.

Cullinane K.P.B., Khanna M. (2000) Economies of scale in large containerships: optimal size and geographical implications. *Journal of Transport Geography*, 8(3): 181–95.

De Domenico M., Sole-Ribalata A., Cozzo E., Kivela M., Moreno Y., Porter M., Gomez S., Arenas A. (2013) Mathematical formulation of multi-layer networks. *Phys. Rev. X*, 3: 041022.

De Monie G., Rodrigue J.P., Notteboom T.E. (2011) Economic cycles in maritime shipping and ports: the path to the crisis of 2008. In: Hall P.V., McCalla R., Comtois C., Slack B. (Eds). *Integrating Seaports and Trade Corridors*. Surrey: Ashgate, pp. 13–30.

Ducruet C. (2012) Ports et routes maritimes dans le monde (1890–1925). *Mappemonde*, 106 (available online at http://mappemonde.mgm.fr/num34/lieux/lieux12201.html [accessed 4 June 2015]).

Ducruet C. (2013a) Mapping global urban interactions: maritime flows and port hierarchies since the late nineteenth century. *Globalisation and World Cities Research Bulletin*, 429. Available online at http://www.lboro.ac.uk/gawc/rb/rb429.html [accessed 4 June 2015].

Ducruet C. (2013b) Network diversity and maritime flows. *Journal of Transport Geography*, 30: 77–88.

Ducruet C. (2015) Asian cities in the global maritime network since the late nineteenth century. In: Bracken G. (Ed), *Asian Cities: From Colonial to Global*. Amsterdam: Amsterdam University Press (in press).

Ducruet C., Marnot B. (2015) *Analyser les trafics portuaires mondiaux en 1890 et 1925 à partir des registres du Lloyd's*. Paper presented at the Second International Congress of Maritime History, Nantes, 26–28 June.

Ducruet C., Gelezeau V., Roussin S. (2008) Les connexions maritimes de La Corée du Nord: Recompositions territoriales dans La péninsule coréenne et nouvelles dynamiques régionales en Asie du Nord-Est. *L'Espace Géographique*, 3: 208–24.

Fayle C.E., Wright C. (1928) *A History of Lloyd's from the Founding of Lloyd's Coffee House to the Present Day*. London: Macmillan and Company Limited.

Fleming D.K. (1968) The independent transport carrier in ocean tramp trades. *Economic Geography*, 44(1): 21–36.

Fletcher M.E. (1958) The Suez Canal and world shipping, 1869-1914. *The Journal of Economic History*, 28: 556-573.

Fry H. (1895) *Lloyd's, its Origin, History and Methods*. Québec: Dawson & Co.

Gerencser M., Weinberg J., Vincent D. (2003) *Port Security War Game: Implications for US Supply Chains*. New York: Booz Allen Hamilton.

Gottmann J. (1961) *Megalopolis, The Urbanized Northeastern Seaboard of the United States*. New York: The Twentieth Century Fund.

Guerrero D., Rodrigue J.P. (2014) The waves of containerization: shifts in global maritime transportation. *Journal of Transport Geography*, 35: 151–64.

Guillaume J. (1998) Les ports de commerce entre ambiance atlantique et mondialisation. *Historiens et Géographes*, 363: 199–205.

Hailey R., Landon F. (Eds) (2009) *275th Lloyd's List Anniversary 2009, the Past, Present and Future of Shipping*. London: Lloyd's List Group.

Heffer J. (1986) *Le Port de New York et le Commerce Extérieur Américain, 1860–1900*. Paris: Publications de La Sorbonne.

Hozier H.M., Watson J.B. (1885) *Hints to Captains of the Mercantile Marine*, Glasgow: Bell and Bain. Available online at http://dbooks.bodleian.ox.ac.uk/books/PDFs/N11431452.pdf [accessed 4 June 2015].

Joly O. (1999) *La structuration des réseaux de circulation maritime.* Unpublished PhD Dissertation in Territorial Planning, Le Havre University, CIRTAI.

Jones S.K. (1982) *A Maritime History of the Port of Whitby, 1700–1914.* Unpublished PhD Dissertation, University College London.

Kaukiainen Y. (2001) Shrinking the world: improvements in the speed of information transmission, *c.* 1820–1870. *European Review of Economic History,* 5(1): 1–28.

Konvitz J.W. (1994) The crisis of Atlantic port cities, 1880 to 1920. *Comparative Studies in Society and History,* 36(2): 293–318.

Lee S.W., Ducruet C. (2009) Spatial glocalization in Asia–Pacific hub port cities: a comparison of Hong Kong and Singapore. *Urban Geography,* 30(2): 162–84.

Lehnof J.L. (2007) Marine marchande, rapidité et gestion du risque en mer dans les derniers temps de La voile au long cours (1780–1940). *Cahiers de La Maison de La Recherche en Sciences Humaines,* 47: 203–16.

Lloyd's Register Foundation, *Infosheet No. 16, Edward Lloyd and his Coffee House,* 2014. Available online at http://www.lr.org/en/research-and-innovation/historical-information/information-sheets [accessed 4 June 2014].

Marcil E. (1990) Fry, Henry. In: Halpenny, F. (Ed.) *Dictionary of Canadian Biography,* vol. 12, Toronto: University of Toronto/Université Laval. Available online at http://www.biographi.ca/en/bio/fry_henry_12E.html [accessed 4 June 2015].

Marnot B. (2005) Interconnexion et reclassements: l'insertion des ports français dans La chaîne multimodale au XIXe siècle. *Flux,* 59(1): 10–21.

Marnot B. (2012) *La Mondialisation au XIXe siècle (1850–1914).* Paris: Armand Colin.

McCusker J.J. (1991) *The Early History of "Lloyd's List." Historical Research,* 64: 427–31.

McCusker J.J. (1997) *Essays in the Economic History of the Atlantic World.* London and New York: Routledge.

McCusker J.J., Gravesteijn C. (1991) *The Beginnings of Commercial and Financial Journalism, the Commodity Price Currents, Exchange Rate Currents, and Money Currents of Early Modern Europe.* Amsterdam: NEHA.

McCusker J.J. (2005) The demise of distance: the business press and the origins of the information revolution in the early modern Atlantic world. *The American Historical Review,* 110(2): 295–321.

McKenzie F.D. (1975) *Maritime Dynamic Traffic Generator. Volume III: Density Data on World Maps.* Working Paper No. AD-A012 498, Transportation Systems Center, Cambridge, Massachusetts.

Merseyside Maritime Museum (2004a) *Information sheet, Holdings of Lloyd's Register and Lloyd's List, Sheet number 47.* Available online at: http://www.liverpoolmuseums. org.uk/maritime/archive/sheet/47 [accessed 3 October 2013].

Merseyside Maritime Museum (2004b) *Information sheet, Lloyd's Marine Insurance Records, Sheet number 52.* Available online at: http://www.liverpoolmuseums. org.uk/maritime/archive/sheet/52 [accessed 3 October 2013].

Miller M.B. (2012) *Europe and the Maritime World. A Twentieth-Century History.* Cambridge: Cambridge University Press.

National Maritime Museum, Greenwich (2006a) *Research guide H1: Lloyd's: Lloyd's List: Brief history.* Available online at: http://www.rmg.co.uk/researchers/library/research-guides/lloyds/lloyds-list-brief-history [accessed 3 October 2013].

National Maritime Museum, Greenwich (2006b) *Research guide H4: Lloyds: Lloyd's List Indexes.* Available online at: http://www.rmg.co.uk/researchers/library/research-guides/lloyds/lloyds-list-indexes [accessed 3 October 2013].

National Maritime Museum, Greenwich (2009) *Research guide C5: The Merchant Navy: Sources for ship histories.* Available online at: http://www.rmg.co.uk/researchers/library/research-guides/the-merchant-navy/research-guide-c5-the-merchant-navy-sources-for-ship-histories [accessed 3 October 2013].

O'Rourke K.H., Williamson J.G. (1999) *Globalization and History: The Evolution of a Nineteenth Century Atlantic Economy.* London and Cambridge: MIT Press.

Palmer C.T., Sattenspiel L., Cassidy C. (2007) Boats, trains, and immunity: the spread of the Spanish Flu on the island of Newfoundland. *Newfoundland and Labrador Studies*, 22(2): 1719–26.

Palmer M. (1999) *Lloyd's List.* Available online at: http://www.mariners-l.co.uk/ResLloydsList.html [accessed 4 June 2014].

Paul J., Maloni M., (2010) Modeling the effects of port disasters. *Maritime Economics and Logistics*, 12(2): 127–46.

Piquet N. (2009) *Histoire du Canal de Suez.* Paris: Perrin.

Pumain D., Swerts E., Cottineau C., Vacchiani-Marcuzzo C., Ignazzi A., Bretagnolle A., Delisle F., Cura R., Lizzi L., Baffi S. (2015) Multilevel comparison of large urban systems. *Cybergeo: European Journal of Geography*, 706. Available online at http://cybergeo.revues.org/26730 [accessed 4 June 2015].

Rees H. (1955) Lloyd's List as a source for port study in schools. *Geography*, 40: 249–54.

Richardson A.M.P., Hurd A. (1923) *Brassey's Naval and Shipping Annual.* London: William Clowes and Sons Ltd. Available online at https://archive.org/details/brasseysnavala1923brasuoft [accessed 4 June 2015].

Rosoff H., von Winterfeldt D. (2007) A risk and economic analysis of dirty bomb attacks on the ports of Los Angeles and Long Beach. *Risk Analysis*, 27(3): 533–46.

Saul S.B. (1960) *Studies in British Overseas Trade, 1870–1914.* Liverpool: Liverpool University Press.

Shi Z., Setlur S., Govindaraju V. (2009) A steerable directional local profile technique for extraction of handwritten Arabic text lines. Proceedings of the 10th International Conference on Document Analysis and Recognition, pp. 176–80.

Solar P.M. (2013) Opening to the East: Shipping between Europe and Asia, 1770–1830. *The Journal of Economic History*, 73(3): 625–61.

Solomon L.P., Barnes A.E., Alessi T., Draper P.J., Weinstein J.J., Lunsford C.R. (1978) *Historical Temporal Shipping (HITS).* Long Range Acoustic Propagation Project, Naval Ocean Research and Development Activity, Bay St. Louis, Mississippi.

Starkey D.J. (1999) *Shipping Movements in the Ports of the United Kingdom, 1871–1913. A Statistical Profile.* Exeter: University of Exeter Press.

Swedish Maritime Administration (2000) *Baltic Maritime Outlook.* Norrköping.

Veenstra A.W., Mulder H.M., Sels R.A. (2005) Analysing container flows in the Caribbean. *Journal of Transport Geography*, 13(4): 295–305.

Verne J. (1995), *The Extraordinary Journeys: Around the World in Eighty Days.* Oxford and New York: Oxford University Press.

Vigarié A. (1964) *Les Grands Ports de Commerce de La Seine au Rhin, leur Evolution devant l'Industrialisation des Arrière-pays.* Paris: SABRI.

Vigarié A. (1998) Une façade portuaire: le Northern Range. In: Gamblin A. (Ed), *Les Littoraux, Espaces de Vies*, Paris: SEDES, pp. 267–75.

Wang C., Ducruet C. (2013) Regional resilience and spatial cycles: long-term evolution of the Chinese port system (221BC–2010AD). *Tijdschrift voor Economische en Sociale Geografie*, 104(5): 524–38.

Part III

Topology and spatial distribution of maritime networks

10 Time considerations for the study of complex maritime networks

Frédéric Guinand, Yoann Pigné

The globalization of exchanges coupled with containerization considerably increased maritime traffic during last decades. Thanks to the standardization of containers, goods can be transported on long distances by container ships, trains, and trucks, without any change in their condition. Containers represent universal transportation boxes that ease the mechanization of the handling system. Today, most of world trade is carried by sea and most of the goods are carried by container ships.

This globalization has been accompanied by rapid changes in port infrastructures, shipping companies' organization with consequences on the global shipping network itself. The strategy of major companies has led to a multilevel network structure. At the higher level, this global network is composed of multi-port calling networks (a kind of mesh between main ports, linked by mega-containerships) and hub-and-spoke networks (star networks at the regional level).

Motivated by these changes, an increasing amount of work has been conducted on various related subjects. Network optimization problems have been widely studied (Tran and Haasis, 2013) such as network design, route optimization, and hub location, combined or not with the problem of allocation of nodes to hubs (O'Kelly and Miller, 1994; Alumur and Kara, 2008; Imai *et al.*, 2009; Gelareh *et al.*, 2010). The analysis of the evolution of the shipping network at worldwide or regional scales also received much attention (Frémont, 2007; Ducruet *et al.*, 2010; Wang and Wang, 2011; Gonzalez-Laxe *et al.*, 2012; Freire-Seoane *et al.*, 2013; Tran and Haasis, 2014). Most of this research complemented statistical analyses with graph-theoretical tools and metrics. Such an approach is not a novelty (Kansky, 1963; Garrison and Marble, 1964; Joly, 1999) and has provided multiple applications since the popularization of complex networks theory (Watts and Strogatz, 1998; Newman, 2003).

In many of these works some properties are recurrent. Depending on the period and data, it was proved that the distribution of port degrees follows a power law or is an exponential-like distribution. Small-world property and the scale-free nature of the shipping network is also often mentioned. In addition, many works analyzed centralities, clustering coefficients, average nearest neighbours degrees, and many other graph metrics (Kaluza *et al.*, 2010), drawing conclusions about the performance of ports (Deng *et al.*, 2009), changes in their hierarchy (Ducruet and

Notteboom, 2012), and the evolution of the network's topological structure (Tran and Haasis, 2014), which were explained by several complementary causes, such as the hub-and-spokes strategies of ports and carriers leading to a rich-club phenomenon (Hu and Zhu, 2009; Ducruet and Zaidi, 2012; Ducruet *et al.*, 2010) or world trade conditions (Gonzalez-Laxe *et al.*, 2012; Freire Seoane *et al.*, 2013).

In all these works, graphs correspond to all ship movements. Unlike continental transport networks, where traffic paths rely on existing and real infrastructures (roads, channels, railways, waterways), the maritime network is not characterized by physical links (Kansky, 1963) but by links corresponding to "the reality of regular lines defined by container ships' movements" (Joly, 1999) and "information about the itineraries of [...] cargo ships [are used] to construct a network of links between ports" (Kaluza *et al.*, 2010). These movements can be obtained from various sources, like databases (Hu and Zhu, 2009), websites of major shipping companies (Deng *et al.*, 2009), annual reports (like *Containerisation International Yearbooks*) (Tran and Haasis, 2014), automatic identification system (AIS)[1] (Kaluza *et al.*, 2010), and *Lloyd's List* reports (Ducruet *et al.*, 2010). The models and results presented in this chapter were obtained using data coming from *Lloyd's List Intelligence*. The Lloyd's corporation collects regularly (on a daily basis) information about ships and more than 90 percent of container ships are tracked by the corporation. These registers report much information about ports–ships events like the date at which a ship enters a port, the date at which it leaves this port, its next destination, and its previous port.

In most research, graphs representing shipping networks are built from all ships' movements for the whole considered period (usually one year), whatever their number between two given ports and whatever the dates of departures from these ports. This may be explained by the regularity of maritime routes used by the main carriers. Thus we can say that the temporal granularity of the studied graphs corresponds to a coarse grain. However, depending on the quality and the accuracy of the data, it is possible to consider a finer temporal granularity. In this chapter we propose to take into account this granularity in two different ways, leading to two different graph models.

Instead of building the graph from all the events occurring during one year, in our first model, we propose to build graphs from events occurring during a given period of time. This period of time corresponds to a temporal granularity J where J is the number of consecutive days of a time window. The graph, called TG-graph, results from the events occurring during this time window. We then build the time series of such graphs of temporal granularity J for the whole year ($365 - J$ graphs). From these series we compute and study a set of simple metrics like number of nodes, average degree, size of the giant connected component, and some other measures detailed later in the chapter. We have noticed that during the year some metrics present particular shapes and are sometimes linked, opening the way to some interpretations.

For the second model we have considered, given the data, the smallest temporal granularity. We propose the use of a model able to keep in its own structure all the events changing its topology. Temporal networks (Holme and Saramäki, 2012) and evolving graphs (Ferreira, 2002) are two examples of families of graphs allowing such a representation. We will see that keeping all these events in the structure allows an analysis of the shipping networks using the container point of view.

The rest of the chapter consists of three main parts. In the next section, a complete analysis of the commonly used graph model is performed. Afterwards, a new model is introduced for studying the evolution of the shipping networks based on the analysis of time series of TG-graphs. In the last section temporal networks are described and resulting shipping networks analyzed. A conclusion and graphics, gathered in the appendices, end this chapter.

Static graphs

From the data, several static graph models can be derived. Nodes are always associated with ports and only the links have a different semantic. Some models are built from maritime routes defined by main carriers companies. A maritime route is a directed cycle, starting from port A, to destination port B with several calls along the way, and coming back to the original port A.

A first graph model can be built, in which the arcs correspond to the travel of the ships from one port to another on the route. This model corresponds to the space *L* topology described in (Sienkiewicz and Holyst, 2005) or to the GDL (graph of direct links) mentioned in Ducruet *et al.* (2010). This graph is generally the model considered by a majority of studies on the evolution of maritime networks. The Global Cargo Ship Network (GCSN) described in (Kaluza *et al.*, 2010) is built according to the same principles but without being restricted to container ships.

From the same dataset and still based on the notion of maritime route, another graph can be built by joining all the ports belonging to the same route. This corresponds to the space *P* topology (Sienkiewicz and Holyst, 2005) or to the GAL (graph of all links) (Ducruet *et al.*, 2010). This second graph model highlights the connectivity between ports relying on ship movements. A path requiring more than one link for reaching port B from port A implies that transhipments are needed.

Though some studies take into consideration both models (Sienkiewicz and Holyst, 2005; Deng *et al.*, 2009; Hu and Zhu, 2009), most analyses emphasize the space *L* topology or GDL model. In this section, we focus on such a graph built from the 1996 and 2006 data extracted from *Lloyd's List*. In the obtained graphs (one per year), one node represents one port and the set of nodes represents all ports that were active at least once during the year (1996 or 2006). A port is said to be active if a ship left or arrived in that port during the year. One arc is added between two nodes *s* (a source node) and *d* (a destination node) if and only if there exists in the data at least one record indicating that one ship made a direct journey from *s* to *d*.

Different kinds of analyses can be carried out on this static network at different scales. The network can be measured as a whole, with global measures, or at a lower scale, at the node level. Global measures usually are scalar values like the average degree, radius, and diameter of the network (Table 10.1 gathers some global measures for 1996 and 2006), while the degree of all nodes, or

Table 10.1 Common graph measures on the two static networks in 1996 and 2006

Measure	1996	2006
Nodes	872	1137
Arcs	7778	13704
Connected Components	2	2
Connected Components > 1	2	2
Giant Component Size	869	1134
Giant Component Ratio	99.66%	99.74%
Strongly Connected Components	36	30
Strongly Connected Components > 1	2	2
Giant Strongly Component Size	835	1106
Giant Strongly Component Ratio	95.76%	97.27%
Average Degree	17.84	24.11
Average Clustering Coefficient	0.53	0.53
Diameter	7	7
Radius	4	4
Path Length	3.22	3.06
Average Eccentricity	5.6018	5.3201

their clustering coefficients are local measures providing vectors of values often analyzed as distributions. The focus is first given to global measures with the study of connected components and of the small-world property. Then node-level measures are investigated with the scale-free property.

Connected components

A connected component is a subset of the network where each node is somehow connected (directly or indirectly) to all the other nodes of the subset. The direction of arcs is not considered in connected components: there exits an undirected path between any pair of nodes. A more restrictive type of subset, which are strongly connected components, impose that any two nodes in the sub-set connect through a directed path (following actual arcs directions). Table 10.1 shows two connected components of respective sizes 869 and 3 in 1996 (respectively 1,134 and 3 in 2006). This 3-node component is identical in both datasets and will be ignored in the remaining. Apart from those three ports, the network is connected.

When it comes to strongly connected components, in 1996, 36 components are identified but only two are larger than 1 (components of size 1 are isolated nodes). One of the two components is again the 3-node component. This leaves 34 nodes out of the giant strongly connected component. These nodes are leaves in the network: whether no path can reach them (only path initiated from them is possible) or the opposite (they can be reached but have no departure). The same observation can be done for 2006, with 1,106 strongly connected nodes and 28 leftovers.

Small-world property

When considering network path lengths (number of hops between nodes), in both networks, each node's most distant destination ranges between the network radius and its diameter (4 and 7) and the average path length for any pair of nodes is 3.22 in year 1996 (3.06 in 2006). Moreover, the average clustering coefficient for both networks is relatively high. These measures suggest that a small-world property (Watts and Strogatz, 1998) should be investigated. Following the ω test (Telesford *et al.*, 2011), we compare the clustering coefficient of our datasets to the one of an equivalent lattice network (a regular network with the same number of nodes and same average degree). We also compare the path length to an equivalent random network: a network with the same number of nodes and same average degree as our network (Erdős, 1959). Let L be the path length of our dataset and C its clustering coefficient, L_{rand} is the path length of the random network and C_{latt} is the clustering coefficient of the lattice. Then the small-world measurement ω proposed by Telesford *et al.* (2011) is as such:

$$\omega = \frac{L_{rand}}{L} - \frac{C}{C_{latt}}$$

Measures indicate a ω value of 0.0716 for 1996 (0.1017 for 2006) (Table 10.2). Values close to zero witness the small-world property. Positive values indicate that the networks have more random characteristics than regular ones. From these results we conclude with $\omega \approx 0.1$, $L > L_{rand}$, and $C > C_{latt}$, that the 1996 and 2006 maritime networks present a small-world property but with slightly more random characteristics due to a lower clustering coefficient than the lattice equivalent graph.

Scale-free property

Additional information can be obtained from local measures when analyzing the distribution of their values. Networks with degree distributions following a power law are classically called scale-free networks. Verifying such a property for maritime networks would help to classify them and understand their underlying mechanisms. However, concluding that a network is scale-free requires careful analysis and comparison. Scale-free networks basically have a degree distribution that follows a power law.

Table 10.2 Comparison with random and regular networks in order to point out small-world properties

Year	L	L_{rand}	C	C_{latt}	ω
1996	3.226	2.662	0.527	0.700	0.0716
2006	3.062	2.558	0.527	0.717	0.1017

Plotting the degree distribution of a supposedly scale-free network is, however, not very informative. Indeed, since very few nodes in the network gather the highest degrees, the visual representation on the right of the distribution gets statistically noisy as fewer samples express more values. This phenomenon, also called fat tail, prevents from precise observation. It is thus desirable not to draw the distribution itself (its probability density function) but its cumulative distribution function (CDF) which also follows a power law if the original distribution follows one (Newman, 2005).

It is also rare that the degree distribution of the network can be identified as a power law on the full range of the distribution. It is admitted (Clauset *et al.*, 2009) that there exists a threshold value $x_{\min}$ from which a distribution obeys a power law. If a power law can be fitted to a real dataset, it is also desirable to try to match it against other random distributions that might fit the data better. In this chapter, guidelines from Clauset *et al.* (2009) have been followed in order to analyze and fit our two datasets. This method follows three main steps.

1.   Estimate the $x_{\min}$ threshold and α parameter of the power law that would fit the real data. The power law parameter α is estimated with the method of maximum likelihood (MLE). The lower bound $x_{\min}$ is estimated by minimizing the distance between the CDF and the data using the Kolmogorov–Smirnov (KS) distance.

2.   Quantitatively estimate how good is the fit between the data and the power law. This method generates synthetic data based on α and tries to recover the $x_{\min}$ lower bound with the MLE. The result is mainly a standard deviation for the given value of $x_{\min}$. The lower the deviation, the better the fit. Also, the KS distance is used to estimate if those synthetic generated data are closer or not to the theoretical power law than the data itself. If the data outperforms at least 10 percent of the synthetic data (its p-value) then it is considered a plausible match for that power law.

3.   Compare the power law with other distributions. Other random distributions might fit the data. The two first steps can be applied to evaluate them. Finally, a likelihood test ratio can give a pairwise comparison between distributions.

Figure 10.1 displays the CDF of the degree distribution of the 1996 dataset along with estimates for power-law, log-normal, and exponential distributions. Each distribution is drawn with its own estimated value for the lower bound $x_{\min}$. These results and the subsequent tables and figures where all generated using the R package poweRlaw (Gillespie, 2015). Distribution estimates for the year 2006 dataset, not shown here, show comparable behaviour.

The estimation of parameters visually shows that the $x_{\min}$ estimated for the power law is very high, making the distribution fit only a fraction of the dataset while the log-normal distribution has a lower $x_{\min}$ estimated which fits more data. The quantitative estimate of those parameters with a bootstrapping methods (Table 10.3) shows that not only the power law has a very high $x_{\min}$ estimate, making it fit less real observations (n_{tail}), but the estimate is statistical unstable

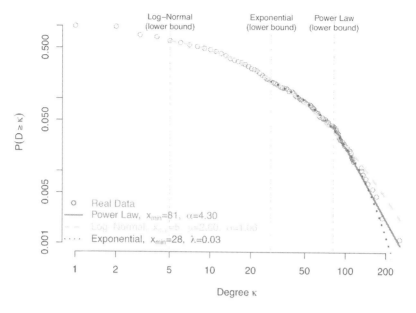

Figure 10.1 Degree distribution's cumulative density function estimated with various discrete probability distributions (year 1996).

Each distribution has fitted parameters estimated with the method of maximum likelihood and lower bonds x_{min} optimized with the KS distance method.

Table 10.3 Various discrete probability distributions fits with *p*-values for the two datasets

Year	Law	x_{min}	n_{tail}	*p-value*
1996	Power law	81 ± 20	37 ± 37	0.89
	Log-normal	5 ± 5	548 ± 458	0.53
	Exponential	28 ± 10	152 ± 133	0.94
2006	Power law	71 ± 22	102 ± 108	0.32
	Log-normal	27 ± 11	295 ± 196	0.67
	Exponential	53 ± 17	145 ± 127	0.52

Note: x_{min} is the estimated lower bound on the considered law (with standard deviation). n_{tail} is the quantity of observations involved (with standard deviation). The *p*-value is the ratio of comparisons between the real data and synthetic datasets that gives the real data a better fit for the considered distribution. *P*-values above 0.1 are considered a plausible match for the considered distribution.

with high standard deviation, meaning that the x_{min} value is barely estimated on synthetic datasets with same characteristics. The log-normal distribution, on the other hand, behaves well on both datasets fitting the largest quantity of observation. P-values, which indicate how close the data is to the distributions compared to synthetically generated datasets, are all above the 0.1 threshold.

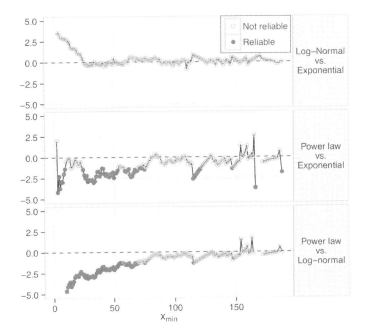

Figure 10.2 Distributions comparison with likelihood ratio test and estimation of reliability with Vuong's test.

The power law fit is always ruled out by the two other distributions, especially for small values of the x_{min} lower bound. The Vuong's tests do not allow any conclusion about the log-normal vs. exponential comparison.

This indicates that the three distribution, independently, are a plausible fit to the dataset.

Distributions are then compared with one another. The sign of the likelihood ratio test (Clauset *et al.*, 2009) indicates which distribution is the best fit for the dataset and Vuong's test indicates the reliability of the likelihood ratio test based on its standard deviation. In order to test the distributions, the lower bound x_{min} must be equal for both. Figure 10.2 shows pairwise comparison between the three considered laws depending on the value of x_{min} for the 1996 dataset. The power law fit is always ruled out by the two other distributions, especially for small values of the x_{min} lower bound. The log-normal distribution overpasses the exponential but the Vuong's test gives no credit to that last assumption. Comparable comments can be made on the year 2006 dataset (not shown here).

A first conclusion would be that MLE estimation for a power law to fit the dataset is not ruled out. There exists a power law for the data and we can qualify the networks as scale-free. However, further analysis show that other distributions, especially log-normal is a better candidate to fit these data. For more comparison with sub-exponential distributions, and comparable datasets, see Chapter 14 (Gastner and Ducruet).

Graphs based on time granularity: TG-graphs

Graph models described in the previous section are built from the whole set of ship movements recorded on a long time period (usually one full year). However, the quality and accuracy of the data allow to consider a smaller time granularity and to build graphs from a restricted set of ship movements. This restriction can be spatial (restriction to a given region) or temporal (restriction to a given time period). We chose the latter in subsequent analyses. The time window considered can last one day up to several months. A TG-graph (time granularity-based graph) is defined by a starting date t and a time granularity J. t and J define a time window Wt, J of length J (days) and starting at t. The TG-graph $TGG(t, J)$ is built from all ships' departures (and not arrivals) occurring during Wt, J. An arc (s, d) is added to the graph if and only if one ship, at least, left the port s to port d at a date belonging to the time interval $[t, t + J - 1]$ (or equivalently during Wt, J).

Nodes are added to the graph accordingly: a node (port) p belongs to $TGG(t, J)$ if and only if there exists a ship departure in Wt, J for which p is either the source port or the destination port. Let us consider the set of departures given in Table 10.3. $TGG(1, 3)$ and $TGG(3, 3)$ are represented in Figure 10.3.

Time granularity and measures

Given a time granularity J we can build $365 - J$ TG-graphs for 2006 and $366 - J$ for 1996, with starting dates from $t = 1$ to $t = 365 - J$ ($t = 366 - J$ for 1996), leading to time series of TG-graphs. For each TG-graph we can measures classical indices: graph order, diameter, radius, eccentricity, average degree, giant component size, and many others. From the time series, we can study their evolution along the year, looking for tendencies or particular shapes of the graphics. We denote by $TGG(J, 1996)$ the series of TG-graphs with granularity J for year 1996 for starting dates from $t = 1$ to $t = 366 - J$. In this work, we consider non-directed TG-graphs and we focus mainly on graph order (number of nodes), average node

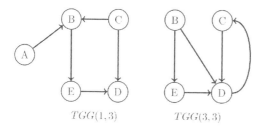

$TGG(1,3)$ $TGG(3,3)$

Figure 10.3 TGG(t, J) are graphs built from ships' departures occurring during the time window W(t, J), or equivalently during the time interval $[t, t + J - 1]$.

On the left side of the figure, TGG(1, 3) is the TG-graph built from ships' departures occurring at dates 1, 2, and 3. On the right side, TGG(3, 3) is the graph built from ships' departures occurring at dates 3, 4, and 5.

degree, size of the giant connected component, average eccentricity, and path length. But for studying time series of TG-graphs we first have to choose time granularities. How to choose a relevant set of time granularities is an open question, so we have chosen, empirically, the following set of values: 1, 7, 14, 21, and 28 days. All graphics obtained for the different measures are reported in Appendices 10.1 to 10.10 (the giant strongly connected component ratio was the only measure obtained from directed TG-graphs).

Observations and analyses

One of the most interesting measures of the obtained results is the evolution of the number of nodes for different values of time granularity. For TGG(1, 1996) we can see in Figure 10.4 a Sunday effect, that plays an important role in the variability of the number of nodes in the network on a daily basis. We can see that between 1996 and 2006 this effect has been levelled as illustrated by Figure 10.5, but we leave the interpretation of this effect to further research.

At this level of granularity ($J = 1$), the signal is noisy but it is already possible to notice a tendency for the whole year: an increase in the number of nodes involved in maritime traffic. This tendency is verified for both 1996 and 2006. If we consider the growth rate in 1996, obtained by linear regression, and if we assume that it remained unchanged between 1996 and 2006, the number of nodes at the end of 2006 would have been about 480. The actual number is 350. This suggests a slowdown in the number of ports involved in the shipping network

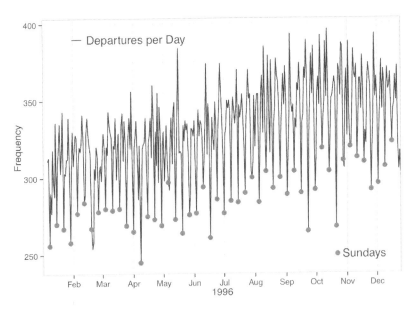

Figure 10.4 Day-per-day departures frequencies for all ports during year 1996. Dots indicate Sundays.

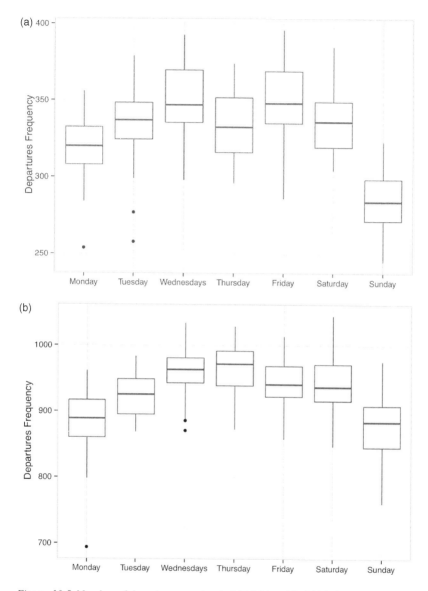

Figure 10.5 Number of departures per day in 1996 (a) and in 2006 (b).

(on a daily basis) between 1996 and 2006. This is verified, at least for 2006, since the value of the growth rate in 2006 is more than three times smaller than the one of 1996, as illustrated by Figure 10.6. If the regularity of the slowdown between 1996 and 2006 could be proved, which might be confirmed by additional data for years between 1996 and 2006 and after 2006, this would suggest that the shipping

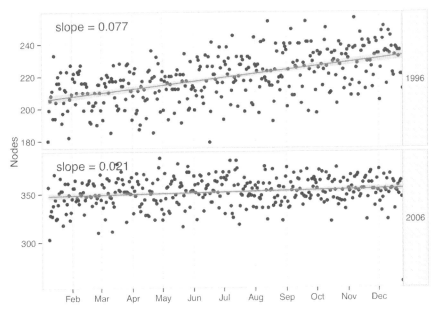

Figure 10.6 Rate of growth of the number of nodes for time granularity $J = 1$ in 1996 (top) and 2006 (bottom).

network would reach (quite quickly) a threshold on the number of ports involved in container shipping. Then, the main evolution process of the network would be an enhancement of the connectivity of ports.

Increasing the value of time granularity clearly affects graphics. However, metric sensitivity to time granularity varies. Increasing time granularity reduces the variability of values and changes these values. For instance, the number of nodes in TGG(1, 1996) belongs to the interval [200, 240] while this interval is equal to [490, 540] for TGG(28, 1996). Moreover, in the graphics presented in Figure 10.7, structures emerge as time granularity increases. Patterns appear and become more visible when sequentially observing time series of nodes' evolution for graphs TGG(1, 1996), TGG(14, 1996), TGG(21, 1996), and TGG(28, 1996); yet the interpretation of such patterns is still under investigation.

However, such sensitivity is not a general rule. Average eccentricity belongs to the interval [6, 8] for the vast majority of measures for $J \geq 7$ in 2006 or $J \geq 14$ in 1996. One can also notice that for $J = 1$ this value is much larger in 2006, as it is the case for $J = 1$ and $J = 7$ in 1996. While a deeper analysis still needs to be done, this could indicate that for some metrics there exists a threshold value, for time granularity, from which the graph becomes stable. For the average eccentricity, this stability is reached in 2006 for lower values of J than in 1996, which could be interpreted as an increase in the frequency of maritime traffic.

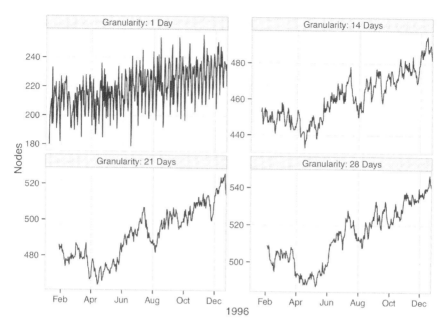

Figure 10.7 Evolution of the number of nodes in TG-graphs according to the value of *J* (from 1 to 28).

Another way of analyzing time series of TG-graphs is to compare the evolution of couples of measures. Such comparison can infer certain hypotheses on the corresponding graphs that could help understanding shipping networks evolution. The most illustrative example for our data is given by the compared evolution of the number of nodes and the average node degrees, for both years, and especially for $J = 28$. Figures 10.8 and 10.9 highlight this link. Both graphics suggest that when the number of nodes increases, the average degree decreases. From a graph perspective, this could indicate that all TG-graphs have in common a set of always present nodes characterized by a high degree. Along the year, some low-degree nodes are linked to this common structure and leave it later. From the maritime network perspective, this could be interpreted as a manifestation of the hub-and-spokes configuration.

Another set of measures seems to be linked: number of nodes and average path length. When studying the graphics it appears that the faster the increase of the number of nodes, the slower the decrease of the average path length as illustrated by Figure 10.10.

From a graph perspective, when new nodes are added to a graph, and if they are sparsely linked to other nodes (low degrees), these arrivals entail an increase of the average path length. Conversely, if new links are added to the graph, some paths between nodes are shorter, which decreases the average path length. We thus have two opposite processes explaining network growth. The comparison between

Figure 10.8 Compared evolution of the number of nodes of the TG-graph and of its average nodes degree for 1996.

1996 and 2006 suggests that the proportion of new nodes compared to new links was more important for the shipping network of 1996 than it was for 2006. In other words, in 1996 the main driving force of network growth was expansion while in 2006, it was densification. We should, however, remain cautious because slope values on which this interpretation is built are very small, but the tendencies were the same for every time granularity values.

Temporal networks

The previous sections focused on the analysis of maritime data when viewed as static graphs or sets of static graphs, with nodes being ports and arcs indicating a possible route between two ports. Within such a static network, time is not considered. Useful time information could complement our analysis. Indeed, from the Lloyd's dataset, an arc could actually hold more information: number and dates of departures on arcs, trip distribution through time, arrival dates, and measures related to the duration of the journeys on this arc (distribution, average, median). Classical complex networks usually do not contain time-related information. In this section we introduce temporal networks, a graph model that contains all time-related events of ship movements.

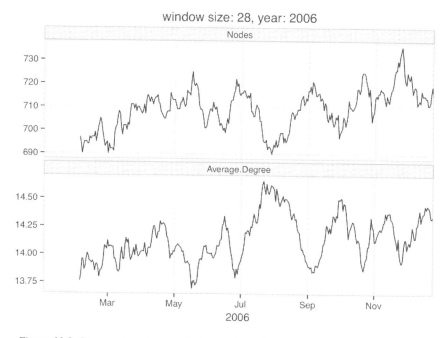

Figure 10.9 Compared evolution of the number of nodes of the TG-graph and of its average nodes degree for 2006.

Temporal network model

The graphs considered in the two previous sections are 1-graphs, meaning that whatever the number of ships moving from one port A to the next call C , there will be only one arc linking A to C. If we want to represent all the ships moving from A to C we should model it using a multigraph. Tran and Haasis (2014) consider a multigraph based on the notion of route, "characterised by a predetermined sequence of ports, arrival schedule, frequency, and deployed ships" and the combination of such routes forms directed maritime networks, but they restrict their analysis to the top 20 shipping lines for 1995–2011. Joly (1999) also raised this question of multigraph modelling but his study took place in a long-term perspective. Adding one arc per ship would have been an unnecessary complication of the problem. The issue of time remains, because such a graph implies synchronicity of ship movements (Joly, 1999).

For tackling this problem, we propose to consider a graph model that is able to carry time-related information: temporal networks (or evolving graphs). Based on ship movements we build such a graph by associating one node to each port and one arc between two ports A and C whenever at least one ship, during the considered period of time, moved from port A to the next one C . If the date of the departure from A was t, then the arc is valuated with t. More generally, if there are n dates

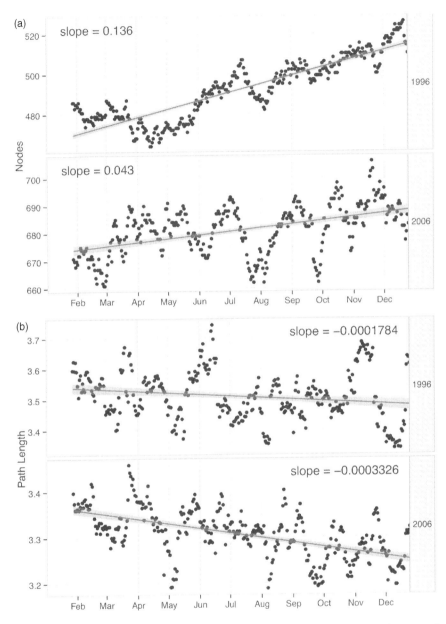

Figure 10.10 The faster the increase of the number of nodes, the slower the decrease of the average path length (for both years).

of departures of ships from port A to C during the period, then the arc (A, C) will be valued by the *n* dates. TG-graphs presented in the previous section can be considered variants of temporal networks. A TGG(t, J) is a non-weighted subgraph of a temporal network T, a sub-graph that only contains the set of arcs of T that are labelled by dates $d \in [t, t + J - 1]$, and, of course, corresponding nodes.

Numerous models exist to analyze time-enabled networks, often called temporal networks (Holme and Saramäki, 2012). In addition to a classical network structure, each edge (or arc) is labelled with a list of dates (or intervals) indicating when it is active. As in distributed computing this corresponds to a weighted graph where edges are qualified by values. When an edge (or arc) is active it is identical to a classical edge; it is non-existing otherwise. Consider a node A connected to a node B, and B connected to a node C. In a classical network, A and C are indirectly connected through B. In a temporal network, time constraints imply that the link (A, B) needs to be active first and then link (B, C) in order to consider that A and C are indirectly connected. Even if edges are undirected, a path existing from A to C does not prevail a path from C to A. Edges (A, B) and (B, C) must be active for the path to exist. A path in a network with such a time constraint is called a journey (Xuan *et al.*, 2003), a non-decreasing path, or a time-respecting path (Kempe *et al.*, 2000).

Figure 10.11 illustrates such a temporal network. A journey exists in this network from node A to node E because time constraints are respected. The path {A, B, C, D, E} can be traversed with respect to time: (A, B) at time 1, then (B, C) at time 1, then (C, D) at time 2, and finally (D, E) at time 4. The reverse path is not a valid journey. Thus the concept of path and related measures (diameter,

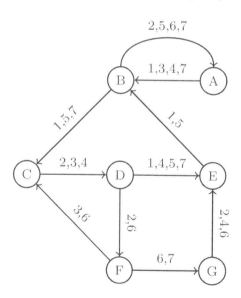

Figure 10.11 An example of temporal network with labelled edges for time steps when they are active.

radius, eccentricity, and most centralities) are redefined by temporal constraints. In the given example, no stop on nodes is assumed, travelling times of edges are neglected, and only the activity of edges is considered. In the following section, stops on nodes and travelling times on edges will both be taken into account for the computation of the journeys.

Least-cost journeys in maritime temporal networks

We propose a new point of view for studying maritime networks. Temporal information and related graph algorithms allow expressing new problems. Instead of analyzing shipping networks from the port or vessel point of view, we describe the network from the container point of view. Let us consider that a given container located at a given place needs to reach a destination. To that purpose it will be shipped through one or several vessels in order to reach the destination. Under various assumptions, multiple constraints can be considered. From the data it is assumed that each arc of the network is labelled with the following information:

- list of departure dates with each vessel's departure on this arc (from source port to destination port)
- list of travel duration associated with the mentioned departures on this arc
- average, standard deviation, and median travel duration on this arc

Based on these elements it is possible to consider new problems for the shipment of one container from one place to another:

1 Minimization of transhipments. The number of calls and subsequent need for transhipment has an inevitable economic cost that could be considered for minimization, so that a journey with a minimum number of transhipments would be more desirable, at the cost of an overall longer journey.
2 Minimization of the arrival date. If the goal is to ship container as fast as possible, then the overall duration from the moment we try to ship the cargo has to be minimized.
3 Minimization of time at sea. It corresponds to finding a fast journey but when the start date does not matter. This case is useful for instance for renewable resources with a freshness to be maximized.

Those three open questions remain to be investigated using the temporal network framework in the field for maritime networks analysis. The remainder of the section focuses on the minimization of the arrival date.

Horizon and foremost journeys

Various adaptations of the classical shortest path problem have been widely investigated in the field of temporal networks (Xuan *et al.*, 2003). As stated, we consider the list of departures on each arc as a constraint. For the sake of statistical relevance and to avoid extreme (and perhaps erroneous) values with high standard deviation, we define travel duration on edges as the median value of the observed real durations. Moreover the minimum stay at a location for a container is set to one day in order to consider transhipment delay.

In the case of maritime networks, before considering the optimization of the arrival date we first consider if an arrival is possible during this observation window. Since data is available year-round, one year is the maximum accepted journey duration. Each port is a potential starting point for a container; it can reach a number of destinations throughout the year based on possible journeys, based on time constraints. The horizon is the average number of reachable destinations for a given port. When time is not considered, the horizon of a port is expected to be large, according to the size of its belonged strongly connected component. When time is considered, due to time constraints, this number is expected to be lower. Some ports were identified in the previous section as leaves in the giant connected components: they are reachable, but cannot reach any destinations. These 32 ports in 1996 (34 in 2006) have no horizon and a potentially infinite journey duration to any destination. Moreover, the duration of journeys can also be investigated. Time

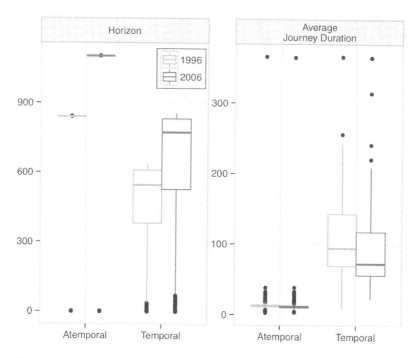

Figure 10.12 Temporal versus atemporal analysis of average journey durations and ports horizon.

When atemporal, the horizon (in number of nodes/ports) is in the order of the size of the connected component of each node and the average journey duration (in days) only considers arcs median duration as a simple weight. When temporal, the horizon is inferior to the Atemporal and the average journey duration is much more important than the naive weighted shortest path. Years 1996 and 2006 are investigated and show similar behaviour.

and duration are usually considered (mixed-up) with weights such that a shortest path on a classical network with arcs durations used as weights is computed. This gives an artificial value for the journey duration since actual vessel departures are omitted. We compute here the actual foremost journeys in the network and compare them with this naive approach.

Figure 10.12 shows an important difference in average for the horizon when time is truly considered for reaching destinations. On average, in 1996, the horizon is 820 nodes, which is close to the size of the strong giant component (835), whereas it is 460 when time is considered with a wide standard deviation (± 130). A similar difference occurs in 2006. The difference between temporal and atemporal approaches for average journey duration is very important. While the naive weighted shortest path provides an average journey duration of 20 ± 47 days in 1996 and 17 ± 42 in 2006, the time respecting foremost journey computation gives an average of 112 ± 55 and 96 ± 54 for respective years. This difference between the supposed classical time consideration on the static network and the effective computation of time dependent paths is of paramount importance for the analysis of maritime networks. While it is commonly believed that the maritime network is strongly connected and that goods can cross the globe in about 20 days, this analysis shows a different point of view. If indeed the network shows scale-free properties, ports that are not directly connected to the large hubs are actually isolated. Such evidence echoes the findings of Mareï and Ducruet (Chapter 19) about the evolution of regional liner shipping networks.

Conclusion

Classical analyses of maritime networks neglect the temporal information contained within the data. We introduce temporal information within graph models built from ship movements recorded by *Lloyds' List Intelligence*. We consider three different graph models, starting from classical static that groups all ship movements into one unique graph, showing that the network carries expected properties like small-worldiness and scale-freeness (to a certain extent).

The second model time granularity-based graph (TG-graph) is characterized by a time granularity allowing building time series of TG-graphs for studying the evolution of many metrics during a given period of time. The temporal evolution of simple metrics like graph order or other metrics provides interesting insights into the understanding of shipping network evolution.

The introduction of time granularity for building TG-graphs raises multiple questions, such as the choice of granularity to reveal certain phenomena, the sensitivity of metrics to granularity changes, and the consistency of results obtained from different granularity values. At this stage we are not yet able to answer these questions but this chapter opened the discussion about the relevance of such a graph model. We focused on a few different time granularities (1, 7, 14, 21, and 28 days) and we have restricted our study to global metrics. However, similar studies can be driven for nodes and edges. These analyses could lead to the comparison of the evolution, stability, and robustness of a given set of ports at different periods of time to observe their response to events like crises, for instance (see Chapter 9 by Ducruet *et al.* about port growth trajectories as well as Chapter 13 by Lhomme on port and maritime network vulnerability analysis).

The temporal network, our last model, takes more explicitly time into account by including time-related data directly in the graph. This model provides allows renewing the analysis of maritime networks by formulating problems and answering questions on how cargo can be shipped through the network, which path should be used and when in order to optimize the transit of goods for different optimization functions. The analysis of these graphs brought new results that change the way those networks should be considered. Despite its small-world property and its hubs, when time is considered, the network exhibits an average journey duration that is five times longer than for a standard off-time network.

Acknowledgements

The authors would like to thanks César Ducruet and his team for providing us with their data and for their availability for the questions we had about these data. All experiments were conducted using GraphStream (Dutot *et al.*, 2007), a tool for designing, analyzing and visualizing dynamic graphs. Figures in the appendices illustrate graph measures with various granularity sizes for the two datasets.

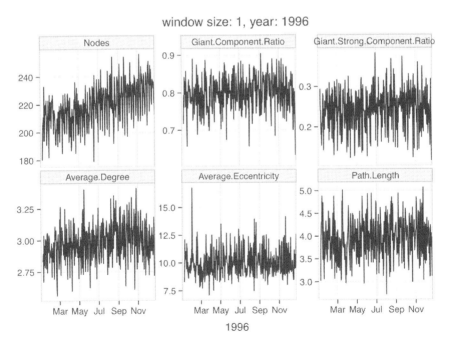

Appendix 10.1 Evolution of network properties in TG-graphs for $J = 1$ in 1996.

window size: 7, year: 1996

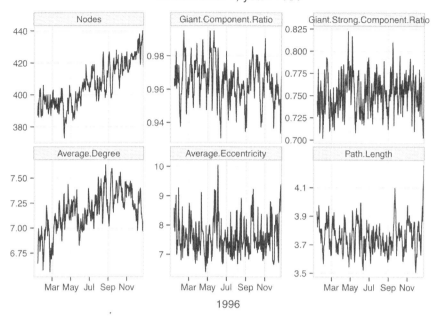

Appendix 10.2 Evolution of network properties in TG-graphs for $J = 7$ in 1996.

window size: 14, year: 1996

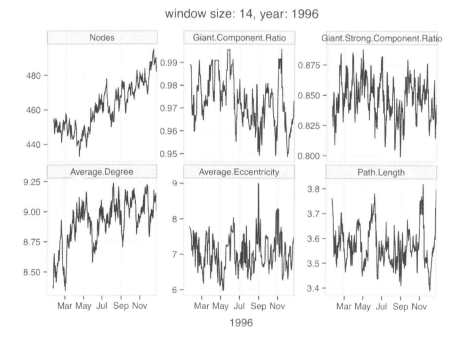

Appendix 10.3 Evolution of network properties in TG-graphs for $J = 14$ in 1996.

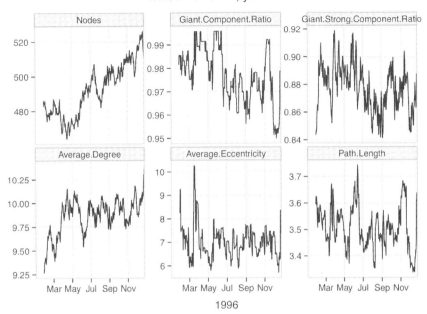

Appendix 10.4 Evolution of network properties in TG-graphs for $J = 21$ in 1996.

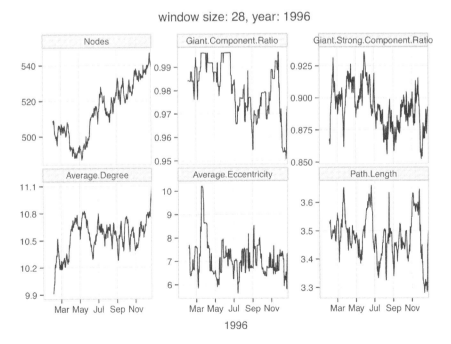

Appendix 10.5 Evolution of network properties in TG-graphs for $J = 28$ in 1996.

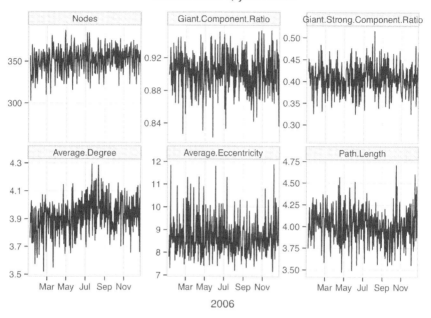

Appendix 10.6 Evolution of network properties in TG-graphs for $J = 1$ in 2006.

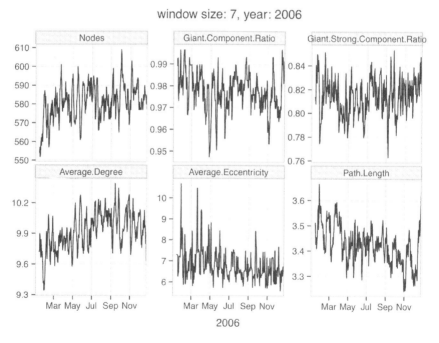

Appendix 10.7 Evolution of network properties in TG-graphs for $J = 7$ in 2006.

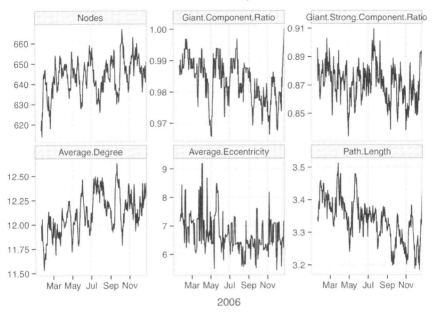

Appendix 10.8 Evolution of network properties in TG-graphs for $J = 14$ in 2006.

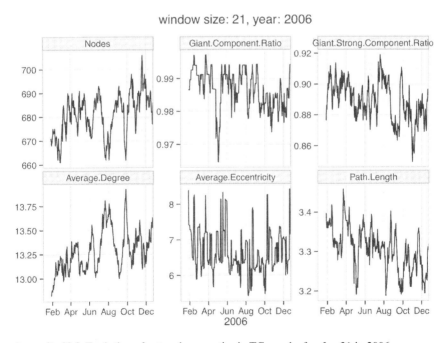

Appendix 10.9 Evolution of network properties in TG-graphs for $J = 21$ in 2006.

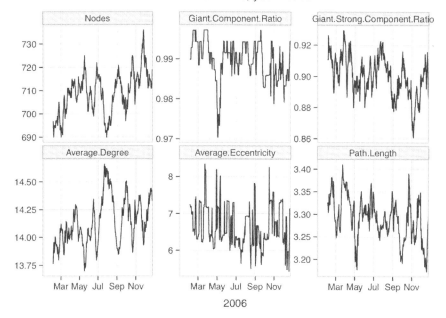

Appendix 10.10 Evolution of network properties in TG-graphs for $J = 28$ in 2006.

Note

1 AIS is a radio-based system located on ships providing information about the position, course, and speed of the ship. Its usage is limited to the transmission range of the radio (less than 30 nautical miles).

References

Alumur S., Kara B.Y. (2008) Network hub location problems: the state of the art. *European Journal of Operational Research*, 190(1): 1–21.

Clauset A., Shalizi C.R., Newman M.E.J. (2009) Power-law distributions in empirical data. *SIAM Rev.*, 51: 661–703.

Deng W.B., Long G., Wei L., Xu C. (2009) Worldwide marine transportation network: efficiency and container throughput. *Chinese Physics Letters*, 26(11): 118901.

Ducruet C., Notteboom T.E. (2012) The worldwide maritime network of container shipping: spatial structure and regional dynamics. *Global Networks*, 12(3): 395–423.

Ducruet, C., Zaidi, F. (2012) Maritime constellations: a complex network approach to shipping and ports. *Maritime Policy and Management* 39(2): 151–68.

Ducruet C., Rozenblat C., Zaidi F. (2010) Ports in multi-level maritime networks: evidence from the Atlantic (1996-2006). *Journal of Transport Geography*, 18(4): 508–18.

Dutot A., Guinand F., Olivier D., Pigné Y. (2007) Graphstream: a tool for bridging the gap between complex systems and dynamic graphs. In Alaoui A., Bertelle C. (Eds), *Proceedings of Emergent Properties in Natural and Artificial Complex Systems*. Satellite Conference within the 4th European Conference on Complex Systems (ECCS'2007), October 4–5. Dresden, Germany, pp. 63–72.

Erdős P. (1959) On random graphs. *Publicationes Mathematicae (Debrecen)*, 6: 290–7.

Ferreira A. (2002) On models and algorithms for dynamic communication networks: the case for evolving graphs. In: *4e Rencontres Francophones sur les Aspects Algorithmiques des Telecommunications (ALGOTEL'2002)*, Mèze, France.

Freire Seoane M.J., Gonzalez-Laxe F., Montes C.P. (2013) Foreland determination for containership and general cargo ports in Europe (2007–2011). *Journal of Transport Geography*, 30: 56–67.

Frémont A. (2007) Global maritime networks: the case of Maersk. *Journal of Transport Geography*, 15(6): 431–42.

Garrison W.L., Marble D.F. (1964) Factor-analytic study of the connectivity of a transportation network. *Papers in Regional Science*, 12: 231–8.

Gelareh S., Nickel S., Pisinger D. (2010) Liner shipping hub network design in a competitive environment. *Transportation Research Part E*, 46(6): 991–1004.

Gillespie C.S. (2015) Fitting heavy tailed distributions: the poweRlaw package. *Journal of Statistical Software*, 64(2): 1–16.

Gonzalez-Laxe F., Freire Seoane M.J., Montes C.P. (2012) Maritime degree, centrality and vulnerability: port hierarchies and emerging areas in containerized transport (2008–2010). *Journal of Transport Geography*, 24: 33–44.

Holme P., Saramäki J. (2012) Temporal networks. *Physics Reports*, 519(3): 97–125.

Hu Y., Zhu D. (2009) Empirical analysis of the worldwide maritime transportation network. *Physica A*, 388(10): 2061–71.

Imai A., Shintani K., Papadimitriou S. (2009) Multi-port vs. hub-and-spoke port calls by containerships. *Transportation Research Part E*, 45(5): 740–57.

Joly O. (1999) *La structuration des réseaux de circulation maritime*. Unpublished PhD Dissertation in Territorial Planning, Le Havre University, CIRTAI.

Kaluza P., Kölzsch A., Gastner M.T., Blasius, B. (2010) The complex network of global cargo ship movements. *Journal of the Royal Society Interface*, 7(48): 1093–103.

Kansky K.J. (1963) *Structure of Transportation Networks: Relationships between Network Geometry and Regional Characteristics*. Chicago: University of Chicago.

Kempe D., Kleinberg J., Kumar A. (2000) Connectivity and inference problems for temporal networks. In: *Proceedings of the Thirty-second Annual ACM Symposium on Theory of Computing, STOC '00*, New York, USA, pp. 504–13.

Newman M.E.J. (2003) The structure and function of complex networks. *SIAM Review*, 45: 167–256.

Newman M.E.J. (2005) Power laws, Pareto distributions and Zipf's law. *Contemporary Physics*, 46(5): 323–51.

O'Kelly M.E., Miller H.J. (1994) The hub network design problem: a review and synthesis. *Journal of Transport Geography*, 2(1): 31–40.

Sienkiewicz J., Holyst J.A. (2005) Statistical analysis of 22 public transport networks in poland. *Physical Review E*, 72: 046127.

Telesford Q.K., Joyce K.E., Hayasaka S., Burdette J.H., Laurienti P.J. (2011) The ubiquity of small-world networks. *Brain Connectivity*, 1(5): 367–75.

Tran N.K., Haasis H.D. (2013) Literature survey of network optimization in container liner shipping. *Flexible Services and Manufacturing Journal*, 1–41.

Tran N.K., Haasis H.D. (2014) Empirical analysis of the container liner shipping network on the East-West corridor (1995–2011). *Netnomics* (in press).

Wang C., Wang J. (2011) Spatial pattern of the global shipping network and its hub-and-spoke system. *Research in Transportation Economics*, 32(1): 54–63.

Watts D.J., Strogatz S.H. (1998) Collective dynamics of "small-world" networks. *Nature*, 393(6684): 440–2.

Xuan B., Ferreira A., Jarry A. (2003) Evolving graphs and least cost journeys in dynamic networks. In: *WiOpt'03: Modeling and Optimization in Mobile, Ad Hoc and Wireless Networks*, Sophia Antipolis, France, p. 10.

11 Maritime network monitoring

From position sensors to shipping patterns

Laurent Etienne, Erwan Alincourt,
Thomas Devogele

The maritime environment has a huge impact on the world economy and our everyday lives. The volume of maritime trade has doubled since the 1970s and reached about 90 percent of global trade in terms of volume and 70 percent in terms of value. Oceans are a shared space where marine species live and human activities (sailing, cruising, fishing, cargo transportation) are conducted. These activities generate traffic, which can lead to navigation difficulties and risks in coastal and crowded areas. The spectrum of ships goes from small sail boats to super tankers. Ships navigate using patterns that depend on their activities and objectives. These movements can conflict and can lead to collisions, posing a serious threat to the environment and human lives. Safety and security have therefore become a major concern, especially in Europe. Consideration of security by the International Maritime Organization (IMO) in the last decade has gone from ship design, education, and navigational rules (e.g. International Regulations for Preventing Collisions at Sea: COLREGS (IMO, 1972); International Convention for the Safety of Life at Sea: SOLAS (IMO, 1974)), to technical solutions for traffic monitoring. Nowadays ships are fitted out with sensors and position report systems whose objective is to identify and locate other vessels. All the information collected from these sensors can be shared on worldwide networks and stored in spatio-temporal databases. Figure 11.1 shows an example of maritime traffic collected in one day (1 April, 2012, 4M positions).

However, the huge amounts of data provided by these systems are rarely used for knowledge discovery. Most analyses of maritime network flows are based on departure and arrival ports (Kaluza *et al.*, 2010; Ducruet, 2013). These databases can be mined to extract more detailed maritime traffic patterns, which are useful for classifying ships' behaviour. The combination of real-time worldwide ship location, traffic pattern, and traffic monitoring gives a better understanding of global maritime traffic.

This first section introduces the problem addressed in this chapter. Then, the second section presents different cooperative and non-cooperative vessel detection and tracking techniques. The third section introduces data distribution and collaborative networks. The fourth section focuses on data fusion and trajectory processing. The fifth section shows how patterns can be mined from

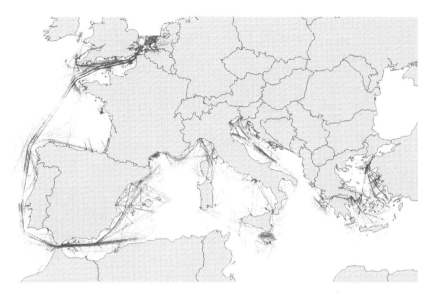

Figure 11.1 One day of maritime traffic collected from different shore base stations using the Automatic Identification System (AIS).

maritime traffic databases. Finally, the last section considers the recent evolution of maritime traffic analysis and monitoring.

Vessel detection and tracking

Different ship tracking systems have been designed to ensure the security and safety of maritime navigation. These tracking systems can be divided into two general categories: cooperative and non-cooperative. Cooperative systems rely on vessels to identify themselves and report their positions. This category includes automated identification system (AIS), long-range identification and tracking (LRIT), and vessel monitoring systems (VMS). Non-cooperative systems are designed to detect and track vessels that do not voluntarily provide information about their location. Coastal radar and visual observation are common types of non-cooperative detection and tracking systems. Most of these systems are designed to detect and track vessels in a limited area around a ship or a traffic monitoring centre. The use of satellites has recently widened the coverage of these tracking systems to the entire planet (Greidanus, 2007; Orr *et al.*, 2013).

These two types of systems complement each other (Pettersson, 2004). The weakness of cooperative systems is that they rely on vessels to truthfully report information. Vessels may misreport their locations or identities in order to hide their intentions, or they may not report them at all. There may also be errors or gaps in their transmissions even if they have no bad intentions. Non-cooperative systems can counterbalance this weakness by detecting and tracking vessels that have chosen not to self-report. However, many non-cooperative systems only provide vessel detection and do not provide an identity or vessel type. Thus, after a non-cooperative target has been detected it still needs to be characterized or identified. Data fusion algorithms are used to fuse the information provided by these different sensors into a single track for each ship. These tracks are used by vessels and vessel traffic services (VTS) on shore to facilitate navigation decisions and warn about possible collisions. Vessel traffic services also take advantage of their higher computing and networking resources to store data locally, share them at national and worldwide levels (e.g. the SafeSeaNet program of the European Maritime Safety Agency), and process them to extract meaningful knowledge about traffic patterns.

Cooperative tracking systems

Automatic identification system (AIS)

The automatic identification system was implemented in the early 2000s and made mandatory on commercial and passenger ships (IALA, 2004). It was originally introduced as a safety measure for collision avoidance (IMO, 1998). It allows vessels to detect and identify other vessels in their vicinity and to easily coordinate movements to avoid unsafe situations. It automatically broadcasts location-based information through self-organized wireless communications (VHF). AIS usually integrates a transceiver system, a GPS receiver, and other navigational sensors on board, such as a gyrocompass and a rate of turn indicator. An AIS transponder runs in an autonomous and continuous mode. It regularly broadcasts a position report according to the ship's cinematic (Table 11.1). The information is broadcast within a range of 35 nautical miles to surrounding ships and maritime authorities on the ground. The AIS signal can also be received by satellite. There are two different classes of AIS on ships, search and rescue aircraft, and ground base stations: mandatory AIS (class A) for large vessels, and low-cost AIS (class B) for smaller vessels. Devices from these two classes broadcast information at different time intervals (Table 11.1), and at different ranges (typically 20–40 miles for class A and 5–10 miles for class B).

Authorities soon discovered they could use AIS to monitor vessel traffic for security and law enforcement purposes. Many countries have set up AIS receiver base stations on their maritime borders, especially in dense maritime traffic areas such as ports and choke points. However, in remote and underdeveloped areas (polar zones, open ocean), installers encountered the twin challenges of getting power to the installation and the data out of it. Satellite AIS (S-AIS) is able to collect AIS signals in remote areas and forward the data to ground base stations.

One important drawback of the AIS system is that the AIS signal is not encrypted. Anybody having an AIS receiver can collect the data broadcast in the coverage area. The data collected are then considered to be "public" information even if they are controversial. The IMO recognized that there might be dangers associated with freely available real-time AIS data on the Internet. Private organizations and companies got into the business of installing ground-based or satellite AIS receivers and built worldwide networks to collect, distribute, and

Table 11.1 AIS shipborne mobile equipment reporting intervals

Ship's dynamic conditions – AIS Class A	Update frequency
Ship at anchor or moored and not moving faster than 3 knots	3 m
Ship at anchor or moored and moving faster than 3 knots	10 s
Speed between 0 and 14 knots	10 s
Speed between 0 and 14 knots and changing course	3.33 s
Speed between 14 and 23 knots	6 s
Speed between 14 and 23 knots and changing course	2 s
Speed over 23 knots	2 s
Speed over 23 knots and changing course	2 s
Ship's dynamic conditions – AIS Class B	Update frequency
Speed below 2 knots	3 m
Speed between 2 and 14 knots	30 s
Speed between 14 and 23 knots	15 s
Speed over 23 knots	5 s
Other equipments	Update frequency
Search and rescue aircraft	10 s
Aids to navigation	3 m
AIS base station	10 s

sell the data. The most recent innovation came with the collection of AIS signals from satellites. In the mid-2000s public and private organizations realized that they could collect AIS signals using receivers on satellites and that this would be a valuable source of data on maritime traffic in the open ocean. Within a few years there were a number of government and commercial sources of this data.

Satellite-collected AIS provides great benefits. Because terrestrial systems are line of sight, countries can potentially monitor their territorial waters. However, in most cases terrestrial systems will not cover the far reaches of their exclusive economic zone (EEZ). Satellite AIS provides countries a view of vessel activity within their EEZ. Terrestrial and satellite systems complemented each other. Terrestrial systems provided frequent updates of vessels in their areas. Satellites are limited by their orbits. On the equator, for example, a single satellite in a polar orbit may have two collection windows per day for any given area. While initially this was a significant limitation, the number of satellites with AIS receivers has increased, and thus the collection periodicity has decreased, though not to the extent of terrestrial systems.

Long-range identification and tracking (LRIT)

The long-range identification and tracking (LRIT) is another international mandatory cooperative tracking system, and its carriage requirements are similar to those of AIS. Unlike the AIS system whose role is mostly related to safety, the LRIT was created specifically for security purposes. LRIT allows nations to track vessels that inbound to their ports or are in transit in their vicinity (within 1,000 nm). Vessels are required to report their locations to their flag states (or their representatives) every six hours. The transmission of the ship location is done using a point-to-point satellite communication, which is a more secure communication system, as the data is not broadcast on the VHF. However, it generates satellite communication costs for the shipowner. Once collected by the flag states' data centres, the data is distributed to all those who are entitled to it. LRIT data is not broadcast "publicly" like AIS. Thus there is generally more control over who within a government is allowed to receive it. Piracy is a good example of the use of the two systems. In a piracy area, ships which turned off their AIS broadcasts keep reporting their LRIT information. The flag states are encouraged to provide this LRIT information to counter-piracy forces. There is more control over vessels' self-reported LRIT data because it is reported directly to the flag state. If a vessel stops reporting LRIT data during a voyage, it would be noticed. In contrast, changing an AIS broadcast is very simple and no one is necessarily doing any quality control on the transmitted data. This is why the LRIT system is still complementary to the AIS, even if the recent increase of satellite AIS coverage can now be used to track ships worldwide (Chen, 2013).

Vessel monitoring system (VMS)

Another cooperative system is the vessel monitoring system (VMS), which is implemented by some nations to monitor fishing activities in their waters. The fishing authorities can monitor fishing vessels and ensure that they comply with their licenses. The use of VMS data is restricted to the analysis of fishing activities. It cannot be used for general security or law enforcement purposes.

Non-cooperative systems

Despite the ubiquity and ease of collecting AIS data, non-cooperative vessel detection and tracking systems are still vital to monitor maritime traffic. Non-cooperative detection systems such as visual observations and radar provide the ability to detect and track vessels that do not broadcast their positions. However, they generally require more effort to characterize and identify a target.

The most common non-cooperative detection and tracking systems are radar, radar imaging, and visual observations. These systems may be set up in vessels, shore stations, aircraft, drones, or satellites. Many important locations such as ports and vessel traffic corridors are monitored by an integrated AIS and coastal radar system. This provides operators with a persistent, fused, real-time display of AIS and radar tracks.

Radio detection and ranging (RADAR)

Marine radar with automatic radar plotting aid (ARPA) tracks vessels using radar contacts. Radar transmitters generate very short pulses of radio waves. When the radio waves encounter an obstacle (such as a ship, shoreline, or big waves), part of the radiated energy is reflected and received by the emitting radar. The reflected pulse generates an echo. The time between the pulse and the echo can be measured and used to compute the distance between the radar emitter and the echo. The direction of the echo reflects the direction of the pulse. Thanks to the relative motion of the echo, the target's course and speed can be computed.

However, the radar horizon is limited by the line of sight, and thus it cannot provide long-range monitoring. The maximum range of an object detected is affected by the height of the radar antenna as well as the height of the target object due to the curvature of the Earth. Coastlines or islands can also cause blind areas which prevent target objects from being detected. Bad weather conditions can also significantly affect the effectiveness of radar tracking. ARPA systems keep track of the echoes and fuse them onto a track with an identifier and coordinates if the echo is confirmed over time (Wall *et al.*, 2005). Maritime patrol aircraft can extend this horizon and collect AIS, radar, and visual observations. However, these sensors are not persistent and they can monitor only a limited range.

Commercial radar imaging satellites are a relatively new and powerful tool for detecting ships beyond the shore-based radar and AIS horizon and without using maritime patrol aircraft. Several commercial companies are in this market. They provide raw imagery or value-added products such as ship detection reports. If available, AIS position reports can also be correlated with radar detections. Generally radar ship detections must be correlated with other data, typically AIS, to identify targets. If other data feeds are not available due to missing equipment like an AIS receiver or antenna, it becomes very difficult or impossible to characterize or identify a target.

Synthetic aperture radar (SAR) satellites can capture scenes at any time of day and are not affected by cloudy weather. Different technical parameters such as the width of swath, the angle of incidence, spatial resolution, and polarization can influence the ship detection capacity. The state of the sea must also be taken into account to be able to differentiate a big wave from a vessel. Narrow swaths are useful to monitor small areas such as coasts or ports, while wide swaths are mostly used on the open sea.

The ability to monitor a given region of ocean is highly related to the satellite's orbits. Most radar imaging satellites use sun-synchronous orbiting. This means that the satellite will cover the equatorial region twice a day (sunrise and sunset). Radar satellites are unable to provide information outside those time windows. Moreover, once collected, the data needs to be sent back to ground stations and processed to detect ships. Satellites must store the data until they orbit to a suitable downlink. Due to all these constraints, delivery and processing of the data can take several hours. The time depends on the number of satellites and ground stations available. However, satellite images bring an added value to the existing systems in terms of spatial cover (it can target either wide or small areas).

Optical sensors

Ships can also be tracked using optical sensors. These range from a traffic monitoring operator who screens the sea using goggles to automated video cameras or satellite pictures. The pictures produced by optical sensors help in the identification of ships. However, optical sensors are limited by weather conditions.

Data distribution networks

As detailed above, many different sensors can be used to detect ship movements. These sensors have different strengths and weaknesses (spatial and temporal resolution, attributes availability, cooperative versus non-cooperative). All these sensors generate a huge amount of data which depend on local country monitoring systems and often focus on the country's EEZ. However, as ships are navigating worldwide, they go from one surveillance zone to another. When shared, these data can be used to create a global maritime situation picture and to trace a complete transit history for each vessel. Thanks to the growth of electronic networks capability, governments, academic organizations, and companies have created maritime data distribution networks.

Many governments would like to share information with their immediate neighbours. Several regional AIS sharing networks exist throughout the world. Flag states also have some interest in vessels carrying their flag regardless of where they are on the ocean. Participation in a global network also provides a country with information on these vessels even if it is a great distance from the flag state. Having worldwide coverage is also important for investigating the full path of ships (shores, visited ports, point of departure).

The Maritime Safety and Security Information System (MSSIS) is one of the largest government-to-government networks for sharing AIS data. Each nation that contributes information to the network is entitled to receive all of the shared information in this network. The MSSIS network comprises 60 to 70 countries all over the world providing data to the network. Governments are free to use the data they receive from MSSIS for any safety and security purpose. MSSIS provides the raw AIS messages, and recipients can process and display them freely. This network can be seen as an aggregated worldwide sensor which can be integrated into maritime surveillance systems.

Business and academic institutions created their own AIS collection and distribution networks. The website Marinetraffic.com is an example of an academic, open, crowd-sourced, community-based project. It relies on AIS data provided by academic institutions and individuals that set up AIS receivers and forward their data to this worldwide shared network. In addition to AIS, contributors can also upload photos of vessels. Some companies (AISLive.com, vesseltracker.com) also sell AIS and other maritime data over the Internet.

> Currently, the C-SIGMA initiative on international cooperation for global maritime awareness is exploring ways how users and providers of space-based maritime surveillance data may work together to increase the joint awareness of the global maritime domain, by facilitating the sharing of, and access to, satellite data.
>
> Greidanus *et al.* (2012)

From position reports to worldwide maritime trajectories

Once the position data are collected by sensors, they can be fused into different tracks. Modelling how position reports can be fused is an interesting research problem (Hägerstrand, 1970). Classical trajectory models rely on the definition of stops to split a sequence of positions reports into different trajectories (Hornsby and Egenhofer, 2002; Thériault *et al.*, 2002). Stops are usually defined as a function of time and distance between two consecutive position reports. However, as explained above, the AIS position report frequency depends on the ship cinematic (Table 11.1). In this maritime case study based on AIS position reports, real ship stops need to be differentiated from a communication loss or VHF transmission disturbance. AIS position report frequency is higher when the ship is moving fast or manoeuvring. This higher frequency allows a better representation of the ship trajectory. However, this transmission mode affects the trajectory model and the data quantity and quality that can be stored in movement databases.

Trajectory generation process

In order to analyze ship behaviour, it is important to focus on trajectory (Laube *et al.*, 2007; Spaccapietra *et al.*, 2008). As soon as a new AIS position report is collected by the system, this position must be integrated into a ship trajectory. If the system has multiple sensors, position reports can be collected at different time scales (online or offline, with time delays due to satellite orbits, etc.). This will induce position reports that are not always ordered in time. In the following section of this chapter, we focus on a trajectory generation process that can cope with a discontinuous, unordered flow of AIS position reports. Figure 11.2 illustrates the different steps of this process.

For each new AIS frame, the trajectory generation process first parse the AIS frame to extract important features such as the ship identifier (id), the timestamp (t), its location (x, y), heading (c), and speed (v) (Figure 11.2 step 1). A position is thereafter presented as a tuple $p(id, t, x, y, c, v)$. Thanks to this information, the process searches for a set of possible matching positions (εpc) already in the database using a spatio-temporal windows query (Figure 11.2 step 2). This spatio-temporal search window is illustrated in Figure 11.4 by a grey dashed square around the position p (strip point with an arrow indicating the heading). Matching positions are illustrated by grey circles with arrows indicating their headings. All the matching positions of the set (εpc) are spatially ($\pm \Delta s$) and temporally ($\pm \Delta t$) close to the position p. These matching positions have previously been individually matched to trajectories. Δs and Δt parameters rely highly on the frequency of AIS position reports. The wider the spatio-temporal window, the bigger the set of matching positions will be. This will also have a direct impact on the database query speed. If the search window is too small, there might be no matching position, and the new position p would not be integrated into an existing trajectory. Parameters Δs and Δt can be defined using the AIS frequency rate (Table 11.1) multiplied by a maximum number of allowed missed frames.

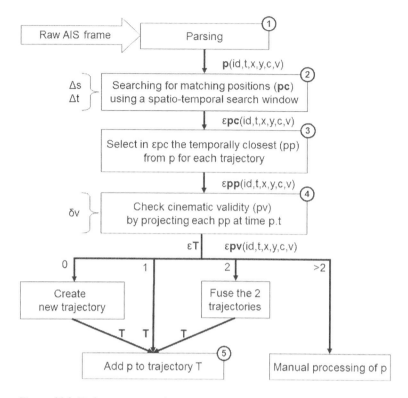

Figure 11.2 Trajectory generation process.

Once the matching position set (εpc) is queried, the next step of the trajectory generation process consists in selecting within the matching positions the temporally closest one for each trajectory (Figure 11.2 step 3). The positions of the temporally closest matching position subset (εpp) are framed with a black square in Figure 11.4.

For each position of the εpp subset, a cinematic validity check is done by extrapolating the position at the timestamp of p (Figure 11.2 step 4). The extrapolated positions (εpe) are illustrated using black points in Figure 11.3b and Figure 11.4. The extrapolated positions are computed using the pp location (x, y), timestamp (t), speed (v), and heading (c). To be considered as valid, an extrapolated position must be within a spatial distance threshold (δv) from p (grey circle around p on Figure 11.4). The subset of valid positions (εpv) is finally used to select the matching trajectories (εT) where p can be inserted. In small areas, the ship identifier (MMSI number) can also ease the matching process. However, in wide areas monitored by satellites, duplicate ship identifiers have been detected. Sometimes communications errors can generate erroneous GPS locations. Without a cinematic validity check, adding the erroneous positions or duplicated identifiers

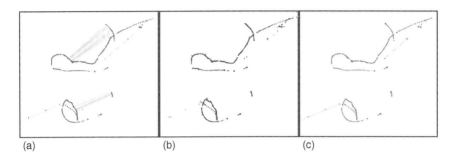

(a)   (b)   (c)

Figure 11.3 Results of the trajectory generation process.

to one single trajectory can create wrong segments, as displayed in Figure 11.3a. Extrapolated positions whose distances are below the validity threshold δv correspond to black points in Figure 11.3b. The final trajectories computed by the process are displayed in Figure 11.3c.

The trajectory generation process relies on the AIS position reports' speed and heading to interpolate positions. It can differentiate two different trajectories of ships using the same identifier. However, if two ships are navigating spatio-temporally very close to each other and are following the same path, depending on the number of matching trajectories in εT, four different scenarios can occur (Table 11.2).

Within these four scenarios, sub-cases can be defined depending on the cinematic validity check (Table 11.3).

When no existing trajectory exists (C0), a new one needs to be created. Once created, the position p is added to this new trajectory. If there is only one matching trajectory T (C1) the position p is added to that trajectory. In case there are two matching trajectories (C2), it means that the position p is likely to be a position in-between the two trajectories which can then be fused into one single trajectory. The process will add position p to the trajectory T_1 and then move all the positions from T_2 to T_1 before deleting T_2. Finally, if more than two trajectories can be matched to position p, this position is flagged to be manually investigated (C3). This case is very unlikely, as it would mean that the two ships were using similar identifiers and were navigating very close to each other. These different scenarios are illustrated in Figure 11.4. One important advantage of this technique is its ability to integrate unordered sets of AIS position reports with uneven frequency rates and duplicated ship identifiers (or even unknown identifiers).

Maritime case study

The trajectory generation process has been applied to a test case of 112,266 AIS ship positions located in the Strait of Gibraltar during a full day (2012-04-01). Only positions of moving ships have been processed (73,767). The trajectory generation process has been applied twice on this dataset (timely and randomly ordered).

Table 11.2 Different scenarios of position-to-trajectory matching

Scenario	Description	εT
C0	No matching trajectory found	$\{\}$
C1	Only one trajectory matching	$\{T1\}$
C2	Two trajectory matching	$\{T1,T2\}$
C3	More than 2 trajectories matching	$\{T1, T2, \ldots, Tn\}$

Table 11.3 Scenarios that can occur when matching extrapolated position to a trajectory

Scenario	Description	εpp	εpv	εT
C00	No matching trajectory found	$\{\}$	$\{\}$	$\{\}$
C10	There exist one matching position but not valid when extrapolated	$\{pp1\}$	$\{\}$	$\{\}$
C11	Only one trajectory matching	$\{pp1\}$	$\{pv1\}$	$\{T1\}$
C20	There exist many matching positions but none of them are valid when extrapolated	$\{pp1,\ldots,ppn\}$	$\{\}$	$\{\}$
C21	There exist many matching positions and one of them is valid when extrapolated	$\{pp1,\ldots,ppn\}$	$\{pv1\}$	$\{T1\}$
C22	There exist many matching positions and two of them are valid when extrapolated	$\{pp1,\ldots,ppn\}$	$\{pv1,pv2\}$	$\{T1,T2\}$
C23	There exist many matching positions and more than two of them are valid when extrapolated	$\{pp1,\ldots,ppn\}$	$\{pv1,pv2,\ldots,pvn\}$	$\{T1, T2, \ldots, Tn\}$

Figure 11.5 illustrates the results of the trajectory generation process on the time ordered dataset. Starting positions of the trajectories are displayed as squares and ending positions as stars. Grey dots correspond to the positions added to existing trajectories. Some of these dots can have more than two matching trajectories and cannot be automatically integrated into one single trajectory (C23). Light grey lines segments represent the generated trajectories.

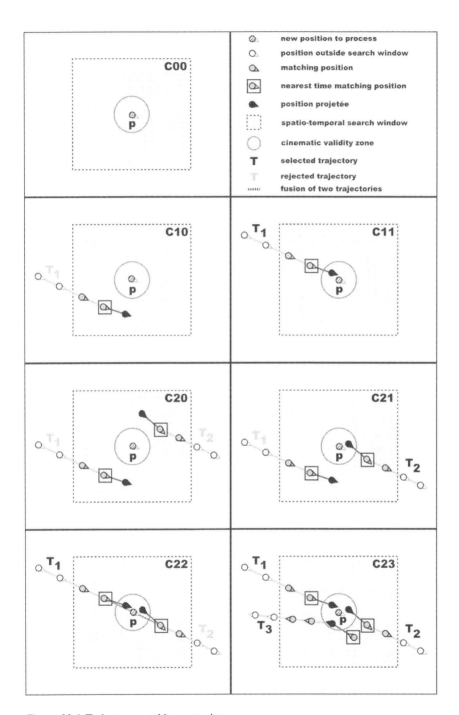

Figure 11.4 Trajectory matching scenarios.

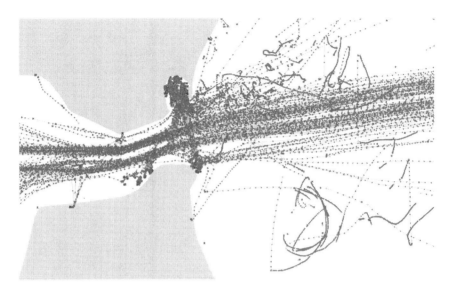

Figure 11.5 Results of the trajectory generation process.

Table 11.4 Trajectory to position matching scenario statistics on test case

Scenario	Description	Time ordered dataset		Randomly ordered dataset	
		Count	*Ratio (%)*	*Count*	*Ratio (%)*
C00	Starting position	3,625	4.91	9,904	13.42
C10	Cinematic filtered position	1,680	2.28	2,199	2.98
C11	One trajectory matching	61,079	82.77	45,454	61.59
C20	Cinematic filtered positions	1,245	1.69	1,576	2.14
C21	One trajectory matching	5,947	8.06	7,581	10.27
C22	Two trajectory matching	216	0.29	7,039	9.54
C23	More than two trajectory matching	5	0.01	44	0.06
All		73,797	100.0	73,797	100.0

A statistical analysis of the different scenarios met by the trajectory generation process is presented in Table 11.4. For the time ordered dataset, 4,182 trajectories were created and 670 of them were fused. The dataset has been processed at a speed of 265 positions per second (using an Intel Core I3 [4 cores 2.13 GHz] PC with 4Go RAM). Regarding the randomly ordered dataset, 4,309 trajectories were created and 1,045 of them were fused. The dataset has been processed at a speed of 293 positions per second.

An analysis of Table 11.4 shows that, most of the time, only one matching trajectory is selected by the process. When the dataset is not ordered, many parts

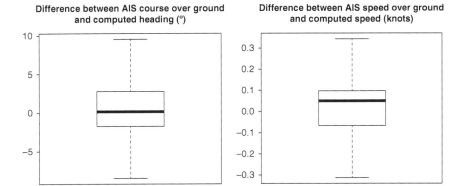

Figure 11.6 Boxplots of differences between the computed and AIS speeds and headings.

of trajectories are created and then fused together. This situation generates more starting positions (C00) and fused trajectories (C22). It is also interesting to note that the unordered dataset was processed faster than the time-ordered one. This can be explained by the important number of C00 cases which are simpler to process, as there is no position to extrapolate. The problematic scenario C23 has a ratio below 0.1 percent. This process is robust and can deal with unordered datasets. It can be parallelized to improve its processing time.

Normally every AIS transceiver should have its own unique identification number (MMSI). However, in this case study, we detected different vessels using the same identifier. This problem can be solved using the cinematic information to extrapolate existing trajectories. One major drawback of this algorithm is that it relies on the position, speed, and heading given by the AIS position report itself. As for the unique identifier, this cinematic information could be fake or erroneous. Once the trajectories are computed, the speed and heading of ships can be computed in order to compare them to the AIS data. Figure 11.6 presents the box plots of differences between the computed and AIS speeds and headings.

The statistical analysis shows that the heading and speed given by the AIS is very close to the computed one using the trajectories. This means that this information is reliable enough to be used to extrapolate ship positions in the trajectory generation process.

From trajectories to maritime traffic patterns

Thanks to the different sensors that monitor ships all over the world, a big shipping movement database can be created. The real-time positions can be directly visualized on traffic monitoring operator screens. They can also be stored in databases in order to extract meaningful information about worldwide maritime traffic patterns. This data-mining operation (Piatetsky-Shapiro and Frawley, 1991) is done

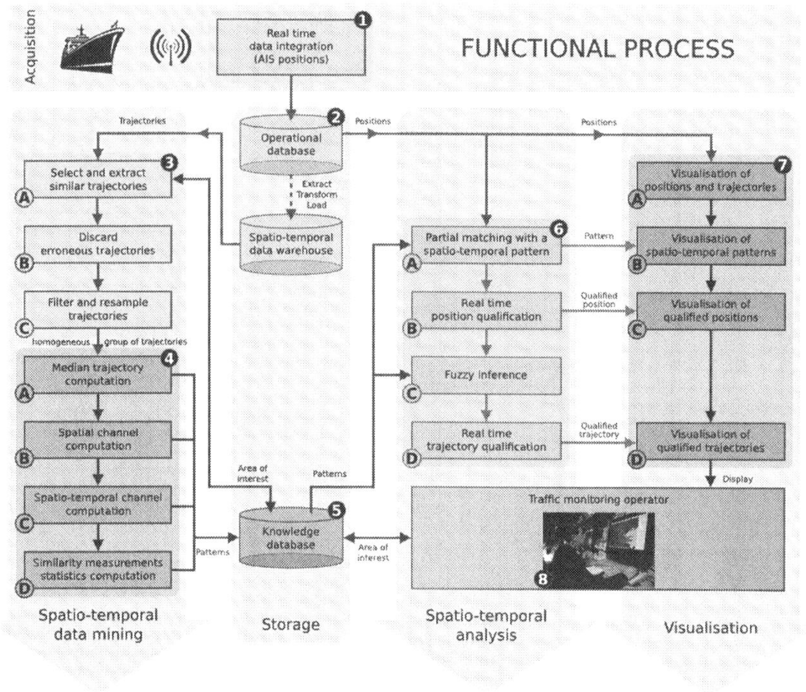

Figure 11.7 Global maritime traffic analysis and monitoring process.

offline. Figure 11.7 shows the different steps required to mine a maritime traffic database and to use the patterns to classify ship movements and detect outliers.

The first step consists in acquiring ship positions using various sensors (Figure 11.7, 1). These positions can be stored into a spatio-temporal data warehouse (Figure 11.7, 2) and fused into trajectories using the trajectory generation process presented earlier. The resulting trajectories need to be filtered in order to be processed. Erroneous positions can be detected by the trajectory generation process thanks to the cinematic check. A spatio-temporal Douglas–Peucker filter can then be applied to reduce the number of positions required to represent the ship trajectory (Bertrand *et al.*, 2007).

These trajectories are then clustered together (Figure 11.7, 3) depending on their path (same starting and ending location). Spatio-temporal clustering is a process that groups objects based on their spatial and temporal similarity (Kisilevich *et al.*, 2010), which results in a collection of homogeneous groups characterized by one or more salient properties (Renso *et al.*, 2013). Several patterns have been defined to describe commonalities seen in clusters of trajectories following the same itineraries (or routes). Spatio-temporal sequential patterns (Cao *et al.*, 2005), T-pattern (Giannotti *et al.*, 2007), and partition and group patterns (Lee *et al.*, 2007) are well-known.

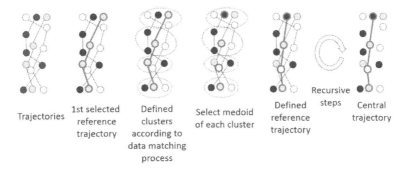

Figure 11.8 Central trajectory computation.

The trajectory cluster can then be synthetized into a pattern that depicts the spatial and temporal variations of the cluster (Figure 11.7, 4) (Etienne *et al.*, 2012, 2014). The results of this offline data-mining process are stored into a knowledge database (Figure 11.7, 5). This knowledge database is useful for classifying ship movements and comparing them to known patterns (Figure 11.7, 6). Once classified, patterns can be used to detect outliers (Vespe *et al.*, 2012) and highlight abnormal ship behaviour to traffic monitoring operators (Figure 11.7, 7).

The pattern computation process (Figure 11.7 step 4) is done offline and can be recomputed on a regular basis to improve the patterns and reflect the change in the maritime traffic. This process (detailed in Etienne *et al.*, 2014) consists in matching all the trajectories of a cluster to a central trajectory (Petitjean *et al.*, 2011). This central trajectory is iteratively created using the ordered clusters of positions to compute a set of medoïd positions (Figure 11.8). The central trajectory corresponds to an extension of the median concept to trajectory cluster. Figure 11.9 shows a cluster of 506 passenger ship trajectories (grey lines) following the same itinerary (Etienne *et al.*, 2010) and the computed median trajectory (white line).

Once the central trajectory is computed, the spatial and temporal dispersion around the median trajectory can be computed. Etienne *et al.* (2014) proposed an extension of the box plot concept to trajectory clusters (trajectory box plot). The spatial and temporal dispersion is visualized in 3D using boxes to define the interquartile range (inner 3D grey box) and the whiskers (outer 3D black box). The time dimension is projected on the z axis. The trajectory box plot of the 506 passenger ships example cluster is presented in Figure 11.10.

As this process relies on statistical computation, the more data available in the historical database, the more precise the pattern is. The computed patterns can be either usual behaviour of normal vessels (base pattern) or the behaviour of vessels known to have illegal or unusual activities (suspicious pattern). These patterns and expert knowledge (rules) are very useful for qualifying the huge real-time position data feed from various sources. Efficient comparison metrics needs to be defined to be able to compare and match the real-time positions and tracks to experts' rules or patterns in order to detect suspicious behaviour (Figure 11.7 step 6).

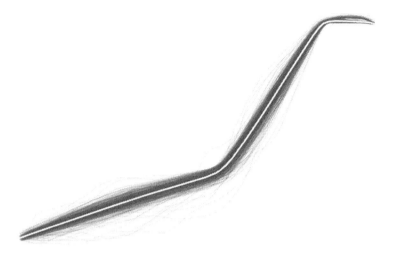

Figure 11.9 A cluster of 506 passenger ship trajectories and its median trajectory.

Figure 11.10 Trajectory box plot of the 506 passenger ship trajectory cluster.

The global maritime situation picture is computed with all the raw and qualified data. This picture is displayed and shared with maritime traffic monitoring operators who can focus their attention on vessel paths that have been qualified as suspicious by the system (Figure 11.7 step 7). As the user is also part of the data qualification process, he can detect abnormal behaviour that is not yet automatically detected and classified by the system. Moreover, the system itself can generate false detections. This is why it is important to integrate the traffic monitoring operator feedback into the system in order to improve the qualification process by creating new rules/patterns or giving different weight to the patterns/rules depending on their effectiveness.

Beyond simple awareness of which vessels are in an area of interest, the data can be analyzed to detect suspicious characteristics or behaviour. Due to the ever-increasing amount of available sensors and worldwide coverage data streams, it is now mandatory to use intelligent systems to ease traffic monitoring operators' work and lower their cognitive load. The goal is to find a manageable subset of vessels for more detailed investigation from the larger universe of vessels operating in the ocean. The worldwide data feed is enormous, and ships performing illegal activities try to hide in this flow.

Conclusion

Thanks to the advances in ship tracking systems, and especially with the emergence of satellite monitoring ships can now be continuously tracked worldwide. However, the various types of sensors give different information at different time frequencies. This raises numerous problems related to data fusion. In this chapter, we presented a trajectory generation algorithm that can fuse position reports from the automatic identification system into trajectories. This algorithm is robust for erroneous position reports and can deal with uneven report rates and integrate old or past datasets to enhance trajectory resolution. A statistical analysis of the AIS position reports' cinematic parameters (speed and heading) compared to the computed speed and heading of the trajectories highlight the reliability of these parameters.

All these sensors used to track ships generate enormous data feeds that can be stored and mined. Research on maritime networks using a graph network often does not really take into account the navigation path used by ships between nodes (ports) of the graph. In this chapter, a full trajectory analysis process has been presented. This process relies on clustering techniques to group similar trajectories (Etienne *et al.*, 2014). Once grouped, a pattern synthesizing the spatial and temporal behaviour of the trajectory cluster is computed. These patterns are useful for better understanding the ship's spatial and temporal behaviour between ports. They can be used to detect abnormal behaviour and alert traffic monitoring operators, who can focus their attention on a smaller subset of ships. Analysis of the statistical parameters of the spatial and temporal distributions along the pattern can also yield interesting knowledge about the quality of the clustering process. This information could be used to detect specific locations where traffic lanes split or merge. These locations could then be integrated into a graph-based model to better understand maritime network flows.

References

Bertrand F., Bouju A., Claramunt C., Devogele T., Ray C. (2007) Web architecture for monitoring and visualizing mobile objects in maritime contexts. In: *Web and Wireless Geographical Information Systems*. Heidelberg: Springer Berlin, pp. 94–105.

Cao H., Mamoulis N., Cheung D.W. (2005) Mining frequent spatio-temporal sequential patterns. *Proceedings of the Fifth IEEE International Conference on Data Mining*. IEEE Computer Society, pp. 82–9.

Chen Y. (2013) Will satellite-based AIS supersede LRIT? In: Weintrit, A. (Ed.) *Marine Navigation and Safety of Sea Transportation: Advances in Marine Navigation*, Florida: CRC Press, pp. 91–4.

Ducruet C. (2013) Network diversity and maritime flows. *Journal of Transport Geography*, 30: 77–88.

Etienne L., Devogele T., Bouju A. (2010) Spatio-temporal trajectory analysis of mobile objects following the same itinerary. In: *Proceedings of the International Symposium on Spatial Data Handling (SDH)*, 86–91.

Etienne L., Devogele T., Bouju A., (2012) Modeling space and time: spatio-temporal trajectory analysis of mobile objects following the same itinerary. In: Wenzhong Shi et al. (Eds) *Advances in Geo-Spatial Information Science*, London: Taylor and Francis, pp. 47–58.

Etienne L., Devogele T., McArdle G. (2014) State of the art in patterns for point cluster analysis. *14th International Conference on Computational Science and its Applications*, Dordrecht: Springer, pp. 252–66.

Giannotti F., Nanni M., Pinelli F., Pedreschi D. (2007) Trajectory pattern mining. *Proceedings of the 13th ACM SIGKDD international conference on Knowledge discovery and data mining*, ACM, pp. 330–9.

Greidanus H. (2007) *Detection, Classification and Identification of Marine Traffic from Space Final Report*. DECLIMS, Joint Research Centre, Ispra, Italy.

Greidanus H., Thomas G., Campbell G., Bryan K. (2012) *International Cooperation For Space-Based Global Maritime Awareness: The Next Step*. ESA, SEASAR Conference, Tromsø, Norway.

Hägerstrand T. (1970) What about people in regional science? *Papers in Regional Science*, 24(1): 6–21.

Hornsby K., Egenhofer M.J. (2002) Modeling moving objects over multiple granularities. *Annals of Mathematics and Artificial Intelligence*, 36(1): 177–94.

IALA (2004) International Association of Marine Aids to Navigation and Lighthouse Authorities *IALA Guideline No. 1028 On The Automatic Identification System (AIS)*, Volume 1, Part I.

International Maritime Organization (1972) *International Regulations for Preventing Collisions at Sea (COLREG)*.

International Maritime Organization (1974) *International Convention for the Safety of Life at Sea (SOLAS)*.

International Maritime Organization (1998) *Resolution MSC.74(69) Annex 3, Recommendation on performance standards for AIS*.

Kaluza P., Kölzsch A., Gastner M.T., Blasius, B. (2010) The complex network of global cargo ship movements. *Journal of the Royal Society Interface*, 7(48): 1093–103.

Kisilevich S., Mansmann F., Nanni M., Rinzivillo S. (2010) Spatio-temporal clustering. *Data Mining and Knowledge Discovery Handbook*, pp. 855–74.

Laube P., Dennis T., Forer T., Walker M. (2007) Movement beyond the snapshot: dynamic analysis of geospatial lifelines. *Computers, Environment and Urban Systems*, 31(5): 481–501.

Lee J.G., Han J., Whang K.Y. (2007) Trajectory clustering: a partition-and-group framework. In: *Proceedings of the 2007 ACM SIGMOD International Conference on Management of Data*. ACM, pp. 593–604.

Orr N.G., Cain J., Stras L., Zee R.E. (2013) Space based AIS detection with the maritime monitoring and messaging microsatellite. 64th International Astronautical Congress.

Petitjean F., Ketterlin A., Ganarski P. (2011) A global averaging method for dynamic time warping, with applications to clustering. *Pattern Recognition*, 44(3): 678–93.

Pettersson B. (2004) *Automatic Identification System*. Technical Report, Swedish Maritime Administration.

Piatetsky-Shapiro G., Frawley W.J. (1991) *Knowledge Discovery in Databases*. Cambridge MA and London: AAAI Press & MIT Press.

Renso C., Spaccapietra S., Zimanyi E. (2013) *Mobility Data*. Cambridge: Cambridge University Press.

Spaccapietra S., Parent C., Damiani M.L., de Macedo J.A., Porto F., Vangenot C. (2008) A conceptual view on trajectories. *Data and Knowledge Engineering*, 65(1): 126–46.

Thériault M., Claramunt C., Séguin A.M., Villeneuve P. (2002) Temporal GIS and Statistical Modelling of Personal Lifelines: Advances in Spatial Data Handling, *10th International Symposium on Spatial Data Handling*, Springer Verlag, pp. 433–49.

Vespe M., Visentini I., Bryan K., Braca P. (2012) Unsupervised learning of maritime traffic patterns for anomaly detection. *Data Fusion and Target Tracking Conference: Algorithms & Applications*, 9th IET, pp. 1–5.

Wall A., Bole A.G., Dineley W.O. (2005) *Radar and ARPA Manual: Radar and Target Tracking for Professional Mariners, Yachtsmen And Users Of Marine Radar*. Oxford: Elsevier.

12 Cluster identification in maritime flows with stochastic methods

Charles Bouveyron, Pierre Latouche,
Rawya Zreik, César Ducruet

Since the original work of Moreno (1934), network data has become ubiquitous in computational social sciences (Snijders and Nowicki, 1997). Applications range from the study of social interactions in historical sciences (Jernite *et al.*, 2014; Villa *et al.*, 2008) to the analysis of maritime flows in geography (Ducruet, 2013). In particular, network analysis was applied recently to a medieval social network in Jernite *et al.* (2014), where the authors consider the clustering of an ecclesiastical network in Merovingian Gaul. Cluster analysis in the network context consists in grouping vertices sharing homogeneous connection profiles.

Both deterministic and probabilistic methods have been used to seek structure in these networks, depending on prior knowledge and assumptions on the form of the data. For example, Hofman and Wiggins (2008) look for specific structures called communities where nodes of the same community are preferentially connected. The alternative strategy of Handcock *et al.* (2007), which is a generalization of Hoff *et al.* (2002), assumes the relations to be conditioned on the projection of the vertices in a social latent space. Another popular method among the community discovery approaches is based on the modularity score of Girvan and Newman (2002), though asymptotically biased (Bickel and Chen, 2009).

Most of the currently used methods derive from the stochastic block model (SBM) (Wang and Wong, 1987; Nowicki and Snijders, 2001). The SBM model assumes that each vertex belongs to a hidden cluster and that connection probabilities between pairs of vertices depend exclusively on their unobserved clusters, as in Frank and Harary (1982). In order to perform inference, standard approaches cannot be used in practice. In particular, the expectation maximization (EM) algorithm (Dempster *et al.*, 1977) cannot be derived because the conditional distribution of the latent groups is intractable. To overcome this issue, variational and stochastic approximations are often used. Thus, Latouche *et al.* (2011) used an approximation of the marginal log-likelihood, while Daudin *et al.* (2008) considered a Laplace approximation of the integrated classification log-likelihood. A non-parametric Bayesian approach was also proposed by Kemp *et al.* (2006) for estimating the number of groups while clustering the vertices.

Extensions of SBM include the mixed membership stochastic block model (MMSBM) (Airoldi *et al.*, 2008) and the overlapping stochastic block model (OSBM) (Latouche *et al.*, 2011). They both allow a vertex to belong to multiple clusters at the same time. More recent work focused on extending random graph models to dynamic networks (Sarkar and Moore, 2005; Xing *et al.*, 2010; Yang *et al.*, 2011; Dubois *et al.*, 2013; Heaukulani and Ghahramani, 2013; Xu and Hero III, 2013), or dealing with non-binary networks such as those with weighted edges (Mariadassou *et al.*, 2010; Soufiani and Airoldi, 2012). Some efforts were also made to take into account covariate information (Zanghi *et al.*, 2010). For instance, the random subgraph model (RSM) (Jernite *et al.*, 2014) was proposed to analyze directed networks with typed edges for which a partition of the vertices is available. For more details, we refer to Goldenberg *et al.* (2010); Salter-Townshend *et al.* (2012); and Matias and Robin (2014) who provided extensive reviews of statistical network models.

In this chapter, we aim to uncover clusters in a maritime flow network extracted from *Lloyd's List* where geographical information is available as well as the type of preferential commodities. The main goal of this research is to determine the possible influence of geography and cargo specialization on the emergence of clusters in a maritime network. On the one hand, a maritime network is a multilayered system (or multigraph, multiplex graph), as different fleet types have different logics of circulation that more or less overlap and connect via port nodes. On the other, it is also a multilevel system where global, regional, and local dynamics take place simultaneously to ensure maritime freight and passenger distribution. Such an approach complements the works of Kaluza *et al.* (2010) and Ducruet and Zaidi (2012), which used other clustering methods and analyzed the different fleets separately, without explicitly including the geographic factor in the partition. Previous works found a strong influence of geographic proximity but other possible logics remained hidden, except for hierarchical tendencies caused by hub-and-spokes configurations in container shipping. It can be hypothesized that the connections between ports are not only determined by geographic proximity but also depend on the intensity and type of circulation, but these elements need to be analyzed simultaneously.

The remainder of the chapter is organized as follows. The next section presents the probabilistic model of SBM and RSM. Inference and model selection are also briefly discussed. The data and experimental setup are given afterwards, followed by an experimental comparison of both methods on the Lloyd's dataset, highlighting the advantages of using such techniques.

Probabilistic models for network clustering

This section presents the stochastic block model and the random subgraph model. Inference and model selection are also briefly discussed.

Context and notations

We consider a directed graph G with N vertices represented by its $N \times N$ adjacency matrix X. Each edge X_{ij}, describing the relation between the vertices i and j, takes its values in a finite set $\{0, \dots, C\}$. Note that $X_{ij} = 0$ corresponds to

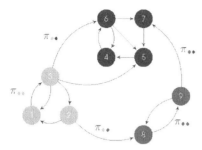

Figure 12.1 An example of an SBM network.

Note: The network is made of nine nodes split into three groups (indicated by the colors). According-ing to the SBM model, the directed edges between the nodes are assumed to be drawn from a Bernoulli distribution with probability πkl, where k, l are here colors.

the absence of an edge. We assume that G does not have any self-loop, and there-fore the entries X_{ii} will not be taken into account. In RSM, a partition P of the vertices into S classes is also assumed to be available. In both cases, our goal is to cluster the network into K groups with homogeneous connection profiles, i.e. estimating a binary matrix Z such that $Z_{ik} = 1$ if vertex i belongs to cluster k, 0 otherwise.

The stochastic block model

The SBM model (Figure 12.1) associates to each vertex of a network a latent variable Z_i drawn from a multinomial distribution:

$$\mathbf{Z}_i \sim \mathcal{M}(1, \alpha),$$

where α denotes the vector of class proportions. As in other standard mixture models, the vector Z_i sees all its components set to zero except one such that $Z_{ik} = 1$ if vertex i belongs to class q. The model then verifies:

$$\sum_{k=1}^{K} Z_{ik} = 1, \quad \forall i \in \{1, \ldots, N\}, \tag{12.1}$$

and

$$\sum_{k=1}^{K} \alpha_k = 1, \tag{12.2}$$

where K denotes the number of components (clusters) of the mixture. Finally, the edges of the network are drawn from a Bernoulli distribution:

$$X_{ij} \mid \{Z_{ik} Z_{jk} = 1\} \sim \mathcal{B}(\pi_{kl}),$$

where $\Pi = (\pi kl)kl$ is a $K \times K$ matrix of connection probabilities. According to this model, the latent variables $Z_1, \ldots, Z_N$ are *iid* and given this latent structure, all the edges are supposed to be independent. Note that SBM was originally described in a more general setting, allowing any discrete relational data. However, in the following we concentrate on binary edges only, i.e. $C = 1$.

Figure 12.1 presents an example of an SBM network made of nine nodes split into three groups (indicated by the colors). As one can see, on this specific example, the within-cluster connexion probabilities ($\pi_{\bullet\bullet}$, $\pi_{\bullet\bullet}$, and $\pi_{\bullet\bullet}$) seem to be rather large since the nodes of each group are well interconnected. Conversely, connections between nodes of different groups are less frequent, which is due to low values of the between-group connexion probabilities ($\pi_{\bullet\bullet}$, $\pi_{\bullet\bullet}$, ...). Such a matrix Π corresponds to networks made of communities, which are frequent in social networks, for instance. However, situations where between-group connexion probabilities are larger than within-group connexion probabilities are possible with the SBM model. This type of network is, for instance, very frequent in biology when studying networks of genes. Indeed, it is of interest in such a context to characterize, on the one hand, the regulatory genes and, on the other, the regulated genes. The Figure 12.2a presents the graphical model associated with SBM, and Table 12.1 summarizes the model notations.

The random subgraph model

We consider now the directed graph G with a known partition P of the vertices into S classes, where each edge X_{ij} is categorical, i.e. takes its values in a finite set $\{0, \ldots, C\}$. Contrary to SBM, RSM can deal with networks where $C > 1$. In order to simplify the notations when describing the model, we also consider the binary matrix A with entries A_{ij} such that $A_{i,j} = 1 \Longleftrightarrow X_{i,j}; = 0$. We also emphasize that the observed partition P induces a decomposition of the graph into subgraphs where each class of vertices corresponds to a specific subgraph. We introduce the variable s_i which takes its values in $\{1, \ldots, S\}$ and is used to indicate to which of the subgraphs vertex i belongs, for $i \in \{1, \ldots, N\}$.

The data is assumed to be generated in three steps. First, the presence of an edge from vertex i to vertex j is supposed to follow a Bernoulli distribution whose

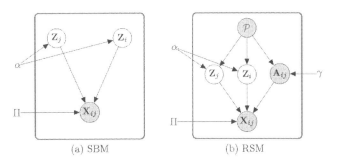

(a) SBM   (b) RSM

Figure 12.2 Graphical models of (a) SBM and (b) RSM (in their frequentist form).

Table 12.1 Summary of the notations used

Notations	Description
SBM & RSM	
X	Adjacency matrix. $X_{ij} \in \{0, 1\}$ (SBM) or $\{0, \ldots, C\}$ (RSM)
Z	Binary matrix. $Zik = 1$ indicates that i belongs to cluster k
N	Number of vertices in the network
K	Number of latent clusters
α	αk is the prior probability of cluster k
Π	πkl is the connexion probability between cluster k and □
RSM	
A	Binary matrix. $A_{ij} = 1$ indicates the presence of an edge
S	Number of subgraphs
C	Number of edge types
γ	γ_{rs} probability of having an edge between vertices of subgraphs r and s

parameter depends on the subgraphs s_i and s_j only:

$$A_{i,j} \sim \mathcal{B}(\gamma_{s_i, s_j}).$$

Each vertex i is then associated to a latent cluster with a probability depending on s_i. In practice, the variable Z_i is drawn from a multinomial distribution:

$$\mathbf{Z}_i \sim \mathcal{M}(1; \alpha_{s_i}),$$

where

$$\forall s \in 1, \ldots, S, \quad \sum_{k=1}^{K} \alpha_{sk} = 1.$$

A notable point of the model is that we allow each subgraph to have different mixing proportions α_s for the latent clusters. We denote hereafter $\alpha = (\alpha 1, \ldots, \alpha S)$. Finally, if an edge between i and j is present, i.e. $A_{ij} = 1$, its type X_{ij} is sampled from a multinomial distribution with parameters depending on the latent clusters. Thus, if i belongs to cluster k and j to cluster l:

$$X_{i,j} \mid Z_{ik} Z_{jl} = 1, \quad A_{ij} = 1 \sim \mathcal{M}(1, \pi_{kl}),$$

where the sum over the C types of each vector $\pi_{kl} = (\pi_{kl} 1, \ldots, \pi_{kl} C)$ is:

$$\forall (k, l) \in \{1, \ldots, K\}^2, \quad \sum_{c=1}^{C} \pi_{klc} = 1.$$

If there is no edge between the two vertices, the entry X_{ij} is simply set to $X_{ij} = A_{ij} = 0$.

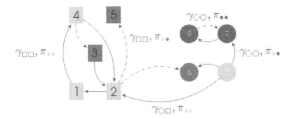

Figure 12.3 An example of an RSM network.

Note: The network is made of nine nodes belonging to two subgraphs (denoted through the form of the nodes) and split into three groups (indicated by colors). According to the RSM model, the directed edges between the nodes can be of different types (two types are considered here). The presence of an edge depends on the connexion probabilities between subgraphs (γ) and on connexion probabilities between groups (Π).

We point out that the choice of separating the role of the known subgraphs and the latent clusters was originally motivated by a parsimony concern. An alternative approach would consist in allowing the presence of an edge and its type to depend on both the subgraphs and latent clusters. However, this would dramatically increase the number of model parameters to be estimated. Indeed, for a network with $S = 6$, $K = 6$, and $C = 4$, it would require $K2S2(C + 1) + SK = 6516$ parameters while RSM only involves $S2 + K2C + SK = 216$ parameters.

The Figure 12.2b presents the graphical model associated with RSM, and Table 12.1 summarizes the model notations. Figure 12.2 allows us to see the conceptual differences between the SBM and RSM models. In particular, the specific role of A_{ij} appears here clearly.

Figure 12.3 presents an example of an RSM network made of nine nodes belonging to two subgraphs (denoted through the form of nodes) and split into three groups (indicated by the colors). A main difference with an SBM network is, of course, the presence of several (here $C = 2$) types of edges and a partition, assumed to be known, of the network into (here $S = 2$) subgraphs. In this specific case of a network generated according to the RSM model, the probability of an edge relies on two different parameters: γ and Π. The parameter γ governs the possibility of an edge (of any type) between two nodes, and this depends on the subgraphs they belong to. For instance, the presence of an edge between nodes 2 and 7 relies on γQD. Then, if the method decides that an edge exists between those two nodes, the type of the edge is drawn from a multinomial distribution with probabilities $\pi_{\bullet\bullet}$. Let us recall that $\pi_{\bullet\bullet}$ is here a vector of C probabilities. It turns out that the specific edge between nodes 2 and 7 was chosen to be of the type "continuous line" and not of the type "dashed line."

Inference and model selection

Given a network, the inference task consists in looking for estimates of the model parameters and cluster memberships. SBM and RSM fall in the family of mixture models for which the expectation maximization (EM) algorithm is the standard inference procedure (Dempster *et al.*, 1977). It is an algorithmic procedure which iteratively maximizes the likelihood relying on the expected complete data likelihood (McLachlan and Krishnan, 1997). Unfortunately, the EM algorithm depends on the conditional distribution of the cluster membership matrix Z given the network, which is here intractable. As an alternative, variational approaches can be used to derive an approximate inference scheme (see for instance Jordan *et al.*, 1999). The key point is to approximate the conditional distribution of Z by assuming the conditional independence of $Z_1, \ldots, Z_N$. The corresponding algorithm is called variational EM (VEM) (Daudin *et al.*, 2008). Note that an alternative strategy consists in focusing on the optimization of the complete data likelihood (Zanghi *et al.*, 2008). This strategy is often called classification EM (CEM). In this case, the choice of the number K of latent groups cannot be based on the observed likelihood, which is not tractable, but can be done using criteria such as the integrated classification likelihood (ICL) criterion (Daudin *et al.*, 2008).

In order to perform model selection, it is also possible to consider the two models presented above in a Bayesian framework. The principle is to see the model parameters as random variables and to make assumptions on their distributions. In practice, conjugate prior distributions are chosen to simplify the inference, which can be done either by relying on sampling techniques (as used in Nowicki and Snijders, 2001), such as Markov chain Monte Carlo (MCMC), or Bayesian extensions of the VEM algorithm (Latouche *et al.*, 2012; Jernite *et al.*, 2014). The latter, called variational Bayes EM (VBEM), is preferred in the context of networks for scaling reasons. Contrary to VEM which maximizes an approximation of the likelihood, VBEM focuses on an approximation of the marginal likelihood where all model parameters and cluster memberships are integrated out. Alternative strategies rely on allocation sampler (McDaid *et al.*, 2013) or greedy search (Côme and Latouche, 2015).

The model selection, which mainly consists here in choosing the appropriate number K of groups, can be done afterwards by considering the approximate marginal likelihood. Thus, K is chosen such that the corresponding criterion is maximized.

Application to the maritime network

This section now focuses on the application of both the SBM and RSM methods to a maritime flow network, extracted from the well-known *Lloyd's List*.

The Lloyd's data

Data was obtained from the printed *Lloyd's Voyage Record* published in October and November 2004, which details for each merchant vessel its successive movements from one port to another. Four main types of vessels are retained (containers, solid bulk, liquid bulk, and passengers/vehicles) calling at the world's 500 largest ports based on their degree (number of connected neighbours in the graph), from the original 2,737 ports or 1,815 port cities referenced in the original dataset, and are complemented by additional sources to retrieve their tonnage capacity (see Ducruet, 2013). Each port was assigned to a large region or continent, namely Asia, Europe/Mediterranean, North America, Latin America, Oceania/Pacific, Middle East/Red Sea, and Africa.

Experimental setup

From the raw database of vessel flows, we constructed an adjacency matrix between ports as follows: first, for every pair of ports, we considered the total tonnage of each commodity type by summing overall ship movements between those ports; second, we retained the main commodity type associated to each pair and drew an edge of the corresponding type between the two ports. In practice, the adjacency matrix contains entries ranging from 0 (no movements) to 4 (for the 4 commodity types taken into account). Figure 12.4 presents the adjacency matrix where commodity types are denoted using colors.

In order to apply the SBM and RSM model to those data, we used the mixer and Rambo packages for the R software. The mixer package (version 1.8) implements the VEM, VBEM, and CEM algorithms for SBM. We used the latter method for the inference, mainly because of its scaling properties. The package also allows the selection of an appropriate number K of groups for the data at hand with two criteria, and provides insightful visualizations of the results. We considered the

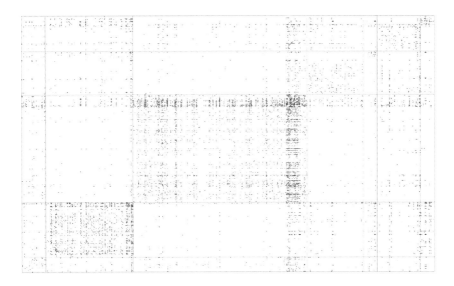

Figure 12.4 Adjacency matrix of the Lloyd's data organized by continent with categorical edges: containers (black), solid bulk (red), liquid bulk (green), and passengers (blue).

Note: Please refer to www.routledge.com/9781138911253 to see Figure 12.4 in full colour.

ICL criterion, which is the one available for the CEM algorithm. On the other hand, the Rambo package (version 1.1) proposes the VBEM algorithm for the inference of the RSM model. Model selection is considered based on an approximation of the marginal likelihood. Some meaningful plots allow the visualization of the clustering results as well. Both algorithms were run for a number K of clusters ranging from 2 to 20 and, for each method, the value of K was chosen such that the associated criterion was maximum.

Analysis of the network with SBM

We first analyze the network with SBM. Listing 1 gives the command lines in the R language to run mixer on a binary version of the adjacency matrix (named hereafter X).

Listing 1: Analysis of the network with SBM

```
# Loading the library library(mixer)
# Binarization of X
X = as.numeric (X! = 0)
# Clustering with mixer
  res.sbm = mixer (X, q min = 2, q max = 20, method =
                    "classification")
# Visualization of the clustering results
  plot(res.sbm)
# Selection of the best SBM model res Best = get
  Model(res.sbm)
```

Figure 12.5 presents the output of the mixer function. As one can observe, the ICL criterion peaks at $K = 10$, meaning that an appropriate number of groups for this network seems to be ten groups for the SBM model. The reorganized adjacency matrix allows us to see different kinds of groups. First, the network comprises one large and sparse group (cluster 1) of ports with few connections. Second, the nine other groups have much larger intra-connection probabilities. We can also note the presence of clusters which tend to connect with nodes of other clusters. Those ports can be considered as hubs. As shown in Figure 12.6, except for cluster 1, most clusters correspond to geographical regions. For instance, it appears that clusters 2 and 3 can be associated with the Europe/Mediterranean and/or North American regions while clusters 4 and 6 mainly include ports from the Oceania/Pacific and Asia regions. Some other clusters, such as cluster 9, are made of hubs which allow ports of different geographic regions to connect.

Interestingly, the original SBM model cannot take a priori geographical information into account. Moreover, it only focuses on binary edges and cannot deal with categorical relationships. Nevertheless, by only looking at the presence and absence of flows between ports, one can see that the geographic information is retrieved. This tends to show that the organization of the maritime network

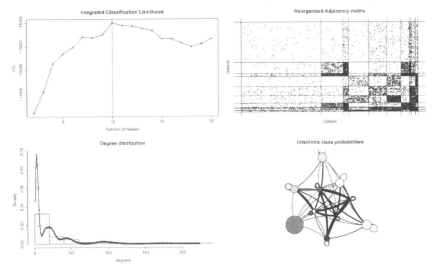

Figure 12.5 Outputs of the mixer function: values of the ICL criterion for the different values of K (top left), reorganized adjacency matrix according to the partition into ten groups found by mixer (top right), empirical and estimated distributions of the node degrees (bottom left), and network summarizing the relationships between the found latent clusters (bottom right).

is mainly explained by the geography where the domination and competition between ports occurs within regions.

Analysis of the network with RSM

We then used the Rambo package to cluster the data according to the RSM model. In this case, the adjacency matrix with categorical entries was used in addition to the partition of the ports by continents. Since we provide geographic information about the network nodes to the algorithm, it should be able to focus on other patterns hidden in the data. Listing 2 gives the command lines in the R language to run the RSM function on the adjacency matrix.

Listing 2: Analysis of the network with RSM

```
# Loading the library library(Rambo)
# Clustering with mixer
res.rsm = rsm (Z, sub, Klist = 2:6, nbredo = 1,
  maxit = 50, disp = TRUE)
# Visualization of the clustering results
  plot(res.rsm)
# Selection of the best SBM model res Best = res.
  rsm $ output [[5]]
```

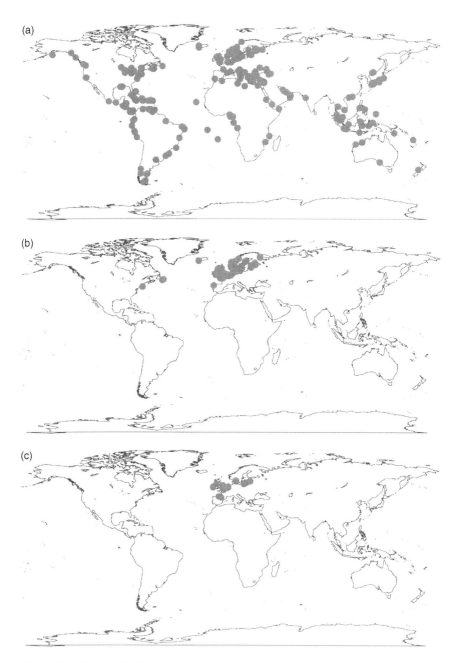

Figure 12.6 Geographic distribution of the ten clusters found by mixer for the SBM model.

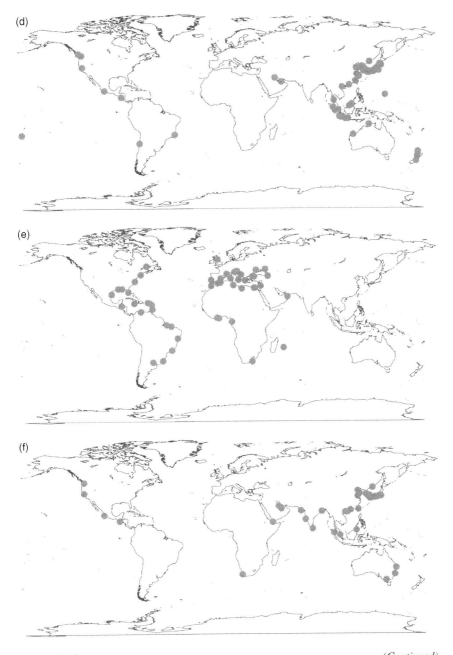

Figure 12.6

(Continued)

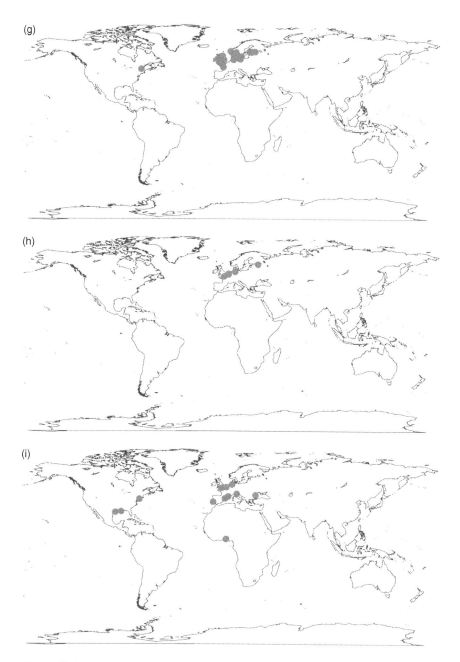

Figure 12.6 (Continued)

(j)

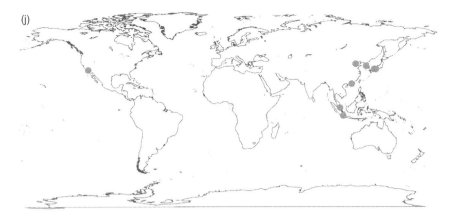

Figure 12.6

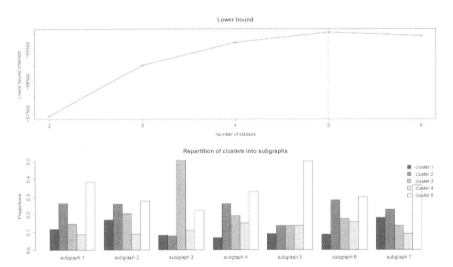

Figure 12.7 Outputs of the RSM function: values of the model selection criterion for the different values of K (top) and proportions of the latent clusters in the seven subgraphs (bottom). The subgraphs are here associated with continents.

Figure 12.7 presents the output of the RSM function. The variational approach finds $K = 5$ clusters. The reorganized adjacency matrix according to the clusters found is given in Figure 12.8. We observe that clusters can be associated with the use of specific types of vessels. Thus, cluster 2 is made of ports which tend to connect mainly through passenger/vehicle vessels. Moreover, cluster 3 contains ports interacting through solid bulk vessels. Similarly, cluster 4 can be associated with containers and cluster 5 with liquid bulk vessels. Interestingly, there are no strong connection profiles from ports in different clusters. We could have expected

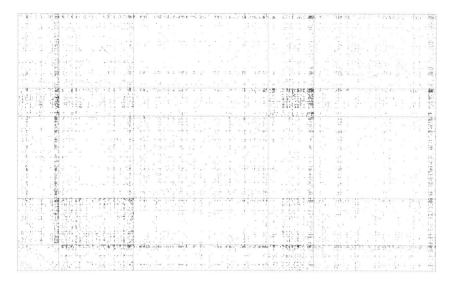

Figure 12.8 Reorganized adjacency matrix according to the partition into five latent groups
found by Rambo: containers (black), solid bulk (red), liquid bulk (green), and
passengers (blue).

Note: Please refer to www.routledge.com/9781138911253 to see Figure 12.8 in full color.

ports interacting through a type of vessels to have notable connections with ports
associated to other types of vessels. Overall, this is not the case. The clusters found
are essentially defined by their ports interacting through specific types of vessels.

As shown in Figure 12.9, the clusters found are not related to geographic
regions, although cluster 3 mainly contains ports from the Europe/Mediterranean
region. This is the key advantage of relying on RSM rather than SBM. Since the
geographic information is given a priori, the clustering technique for RSM can
uncover other patterns present in the data. Here, the results highlight that all the
regions are organized through clusters of interacting types of vessels. Moreover,
we point out that this methodology allows, by removing the geographical factors
present in the data (as shown in the previous section), to assign roles to ports
depending on maritime flows.

Conclusion

In this chapter, we considered the SBM and RSM models for the clustering of ports
in a maritime network created from the printed *Lloyd's Voyage Record* published
in October and November 2004. We pointed out the advantages and the flexibility
of the two models, and gave a short review of some of the existing approaches for
their inference. In particular, we mentioned the use of variational approximations
to derive tractable quantities. The two models gave rise to different and complementary results. By only looking at the presence or absence of connections between

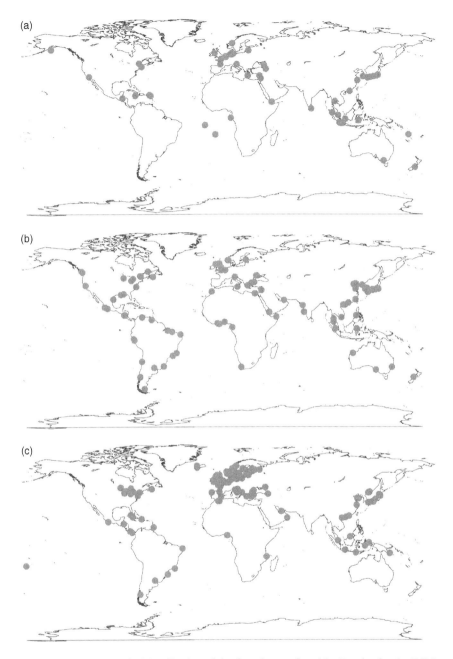

Figure 12.9 Geographical localization of the five clusters found by Rambo for the RSM model. *(Continued)*

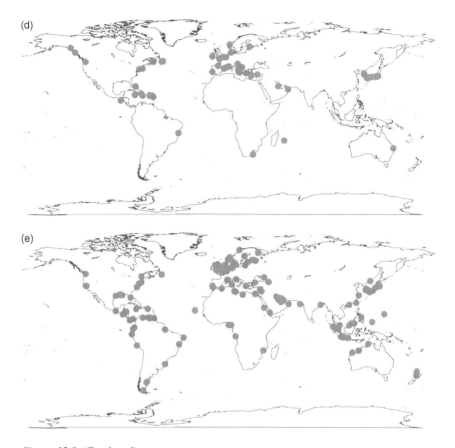

Figure 12.9 (Continued)

ports (SBM), we retrieved mainly geographical clusters highlighting the influence of physical geography and regional markets on port competition and maritime network configuration. However, using the known regions as subgraphs (RSM) and taking into account fleet types uncovered other types of clusters hidden in the data. These clusters are made of ports interacting through specific types of vessels. This allows us to assign a role to each port, by removing the geographical factors.

Acknowledgements

The authors would like to thank Olivier Joly, Marine Le Cam, and Brahim Ould Ismail at UMR IDEES (Le Havre) for their help on data provision and preparation.

References

Airoldi E.M., Blei D.M., Fienberg S.E., Xing, E.P. (2008) Mixed membership stochastic blockmodels. *The Journal of Machine Learning Research*, 9: 1981–2014.

Bickel P.J., Chen A. (2009) A nonparametric view of network models and Newman–Girvan and other modularities. *Proceedings of the National Academy of Sciences*, 106(50): 21068–73.

Côme E., Latouche, P. (2015) Model selection and clustering in stochastic block models with the exact integrated complete data likelihood. *Statistical Modelling* (in press).

Daudin J.J., Picard F., Robin S. (2008) A mixture model for random graphs. *Statistics and Computing*, 18(2): 173–83.

Dempster A.P., Laird N.M., Rubin D.B. (1977) Maximum likelihood for incomplete data via the EM algorithm. *Journal of the Royal Statistical Society*, B39: 1–38.

Dubois C., Butts C.T., Smyth P. (2013) Stochastic blockmodelling of relational event dynamics. *Proceedings of the International Conference on Artificial Intelligence and Statistics, Journal of Machine Learning Research Proceedings*, 31: 238–46.

Ducruet C. (2013) Network diversity and maritime flows. *Journal of Transport Geography*, 30: 77–88.

Ducruet, C., Zaidi, F. (2012) Maritime constellations: A complex network approach to shipping and ports. *Maritime Policy and Management*, 39(2): 151–68.

Frank O., Harary F. (1982) Cluster inference by using transitivity indices in empirical graphs. *Journal of the American Statistical Association*, 835–40.

Girvan M., Newman M.E.J. (2002) Community structure in social and biological networks. *Proceedings of the National Academy of Sciences*, 99(12): 7821–6.

Goldenberg A., Zheng A.X., Fienberg S.E. (2010) A survey of statistical network models. *Foundations and Trends® in Machine Learning*, 2(2), 129–233.

Handcock M.S., Raftery A.E., Tantrum, J.M. (2007) Model-based clustering for social networks. *Journal of the Royal Statistical Society: Series A*, 170(2): 301–54.

Heaukulani C., Ghahramani Z. (2013) Dynamic probabilistic models for latent feature propagation in social networks. *Proceedings of the 30th International Conference on Machine Learning (ICML-13)*, pp. 275–83.

Hoff P.D., Raftery A.E., Handcock M.S. (2002) Latent space approaches to social network analysis. *Journal of the American Statistical Association*, 97(460): 1090–8.

Hofman J.M., Wiggins C.H. (2008) Bayesian approach to network modularity. *Physical Review Letters*, 100(25): 258701.

Jernite Y., Latouche P., Bouveyron C., Rivera P., Jegou L., Lamasse S. (2014) The random subgraph model for the analysis of an ecclesiastical network in merovingian Gaul. *The Annals of Applied Statistics*, 8(1): 377–405.

Jordan M.I., Ghahramani Z., Jaakkola T.S., Saul L.K. (1999) An introduction to variational methods for graphical models. *Machine Learning*, 37(2): 183–233.

Kaluza P., Kölzsch A., Gastner M.T., Blasius, B. (2010) The complex network of global cargo ship movements. *Journal of the Royal Society Interface*, 7(48): 1093–103.

Kemp C., Tenenbaum J.B., Griffiths T.L., Yamada T., Ueda N. (2006) Learning systems of concepts with an infinite relational model. *Proceedings of the National Conference on Artificial Intelligence*, 21: 381.

Latouche P., Birmele E., Ambroise C. (2011) Overlapping stochastic block models with application to the French political blogosphere. *Annals of Applied Statistics*, 5(1): 309–36.

Latouche P., Birmele E., Ambroise C. (2012) Variational Bayesian inference and complexity control for stochastic block models. *Statistical Modelling*, 12(1): 93–115.

McDaid A., Murphy T.B., Frieln N., Hurley N.J. (2013) Improved Bayesian inference for the stochastic block model with application to large networks. *Computational Statistics and Data Analysis*, 60: 12–31.

McLachlan G., Krishnan T. (1997) *The EM Algorithm and Extensions*. New York: John Wiley.

Mariadassou M., Robin S., Vacher C. (2010) Uncovering latent structure in valued graphs: a variational approach. *Annals of Applied Statistics*, 4(2): 715–42.

Matias C. Robin S. (2014) Modeling heterogeneity in random graphs through latent space models: a selective review. *Esaim Proc. and Surveys*, 47: 55–74.

Moreno J.L. (1934) *Who Shall Survive? A New Approach to the Problem of Human Interrelations*. Washington: Nervous and Mental Disease Publishing Co.

Nowicki K., Snijders T.A.B. (2001) Estimation and prediction for stochastic blockstructures. *Journal of the American Statistical Association*, 96(455): 1077–87.

Salter-Townshend M., White A., Gollini I., Murphy T.B. (2012) Review of statistical network analysis: models, algorithms, and software. *Statistical Analysis and Data Mining*, 5(4): 243–64.

Sarkar P., Moore A.A.W. (2005) Dynamic social network analysis using latent space models. *ACM SIGKDD Explorations Newsletter*, 7(2): 31–40.

Snijders T.A.B., Nowicki K. (1997) Estimation and prediction for stochastic blockmodels for graphs with latent block structure. *Journal of Classification*, 14(1): 75–100.

Soufiani H.A., Airoldi E.M. (2012) Graphlet decomposition of a weighted network. *Journal of Machine Learning Research, Workshop & Conference Proceedings*, 22 : 54–63.

Villa N., Rossi F., Truong Q.D. (2008) Mining a medieval social network by kernel SOM and related methods. Arxiv preprint arXiv:0805.1374.

Wang Y.J., Wong G.Y. (1987) Stochastic blockmodels for directed graphs. *Journal of the American Statistical Association*, 82: 8–19.

Xing E.P., Fu W., Song L. (2010) A state-space mixed membership blockmodel for dynamic network tomography. *The Annals of Applied Statistics*, 4(2): 535–66.

Xu K.S., Hero III A.O. (2013) Dynamic stochastic blockmodels: statistical models for time-evolving networks. *Proceedings of the 6th International Conference on Social Computing, Behavioral-Cultural Modeling, and Prediction*, pp. 201–10.

Yang T., Chi Y., Zhu S., Gong Y., Jin R. (2011) Detecting communities and their evolutions in dynamic social networks: a Bayesian approach. *Machine Learning*, 82(2): 157–89.

Zanghi H., Ambroise C., Miele V. (2008) Fast online graph clustering via Erdős–Renyi mixture. *Pattern Recognition*, 41: 3592–9.

Zanghi H., Volant S., Ambroise C. (2010) Clustering based on random graph model embedding vertex features. *Pattern Recognition Letters*, 31(9): 830–6.

13 Vulnerability and resilience of ports and maritime networks to cascading failures and targeted attacks

Serge Lhomme

A key question in the context of large-scale technological and infrastructural networks concerns their response to local failure and resilience to partial accidental breakdown or anticipated attacks (Woolley-Meza *et al.*, 2011). Moreover ports and maritime networks are subject to unpredictable, recurrent and extreme weather conditions that lead to repetitive and regionally-localized failure that must be compensated for by re-routing traffic or re-planning schedules (Woolley-Meza *et al.*, 2011). That is why it seems relevant to study vulnerability and resilience of ports and maritime networks.

In the literature, technological and infrastructural network vulnerability models have been grouped into two types. The first are the complex-network-based vulnerability models, which do not consider the flow transportation and redistribution or measure the system performance drop only according to topological change, where the performance is usually measured by the size of the largest connected sub-grid, the connectivity level or loss, the fraction of affected customers, and so on (Ouyang *et al.*, 2014). The second type are real flow models, which use equations and engineering constraints to describe the performance drop of networks undergoing a disruptive event (Ouyang *et al.*, 2014). For instance, commodity (electric energy) flows in electricity networks are governed by Ohm's law and Kirchhoff's laws, which are not captured in simple topological models (Hines *et al.*, 2010). Thus, to capture power grid behaviour, the alternative current (AC) power-flow model is used. This model analytically determines the real and reactive flows over all lines by using real and reactive balance equations to solve the voltage magnitude and phase angles at each substation, and is used for vulnerability studies (Ouyang *et al.*, 2012).

For studying vulnerability and resilience of ports and maritime networks, it seems relevant to use the first type of vulnerability models. Indeed a maritime network in its simplest form is just a set of nodes or vertices joined together in pairs by lines or edges (Gastner and Newman, 2006). Moreover, there is no accurate model to capture maritime network behaviour. So, we choose to investigate network representation of the maritime network from topological and geometrical perspectives in the hope of finding properties and behaviours that transcend the abstraction (Albert *et al.*, 2004). In this context, nodes correspond to ports and edges correspond to the relationships between ports. The data comes from *Lloyd's List Intelligence*. *Lloyd's List* is the world leader in maritime intelligence and produces vessel movement data in digital form. That is why this analysis is principally based on the extraction of worldwide vessel movements reported in 2006. More accurately, data refer to container movements from port to port. In this context, edges can be valued by the number of relationships.

Starting with the state of the art, we distinguish three ways for studying network vulnerability: basic vulnerability measures; dynamic approaches; and error and attack approaches. The objectives are to assess global vulnerability of the world maritime network and identify the most critical ports. To this end, new methods and algorithms have been developed.

State of the art

From topological and geometrical perspectives, networks vulnerability and resilience have been studied in three ways, which we describe in the following sections.

Basic measures: network vulnerability to single component (node or edge) breakdown

The easiest way of studying network vulnerability and identifying the most critical components is to assess network disruptions due to a single component break-down without taking into account cascading failures (Kinney *et al.*, 2005; Winkler *et al.*, 2010). Such studies focus only on the static properties of the network. This kind of measure is commonly used to determine the importance of nodes or edges in a graph and may be considered as a centrality index (Brandes and Erlebach, 2005). In this context, one indicator is chosen to assess network performance. For instance, two common indicators are used to assess transportation network performance: closeness accessibility and geographic accessibility (Gleyze, 2005). Nevertheless, it is also possible to use the size of the largest connected component (LCC) (Winkler *et al.*, 2010). However, this performance indicator is computed for the 'normal network' (network with all components) and for a 'disturbed network' (network with all components but without a single component). To conclude, vulnerability to single node breakdown is assessed by the difference between these two values.

Basic measures can be easily computed for each component. Thus network components can be ranked in order to identify most critical components. Then there is no problem for mapping a drop in network performance due to a single component breakdown. Moreover, for transportation networks correlations between vulnerability and centrality have been identified (Gleyze, 2005). So basic measures have many advantages and are a good starting point for studying vulnerability and resilience of ports and maritime networks. Nevertheless these measures remain too simple to capture real network behaviour. That is why it seems relevant to use more complex approaches.

Dynamic approaches: network vulnerability to cascading failures

A network is notably characterized by a specific capacity to absorb disturbances. Thus most of the frequent disruptions are locally absorbed by the networks, and the end users remain unaware of their occurrence (Dueñas-Osorio, 2005). This fact results from the ability of the networks to redistribute the flow at the location of the disruption. In fact, severe incidents, like the 2003 North American blackout, have been attributed to cascading behaviours. One typical feature of blackouts is that they involve several network components. Even though intentional attacks and random failures emerge very locally, the entire network can be affected, even resulting in global collapse (Wang and Rong, 2011). So, taking into account the intrinsic dynamics of the flow in the network using only topologic properties has been discussed in the literature, and many valuable results have been found with the design of load models.

Cascading failures are common in most complex networks (Zhang *et al.*, 2011). Although most failures emerge and dissolve locally, largely unnoticed by the rest of the world, a few trigger avalanche mechanisms can affect entire networks (Crucitti *et al.*, 2004). For instance, cascading failures take place on the Internet, where traffic is rerouted to bypass malfunctioning routers, eventually leading to an avalanche of overloads on other routers that are not equipped to handle extra traffic (Crucitti *et al.*, 2004). The redistribution of traffic can result in a congestion regime with a large drop in performance. In fact, dynamic approaches study how the breakdown of a single node is sufficient to collapse the entire system simply because of the dynamics of flow redistribution on the network.

In dynamic approaches, nodes are characterized by their loads (degree, betweenness) and by a given capacity to handle traffic. Initially the network is in a stationary state in which the load at each node is smaller than its capacity (Ash and Newth, 2007). It is generally assumed that the capacity of a node is proportional to its initial load, corresponding to the capacity (tolerance) parameter (Wang *et al.*, 2011). In fact, the breakdown removal of a node changes the balance of flows and leads to a redistribution of loads over other nodes (Motter and Lai, 2002; Crucitti *et al.*, 2004; Motter, 2004). So a redistribution rule is needed to capture this network behaviour. For instance, after a node i is attacked, its load will be redistributed to its neighbouring nodes (Wang and Rong, 2009). The additional load received by the node j can be proportional to its initial load. If the capacity of these nodes cannot handle the extra load this will be redistributed, in turn triggering a cascade of overload failures and eventually a large drop in network performance such as those observed in real systems like the Internet or electrical power grids (Crucitti *et al.*, 2004). Finally, the damage caused by a cascade is quantified in terms of the decrease in the network efficiency or in terms of the increase in the number of broken nodes (Koc *et al.*, 2013).

Dynamic approaches are the first step to take into account breakdowns of a group of components. Nevertheless there is no standardized or acknowledged method for mapping results. Moreover comparison between networks (in order to compare network vulnerabilities) is difficult.

Attack and error approaches: the worst-case scenario

In order to assess network vulnerability, resistance of networks to the removal of nodes or edges, due either to random breakdowns or to intentional attacks, has been studied. Such studies have focused on the static properties of the network showing that the removal of a group of nodes altogether can have important consequences (Albert *et al.*, 2000; Holme *et al.*, 2002). Consequences are commonly assessed using connectivity loss indices (Murray and Grubesic, 2011). Connectivity loss indices quantify the decrease in the number of relationships between each node.

The emphasis has long been on the need to identify network elements that would degrade system performance the most if disrupted (Murray and Grubesic, 2011). This worst-case approach to vulnerability assessment stems from the early work of Wollmer (1964), who was concerned with examining the maximal flow possible through a networked system if arcs, nodes or a combination of each is interdicted. Similarly, work conducted by Fulkerson and Harding (1977) and Corley and Sha (1982) examined impacts of disruptions on the shortest path in the network. More recently, additional measures of network performance and vulnerability have been used, including connectivity (Albert *et al.*, 2000; Myung and Kim, 2004), degree of node (Grubesic *et al.*, 2003), and betweenness and clustering coefficients (Demsar *et al.*, 2008).

This approach obtained significant results. For instance, Albert *et al.* (2004) removed transmission nodes of the North American power grid one by one, first randomly, then in decreasing order of their degree or load (betweenness). It appears that connectivity loss is significantly higher when targeting high degree or high load transmission hubs. Finally, Albert *et al.*. used a cascading scenario, where the loads are periodically recalculated, and show that this cascading failure has the most damaging effect.

One of the most important findings of these studies was that scale-free networks with power-law degree distributions respond very differently in scenarios that reflect random failures as opposed to selected removal of central nodes (Woolley-Meza *et al.*, 2011). For instance, scale-free networks are relatively immune to random removal of nodes and extremely sensitive to targeted removal of high centrality nodes. Since centrality measures such as degree, betweenness andflux typically correlate in these networks, this effectively amounts to removal of nodes that function as hubs (Woolley-Meza *et al.*, 2011).

Basic vulnerability measures

In order to start with basic vulnerability measures and identify the most critical ports, a closeness vitality indicator has been computed first. Indeed this indicator is presented in several books (Brandes and Erlebach, 2005). Moreover, it is implemented in a well-known Python library for network analysis (NetworkX). Closeness vitality of a node is the change in the sum of distances between all node pairs when excluding that node. This first analysis highlights the high criticality of the port of Busan. Nevertheless there is one pitfall in the general idea of closeness vitality: if a node or an edge is a cut-vertex or a bridge the graph will be

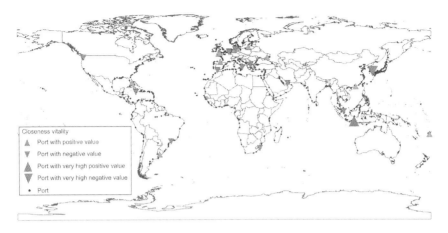

Figure 13.1 Maritime network vulnerability using closeness vitality indicator.

Figure 13.2 Maritime network vulnerability using connectivity loss indicator.

disconnected, and then some distances can be infinite. That is why several nodes are characterized by negative values. This is the case for some small European ports (Wismar, Bilbao, Bremen and Mariupol) but also involves the major port of Honk Kong. Thanks to this indicator, a first vulnerability map of maritime network has been produced (Figure 13.1).

In fact, for assessing maritime network vulnerability, it is useful to determine loss of connectivity due to a single node breakdown. It appears that nodes with negative values of closeness vitality are characterized by connectivity loss (Figure 13.2). But some ports with positive values of closeness vitality, like Singapore, are also characterized by connectivity loss.

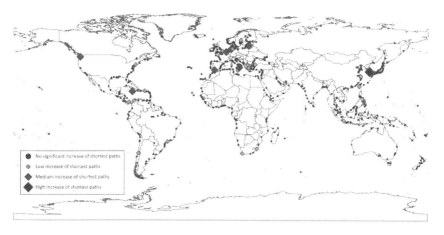

Figure 13.3 Map of maritime network vulnerability using increase of shortest paths.

In order to improve connectivity loss analysis, increase of shortest paths in the network due to a single node breakdown has been assessed without taking into account infinite distance (due to connectivity loss) (Figure 13.3). Indeed, in maritime networks, it is always possible to find an alternative to the loss of connectivity between two ports. This measure highlights not only the high criticality of Busan port, but also that of several European ports (Bremerhaven, Antwerp, Gioia Tauro, Hamburg).

To conclude with basic vulnerability measures, it seems that the most important ports are also the most critical ports. Thus the world maritime network is vulnerable to the disturbance of major Asian ports (like Busan, Hong Kong and Singapore). In fact it appears that there is a correlation between increase of shortest paths and nodes betweenness (Figure 13.4). There is also a correlation between increase of shortest paths and nodes degree. These correlations may partly obscure much more complex situations.

Cascading failures

In the continuity of basic measures, dynamic approaches are used for identifying the most critical ports. Dynamic approaches implementation calls for a definition of methodology. Based on the state of the art, nodes are first characterized by their load (their weighted degree). Then capacity of a node (node tolerance) is proportional to its initial load: it is the capacity parameter. Third, a redistribution rule is needed. To this end, after a node is attacked, its load will be redistributed to its neighbouring nodes. Additional loads received by neighbouring nodes are proportional to their initial load. Finally, the damage caused by a cascade is quantified in terms of the increase in the number of broken nodes.

In order to identify the most critical ports, starting from a single node breakdown, here we assess the capacity parameter involving a number of broken nodes at least

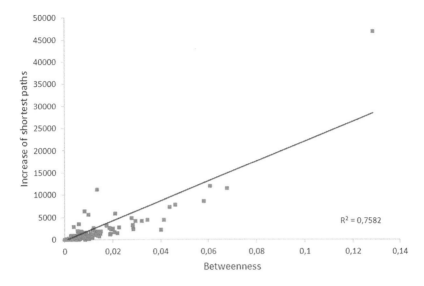

Figure 13.4 Correlation between increase of shortest paths and nodes betweenness ($R^2 = 0.758$).

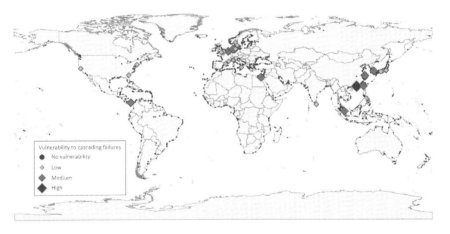

Figure 13.5 Maritime network vulnerability using a dynamic approach.

equal to half the number of nodes. This assessment is carried out for each node. Thus the more the capacity parameter required to break at least half of nodes is high, the more the node is critical. Thanks to this method, nodes can be ranked from the most to the least critical, and results can be mapped (Figure 13.5). It appears that the most critical port is again Hong Kong. Singapore, Hamburg, Rotterdam, Suez Canal and Shenzhen are also highly critical. All can be considered major nodes. In fact there is again a correlation between criticality and betweenness. There is also a strong correlation between criticality and weighted degree (Figure 13.6). The most critical port (Hong Kong) is not so critical compared to the norm (compared to the fitted line), but several ports seem more critical than the norm.

Therefore it seemed relevant to analyse residuals of the linear regression model. To this end a world map has been designed. The results are surprising (Figure 13.7). Indeed this map shows that several European ports are more critical than expected in view of their weighted degree (especially Hamburg, Rotterdam, Felixstowe and Bremerhaven). In fact almost all the ports which appear more critical than expected are European. There is a European singularity.

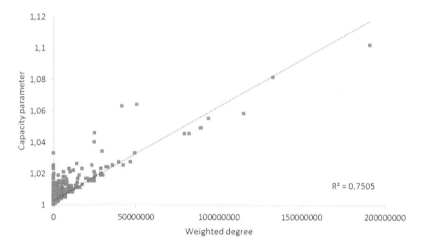

Figure 13.6 Correlation between capacity parameter and weighted degree ($R^2 = 0.750$).

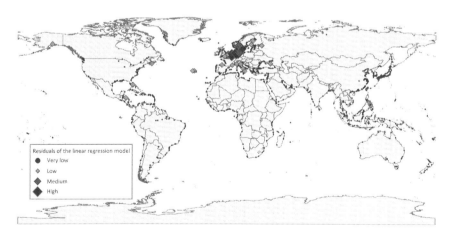

Figure 13.7 Residuals of the linear regression model (capacity parameter and weighted degree).

Vulnerability to targeted attacks

Here the main objective is to assess the global vulnerability of the worldwide maritime network in comparison with other networks. Indeed if we have assessed criticality of ports thanks to basic vulnerability measures and dynamic approaches, we are not yet able to say if the maritime network is vulnerable or not. First, three attack scenarios, commonly used in the literature, have been studied, with nodes being removed one by one in decreasing order:

- of their degree (degree-based attacks)
- of their betweenness (betweenness-based attacks)
- of their betweenness, but nodes betweenness is recalculated after each node removal (cascading-based attacks)

Vulnerability and resilience of maritime networks had already been compared with another large-scale transportation network: worldwide air transportation (Woolley-Meza *et al.*, 2011). That is why we choose here to compare maritime network vulnerability to a technical network: the British electrical network (Figure 13.8). There is no surprise: for the three attack scenarios, the maritime network is less vulnerable. Absence of linear infrastructures explains maritime

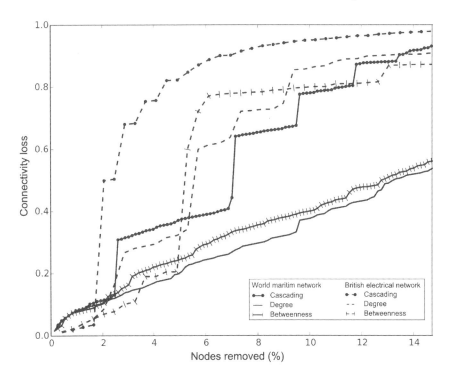

Figure 13.8 Comparison between British electrical network vulnerability and maritime network vulnerability.

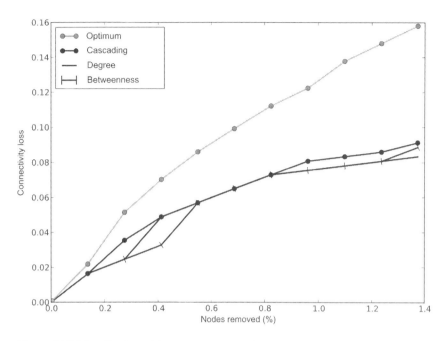

Figure 13.9 Identification of the worst-case scenarios.

network resilience. Nonetheless, the presence of hubs in maritime networks explains that they are quite vulnerable to cascading-based attacks.

Complex networks are commonly vulnerable to cascading-based attacks. In fact this type of targeted attack is close to be the worst-case scenario, and cascading-based attacks can be considered as a good heuristic for identifying worst-case scenarios. Nevertheless sometimes cascading-based attacks may be far from worst-case scenarios. For instance, this is the case for the British electrical network (Lhomme, 2015). So we used a heuristic algorithm in order to identify worst-case scenarios (Figure 13.9).

Maritime networks cannot be considered as highly vulnerable. Nevertheless it appears that cascading-based attacks are quite far from worst-case scenarios (when the number of nodes removed is under 2 per cent). Thus it seemed relevant to look for a better type of attack. That is why we developed an algorithm based on hierarchical clustering. The idea is first to define communities thanks to hierarchical clustering (for a given number of communities). Then each community is disconnected from the network and we assess the number of nodes removed to disconnect each community as well as the loss of connectivity. This algorithm can be carried for several numbers of communities. Finally, for a given number of nodes removed we keep the highest value of loss of connectivity. Results are interesting, but this new algorithm is not better than cascading-based attacks (Figure 13.10).

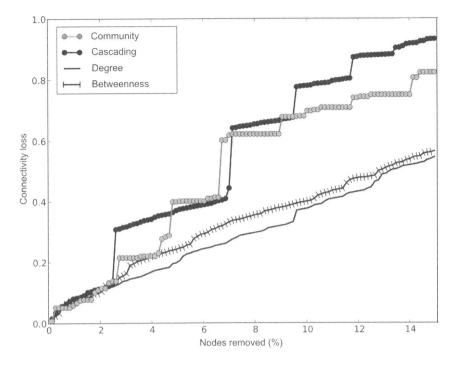

Figure 13.10 Attacks based on hierarchical clustering.

Conclusion

This research highlights that the worldwide maritime network is quite resilient to cascading failures and targeted attacks. However, it is important to pay attention to ports with high betweenness, especially Busan, in case of a single node breakdown. Moreover it is also important to pay attention to ports with high weighted degrees in case of cascading failures. More generally, the most important ports are also the most critical ones. The world maritime network may be vulnerable to the disturbance of major Asian ports (Busan, Hong Kong and Singapore).

Nevertheless this correlation partly obscures a much more complex situation. For instance, it appears that European ports are more critical than expected in view of their weighted degree. Finally, several maps of worldwide maritime network vulnerability have been designed and a new attacks and errors algorithm has been designed.

References

Albert R., Jeong H., Barabasi A. (2000) Error and attack tolerance of complex networks. *Nature*, 406(6794): 378–82.

Albert R., Albert I., Nakarado G.L. (2004) Structural vulnerability of the North American power grid. *Physical Review E*, 69: 025103(R).

Ash J., Newth D. (2007) Optimizing complex networks for resilience against cascading failure. *Physica A: Statistical Mechanics and its Applications*, 380: 673–83.

Brandes U., Erlebach T. (2005) *Network Analysis.* Dordrecht: Springer.

Corley H.W., Sha D.Y. (1982) Most vital links and nodes in weighted networks. *Operations Research Letters*, 1: 157–60.

Crucitti P., Latora V., Marchiori M., Rapisarda A. (2004) Error and attack tolerance of complex networks. *Physica A*, 340(1–3): 388–94.

Demsar U., Spatenkova O., Virrantaus K. (2008) Identifying critical locations in a spatial network with graph theory. *Transactions in GIS*, 12: 61–82.

Dueñas-Osorio L. (2005) *Interdependent Response of Networked Systems to Natural Hazards and Intentional Disruptions.* Dissertation, Georgia Institute of Technology, Atlanta: Georgia Tech Library.

Fulkerson D.R., Harding G.C. (1977) Maximizing the minimum source–sink path subject to a budget constraint. *Mathematical Programming*, 13: 116–18.

Gastner M.T., Newman M. E. J. (2006) The spatial structure of networks. *The European Physical Journal B*, 1–5.

Gleyze J.F. (2005) La vulnérabilité structurelle des réseaux de transport dans un contexte de risques. Unpublished PhD dissertation in Geography, Paris: University of Paris 7 Diderot.

Grubesic T.H., O'Kelly M.E., Murray A.T. (2003) A geographic perspective on commercial Internet survivability. *Telematics and Informatics*, 20: 51–69.

Hines P., Cotilla-Sanchez E. (2010) Do topological models provide good information about electricity infrastructure vulnerability? *Chaos*, 20: 033122.

Holme P., Kim B.J., Yoon C.N., Han S.K. (2002) Attack vulnerability of complex networks. *Physical Review E*, 65: 056109.

Kinney R., Crucitti P., Albert R., Latora V. (2005) Modeling cascading failures in the North American power grid. *The European Physical Journal B*, 46(1): 101–7.

Koc Y., Warnier M., Kooij R.E., Brazier F.M.T. (2013) A robustness metric for cascading failures by targeted attacks in power networks. *Proceedings of the 10th IEEE International Conference on Networking, Sensing and Control (ICNSC)*, April 10–12, Evry, France, pp. 48–53.

Lhomme S. (2015) Analyse spatiale de La structure des réseaux techniques dans un contexte de risques. *Cybergeo: European Journal of Geography*, 711. Available online at http://cybergeo.revues.org/26763 [accessed 5 June 2015].

Motter A.E. (2004) Cascade control and defense in complex networks. *Physical Review Letters*, 93: 098701.

Motter A.E., Lai Y. (2002) Cascade-based attacks on complex networks. *Physical Review E*, 66: 065101.

Murray A.T., Grubesic T.H. (2011) Critical infrastructure protection: the vulnerability conundrum. *Telematics and Informatics*, 29(1): 56–65.

Myung Y.S., Kim H.J. (2004) A cutting plane algorithm for computing k-edge survivability of a network. *European Journal of Operational Research*, 156: 579–89.

Ouyang M., Due nas-Osorio L., Min X. (2012) A three-stage resilience analysis framework for urban infrastructure systems. *Structural Safety*, 36–7: 23–31.

Ouyang M., Zhao L., Pan Z., Hong L. (2014) Comparisons of complex network based models and direct current power flow model to analyze power grid vulnerability under intentional attacks. *Physica A*, 403: 45–53.

Wang J.W., Rong L.L. (2009) Cascade-based attack vulnerability on the US power grid. *Safety Science*, 47(10): 1332–6.

Wang J.W., Rong L.L. (2011) Robustness of the western United States power grid under edge attack strategies due to cascading failures. *Safety Science*, 49(6): 807–12.

Wang W., Cai Q., Suny Y. L., He H. (2011) *Risk-aware Attacks and Catastrophic Cascading Failures in U.S. Power Grid.* Global Telecommunications Conference (GLOBECOM 2011), IEEE, pp. 1–6.

Winkler J., Duenas-Osorio A., Stein R., Subramanian D. (2010) Performance assessment of topologically diverse power systems subjected to hurricane events. *Reliability Engineering and System Safety*, 95: 323–36.

Wollmer R. (1964) Removing arcs from a network. *Operations Research*, 12: 934–40.

Woolley-Meza O., Thiemann C., Grady D., Lee J.J., Seebens H., Blasius B., Brockmann D. (2011) Complexity in human transportation networks: a comparative analysis of worldwide air transportation and global cargo-ship movements. *The European Physical Journal B*, 84: 589–600.

Zhang Y., Cai S., Chen C., Shi J. (2011) Robustness of deterministic hierarchical networks against cascading failures. *Proceedings of the International Conference on Electrical and Control Engineering, Yichang, China*, 16–18 September, pp. 4063–6.

14 The distribution functions of vessel calls and port connectivity in the global cargo ship network

Michael T. Gastner, César Ducruet

Recent years have seen intense research activity in the modelling and analysis of complex networks, mainly driven by the availability of new large-scale databases for social, biological, and technological networks (see for example Newman, 2010 for a review). Maritime transport networks are one area where these new ideas and techniques have found fertile ground (Deng *et al.*, 2009; Hu and Zhu, 2009; Kaluza *et al.*, 2010; Ducruet, 2013). In this study, we analyse a database generated from *Lloyd's Shipping Index*, a weekly publication of cargo ship movements by *Lloyd's List*, over the period 1890 to 2008. For 20 selected years, an entire volume of the *Index*, each containing data for one week, was extracted and the data transformed into a network where the nodes are ports and links are nonstop ship voyages. Because cargo shipping is the dominant transport mode for world trade (UNCTAD, 2013), it is of great economic relevance for understanding the importance of the nodes. Here we measure importance in two ways:

- the number of vessel calls; and
- the degree, defined as the number of ports that the node is connected to by at least one arriving or departing ship.

The call and degree distributions are arguably the two most important summary statistics of the network (see Chapter 4 by Barthelemy for a more general discussion). They may not allow a complete reconstruction of traffic on the links. However, unweighted and weighted degree distributions are an important feature of a network's topology and have often been used as circumstantial evidence for mechanistic models of the network's evolution (Albert and Barabási, 1999; Tadić, 2002; Moore *et al.*, 2006). The call distribution also plays a crucial role for predicting the full origin-destination matrix (i.e. the traffic between all pairs of ports) because it is an input in transport forecasting (e.g. in the gravity model or the intervening opportunities model (Wilson, 1967)).

In the early phase of complex network science, many degree distributions of real-world networks were characterized as power laws (Albert and Barabási, 1999). In the parlance of statistics, an integer-valued power law is a probabilistic model that assigns the probability $\Pr(k)$ to the event that an arbitrary node has degree or weight k so that

$$\Pr(k; \tau) = \frac{k^{-\tau}}{\zeta(\tau)}, \quad k = 1, 2, 3, \ldots \qquad (14.1)$$

Here $\zeta(\tau)$ is the Riemann zeta function and $\tau > 1$ a fixed parameter that has to be fitted to the data. Because $\Pr(ak; \tau) = a^{-\tau} \Pr(k; \tau)$, the distribution of Equation (14.1) is also called scale-free. The interest in power law distributions stems mainly from the fact that these are particularly heavy-tailed (i.e. the tail of the distribution decays more slowly than an exponential function). As a consequence, a power-law distribution has a large range in degrees: while most nodes have only a small degree, some nodes possess a much larger degree than the average. At first glance, such a heterogeneity in degrees is indeed found in many empirical networks (Albert and Barabási, 2002).

Most of the time, a power-law degree distribution was inferred from straight-line fits to the log-log diagram of the degree frequency, but this is now generally viewed as an unsatisfactory approach (Clauset *et al.*, 2009). Identifying a region where the data appear more or less linear is largely arbitrary because most distributions are too noisy and substantially curved on double-logarithmic scales. Straight-line fits based on standard least-squares algorithms can also lead to a bias in the estimated exponents. Most importantly, however, there is no a priori reason why $\Pr(k)$ has to be a power law. Many other common probability distributions are also heavy-tailed and may fit the data better. Recent studies in fact doubt that power laws are as ubiquitous as once believed (Edwards *et al.*, 2007; Willinger *et al.*, 2009; Stumpf and Porter, 2012).

This study proposes that statistical methods should be applied to the maritime network to understand which type of call or degree distribution best explains the observed data. We apply information-based model selection (Burnham and Anderson, 1998) and statistical tests to compare different candidate distributions. Another goal of the chapter is to assess whether the call and degree distributions of the cargo ship network have significantly changed over time. One hypothesis from the geographic literature is that the call and degree distributions may structurally change alongside major technological transformations of the shipping industry and their consequences on port operations and maritime network configurations (McCalla, 2004). The studied period goes across different dominant ship technologies, such as sail, steam, combustion, specialized vessels (e.g. container, tanker), and mega-carriers. Such technological evolutions are believed to have been selective, as some ports were dropped from the network and replaced or superseded by new ones better adapted to changing standards, sometimes resulting in an increasing concentration of port activity favouring fewer and larger ports. Containerization is seen as a revolution in itself with profound impacts on network configuration and world trade (Cullinane and Khanna, 2000; Bernhofen *et al.*, 2013). In this study we find indeed evidence that the call distributions have evolved so that the fraction of small ports has decreased. At the same time the

Gini coefficient, a common measure for inequality of a distribution, has slightly decreased over the study period.

Before proceeding with the statistical analysis, we emphasize one caveat. The voyages reported by Lloyd's certainly form only a subset of the entire global traffic distribution and may possibly be biased, for example if certain ports, ships or routes are systematically underreported. The quality of reporting may also differ between different years. We currently have insufficient knowledge whether such biases are present and thus cannot apply any corrections. *Lloyd's Shipping Index*, however, is the most complete and consistent data source available to study the development of the cargo ship network over the investigated time period. Therefore, we are confident that the trends reported below are genuinely representative of the network's evolution.

Probabilistic models

We investigate eight different models that have frequently been used to fit empirical degree distributions in complex networks (Table 14.1). We restrict our study to discrete distributions

(a)   whose support are all positive integers; and
(b)   that depend on maximally two parameters.

Restriction (a) reflects that degree or port calls only have integer values. One might argue that should also be included and that the maximum degree should have an upper bound because the network is finite. However, from *Lloyd's Shipping Index* we cannot directly infer which ports were in principle open to traffic but remained unused. Consequently, distributions with infinite support but excluding are more appropriate in the present context. The number of ports with $k > 0$ can differ slightly between the call and degree distributions: some ports have a positive number of calls but are degree zero because in the raw data some vessels are reported to call at one, not two ports (namely origin and destination) in their latest known voyage. For the call distribution we kept these isolated ports but removed them from the degree distribution since zero is unlikely to be their true degree. Restriction (b) avoids overfitting of the data but still includes the "usual suspects" for degree distributions in socio-economic networks.

We include four one-parameter models: besides the power law of Equation (14.1) (also known as zeta distribution), we assess the likelihood of Poisson, geometric and Yule–Simon distributions. The Poisson distribution describes the node degrees of large sparse Erdős–Rényi random graphs, a common null model in network studies. The tail of a Poisson distribution decays faster than exponentially so that degrees in Erdős–Rényi graphs are effectively limited to values near the mean degree. The geometric distribution decays exponentially, whereas the Yule–Simon distribution has a power law tail and only differs mildly from a strict power law for small k. Because the Yule–Simon distribution is the exact solution of popular "preferential attachment" models (Simon, 1955) (i.e. models where

Table 14.1 The investigated probabilistic models

Distribution	Parameters	$\Pr(k)$, $k = 1, 2, 3, \ldots$
Poisson (POIS)	$\lambda > 0$	$\dfrac{\lambda^k}{(e^\lambda - 1)k!}$
geometric (GEOM)	$p \in (0, 1)$	$p(1 - p)^{k-1}$
power law (ZETA)	$\tau > 1$	$[\zeta(\tau)k^\tau]^{-1}$
Yule–Simon (YULE)	$\rho > 0$	$\rho B(k, \rho + 1)$
negative binomial (NEGB)	$p \in (0, 1), r > 0$	$\dfrac{\Gamma(K + r)p^k(1 - p)^r}{k!\Gamma(r)[1 - (1 - p)^r]}$
truncated power law (TPOW)	$q \in (0, 1), \tau > 1$	$\dfrac{q^k}{\mathrm{Li}_\tau(q)k^\tau}$
discrete lognormal (DLGN)	$\mu \in \mathbf{R}, \sigma > 0$	$\begin{cases} \dfrac{1}{2} + \dfrac{1}{2}\mathrm{erf}\left(-\dfrac{\mu}{\sqrt{2}\sigma}\right) \\ \quad \text{if } k = 1 \\ \dfrac{1}{2}\left[\mathrm{erf}\left(\dfrac{\ln k - \mu}{\sqrt{2}\sigma}\right) - \mathrm{erf}\left(\dfrac{\ln(k-1) - \mu}{\sqrt{2}\sigma}\right)\right] \\ \quad \text{if } k = 2, 3, \ldots \end{cases}$
discrete Weibull (DWEI)	$q \in (0, 1), \beta > 0$	$\dfrac{1}{q}\left[q^{(k^\beta)} - q^{((k+1)^\beta)}\right]$

nodes are constantly added to the network and linked preferentially to nodes of high degree), we have included it in our list.

As a mixed case we introduce the exponentially truncated power law as one of our two-parameter models in Table 14.1. The negative binomial is another two-parameter example that decays more slowly than an exponential if its parameter r exceeds 1, but with much less weight in the tail than a power law. All the distributions mentioned so far are discrete: they are defined for integer numbers k. In the case of the Poisson and negative binomial distributions, is conventionally included in the distributions' support. In order to restore restriction (a) from above, we constrain these distributions to exclude $k = 0$, which explains why the equations in Table 14.1 differ from the ordinary textbook form.

Among continuous distributions, there are two further canonical candidates whose decay is between an exponential and a power law: the lognormal distribution and the Weibull distribution (also known as stretched exponential if in the formula stated in Table 14.1). We include these models in our study because previous studies have reported lognormal (Stumpf *et al.*, 2005; Bhattacharya *et al.*, 2008; Gómez *et al.*, 2008; Todor *et al.*, 2012) and Weibull distributions (Lahererre and Sornette, 1998; Broido and Claffy, 2001; He *et al.*, 2007; Rocha *et al.*, 2010) in real-world networks. To allow a direct comparison with the other models, we have to discretize the continuous lognormal and Weibull distribution, which can be accomplished in a variety of ways. Here we have chosen to integrate the continuous distributions between subsequent integers k and $k + 1$. In terms of the cumulative distribution F, we can express the integral as the probability $F(K + 1) - F(k)$. For the lognormal distribution, we assign this probability to the integer at the upper boundary $k + 1$ and call this the "discrete lognormal" distribution. In the case of the Weibull distribution preliminary tests showed that the likelihoods are in general slightly larger if $f(K + 1) - F(k)$ is assigned to k instead of $k + 1$. Imposing the constraint (a), yields the expression for the "discrete Weibull" distribution in Table 14.1.

One subtlety to note is that in this study we do not judge the fit of the distributions by the tails alone, as is often done elsewhere ((Albert and Barabási, 1999); Clauset *et al.*, 2009). In the study of continuous phase transitions in physics it is justified to restrict attention to the tails because only these are important for determining "universal" power-law features. However, in the present context it is far-fetched to assume that the cargo ship network has anything to do with a physical phase transition. Instead we will assess the match of the distribution over the full set of positive integers $k = 1, 2, 3, \ldots$ with the same motivation as in the study of city size distributions by Eeckhout (2004). Although it is, in principle, possible to restrict the analysis to the tails by introducing a lower cutoff $k > 1$, this would introduce an additional parameter and ignore the bulk of the data, which consists of ports with only few calls and low degree. On the contrary, we regard it as valuable information for practitioners to model low-traffic ports too, not only the small fraction of busy hubs that make up the distribution's tail.

Akaike information criterion

Assuming that all calls and degrees are independent, the likelihood function for any of the models in Table 14.1 has the general form

$$L(\mathbf{v}) = \prod_{i=1}^{n} \Pr(k_i; \mathbf{v}), \tag{14.2}$$

where k_i is the number of calls (or the degree) at port i, n is the number of ports in the sample, and $\mathbf{v}$ is the set of the parameters in the second column of the table. The calls (or degrees) may in reality depend on each other so that $L(\mathbf{v})$ in Equation (14.2) is more properly thought of as a composite likelihood. We can justify the use of a composite likelihood in our present context because the call (or degree) distribution $\Pr(k)$ that we would like to model is a marginal rather than the complete joint distribution of all calls (or degrees). Therefore, the full dependence structure is in statistical terms a "nuisance parameter" which neither matters to us nor is it clear how to specify the full likelihood. In such cases, composite likelihood methods have proved to be a well-behaved alternative (Cox and Reid, 2004; Varin *et al.*, 2011). Another, more pragmatic, point of view is that there is no straightforward method to establish from our data how the k_i may depend on each other so that assuming independence is the most parsimonious choice.

For a specified model j, we determine the parameter $\hat{\mathbf{v}}_j$ that maximizes L and hence also the log-likelihood $\ln(L)$. A comparison between different models can then be performed by ranking their Akaike information criterion (AIC) (Akaike, 1974),

$$\text{AIC}_j = -2\ln(L(\hat{\mathbf{v}}_j)) + 2K_j, \tag{14.3}$$

where K_j is the number of parameters in the respective model. The AIC not only tells us which model is closest to the data in information content, properly taking into account that higher K_j generally allows better fits to the data, but weakens the explanatory power of the model. We can also make quantitative comparisons between different models based on the differences. If $\text{AIC}_{\min}$ is the minimum AIC over all models, then the difference

$$\Delta_j = \text{AIC}_j - AIC_{\min} \tag{14.4}$$

estimates the relative expected information gain between model j and the estimated best model. Because the likelihood of model j given the number of calls (or degrees) $k_1, k_2, \ldots$ is proportional to $\exp(-\Delta_j/2)$ (Burnham and Anderson, 1998), the relative likelihood is the so-called Akaike weight

$$w_j = \frac{\exp(-\Delta_j/2)}{\sum_i \exp(-\Delta_i/2)}, \tag{14.5}$$

where the summation in the denominator is over all models included in the comparison. Model selection by Akaike weights has become an increasingly popular tool to compare different hypothesized probability distributions (Edwards *et al.*, 2007; Stumpf *et al.*, 2005; Hamilton *et al.*, 2008; Prieto and Sarabia, 2011). The Akaike weights for our data sets are summarized in Table 14.2 for the call distributions and in Table 14.3 for the degree distributions.

As a quick glance at the tables reveals, the maximum Akaike weights are achieved by the discrete lognormal and Weibull distributions and, in the case of the calls, in some years a truncated power law. These two-parameter models always perform better than even the best one-parameter model, which is in all cases the Yule–Simon distribution. The added term $2K_i$ in Equation (14.3) for introducing a second parameter is therefore more than compensated by an increased likelihood for the best-performing models.

The effect of including a second parameter can be seen in Figure 14.1(a) and (b) where we compare the observed call distributions in 1910 and 2000 with the maximum-likelihood estimates for the Yule–Simon, truncated power law, lognormal, and Weibull distributions. Both observed distributions are substantially curved on a log-log scale and thus difficult to fit by an asymptotic power law such as the Yule–Simon distribution. All other plotted candidate distributions have the

Table 14.2 Akaike weights for the distribution of vessel calls

Year	Ports	POIS	GEOM	ZETA	YULE	NEGB	TPOW	DLGN	DWEI
1890	904	0	0	2.61×10^{-16}	1.60×10^{-10}	4.61×10^{-30}	3.64×10^{-1}	$\mathbf{6.10 \times 10^{-1}}$	2.58×10^{-2}
1910	1200	0	0	2.90×10^{-25}	4.56×10^{-17}	4.76×10^{-31}	$\mathbf{9.37 \times 10^{-1}}$	6.13×10^{-2}	2.12×10^{-3}
1915	992	0	0	1.51×10^{-23}	1.23×10^{-16}	3.55×10^{-23}	$\mathbf{7.70 \times 10^{-1}}$	2.26×10^{-1}	3.94×10^{-3}
1920	994	0	0	9.36×10^{-20}	2.07×10^{-13}	2.42×10^{-30}	$\mathbf{8.83 \times 10^{-1}}$	1.10×10^{-1}	6.22×10^{-3}
1925	1205	0	0	2.51×10^{-29}	4.17×10^{-20}	6.09×10^{-30}	6.97×10^{-2}	$\mathbf{8.27 \times 10^{-1}}$	1.03×10^{-1}
1930	1254	0	0	4.78×10^{-33}	3.16×10^{-23}	5.61×10^{-29}	9.64×10^{-3}	$\mathbf{9.64 \times 10^{-1}}$	2.66×10^{-2}
1935	1282	0	0	4.29×10^{-33}	3.15×10^{-22}	5.01×10^{-29}	1.03×10^{-2}	$\mathbf{5.24 \times 10^{-1}}$	4.66×10^{-1}
1940	1309	0	0	1.42×10^{-23}	2.62×10^{-15}	1.50×10^{-41}	$\mathbf{9.79 \times 10^{-1}}$	1.96×10^{-2}	1.20×10^{-3}
1946	1281	0	0	6.05×10^{-26}	7.30×10^{-17}	9.37×10^{-37}	$\mathbf{8.47 \times 10^{-1}}$	8.47×10^{-2}	6.80×10^{-2}
1951	1321	0	0	1.91×10^{-34}	1.06×10^{-23}	1.42×10^{-25}	3.21×10^{-1}	$\mathbf{5.67 \times 10^{-1}}$	1.13×10^{-1}
1960	1541	0	0	1.49×10^{-47}	1.51×10^{-34}	2.66×10^{-23}	8.99×10^{-2}	$\mathbf{8.78 \times 10^{-1}}$	3.22×10^{-2}
1965	1554	0	0	2.58×10^{-59}	1.07×10^{-44}	1.42×10^{-17}	3.52×10^{-3}	$\mathbf{6.40 \times 10^{-1}}$	3.56×10^{-1}
1970	1512	0	0	5.70×10^{-57}	2.29×10^{-43}	4.73×10^{-14}	$\mathbf{5.83 \times 10^{-1}}$	3.44×10^{-1}	7.25×10^{-2}
1975	1610	0	0	6.08×10^{-60}	1.08×10^{-44}	2.98×10^{-22}	1.15×10^{-4}	4.91×10^{-1}	$\mathbf{5.09 \times 10^{-1}}$
1980	1637	0	0	1.40×10^{-76}	1.40×10^{-59}	3.60×10^{-15}	2.23×10^{-6}	2.17×10^{-1}	$\mathbf{7.83 \times 10^{-1}}$
1985	1925	0	0	3.21×10^{-107}	1.22×10^{-84}	2.54×10^{-19}	8.01×10^{-14}	9.46×10^{-2}	$\mathbf{9.05 \times 10^{-1}}$
1990	1903	0	0	1.14×10^{-107}	2.37×10^{-85}	1.12×10^{-18}	6.86×10^{-14}	4.29×10^{-2}	$\mathbf{9.57 \times 10^{-1}}$
1995	1953	0	0	2.93×10^{-107}	6.45×10^{-85}	1.71×10^{-15}	8.34×10^{-11}	2.09×10^{-2}	$\mathbf{9.79 \times 10^{-1}}$
2000	2050	0	0	1.41×10^{-113}	1.36×10^{-89}	2.15×10^{-15}	4.87×10^{-11}	1.13×10^{-2}	$\mathbf{9.89 \times 10^{-1}}$
2008	2157	0	0	1.82×10^{-96}	3.97×10^{-74}	8.03×10^{-15}	5.93×10^{-5}	4.31×10^{-2}	$\mathbf{9.57 \times 10^{-1}}$

Note: Values below 10^{-200} are rounded to zero. The largest Akaike weight in each year is highlighted in bold type.

Table 14.3 Akaike weights for the degree distribution

Year	Ports	POIS	GEOM	ZETA	YULE	NEGB	TPOW	DLGN	DWEI
1890	895	0	3.05×10^{-132}	4.96×10^{-37}	1.22×10^{-25}	8.99×10^{-8}	3.62×10^{-4}	$\mathbf{6.21 \times 10^{-1}}$	3.79×10^{-1}
1910	1186	0	3.66×10^{-186}	1.97×10^{-69}	5.02×10^{-53}	1.20×10^{-9}	1.54×10^{-8}	$\mathbf{9.82 \times 10^{-1}}$	1.80×10^{-2}
1915	970	0	9.77×10^{-140}	4.07×10^{-62}	8.23×10^{-49}	1.48×10^{-4}	1.87×10^{-4}	$\mathbf{6.04 \times 10^{-1}}$	3.96×10^{-1}
1920	955	0	8.66×10^{-147}	4.53×10^{-60}	1.01×10^{-46}	5.13×10^{-7}	1.18×10^{-6}	$\mathbf{9.65 \times 10^{-1}}$	3.49×10^{-2}
1925	1170	0	1.79×10^{-188}	3.85×10^{-67}	3.23×10^{-52}	5.22×10^{-5}	3.74×10^{-4}	1.05×10^{-1}	$\mathbf{8.94 \times 10^{-1}}$
1930	1231	0	1.65×10^{-179}	6.11×10^{-89}	1.59×10^{-71}	9.58×10^{-9}	8.04×10^{-9}	$\mathbf{7.94 \times 10^{-1}}$	2.06×10^{-1}
1935	1259	0	3.08×10^{-181}	1.07×10^{-90}	2.22×10^{-72}	5.79×10^{-11}	5.18×10^{-11}	$\mathbf{9.92 \times 10^{-1}}$	8.34×10^{-3}
1940	1273	0	3.41×10^{-196}	1.25×10^{-85}	6.69×10^{-67}	2.44×10^{-13}	5.43×10^{-13}	$> \mathbf{9.99 \times 10^{-1}}$	4.92×10^{-4}
1946	1220	0	3.38×10^{-197}	5.90×10^{-57}	1.13×10^{-41}	1.13×10^{-6}	1.51×10^{-3}	$\mathbf{5.11 \times 10^{-1}}$	4.87×10^{-1}
1951	1294	0	3.85×10^{-180}	3.94×10^{-88}	2.04×10^{-69}	1.19×10^{-9}	1.29×10^{-9}	$\mathbf{9.94 \times 10^{-1}}$	6.48×10^{-3}
1960	1506	0	0	8.78×10^{-105}	1.09×10^{-83}	3.47×10^{-9}	3.26×10^{-9}	$\mathbf{9.57 \times 10^{-1}}$	4.29×10^{-2}
1965	1534	0	0	6.26×10^{-119}	3.03×10^{-97}	2.53×10^{-7}	1.12×10^{-7}	1.18×10^{-1}	$\mathbf{8.82 \times 10^{-1}}$
1970	1487	0	0	2.72×10^{-109}	2.20×10^{-89}	2.71×10^{-4}	1.74×10^{-4}	6.07×10^{-3}	$\mathbf{9.93 \times 10^{-1}}$
1975	1579	0	0	1.92×10^{-103}	3.00×10^{-82}	1.57×10^{-6}	2.00×10^{-6}	2.75×10^{-1}	$\mathbf{7.25 \times 10^{-1}}$
1980	1591	0	9.20×10^{-198}	3.34×10^{-124}	2.44×10^{-102}	4.49×10^{-5}	2.19×10^{-5}	1.25×10^{-4}	$> \mathbf{9.99 \times 10^{-1}}$
1985	1872	0	0	2.18×10^{-150}	1.57×10^{-123}	1.64×10^{-8}	5.10×10^{-9}	6.41×10^{-4}	$\mathbf{9.99 \times 10^{-1}}$
1990	1875	0	0	4.46×10^{-162}	1.44×10^{-136}	1.96×10^{-5}	7.40×10^{-6}	1.15×10^{-8}	$> \mathbf{9.99 \times 10^{-1}}$
1995	1897	0	4.51×10^{-191}	5.31×10^{-176}	3.15×10^{-149}	3.07×10^{-4}	8.99×10^{-5}	6.78×10^{-10}	$> \mathbf{9.99 \times 10^{-1}}$
2000	1969	0	0	2.60×10^{-148}	6.90×10^{-121}	1.84×10^{-3}	9.28×10^{-4}	1.17×10^{-7}	$\mathbf{9.97 \times 10^{-1}}$
2008	2007	0	8.85×10^{-183}	2.55×10^{-127}	1.78×10^{-99}	2.01×10^{-1}	1.61×10^{-1}	9.33×10^{-8}	$\mathbf{6.38 \times 10^{-1}}$

Note: Values below 10^{-200} are rounded to zero. The largest Akaike weight in each year is highlighted in bold type.

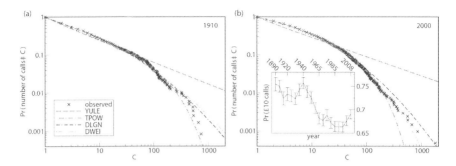

Figure 14.1 Observed complementary cumulative call distribution function in 1910 (a), 2000 (b) together with the maximum-likelihood Yule–Simon, truncated power law, discrete lognormal and discrete Weibull distributions.

flexibility to follow the curvature more accurately. Among these, the truncated power law decays in the limit $k \to \infty$ most rapidly and the lognormal distribution most slowly in the tail.[1]

The one-parameter Yule-Simon distribution fits the data far worse than any of the two-parameter alternatives. In 1910 the truncated power law has the highest likelihood among all models. In 2000 the Weibull distribution fits best (Table 14.2). Inset in (b): The fraction of ports with no more than ten ports has dropped from around 75 percent to approximately 68 percent during the 1960s. This subtle, but statistically significant decrease is responsible for more curvature in later years on the left-hand side of the observed data. Error bars are jackknife estimates.

Comparing the observed call distributions in 1910 and 2000, the most obvious difference is that the initial decay on the left-hand side appears less curved in Figure 14.1(a) than in (b). For this reason, the truncated power law that fits well in 1910 is no longer a suitable candidate in 2000. In general, we observed by visual inspection that in the small to medium port range the complementary cumulative call distribution tends to be more curved in later years. This trend is detected by the Akaike weights in Table 14.2 that have shifted over the years from the truncated power law to the Weibull distribution. In practice, this change in the distribution implies that there is now a smaller fraction of ports listed with maximally ten calls in one week. The inset in Figure 14.1(b) confirms this trend, showing a statistically significant decrease between the years 1890 and 2008 from 75.4 percent to 69.0 percent of ports having no more than ten calls.[2]

The interpretation of the degree distribution is a little trickier. The Akaike weights in Table 14.3 seem to suggest a clear distinction: before the mid-1960s the most likely model is in all but one case a lognormal, but afterwards it is always a Weibull distribution. However, Figure 14.2(a) shows that in 1910 the lognormal and Weibull distributions are visually more or less equally good fits. Only in 2000 (Figure 14.2b) does the maximum-likelihood Weibull distribution clearly fit better in the tail than the lognormal. Unlike for the call distribution, we do not find a

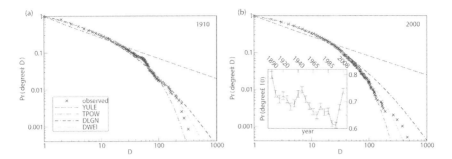

Figure 14.2 Observed complementary cumulative degree distribution function in 1910 (a), 2000 (b) together with the maximum-likelihood Yule–Simon, truncated power law, discrete lognormal and discrete Weibull distributions.

significant trend that the percentage of low-degree ports has decreased (inset in Figure 14.2b). In order to shed light on the significance of the apparent trend in the Akaike weights for the degree distribution, in the next section we will compare the performance of the maximum-likelihood models with another statistical technique.

The highest Akaike weight is achieved by the (a) lognormal, (b) Weibull distribution. Inset in (b): The fraction of ports with degree ≤ 10 does not show a clear trend.

Vuong's likelihood ratio tests

For models with an equal number of parameters, Akaike weights compare the models purely by the differences in their log-likelihood. Proponents of AIC-based model selection have argued that the Akaike weights are sufficient to judge the significance of the best model (Burnham and Anderson, 1998). However, others argue that the log-likelihood alone does not in itself allow an assessment when we should reject the second-ranked model in favour of the model with the highest Akaike weight (Stephens *et al.*, 2005). Likelihood ratio tests, on the other hand, can inform us how significant the difference in the log-likelihood is (Clauset *et al.*, 2009).

In this section we investigate the three two-parameter models that achieved maximal Akaike weight in at least one year for either the call or degree distribution: truncated power law, discrete lognormal, and Weibull distributions. For these non-nested models we apply the likelihood ratio test devised by Vuong (1989). The test statistic for comparing models r and s is the ratio of their likelihoods from Equation (14.2) or equivalently its logarithm

$$R = \ln\left(\prod_{i=1}^{n} \frac{p_r(k_i)}{p_s(k_i)}\right) = \sum_{i=1}^{n}(\ln p_r(k_i) - \ln p_s(k_i)), \qquad (14.6)$$

where $p_r(k_i)$ is the probability $\Pr(k_i; \hat{\mathbf{v}}_r)$ assigned to observing degree k_i in model r with the maximum-likelihood parameters $\hat{\mathbf{v}}_r$. If we assume that all observed k_i

are independent (as we discussed after Equation (14.2)), then all terms $\ln p_r(k_i) - \ln p_s(k_i)$ in the sum on the left-hand side of Equation (14.6) are also independent. With the shorthand notation $l_i = \ln p_r(k_i) - \ln p_s(k_i)$, the variance of one term in the sum can be estimated as

$$\sigma^2 = \frac{1}{n}\sum_{i=1}^{n} l_i^2 - \left(\frac{1}{n}\sum_{i=1}^{n} l_i\right)^2. \tag{14.7}$$

For sufficiently large n, the random variable R thus becomes normally distributed with an estimated variance $n\sigma^2$. We can then apply a conventional Z-test to determine whether the observed value R is significantly different from zero given the observed variance. The p-value can be expressed as

$$p = \text{erfc}\left(\frac{|R|}{\sqrt{2n\sigma^2}}\right), \tag{14.8}$$

where erfc is the complementary error function.

This handwaving derivation, which follows essentially that of Clauset *et al.* (2009), is admittedly oversimplified. For both models r and s in Equation (14.6) we have fitted the parameters $\hat{\mathbf{v}}_r$ and $\hat{\mathbf{v}}_s$ to the same data so that there are nontrivial correlations between R and σ^2. However, Vuong (1989) proved that Equation (14.8) still remains true. One noteworthy point about this equation is the appearance of the variance σ^2. The variance of the data is a crucial piece of evidence whether one of the two models in question is likely to be significantly better. The Akaike weights, by contrast, did not account for the variance.

We list the p-values for all pairwise comparisons between truncated power laws, lognormal, and Weibull distributions in Table 14.4. We highlight in bold type all p-values less than 0.1 and, where the likelihood ratio test indicates a deviation from randomness at this 10 percent significance level, we list in parentheses the more likely model. As an overall pattern for the call distribution (left half of the table), the tests are for most years indifferent between the three candidate models. However, for the degrees (right half of the table) the test strongly rejects for most years the truncated power law, consistent with its small Akaike weights in Table 14.3. Also in agreement with our earlier findings, the tests favour the Weibull distribution in some of the more recent years for both calls and degrees. There are examples where the Akaike weights suggest a high likelihood for one particular model, yet the likelihood-ratio test does not lend strong support to it. For example, in 2008 the Weibull distribution has an Akaike weight 0.957 for the calls, but, after factoring in the variance in the data, the likelihood ratio test does not reject the possibility that the data could be from a lognormal distribution (Akaike weight 0.043) or even a truncated power law despite its much lower Akaike weight (5.93×10^{-5}).

There is thus for most years no simple answer if the call distribution is better described by a Weibull or lognormal distribution. Over the range of observed calls (i.e. between 1 and approximately 2000; the precise upper bound, of course,

Table 14.4 *p*-values for Vuong's likelihood ratio test of the maximum-likelihood distributions

Year	calls			degrees		
	TPOW-DLGN	TPOW-DWEI	DLGN-DWEI	TPOW-DLGN	TPOW-DWEI	DLGN-DWEI
1890	0.83	0.49	0.20	**0.09** (DLGN)	**0.04** (DWEI)	0.67
1910	0.35	0.18	0.18	**0.01** (DLGN)	**0.01** (DWEI)	0.11
1915	0.66	0.22	**0.09** (DLGN)	0.16	**0.05** (DWEI)	0.84
1920	0.47	0.26	0.28	**0.03** (DLGN)	**0.01** (DWEI)	0.16
1925	0.52	0.94	0.34	0.35	**0.09** (DWEI)	0.19
1930	0.25	0.85	0.10	**0.02** (DLGN)	**0.00** (DWEI)	0.64
1935	0.37	0.48	0.94	**0.00** (DLGN)	**0.00** (DWEI)	0.13
1940	0.19	0.15	0.35	**0.00** (DLGN)	**0.00** (DWEI)	**0.02** (DLGN)
1946	0.59	0.66	0.93	0.30	0.18	0.97
1951	0.88	0.84	0.37	**0.01** (DLGN)	**0.00** (DWEI)	0.10
1960	0.64	0.86	0.10	**0.02** (DLGN)	**0.00** (DWEI)	0.33
1965	0.40	0.49	0.68	0.11	**0.00** (DWEI)	0.55
1970	0.92	0.73	0.39	0.64	0.10	**0.07** (DWEI)
1975	0.19	0.22	0.98	0.14	**0.02** (DWEI)	0.72
1980	0.13	**0.08** (DWEI)	0.30	0.84	**0.06** (DWEI)	**0.01** (DWEI)
1985	**0.01** (DLGN)	**0.00** (DWEI)	0.22	0.26	**0.00** (DWEI)	**0.08** (DWEI)
1990	**0.03** (DLGN)	**0.01** (DWEI)	0.18	0.56	0.10	**0.00** (DWEI)
1995	0.12	**0.03** (DWEI)	**0.09** (DWEI)	0.29	0.17	**0.00** (DWEI)
2000	0.16	**0.05** (DWEI)	**0.06** (DWEI)	0.39	0.32	**0.00** (DWEI)
2008	0.70	0.54	0.23	0.19	0.86	**0.00** (DWEI)

Note: We show all pairwise comparisons between truncated power law, discrete lognormal and discrete Weibull distributions. We highlight *p*-values smaller than 0.1 in bold type and add in parentheses the more likely distribution. Values below 5×10^{-3} are rounded to zero.

depends on the year in question) the maximum-likelihood distributions from the lognormal and Weibull family do in fact not differ very much as can be seen in Figure 14.1(a). Likewise, for the degree distribution there is no clear support in favour of the lognormal hypothesis prior to 1960 (except in 1940) despite generally having the highest Akaike weight. Afterwards, there is increasing evidence in favour of the Weibull distribution, which might have to do with an increasing number of ports in the sample that allows us to distinguish more clearly between the models.

One has to bear in mind that neither the Akaike weight nor the likelihood ratio test can tell us that a model is good in an absolute sense, only that it is more plausible than its competitors. In other words, if all our candidate models are bad, then "in the country of the blind, the one-eyed man is king." We will now apply two classic goodness-of-fit tests that show that some of our candidate models are indeed a good match for the observations.

Kolmogorov–Smirnov and Anderson–Darling tests

The key idea behind both the Kolmogorov–Smirnov (KS) and Anderson–Darling (AD) tests is to compare the difference between the observed and hypothesized cumulative distribution functions. If the observed degree (or number of calls) are $k_1, k_2, \ldots, k_n$, then the observed cumulative distribution $F_{\text{obs}}(x)$ is the number of ports with $k_i \geq x$ divided by n. The KS statistic is defined by

$$D_{KS} = \max_{x=1,2,3,\ldots} |F_{\text{obs}}(x) - F_{\text{model}}(x)|, \qquad (14.9)$$

where F_{model} is the cumulative distribution function of the model to be tested (Kolmogorov, 1933). In words, D_{KS} is the maximum absolute difference between observed and hypothesized cumulative distribution function for any possible value x. While D_{KS} has a very intuitive interpretation, it also has one shortcoming when applied to heavy-tailed distributions: $|F_{\text{obs}}(x) - F_{\text{model}}(x)|$ is typically maximized where $F_{\text{model}} \approx 0.5$ and therefore D_{KS} does not effectively sample the tail where $F_{model}(x)$ is close to 1. This phenomenon can be understood as follows. If the model were correct and the difference between F_{obs} and F_{model} only the consequence of random chance, the jackknife estimate of the standard deviation in the difference is $\sqrt{F_{\text{model}}(x)[1 - F_{\text{model}}(x)]/(n - 1)}$, which has a maximum at $F_{\text{model}}(x) = 1/2$.

There is one obvious cure to this problem: we divide the difference to be maximized in Equation (14.9) by the expected standard deviation,

$$D_{AD} = \max_{x=1,2,3,\ldots} \frac{|F_{\text{obs}}(x) - F_{\text{model}}(x)|}{\sqrt{F_{\text{model}}(x)[1 - F_{\text{model}}(x)]}}, \qquad (14.10)$$

where we dropped the term $\sqrt{n-1}$ because it is independent of x. D_{AD} is called the Anderson–Darling statistic (Anderson and Darling, 1952). We have decided to carry out tests for both D_{KS} and D_{AD} because these two statistics measure different features of the distribution. A good model should be able to have small values of D_{KS} as well as D_{AD}.

We test the significance of the same three two-parameter models as in the likelihood ratio test (truncated power law, lognormal, and Weibull distribution), but also include for comparison the Yule–Simon distribution which the Akaike weights identified as the best one-parameter model. We calculate p-values with Monte Carlo simulations based on the following algorithm.

First, we determine for a given model the maximum-likelihood parameters $\hat{\mathbf{v}}_{\mathrm{obs}}$ that fit the *Lloyd's Shipping Index* data best. For the model distribution with parameters $\hat{\mathbf{v}}_{\mathrm{obs}}$ we calculate the observed test statistics $D_{KS,\mathrm{obs}}$ and $D_{AD,\mathrm{obs}}$. Next we generate n random numbers drawn from the model distribution with parameters $\hat{\mathbf{v}}_{\mathrm{obs}}$. We then pretend that we do not know $\hat{\mathbf{v}}_{\mathrm{obs}}$ and determine the maximum-likelihood parameters $\hat{\mathbf{v}}_{\mathrm{md}}$ that fit the random numbers best. In general, $\hat{\mathbf{v}}_{\mathrm{md}}$ will differ slightly from $\hat{\mathbf{v}}_{\mathrm{obs}}$. From the difference between the random numbers (now treated as surrogate observation) and the model with $\hat{\mathbf{v}}_{\mathrm{md}}$ we calculate $D_{KS,\mathrm{md}}$ and $D_{AD,\mathrm{md}}$. We repeat drawing n random numbers 10^5 times and estimate the p-value p_{KS} for the KS test by the fraction of runs with $D_{KS,md} \geq D_{KS,\mathrm{obs}}$. The same calculations are also carried out for the AD statistic. The repeated calculation of $\hat{\mathbf{v}}_{\mathrm{md}}$ slows down the simulation, but is necessary to mimic the steps in the calculation of $D_{KS,\mathrm{obs}}$ and $D_{AD,\mathrm{obs}}$. Otherwise we obtain p-values with a strong downward bias that would lead us to accept the null hypothesis (i.e. that the real data follows the model distribution) more often than truly justified (Clauset *et al.*, 2009).

The p-values are listed in Table 14.5. The highlighted entries in bold type are those cases where there is no reason to suspect at the 10 percent significance level that the model is wrong, either in terms of the KS or the AD statistic. It is striking that the Yule–Simon distribution fails as a null hypothesis for call and degree distributions in all years. The truncated power law is accepted only for the call distribution (left half of the table) and mostly in the early years of our data base. By contrast, the lognormal distribution is a suitable null hypothesis for the call distribution in all except one year (1995), and even then the null hypothesis would not be rejected at a 5 percent significance level. For the degree distribution (right half of the table), a lognormal null hypothesis is accepted in most, but not all years. Especially in the later years, the Weibull distribution shows better performance than the lognormal, confirming the trends we observed in the Akaike weights and the likelihood ratio tests. However, the KS and AD tests in earlier years only sporadically support a Weibull distribution.

Discussion

The overall picture that emerges from the KS and AD tests is a surprisingly consistent performance of the lognormal model for the call distribution. The only rejection, namely by the KS test for the data of 1995, could plausibly be by random chance. After all, at the chosen 10 percent significance level it is likely that at least one false positive exists among the 20 years which we have tested. The lognormal hypothesis also gains support from a recent analysis of world container

Table 14.5 *p*-values for the Kolmogorov–Smirnov test and the Anderson–Darling test

Year	calls								degrees							
	YULE		TPOW		DLGN		DWEI		YULE		TPOW		DLGN		DWEI	
	p_{KS}	p_{AD}	p_{KS}	p_{AD}	p_{KS}	p_{AD}	p_{KS}	p_{AD}	p_{KS}	p_{AD}	p_{KS}	p_{AD}	p_{KS}	p_{AD}	p_{KS}	p_{AD}
1890	0.00	0.06	**0.22**	**0.37**	**0.98**	**0.78**	0.04	0.38	0.00	0.02	0.00	0.11	**0.93**	**0.63**	**0.34**	**0.47**
1910	0.00	0.04	**0.22**	**0.27**	**0.72**	**0.46**	0.01	0.18	0.00	0.00	0.00	0.03	0.07	0.17	0.00	0.10
1915	0.00	0.04	**0.24**	**0.21**	**0.81**	**0.69**	0.01	0.20	0.00	0.00	0.00	0.06	**0.50**	**0.43**	0.03	0.31
1920	0.00	0.05	**0.51**	**0.58**	**0.95**	**0.80**	0.04	0.37	0.00	0.00	0.00	0.03	**0.18**	**0.37**	0.01	0.11
1925	0.00	0.03	0.04	0.06	**0.96**	**0.82**	0.07	0.40	0.00	0.00	0.00	0.07	**0.78**	**0.44**	**0.29**	**0.55**
1930	0.00	0.03	0.02	0.03	**0.84**	**0.70**	0.01	0.26	0.00	0.00	0.00	0.02	**0.69**	**0.55**	0.02	0.28
1935	0.00	0.03	0.00	0.04	**0.91**	**0.77**	**0.42**	**0.49**	0.00	0.00	0.00	0.03	**0.35**	**0.51**	0.00	0.10
1940	0.00	0.04	**0.12**	**0.40**	**0.61**	**0.64**	0.03	0.17	0.00	0.00	0.00	0.02	**0.11**	**0.20**	0.00	0.06
1946	0.00	0.03	0.02	0.02	**0.31**	**0.22**	0.03	0.10	0.00	0.00	0.00	0.06	**0.30**	**0.30**	0.01	0.24
1951	0.00	0.03	0.03	0.06	**0.78**	**0.68**	0.08	0.33	0.00	0.00	0.00	0.03	**0.11**	**0.45**	0.00	0.08
1960	0.00	0.01	0.11	0.04	**0.55**	**0.65**	0.01	0.25	0.00	0.00	0.00	0.02	0.03	0.22	0.00	0.09
1965	0.00	0.00	0.02	0.02	**0.88**	**0.49**	0.08	0.48	0.00	0.00	0.00	0.03	**0.49**	**0.29**	0.06	0.42
1970	0.00	0.00	0.07	0.03	**0.84**	**0.54**	0.00	0.23	0.00	0.00	0.00	0.07	**0.23**	**0.25**	0.09	0.53
1975	0.00	0.00	0.00	0.02	**0.87**	**0.63**	**0.37**	**0.47**	0.00	0.00	0.00	0.04	**0.22**	**0.34**	0.02	0.31
1980	0.00	0.00	0.00	0.01	**0.60**	**0.52**	**0.20**	**0.75**	0.00	0.00	0.00	0.04	**0.23**	**0.14**	**0.21**	**0.75**
1985	0.00	0.00	0.00	0.00	**0.79**	**0.88**	**0.94**	**0.54**	0.00	0.00	0.00	0.01	**0.41**	**0.18**	**0.85**	**0.64**
1990	0.00	0.00	0.00	0.00	**0.26**	**0.46**	**0.26**	**0.24**	0.00	0.00	0.00	0.00	0.02	0.09	**0.34**	**0.58**
1995	0.00	0.00	0.00	0.00	0.06	0.25	0.02	0.40	0.00	0.00	0.01	0.01	0.01	0.06	**0.10**	**0.42**
2000	0.00	0.00	0.00	0.00	**0.60**	**0.25**	**0.56**	**0.16**	0.00	0.00	0.00	0.00	0.09	0.07	**0.16**	**0.34**
2008	0.00	0.00	0.04	0.00	**0.31**	**0.11**	0.04	0.10	0.00	0.00	0.05	0.00	0.03	0.06	0.00	0.18

Note: Values below 5×10^{-3} are rounded to zero. We highlight those distributions in bold type where the null hypothesis (i.e. that the data is generated by the model) is not rejected at a 10 percent significance level.

port throughput (Ding and Teo, 2010) that reported a good fit between the number of containers handled at 300 top ports and a lognormal distribution. There is also a simple mechanistic model that could explain how a lognormal distribution might come about: Gibrat's law of proportionate growth (Gibrat, 1931). It is, in principle, possible to carry out further tests whether *Lloyd's Shipping Index* supports the key principle behind Gibrat's law, namely that the growth rates in calls are independent of the number of calls. Such a test will make more stringent demands on the data quality than what we currently have available. Right now such an effort would be hampered, for example, by the irregular time intervals between the samples. As more data becomes available, an analysis of port growth rates is clearly an intriguing research direction.

For the time being, we can instead view the call distribution from yet another angle. As an alternative to plotting the complementary distribution function directly (Figure 14.1), economists frequently employ Lorenz curves (Lorenz, 1905) to visualize inequality in distributions. Translated to our application, the Lorenz curve $y(x)$ shows the percentage of ship calls that were made at the x percent of lowest ranked ports (ranked by the number of calls). We plot the Lorenz curves for three representative years in Figure 14.3(a). If all ports had an equal number of calls, the Lorenz curve would be the dashed diagonal line. One measure of inequality is the area between this diagonal and the actually observed Lorenz curve: the more unequal the distribution, the larger this area. Multiplied by two, this measure is known as the Gini coefficient (Gini, 1912). The coefficient itself, as well as a jackknife estimate of its standard error, can be conveniently calculated with ordinary least-squares regression (Giles, 2004). The results for all years in our data base (Figure 14.3b) reveal that the Gini coefficient for the calls has decreased from 0.80 in 1890 to 0.74 in 2008. Although this is a subtle decline, it is statistically significant: the values are more than five standard errors apart.

Why is the inequality declining? The maximum number of calls has increased (from 822 in 1890 to 2,422 in 2008), which at first glance suggests increasing inequality. The resolution to this apparent paradox lies in the inset of Figure 14.1(b): the fraction of small ports with ≤ 10 calls has decreased. As the total number of ports has grown over the years, an overproportional number of new medium-sized ports were added to the network. Together with a flattening global hierarchy this has reduced the gap between core and periphery, thereby making the network more polycentric. This trend more than compensates the growth in maximum port size and has led to an overall decrease in the Gini coefficient.

There is more than just the Gini coefficient that we can infer from the Lorenz curve. One complementary measure is the Lorenz asymmetry coefficient (LAC) (Damgaard and Weiner, 2000). A Lorenz curve is defined to be symmetric if it has the same slope as the diagonal "line of equality" (i.e. a slope of 1) at the point where the curve and the antidiagonal line $y = 1 - x$ (i.e. the dotted line in Figure 14.3a) intersect. One can show that for a continuous cumulative distribution F with mean μ the slope equals 1 at $x = F(\mu)$. At this point $y = \int_0^\mu (x/\mu)\,dF(x)$, so a criterion for symmetry is LAC $= F(\mu) + \int_0^\mu (x/\mu)\,dF(x) = 1$.[3] If LAC < 1, the Lorenz curve is skewed such that it has slope 1 below the dotted antidiagonal.

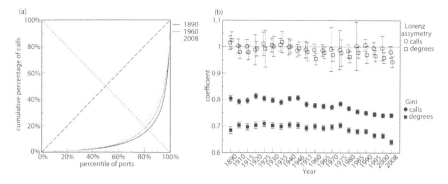

Figure 14.3 Lorenz curves for the call distributions in three exemplary years (a) (black: 1890, dark grey: 1960, light grey: 2008). Gini coefficients and LACs for all 20 years for which we have data (b).

The Gini coefficient measures inequality as twice the area between the Lorenz curve and the line of equality (dashed diagonal). The Lorenz asymmetry coefficient (LAC) measures whether curves have a slope of 1 at the intersection with the dotted antidiagonal line (LAC < 1 if the slope equals 1 below the antidiagonal, LAC > 1 if the slope equals 1 above it). For the three curves in the figure the Gini coefficient has decreased over time, but they all have a slope close to 1 at the symmetry axis. Error bars represent jackknife estimates of the standard deviation. The Gini coefficient for the call and degree distribution both show a slightly decreasing tendency that is statistically significant, similarly the LAC for the degrees. The LAC for the call distribution, however, shows no significant deviation from 1 in any of the investigated years

Conversely, if LAC > 1, the Lorenz curve is parallel with the line of equality above the antidiagonal symmetry axis.

The LAC is of interest because curves with the same Gini coefficient can have different asymmetries. If LAC < 1, the inequality in the distribution is caused by a large gap between a roughly equal number of small and large ports. By contrast, if LAC > 1, the inequality is due to a small number of very busy ports, whereas the majority of ports experiences approximately equally low traffic. The base case is a lognormal distribution where LAC = 1 regardless of the parameters μ and σ (Damgaard and Weiner, 2000). For the call distribution, we see in Figure 14.3(b) that LAC = 1 is always included in the error bar which represents a jackknife estimate of the standard deviation. This observation gives additional credence to the lognormal distribution as a working hypothesis for ship calls.

While the lognormal model is hence a generally promising candidate for the call distribution, it is not equally good for the degree distribution because LAC < 1 in the later years (Figure 14.3b). These numbers confirm the results from Tables 14.3–14.5 showing that the lognormal distribution is in those years not the best model for the degrees. There is, however, no immediate contradiction between this finding and a lognormal call distribution. The relationship between the call and degree distributions is complicated: regardless of whether one or multiple voyages are made between the same two ports, it always only adds 1 to the ports' degrees. In other words, the call distribution is a measure of the weighted multigraph of voyages, whereas the degree distribution is derived from the unweighted network that forms a so-called simple graph. The collapse of multiple voyages into one unweighted link can conceivably change the distribution so that it appears to come from a completely different probabilistic law. In future analysis, we will explore with suitable null models (e.g. random graphs with a fixed weighted degree sequence; see Molloy and Reed, 1995) how the degree distribution changes when a heavy-tailed (in particular lognormal) multigraph is mapped to a simple graph and if this may explain our observations for the cargo ship data.

Conclusion

We have statistically analysed call and degree distributions of the cargo ship network extracted from snapshots of *Lloyd's Shipping Index* in 20 different years between 1890 and 2008. We have applied information-based model selection and statistical hypothesis tests to quantify the empirical distribution in a mathematically principled manner. For the call distribution a lognormal null model passes the Anderson–Darling goodness-of-fit test in all years and the Kolmogorov–Smirnov test in 19 out of 20 years at a 10 percent significance level. In some early years the Akaike weight is higher for truncated power laws than a lognormal distribution; in later years a Weibull distribution is preferred. However, Vuong's likelihood ratio test does not reject the lognormal null hypothesis at a 5 percent significance level for any tested year, neither compared with the maximum-likelihood truncated power law nor Weibull distribution. When the empirical call distribution is replaced by the degree distribution, the lognormal model is plausible in early years, but in later years Weibull distributions fit the data better.

As in all model selection problems, one should bear in mind that reality is, of course, more complex than any of the candidate models. In our case, it might be possible to reduce the AIC further by allowing more than two parameters, but we feel that two parameters are a good compromise between simplicity of the model and goodness-of-fit. With additional data it might become possible to analyse the dynamics of port calls in more detail, especially to test if Gibrat's law applies in our case, which could explain a lognormal call distribution. It may also become feasible to test the assumption of independence between ports and apply full likelihood methods to the dynamics of the network (Wiuf *et al.*, 2006).

Acknowledgment

The research leading to these results has received funding from the European Research Council under the European Union's Seventh Framework Programme (FP/2007-2013)/ERC Grant Agreement n. [313847] "World Seastems." M.T.G. thanks the European Commission for financial support (project number FP7-PEOPLE-2012-IEF 6-4564/2013).

Notes

1 Depending on the parameters, k may have to be larger than the maximum port size for the lognormal to exceed the Weibull distribution. For example, in Figure 14.1(a) we are not

yet far enough in the asymptotic regime on the right-hand side for the Weibull distribution to fall below the lognormal.

2 Because the number of ports, however, has more than doubled between 1890 and 2008 (see second column of Table 14.2), the *absolute* number of ports with less than or equal to ten calls has of course still increased.

3 Strictly speaking, this is the definition only for a continuous distribution F. For discrete distributions the Lorenz curve is a polygon instead of a smooth curve so that there is typically no point where the slope is exactly 1. However, one can generalize the definition so that it still works for the discrete distributions obtained from finite samples, see Damgaard and Weiner (2000) for details.

References

Akaike H. (1974) A new look at the statistical model identification. *IEEE T. Automat. Contr.*, 19: 716–23.

Albert R., Barabási A.L. (1999) Emergence of scaling in random networks. *Science*, 286: 509–12.

Albert R., Barabási A.L. (2002) Statistical mechanics of complex networks. *Rev. Mod. Phys.*, 74: 47–97.

Anderson T.W., Darling D.A. (1952) Asymptotic theory of certain "goodness of fit" criteria based on stochastic processes. *Ann. Math. Stat.*, 23: 193–212.

Bernhofen D.M., El-Sahli Z., Kneller R. (2013) *Estimating the Effects of the Container Revolution on World Trade.* Lund University Working Paper 2013:4, Department of Economics, School of Economics and Management.

Bhattacharya K., Mukherjee G., Saramäki J., Kaski K., Manna S.S. (2008) The international trade network: weighted network analysis and modelling. *J. Stat. Mech.*, 2008: P02002.

Broido A., Claffy K.C. (2001) Internet topology: connectivity of IP graphs. *Proc. SPIE*, 4526: 172–87.

Burnham K.P., Anderson D.R. (1998) *Model Selection and Multimodel Inference.* New York: Springer.

Clauset A., Shalizi C.R., Newman M.E.J. (2009) Power-law distributions in empirical data. *SIAM Rev.*, 51: 661–703.

Cox D.R., Reid N. (2004) A note on pseudolikelihood constructed from marginal densities. *Biometrika*, 91: 729–37.

Cullinane K.P.B., Khanna M. (2000) Economies of scale in large containerships: optimal size and geographical implications. *J. Transp. Geogr.*, 8(3): 181–95.

Damgaard C., Weiner J. (2000) Describing inequality in plant size or fecundity. *Ecology*, 91: 1139–42.

Deng W.B., Long G., Wei L., Xu C. (2009) Worldwide marine transportation network: Efficiency and container throughput. *Chinese Physics Letters,* 26(11): 118901.

Ding D., Teo C.P. (2010) World container port throughput follows lognormal distribution. *Maritime Policy and Management*, 37: 401-426.

Ducruet C. (2013) Network diversity and maritime flows. *J. Transp. Geogr.*, 30: 77–88.

Edwards A.M., Phillips R.A., Watkins N.W., Freeman M.P., Murphy E.J., Afanasyev V., Buldyrev S.V., da Luz M.G.E., Raposo E.P., Stanley H.E., Viswanathan G.M. (2007) Revisiting Lévy flight search patterns of wandering albatrosses, bumblebees and deer. *Nature*, 449: 1044–7.

Eeckhout J. (2004) Gibrat's law for (all) cities. *Am. Econ. Rev.*, 94: 1429–51.

Gibrat R. (1931) *Les Inégalités Economiques.* Paris: Librairie du Recueil Sirey.

Giles D.E.A. (2004) Calculating a standard error for the Gini coefficient: some further results. *Oxford B. Econ. Stat.*, 66: 425–33.

Gini C. (1912) *Variabilità e Mutabilità.* Bologna: P. Cuppini.

Gómez V., Kaltenbrunner A., López V. (2008) Statistical analysis of the social network and discussion threads in Slashdot. *Proc. 17th Int. Conf. World Wide Web*, pp. 645–54.

Hamilton D.T., Handcock M.S., Morris M. (2008) Degree distributions in sexual networks: a framework for evaluating evidence. *Sex. Transm. Dis.*, 35: 30–40.

He Y., Siganos G., Faloutsos M., Krishnamurthy S. (2007) A systematic framework for unearthing the missing links: measurements and impact. *Proc. 4th USENIX Conf. Networked Systems Design & Implementation*, p. 14.

Hu Y., Zhu D. (2009) Empirical analysis of the worldwide maritime transportation network. *Physica A*, 388(10): 2061–71.

Kaluza P., Kölzsch A., Gastner M.T., Blasius, B. (2010) The complex network of global cargo ship movements. *J. R. Soc. Interface*, 7(48): 1093–103.

Kolmogorov A. (1933) Sulla determinazione empirica di una legge di distribuzione. *G. Ist. Ital. Attuari*, 4: 83–91.

Lahererre J., Sornette J. (1998) Stretched exponential distributions in nature and economy: fat tails with characteristic scales. *Eur. Phys. J. B*, 2: 525–39.

Lorenz M.O. (1905) Methods of measuring the concentration of wealth. *Publ. Am. Stat. Assoc.*, 9: 209–19.

McCalla R.J. (2004) From "Anyport" to "Superterminal." In: Pinder D., Slack B. (Eds), *Shipping and Ports in the Twenty-first Century*, London: Routledge, pp. 123–42.

Molloy M., Reed B. (1995) A critical point for random graphs with a given degree sequence. *Random Struct. Algor.*, 6: 161–80.

Moore C., Ghoshal G., Newman M.E.J. (2006) Exact solutions for models of evolving networks with addition and deletion of nodes. *Physi. Rev. E*, 74: 036121.

Newman M.E.J. (2010) *Networks: an introduction*. Oxford: Oxford University Press.

Prieto F., Sarabia J.M. (2011) Fitting the degree distribution of real-world networks. *Int. J. Complex Systems in Science*, 1: 129–33.

Rocha L.E.C., Liljeros F., Holme P. (2010) Information dynamics shape the sexual networks of Internet-mediated prostitution. *Proc. Nat. Acad. Sci.*, 107: 5706–11.

Simon H.A. (1955) On a class of skew distribution functions. *Biometrika*, 42: 425–40.

Stephens P.A., Buskirk S.W., Hayward G.D., Martínez del Rio C. (2005) Information theory and hypothesis testing: a call for pluralism. *J. Appl. Ecol.*, 42: 4–12.

Stumpf M.P.H., Ingram P.J., Nouvel I., Wiuf C. (2005) Statistical model selection methods applied to biological networks. In: Priami C., Merelli E., Gonzalez P., Omicini A. (Eds), Transactions on computational systems biology III, *Lecture notes in computer science*, 3737, Berlin: Springer, pp. 65–77.

Stumpf M.P.H., Porter M.A. (2012) Critical truths about power laws. *Science*, 335: 665–6.

Tadić B. (2002) Temporal fractal structures: Origin of power laws in the world-wide web. *Physica A*, 314: 278–83.

Todor A., Dobra A., Kahveci T. (2012) Uncertain interactions affect degree distribution of biological networks. *IEEE Int. Conf. Bioinformatics and Biomedicine*, pp. 457–61.

UNCTAD (2013) *Review of Maritime Transport*. Geneva: United Nations.

Varin C., Reid N., Firth D. (2011) An overview of composite likelihood methods. *Stat. Sinica*, 21: 5–42.

Vuong Q.H. (1989) Likelihood ratio tests for model selection and non-nested hypotheses. *Econometrica*, 57: 307–33.

Willinger W., Alderson D., Doyle J.C. (2009) Mathematics and the Internet: a source of enormous confusion and great potential. *Not. Am. Math. Soc.*, 56: 586–99.

Wilson A.G. (1967) A statistical theory of spatial distribution models. *Transport. Res.*, 1: 253–69.

Wiuf C., Brameier M., Hagberg O., Stumpf M.P.H. (2006) A likelihood approach to analysis of network data. *Proc. Nat. Acad. Sci*, 103: 7566–70.

Part IV

Maritime networks and regional development

15 The impact of the emergence of direct shipping lines on port flows

Ronald A. Halim, Lóránt A. Tavasszy, Jan H. Kwakkel

World trade over the past couple of decades has proven to be very dynamic. The economies of many developing countries have grown, while the economies of most developed countries have been stagnant or witnessed only sluggish growth. Over time, the world's maritime transport network will continue to adapt itself to these changes. The foreseen increase of trade between the BRICS (Brazil, Russia, India, China, South Africa) countries and the rest of the world, is an example of a trend that will stimulate and promote the emergence of new shipping lines in the world's shipping network. New direct connections might emerge in response to this trend, and existing routes might be adapted. The global maritime shipping network evolves over time to keep providing adequate sea transport services for the growing demand between these developing countries and the rest of the world. Insight into how trends and developments such as the growth in demand for shipping between the BRICS countries and the rest of the world will influence or shape the future global maritime shipping network is therefore highly valuable.

Without understanding future transport demand patterns at the global level, parties such as port authorities, governments, and international organizations such as the United Nations will have to deal with undesired uncertainties. Such uncertainties, when not dealt with systematically, will not only hurt plans to develop adequate transport infrastructure in many countries but also, at the higher level, will negatively affect the world economy. It is clear that under- and over-capacitated maritime transport infrastructure, especially ports, will incur a high cost due to congestion and under-utilization, respectively.

In order to help us gain strategic insight into the future pattern of freight flows, there are essential questions that need to be investigated:

- How will carriers' shipping networks be restructured by demands for freight transport?
- How will the emergence of new service/shipping lines influence the performance of big ports in existing economic blocs such as the European Union, the United States, and East Asia (China, Singapore)?

There have been a few works aimed at studying global maritime shipping networks (Ducruet and Notteboom, 2012; Song *et al.*, 2005). But the majority of these studies aim at interpreting the network structure using graph theory and spatial analysis (Ducruet *et al.*, 2010; Kaluza *et al.*, 2010) or complex adaptive system theory (Caschili and Medda, 2012). Hence, it is clear that there are few studies aimed at predicting how the restructuring of global maritime shipping services affects shippers' behaviour and, consequently, the performance of ports. Another commonly used approach is to use optimization in modelling the most efficient network structure that can connect ports worldwide (Zeng and Yang, 2002). However this approach is not suited for describing and predicting the global maritime shipping network, but rather to design a desirable network.

In this chapter, we aim at sketching the aggregate responses of shipping lines to foreseen growth trends. To this end, we first examine how direct shipping lines between two ports can emerge as a response to change in the demand for freight transport. Second, as a case study, we investigate the influence of the emergence of new direct lines on European ports, in terms of port throughput. For this purpose, a strategic global freight transport model is developed. Third, utilizing the model capacity and scale, we also analyse how the direct lines affect container flows distribution worldwide and how the port choice of the shippers is affected by these lines, particularly for big ports in the United States and East Asia.

The model that has been developed to support these analyses is explicitly exploratory in character. It builds on the widely used freight modelling framework which finds its roots in discrete choice modelling (Tavasszy and de Jong, 2014). The model has been used for exploring alternative scenarios related to changes in origin-destination (OD) demand patterns globally. Here we use it to study the emergence of direct shipping lines in response to demand growth. The model can also be used to analyse the disappearance of direct lines in response to declining demand.

The remainder of our chapter is organized as follows. The next section provides a brief review of the surrounding research environment of our topic. Then we introduce the modelling approach used, before describing the application to global networks and the implications for the port of Rotterdam. The last section summarizes the findings of this chapter and makes recommendations for further research.

Review of model-based analyses of global maritime shipping networks

Our research is focused on the emergence of direct maritime connections between ports throughout the world. A direct maritime connection is a freight transport service from one port to another that is conducted without any transhipment or change in shipping service provider. The actual ship delivering the cargo might call at different ports on the way to its final port of call before heading back to the origin port. It is apparent from empirical observations that direct shipping lines have a significant impact on the throughput and transhipment values of a port. As can be seen in Figure 15.1, ports with a high number of shipping service calls have high corresponding total container throughput. Furthermore, a high correlation

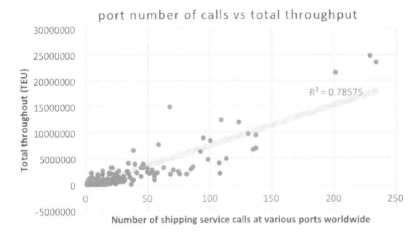

Figure 15.1 Relationship between number of shipping services calling at a port and its total throughput.

factor between number of port calls and total port throughput confirms this observation.

Direct shipping lines are used to transport large volumes of freight/containers between two (typically large) ports. These direct lines carry high volumes and have substantial economy of scale advantages, resulting in reduced transport costs. From our observation, it is clear that the emergence of direct lines is tightly related to the scale of transport demands between two ports. In general, the higher the amount of flows between two ports, the more likely it is that a transport service will be done with less transhipment or even directly. An example of this phenomenon can be seen in the shipping services that connect the port of Rotterdam and the port of Singapore. These are the biggest ports in both Europe and Asia, respectively, with very high transport demand between them, and there are more than 32 direct shipping services connecting them. An important reason for this is that shipping companies benefit from providing services that have better cost–revenue ratio per goods transported. Figure 15.2 provides an illustration of economies gained at the ship level, where increasing ship size can reduce unit costs of transport (Cullinane and Khanna, 2000).

To date, there are many models to optimize the network of a liner shipping company. Generally such models are developed to minimize total transportation costs while fulfilling demand or maximizing the profit of a liner shipping company (Wang and Liu, 2015). Since there are many operational factors that can be considered, a container transport network can be very complex. Therefore the specificity of the models depends on specific factors.

For example, Fagerholt (2004) proposed a model where the main objective is to optimize the routing of individual ships given a delivery time constraint so that total costs can be minimized. Another study uses a model that minimizes both the

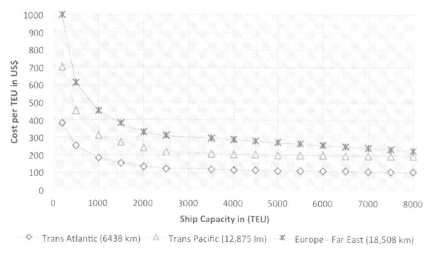

Figure 15.2 The relationship between unit cost of transport and ship capacity.

Source: Cullinane and Khanna (2000).

total distance travelled by the ships and fuel consumption (Jepsen *et al.*, 2011). An example of a more complex model that considers fleet design, ship schedule, and ship routing simultaneously can be found in Mulder and Dekker (2014). Another type of model in this class was developed by considering extra constraints such as maritime cabotage and transit time between routes (Wang *et al.*, 2013). Furthermore this kind of model can take more factors into account; one example is that developed by Liu *et al.* (2014). This model optimizes the strategic routing of the containers on both hinterland and maritime sides using discrete choice model and mixed integer linear programming approach, respectively.

A major drawback of such network design models is they cannot be used to analyze the emergence or disappearance of shipping lines globally or the impact of this trend on the performance of individual ports. There might be several shipping companies that plan to provide a direct shipping service in response to growing global demand. In this case, optimizing the routes of all individual shipping companies would not be computationally tractable.

Another approach to model the global maritime shipping network is applying the graph theory perspective onto the network and using its indicators such as the centrality indices to interpret the structure of the network (Ducruet and Notteboom, 2012). However, this approach does not aim to predict the impact of new trade scenarios on the network, but rather makes use of existing network data to understand the properties of the network.

Therefore, we need a more aggregate and holistic approach for analyzing the plausible impacts of such future trends. This approach should be able to reckon changes in the structure of the global maritime shipping network based on changes in the demand for freight transport and vice versa. For this reason, we develop a rule-based method that can be used on a global scale. This approach is rooted in the science of descriptive freight modelling as described by Tavasszy and de Jong (2014). The next section provides an elaboration of this method.

Approach to evaluate emergence of direct lines

We implement a rule-based method to model changes in shipping networks caused by the emergence of direct shipping lines. This method is integrated into an existing model of world container flows (Cullinane and Khanna, 2000). We investigate how changes in the network of shipping lines affect the throughput and transhipment of the ports in the Le Havre–Bremen range (Bremen, Hamburg, Amsterdam, Rotterdam, Antwerp, Zeebrugge, Dunkirk, and Le Havre).

Descriptive global container flow model

The world container model (WCM) is a strategic network choice model for global container flows (Tavasszy *et al.*, 2011). The model considers more than 400 major ports, 237 countries and more than 800 shipping lines and predicts annual container flows over these lines. Transport costs in the model are based on transport time, distance, toll, value of time of the goods transported, and cost of handling the containers at the ports. The formal definition of the cost model is delineated below:

$$C_r = \sum_{p \in r} A_p + \sum_{l \in r} c_l + \alpha \cdot \left(\sum_{p \in r} T_p + \sum_{l \in r} t_l \right) \tag{15.1}$$

where:

  C_r costs of route r
  p ports used by the route
  l links used by the route
  A_p total cost of transhipment at port p
  c_l total cost of transportation over link l
  T_p time spent during transhipment at port p
  t_l time spent during transportation over link l
  α value of transport time (USD/day/ton)

The WCM enumerates all plausible route alternatives for major countries in the world using the publicly available global shipping network data and shortest path algorithms. Routes which are on both maritime and continental sides are taken into account in the network. The route and port choice algorithms use a path-sized logit model which takes overlaps between the alternative routes into account and distinguishes the transport costs associated with these alternatives. The basis of this model can be found in Ben-Akiva and Bierlaire (1999). The following is the formal definition of the path size logit model:

$$P_r = \frac{e^{-\mu(C_r + \ln S_r)}}{\sum_{h \in CS} e^{-\mu(C_{kh} + \ln S_{kh})}} \tag{15.2}$$

With the path size overlap variable defined as

$$S_r = \sum_{a \in \Gamma_r} \left(\frac{z_a}{z_r}\right) \frac{1}{N_{ah}} \tag{15.3}$$

where:

P_r the choice probability of route r
C generalized costs
CS the choice set
h path indicator
μ logit scale parameter
a link in route r
S_r degree of path overlap
Γ_r set of links in route r
z_a length of link a
z_r length of route r
N_{ah} number of times link a is found in alternative routes

Calibration of the model was done at an aggregate level using available port throughput and transhipment statistics. The model has been used to analyze and explore different long-term scenarios in the European Commission's Trans-European Networks programme and Next Generation Infrastructure Project, respectively. Some of the scenario analyses include:

1   The opening of the Arctic route.
2   The development and use of the Trans-Siberian Railway.
3   A sharp increase in inland transportation costs.
4   A decrease of transhipment costs in the port of Antwerp to the same level as that of Rotterdam.
5   A strong overall increase of transhipment costs.
6   A decrease in shipping speed due to slow steaming behaviour.
7   Incorporation of CO_2 price in the container transport cost.

The model also has been used to perform exploratory analysis to deal with deep uncertainties. In this case, we investigated the impact of massive scenarios representing a vast combination of factors influencing the structure of the network and different cost components in the network. The study has been used to map the worst impact of these uncertainties across the ports in the Bremen–Le Havre range. Scenario discovery technique is also used to gain insight into the scenarios and circumstances that lead to such undesired impacts.

We implemented the WCM using Java technology to achieve good portability in running the model on different operating systems. Furthermore we also use a set of libraries that help us to optimize the computation process such as JUNG (Java Universal Graph) library (O'Madadhain *et al.*, 2005). Specifically, we use JUNG to implement both the global maritime and hinterland transportation networks. Finally, the Unfolding library (Nagel *et al.*, 2013) is also used to create maps that visualize the distribution of the flows over the intermodal freight network worldwide.

To run the computation of the model, we use a desktop PC with 2.4GHz Intel i5 processor, and 4G memory. The total run time of the model is around three minutes, and the memory usage is at 1.5G on average. Computation speed and memory usage have been given proportionate attention since the model is expected to be used in a large-scale experiment involving more than 10,000 model iterations.

Figure 15.3 depicts the global maritime shipping network, which includes hinterland transportation routes with a different mode of transport such as trucks. The thickness of the lines indicates the magnitude of the flows on each of the links, and the pie charts indicate the magnitude of total throughput (in dark grey) and transhipment (in light grey) for each port in Europe.

The WCM describes the demand side of the global container shipping system, where shippers and forwarders make decisions with respect to the use of shipping lines. The model assumes the shipping lines as a given. The linkage to the supply side of the global container shipping system, which concerns changes in the shipping services, is described in the next section.

Emergence of direct shipping lines

To investigate the impact of a new shipping network with more direct shipping lines, we employed an approach which systematically adds new shipping lines between two ports, based on a rule reflecting the impact of the economies of scale on the network. Figure 15.4 gives an overview of the approach used in this analysis. Using the WCM, the port choices of the shippers using the new network can be simulated, and the volumes expected for all ports can be obtained. The following paragraphs elaborate the steps that were taken in the analysis.

Step 1: Identifying port-to-port flow thresholds for availability of a direct connection

As the first step in modelling change in the shipping network, we investigate the threshold value by which shipping companies would provide a direct shipping service or a new shipping line between two ports. We obtain this threshold value by observing the volume of container flow and transhipment in more than 160,000 port-to-port flows where transport is served by the available shipping lines. From this analysis we obtain a flow value above which the transhipment number becomes zero. This is the threshold value.

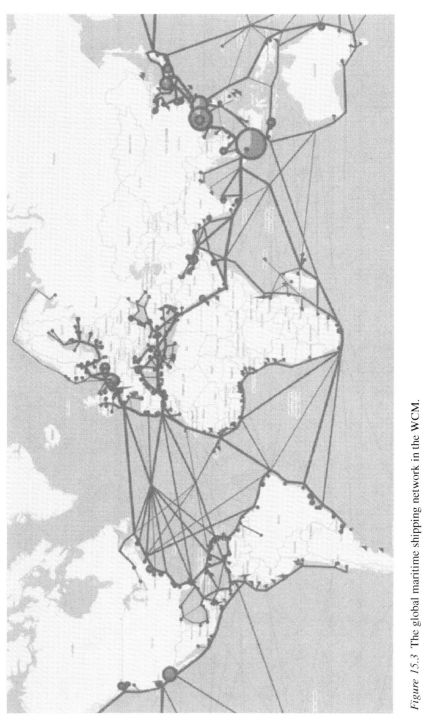

Figure 15.3 The global maritime shipping network in the WCM.

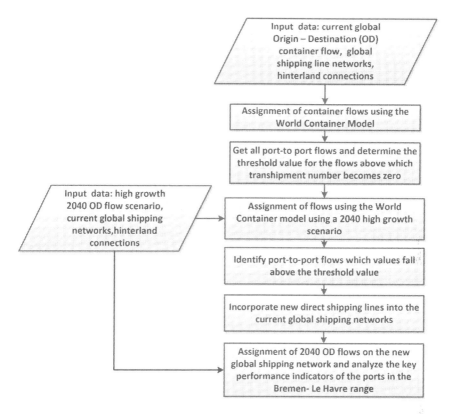

Figure 15.4 Steps used to model how the emergence of direct shipping lines effect the choices of ports by the shippers.

Step 2: Applying growth scenario to flows

Next, we use a scenario for 2040, where there has been a significant increase in transport demand. In this scenario, most of the countries in the world are expected to experience growth in their export and import activities leading to higher transport demand between countries. This growth in transport demand takes into account significant economic growth in developing countries such as Brazil, Indonesia, China, and India. The increase in demand varies between 30 percent and 140 percent depending on the forecasted increase of trade between the corresponding countries. Transport demand data for the scenario was obtained using a global spatial computable general equilibrium model (Ivanova, 2013) that estimates the amount of container flows worldwide as a result of global trade.

Step 3: Identifying port-to-port relations where flow is above the threshold

The high growth scenario is used as an input for the WCM. Subsequently, the WCM is used to assign the scenario OD demand to the existing shipping line

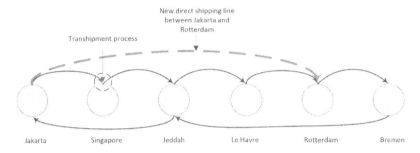

Figure 15.5 The procedure to adding a direct shipping line into the global shipping network.

network. From this assignment, we derive port-to-port container flows. Next, assuming that the threshold value found in step 1 will remain the same, we identify all port-to-port flows that exceed the threshold value. These flows represent flows that are expected to be handled by direct services.

Step 4: Creating direct lines between ports in the shipping line network

Next, based on the identified port-to-port flows, new shipping lines are automatically created and added to the current network. That is, if for a given pair of ports with sufficient flow to warrant direct service no direct service exists, we add such a direct service to the model. The new shipping line provides a direct connection between two ports where flow is above the threshold value. We assume that the capacity and frequency of the new shipping line will suffice to accommodate the increased demand. Furthermore, it is also assumed that all the old shipping lines will remain in the new network. Figure 15.5 illustrates the case where the container flow between Jakarta and Rotterdam is above the threshold value found in step 1. In this case, a new direct shipping line between Jakarta and Rotterdam is added to the current network. This procedure is applied to all port-to-port relations found in step 3. A shortest path algorithm is used to construct the route used by the direct shipping lines.

Step 5: Re-assigning port-to-port flows based on the new shipping network

Once the new shipping lines have been created and have been added to the network, the WCM is used once more to assign the flows for the high growth scenario over the new shipping network. From this assignment of flows the modified service line network arises; we can derive throughput and transhipment for the more than 400 ports in the network given the high growth scenario.

Results

Observed threshold value

In order to obtain flows that are relevant for determining the threshold value, we retrieved the highest flow that is transported by each of the shipping lines in the

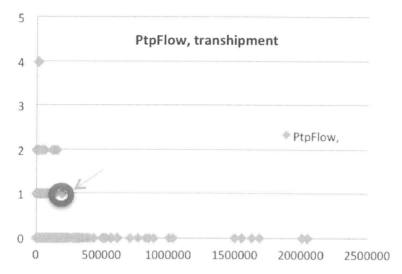

Figure 15.6 Threshold value for ptpFlow with direct connection.

world. Hence, with more than 840 service lines in the world serving global routes, we obtained 840 highest flows of these lines. Figure 15.6 plots the data points for each recorded port-to-port flow and its corresponding number of transhipments. As can be seen, there are many small flows with direct connections. Most of these flows are served by the same shipping lines that transport bigger flows for long-distance destinations. This implies that there is a "piggybacking" phenomenon from the smaller port-to-port flows that can be ignored in our analysis. We determine the threshold value by looking at the highest flow value above which the transhipment number for the flow becomes zero; this value lies at around 200,000 TEU/year.

Next, we run the WCM with the high growth scenario. Given the threshold value of 200,000 TEU/year, we identify 528 port-to-port flows where values exceeded the threshold. New direct shipping lines are created to connect these ports and these new lines are added to the current shipping network.

Impact of direct shipping lines on the ports in the Bremen-Le Havre range

Using the new structure of the global shipping line network, the assignment of flows is done once again, and the throughput and transhipment values of the ports are derived. As can be seen in Figure 15.7, in comparison to the base scenario in 2006, most of the ports in the Bremen–Le Havre range are expected to handle more container flows. This can be seen from the growth in their throughput values, ranging from 95 percent for Amsterdam to 172 percent for Antwerp. This indicates that in 2040, there is substantially high growth of the volume of containers being transported to and from Europe. With regards to transhipment values,

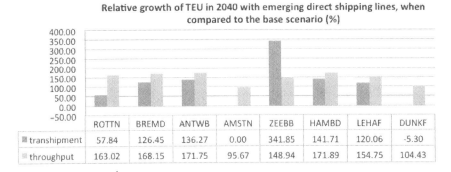

Figure 15.7 Relative change of ports' transhipment and throughput when compared to the base scenario.

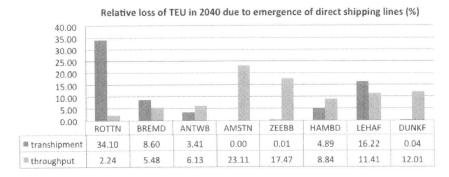

Figure 15.8 KPI percentage change caused by the addition of new shipping lines, high growth scenario.

we can observe an interesting pattern where Rotterdam is expected not to experience as much growth as the other ports in the Bremen–Le Havre range. On the other hand, while Dunkirk loses 5 percent of transhipment volume, Zeebrugge is expected to handle more than 3.5 times the transhipment volume as the base scenario.

Next, we compare ports' performance in 2040 between two scenarios: when direct shipping services emerge and when there is no change in the current shipping services. Figure 15.8 depicts the percentage change in transhipment and throughput values of the ports in the Hamburg–Le Havre range relative to the values when there are no new shipping lines in the high-growth scenario.

As can be seen from the result, most of the ports in the Le Havre–Bremen range suffer from the addition of new lines. In terms of throughput, Rotterdam is not severely impacted by the emergence of these lines. While the rest of the ports in Europe suffer considerable negative impact in their throughput, Rotterdam only has a reduction in throughput. This indicates that the loss in transhipment is well compensated by the flows of containers going from and to Europe through the hinterland of Rotterdam. This also indicates that there are direct lines calling at Rotterdam, connecting it to countries where there is significant economic growth.

It appears that Amsterdam is the most negatively impacted, followed by Zeebrugge. In terms of transhipment, Rotterdam's performance is the most negatively impacted. This is followed by Le Havre and Bremen. Transhipment values of the other ports are not severely affected. For Zeebrugge, this particular trend means that the emergence of direct shipping service does not significantly impact it.

The loss of transhipment by Rotterdam indicates that in the scenario where there is a high growth in trade between countries, many of the emerging shipping lines would not have transhipment anymore in Rotterdam. Several factors might cause this. First, new transhipment hubs might emerge, driven by these new lines and the overall growth of transport demand. These hubs typically emerge in ports where new shipping lines make a call or in nearby ports connected to these ports by previously available shipping lines.

Second, the direct shipping lines take over the transhipment market of the big transhipment ports such as Rotterdam, Bremen, and Le Havre. This is logical, as with better economy of scale, transporting containers using the direct lines would be cheaper and hence more attractive for the shippers. Shipping lines which call at the ports in the Bremen–Le Havre range will have less demand for container transport when there are direct lines calling at these ports. As a result, big transhipment ports such as Rotterdam, Bremen, and Le Havre are foreseen to suffer from the emergence of new direct shipping lines. And third, this also indicates that there are more direct shipping lines calling at competing ports outside the range.

Impact of direct shipping lines on global ports

Figure 15.9 visualizes the effect of the changes in global container flows caused by the addition of new shipping lines. As can be seen in the figure, the new lines have caused certain routes to have more volume and certain ports to have more transhipment.

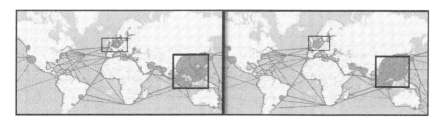

Figure 15.9 The world container flows without (left) and with new shipping lines (right), in high growth scenario in 2040.

The size of the pie charts indicates the magnitude of the total throughput of the port, with light grey section indicates the transhipment fraction of the throughput value.

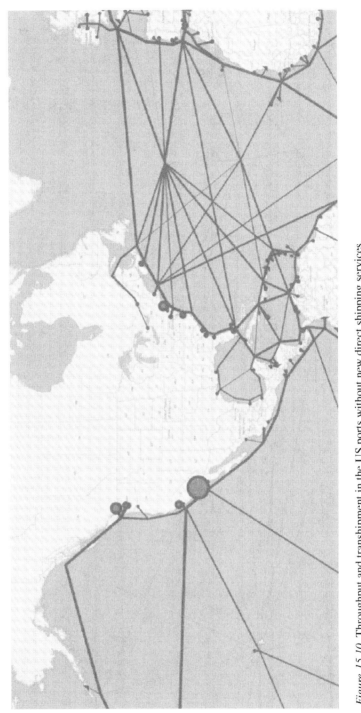

Figure 15.10 Throughput and transhipment in the US ports without new direct shipping services.

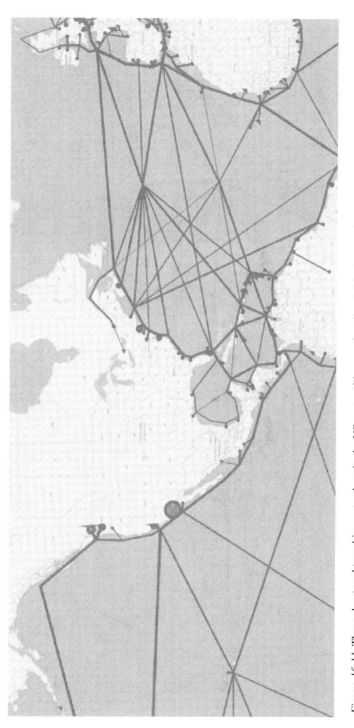

Figure 15.11 Throughput and transshipment values in the US ports with emerging direct shipping services.

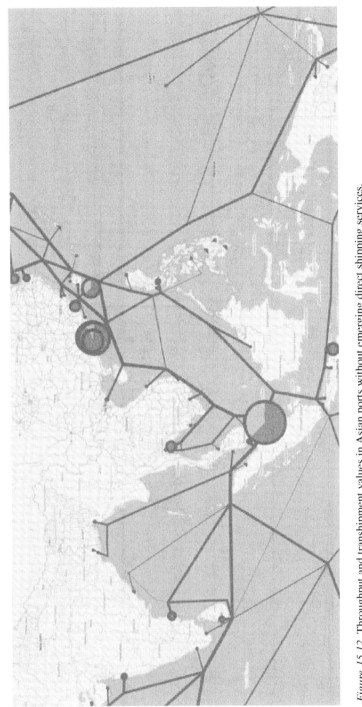

Figure 15.12 Throughput and transhipment values in Asian ports without emerging direct shipping services.

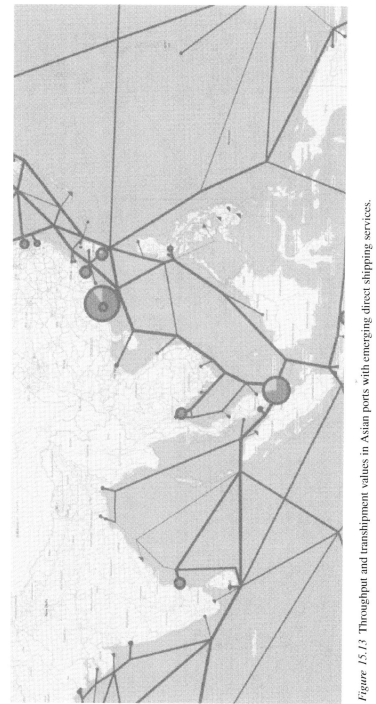

Figure 15.13 Throughput and transhipment values in Asian ports with emerging direct shipping services.

Specifically, there are direct shipping lines that call at ports in South America and connect with ports in East Asia (left box). More flows are also visible in southern Argentina, indicating that there are direct shipping lines that call at the ports in this region. In terms of throughput and transhipment, we see that big ports in the United States like Los Angeles and New York have more transhipment when with less total throughput values when direct shipping services are available. Figures 15.10 and 15.11 provide visualization for the throughput of the ports in the United States where there are no new direct shipping services and where direct shipping services emerge, respectively.

Similarly, big ports in East Asia such as Singapore and Shanghai seem to have a decline in their transhipment market, especially in Singapore, caused by the emergence of direct shipping services. Figures 15.12 and 15.13 illustrate the ports' throughput in Asia with and without direct service shipping services, respectively.

These results seem to indicate that the emergence of new direct shipping lines causes big transhipment ports worldwide to have a decline in their transhipment market, especially those which support the growing trade between the western and eastern countries. Ports that also have a strong hinterland may compensate these losses with the increase of direct flows from these regions. This is the case with Rotterdam.

Conclusion

We have presented a systematic analysis which can explain how demand for freight transport can structure future global maritime shipping networks. Particularly, we have investigated the underlying principle which governs the emergence of direct shipping services between two ports. Furthermore, using this principle, we explored future changes in port flows caused by the emergence of these direct shipping lines. The analysis makes use of a simple rule-based method to model and systematically update existing global shipping networks with plausible direct shipping services. Although the method is simple and straightforward, it has proven to be useful in providing insight into how direct shipping lines can affect the performance of ports worldwide.

We discovered that direct shipping service between two ports was likely to emerge when the volume of flow transported was above 200,000 TEU/year. When we ran the model with the high-growth scenario in 2040, we discovered that the emergence of new shipping lines would have a significantly negative impact on the transhipment of Rotterdam and an overall negative impact on the ports in the Bremen–Le Havre range. Furthermore, our experiment also shows that big transhipment ports in East Asia such as Singapore and Shanghai are also severely affected by this trend. Similarly, big ports in the United States such as Los Angeles and New York seem also to be negatively impacted by these direct lines.

Finally, the model presented here opens up new opportunities to develop a holistic and efficient heuristic to approximate the future structure of global shipping networks. Trade scenarios can be investigated to assess the impact of uncertainty concerning the increase of scale in the maritime transport system. In this regard, it is also highly valuable to have a strategic model which can explain the formation of the global shipping network based on simple rules. With efficient calculations, this type of model can be used to explore vast amounts of scenarios. Eventually, it could be used to assist policy makers in anticipating negative outcomes of major uncertainties in the global freight network.

References

Ben-Akiva M., Bierlaire M. (1999) Discrete choice methods and their applications to short term travel decisions. In Hall R. (Ed), *Handbook of Transportation Science*, New York: Springer US, pp. 5–33.

Caschili S., Medda F.R. (2012) A review of the maritime container shipping industry as a complex adaptive system. *Interdisciplinary Description of Complex Systems*, 10(1): 1–15.

Cullinane K.P.B., Khanna M. (2000) Economies of scale in large containerships: optimal size and geographical implications. *Journal of Transport Geography*, 8(3): 181–95.

Ducruet C., Notteboom T.E. (2012) The worldwide maritime network of container shipping: spatial structure and regional dynamics. *Global Networks*, 12(3): 395–423.

Ducruet C., Rozenblat C., Zaidi F. (2010) Ports in multi-level maritime networks: evidence from the Atlantic (1996-2006). *Journal of Transport Geography*, 18(4): 508–18.

Fagerholt K. (2004) Designing optimal routes in a liner shipping problem. *Maritime Policy and Management*, 31(4): 259–68.

Ivanova O. (2013) Modelling interregional freight demand with input-output, gravity and SCGE methodologies. In: Tavasszy L.A., de Jong G. (Eds), *Modelling Freight Transport*, London: Elsevier, pp. 13–42.

Jepsen M.K., Brouer B.D., Plum C.E.M., Pisinger D. (2011) A path based model for a green liner shipping network design problem. *Proceedings of The International MultiConference of Engineers and Computer Scientists*, Hong Kong: Newswood Ltd., pp. 1379–84.

Kaluza P., Kölzsch A., Gastner M.T., Blasius, B. (2010) The complex network of global cargo ship movements. *Journal of the Royal Society Interface*, 7(48): 1093–103.

Liu Z., Meng Q., Wang S., Sun Z. (2014) Global intermodal liner shipping network design. *Transportation Research Part E*, 61: 28–39.

Mulder J., Dekker R. (2014) Methods for strategic liner shipping network design. *European Journal of Operational Research*, 235(2): 367–77.

Nagel T., Klerkx J., Vande Moere A., Duval E. (2013) Unfolding: a library for interactive maps, in human factors in computing and informatics. In: Holzinger A., Ziefle M., Hitz M., Debevk M. (Eds), *Human Factors in Computing and Informatics*, Berlin and Heidelberg: Springer, pp. 497–513.

O'Madadhain J., Fisher D., Smyth P., White S., Boey Y.B. (2005) Analysis and visualization of network data using JUNG. *Journal of Statistical Software*, 10(2): 1–35.

Song D., Zhang J., Carter J., Field T., Marshall J., Polak J., Schumacher K., Sinha-Ray P., Woods J. (2005) On cost-efficiency of the global container shipping network. *Maritime Policy and Management*, 32(1): 15–30.

Tavasszy L.A., de Jong G. (2014) *Modelling Freight Transport*. London and Waltham: Elsevier.

Tavasszy L., Minderhoud M., Perrin J.F., Notteboom T.E. (2011) A strategic network choice model for global container flows: Specification, estimation and application. *Journal of Transport Geography*, 19(6): 1163–72.

Wang S., Liu Z. (2015) Efficient global container transport network design. In: Lee C.Y., Meng Q. (Eds), *Handbook of Ocean Container Transport Logistics*, Springer International Publishing, pp. 359–95.

Wang S., Meng Q., Sun Z. (2013) Container routing in liner shipping. *Transportation Research Part E*, 49(1): 1–7.

Zeng Z., Yang Z. (2002) Dynamic programming of port position and scale in the hierarchized container ports network. *Maritime Policy and Management*, 29(2): 163–77.

16 The mutual specialization of port regions connected by multiple commodity flows in a maritime network

César Ducruet, Hidekazu Itoh

Throughout port and maritime studies, the link between flows and the socio-economic characteristics of localities has been investigated mostly qualitatively. While systematic international quantitative investigations remain scarce and dispersed, their reliance upon port tonnage statistics tends to ignore maritime linkages. Conversely, maritime network studies remain abstract, where ports are considered only as nodes in a graph. What is the influence of the local economy on the situation in—and specialization of—maritime networks? Are there significant interrelations between types of maritime flows and types of local economies? Using such an approach we shall first discuss the wider scientific literature about transport and regional development, with a particular focus on previous quantitative studies. Second, this chapter provides an analysis of the Pacific Rim area based on the comparison of vessel movement data and regional socio-economic data collected at the level of subnational entities or port regions. The fact that populations and markets are concentrated on the coastlines of North America, Asia, and Oceania (Lee *et al.*, 2008) motivated the search for spatial and functional interdependencies between traffic and local economic structure. In addition, the Asia–Pacific Rim "had become the indisputed main generator of containers" in the world (Rimmer, 2014: 91) and a major concentration of multinational industrial and logistics corporations.

Regions, material flows, and maritime networks

A great variety of research throughout the academic literature has addressed the link between regional development and material flows. Reference to such flows is often implicit, however, as for instance in urban economics and location theory (Fujita *et al.*, 1999; McCann and Shefer, 2004; Beyers and Fowler, 2012), in regional development theory (Dawkins, 2003), and in studies of economic growth and globalization (Scott and Storper, 2003), and of commodity chains, global production networks, and world cities (Leslie and Reimer, 1999; Dicken, 2001; Derudder and Witlox, 2010). Empirical investigations are often qualitative case studies of particular places and contexts. Quantitative analyses are done mostly at the national level (Harrigan, 2004), while those done at the regional (subnational) level mainly focus on mobility and communication flows, without always measuring their interdependence with local socio-economic development. One example is evolutionary economic geography, which analyzes regional branching and industry relatedness by looking at flows of labour, firms, and knowledge (Boschma and Frenken, 2011a). More specialized studies of (freight) traffic flows do exist, but they often ignore the local context, such as studies of transport networks addressing issues of accessibility and connectivity (Ducruet and Lugo, 2013).

The few existing empirical studies of material flows in relation to their local environment come from very diverse schools of thought and methods, of which urban ecology and regional science. As reviewed by Ducruet and Itoh (2015), regional scientists focused on the impact of transport infrastructure on the intensity of trading flows and on the location of economic activities, with applications to ports focusing on infrastructure quantity, quality, its influence on trade, economic development, manufacturing costs, private investment, capital stock, employment, etc. Other approaches included measuring the local determinants of regional exports in terms of transport costs and sea access, the influence of gross regional product (GRP) on airline accessibility and urban centrality of cities, and the distribution of supply chain networks in relation to urban hierarchy (see Guerrero and Proulhac, 2014).

The case of ports and port regions offers mixed evidence, and local socio-economic development in relation to ports has not been fully studied from a maritime network perspective. On the one hand, certain studies confirmed the weakening spatial fix of port traffic as a combined effect of shipping line concentration and service rationalization, new port development outside urban cores to avoid congestion, with a growing gap between white-collar urban regions and blue-collar port regions in terms of economic structure, wage level, economic productivity, and presence of advanced producer services. But despite their sometimes global focus, such empirical studies mostly focused on Western cases, such as the United States, Canada, and Europe (Ducruet *et al.*, 2010) or richer countries (Ducruet, 2009; Ducruet *et al.*, 2015). Yet, large European port gateways may expand their hinterlands further inland but at the same time maintain strong local linkages through heavy industrial complexes (Merk *et al.*, 2013; Bottasso *et al.*, 2013; Guerrero, 2014). Nevertheless, the majority of studies contradicting the erosion of port-region linkages are of Asian essence (see Fujita and Mori (1996) for a general discussion). In Japan, port investment had significantly positive effects on gross domestic product (GDP) and private capital (Kawakami and Doi, 2004) as did port efficiency on shipping cost and GDP growth (Doi *et al.*, 2001). In China, industrial productivity had a positive influence on port traffic growth (Cheung and Yip, 2011), while port-related added value had a positive impact on regional economic growth (Deng *et al.*, 2013), sometimes depending on the location, stage of economic development, and land-transport density of the different provinces (Song and van Geenhuizen, 2014). Despite a diversity of methods and outcomes, these studies remain bound to single-country datasets and neglected the importance of maritime linkages between (subnational) port regions (see a complementary discussion in Chapter 20 by Ducruet *et al.* on port cities).

The network analysis of maritime flows has progressed rapidly in the last decade or so (see Chapter 1 for an overview), but little has been done about their local socio-economic embedding. In terms of commodity specialization, Ducruet (2013) demonstrated the strong influence of commodity diversity on port centrality and maritime network structure, but without discussing the role of industrial linkages. Crossing port throughput and regional data across both developed and developing countries could show that core economic regions, which are richer and more densely populated, concentrate international and valued traffic (general cargo, containers), while peripheral regions, which specialize in the primary sector, concentrate more bulky flows (Ducruet and Itoh, 2015). Such an analysis was inspired by recent works on place- and path-dependency in economic geography (Boschma and Frenken, 2011a, 2011b; Neffke *et al.*, 2011) as well as previous discussions on commodity specialization and regional specialization (Tabuchi and Thisse, 2002).

A network methodology can push further our understanding of port-region linkages in several ways. In line with previous research based on port throughput data, it can elucidate whether maritime traffic specialization is related with economic sector specialization, if certain socio-economic characteristics influence nodes' position in the network, and if similar types of port regions strongly connect each other, and through which type of commodity flow. To some extent, this chapter searches for technological coherence (Boschma and Frenken, 2011b) between flows and spaces.

Mutual specialization effects across Pacific Rim port regions

Data and methodology

One first step has been to obtain vessel movement data from one issue of the *Lloyd's Shipping Index* published in 2008, which covered 88.8 percent of the world fleet capacity measured in deadweight tonnage according to UNCTAD (2008). This source details the technical characteristics of the vessels and their last known voyage between two ports in April 2008. The 23,675 recorded vessels were categorized into five main types for the sake of simplicity (general cargo, container, liquid bulk, solid bulk, and passenger/vehicle), measured in deadweight tons (DWT). A total of 518 ports were recorded in 13 countries of the Asia–Pacific region, for which socio-economic data at the regional (subnational) level was available (Table 16.1), resulting in 124 port regions. Regional data was collected for the year 2009 except for China and Taiwan (2010) and selected according to potential effects and links with vessel traffics (Table 16.2). The local economy is described via seven variables: employment in three main economic sectors (primary, secondary, and tertiary), demographic weight (or population share), population density, GRP, and unemployment rate. Regional variables were transformed into location quotients (LQ) based on national average to avoid possible biases caused by structural differences among countries in terms of economic structure and statistical definitions.

Five traffic categories cover the whole spectrum of port and maritime activities, alongside the shares of inbound and domestic traffic and the share of regional

Table 16.1 Study sample

Country	No. ports	No. port regions	Administrative unit*	Data source for regional data
Australia	62	7	State/TL2	OECD Territorial Database
Canada	7	1	TL2	OECD Territorial Database
Chile	31	11	TL2	OECD Territorial Database
China	81	15	Province	National Bureau of Statistics
India	41	10	State	Ministry of Labour and Employment & Central Statistics Office
Japan	140	40	Prefecture/TL3	Statistics Bureau, Ministry of Internal Affairs and Communications
Malaysia	24	12	State	Department of Statistics
Mexico	16	9	State/TL2	Instituto Nacional de Estadistica y Geografia
New Zealand	14	2	Island/TL2	OECD Territorial Database
Russia	23	1	Federal district	Federal State Statistics Service
South Korea	21	7	TL2	OECD Territorial Database
Taiwan	8	4	Region	National Statistics & Directorate-General of Budget, Accounting and Statistics
United States	50	5	State/TL2	OECD Territorial Database
Total	**518**	**124**		

traffic in the national total for 2009. Traffic categories were weighted (Charlier, 1994) in order to better reflect their potential cargo value and employment generation power at the docks and terminals. The variables (indicators) of (port) traffic categories for each region indicate the share in total regional traffic except for the share of regional traffic in (total) national traffic. Lastly, this empirical analysis includes network centrality variables (indicators) calculated at the global level of the worldwide graph: degree centrality (or number of links) and clustering coefficient (connectivity share among a node's neighbors), for discussing interdependencies between the socio-economic profile of the port region and its connectivity in the maritime network. The hub function of the port region is the inverse value of its clustering coefficient:[1] higher values underline a strong bridge or hub position towards immediate neighbours in the graph.

The study sample represents 49.9 percent of total world traffic, with a slightly higher share for containers (60.5 percent) and solid bulk (67.4 percent) than passengers and vehicles (47.1 percent), general cargo (36.9 percent), and liquid bulk (32.9 percent). This traffic structure reflects the intensity of container flows across the Asia–Pacific region, such as between China and the United States, and the growing trade of raw materials such as cement, coal, metals, and minerals from Australia. The selected port regions constitute subnational administrative entities in each country, such as Chinese provinces and American states, where one or

Table 16.2 Selected indicators

Traffic indicators		Unit	Regional indicators		Unit
P_DWT%	Share in total national traffic	%	R_Pop(%)	Share in total national population	%
P_Container	Container traffic in regional total	%	R_Density	Regional density/ national density	index
P_General	General cargo traffic in regional total	%	R_Unemployment	Regional unemployment/ national unemployment	index
P_Liquid	Liquid bulk traffic in regional total	%	R_Primary	Employment in primary activities (LQ)	index
P_Solid	Solid bulk traffic in regional total	%	R_Secondary	Employment in secondary activities (LQ)	index
P_Passenger	Passenger and vehicle traffic in regional total	%	R_ Tertiary	Employment in tertiary activities (LQ)	index
P_Inbound	Inbound traffic in region	%	R_GDPpc	GRP per capita/GDP per capita	index
P_Domestic	Domestic traffic in region	%			
P_Degree	No. of connected nodes				
P_Inv_cc	Share of adjacent triangles				

more ports operate. Such a level of analysis allows mixing regional and port traffic variables in a common database and takes into account the local or captive hinterland of ports, where most clients are located and where port-related activities concentrate, such as in the port city or port cluster. It is unfortunately impossible to distinguish local trade from transit trade in maritime statistics as the same region may be the origin/destination of flows but also a gate to access inland core regions beyond local needs (Itoh, 2013). For instance, inland rural regions may ship their exports through a port situated in an urban region acting as the main gateway (Löfgren and Robinson, 1999), and vice-versa.

A simple, linear regression between total vessel traffic and total port tonnage showed a significant relationship with a determination coefficient of 0.49 and 0.57 for non-weighted and weighted figures, respectively (Figure 16.1).[2] The fitness of weighted figures is slightly better than for non-weighted figures due to the higher efficiency of shipping networks and their high load factors for valued cargoes such as containers. Therefore, this empirical analysis adopted weighted figures as indicators for discussion of the relationship with regional activities. Differences in data sources such as time coverage and measurement unit may lower

Figure 16.1 Total port tonnage by region in 2009 (000s metric tons).

the relationship as well as the inclusion of landward (hinterland) flows in port tonnage.

Preliminary results

A principal components analysis (PCA) was applied to the 17 port and regional variables (see also Table 16.2), from which Figure 16.2 presents the two first main factors (see also Appendix 16.1 for more detailed results). Overall, the results point to a very significant relationship between traffic specialization and regional specialization. As such, regions specialized in primary activities tend to have a higher share of solid bulk, standing apart from other variables (the second quadrant in the figure). An opposite trend is that regions specialized in services (tertiary sector) while being richer and more densely populated concentrate container flows (the fourth quadrant in the figure). This opposition already underlined by Ducruet and Itoh (2015) based on port throughput statistics in a global perspective, confirms that (maritime) traffic is not randomly distributed across space and therefore reflects the dominant character of the place where it is handled, despite the

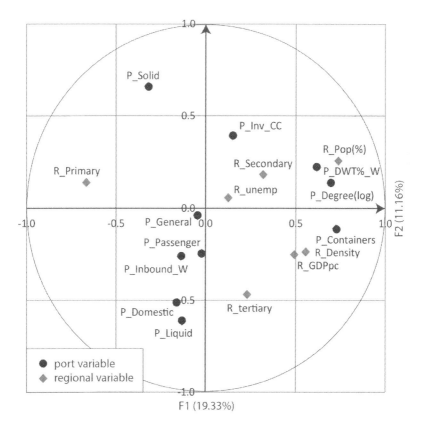

Figure 16.2 Coordinates of port and regional variables on the two main factors.

impossibility of distinguishing transit flows (transhipment) from trade flows (hinterland) in total shipping activity, and correcting for possible spatial and functional mismatches between administrative regions and port hinterlands.

In addition, on the first factor, degree centrality is clearly, if only partly, determined by demographic concentration and GRP per capita and high traffic share, which corroborates the aforementioned works on airline networks and cities. Regions specialized in the secondary (industrial) sector are likely to act as hubs in the maritime network, i.e. to be distribution platforms of hub-and-spokes configurations with an average hub function. When considering the second factor alone, negative scores underline some affinity between the tertiary sector, liquid bulk, domestic, and inbound traffic, as service or urban regions are important consumption centres for fuels (Graham, 1997; Decker *et al.*, 2000). The remaining variables have less significance along the two first factors. However, results show that passenger and vehicle traffic is closer to the tertiary sector and to population share and population density to a lesser extent for the third factor, while general cargo traffic is closer to the industrial (secondary) sector, and density to GRP for the fourth factor.

Eight coherent groups of port regions were obtained from a non-hierarchical clustering based on the PCA (see Appendix 16.2 for an overview[3]). The first cluster (*industrial centre*) is the largest by the number of port regions and its share in total vessel traffic (36.8 percent). It is also the only cluster with a positive, pronounced specialization in the industrial sector rather than services. Yet, its traffic profile is only slightly specialized in solid bulk, containers, outbound, international, and degree centrality, but a negative score for hub function. The second cluster (*value-added city-hub*), with only ten regions but 18 percent of the sample's traffic, is highly specialized in containers, general cargo, and international outbound traffic, with important degree centrality, traffic share, and hub function. Interestingly, such a profile goes along with the concentration of population, density, but also unemployment and a balanced role of the tertiary and industrial sectors. The third cluster (*agri-bulk hub*), with only seven regions, still captures 17.4 percent of total traffic as it shares the same profile than the former as a hub concentrating traffic and population, but with a specialization in primary activities and solid bulk and traffic share, and a lower density. The second and third clusters only have higher degree centrality and hub function both with high traffic share and population share, but a higher unemployment rate than the national average, probably caused by excessive immigration inflows. The fourth cluster (*energy centre*), with 25 regions, accounts for only 10.3 percent of total traffic. Such regions are smaller in size (traffic, demography) and are mostly domestic import regions for liquid bulk to fuel primary and tertiary activities.

The fifth cluster (*transit centre*) is a special case with only three regions and less than 1 percent traffic, mostly defined by passengers and vehicles, tertiary activities and to a lesser extent some primary activities as well as containers and international outbound. The sixth cluster (*construction centre*), with 19 regions, has only a small traffic share (7.5 percent), as these regions handle small traffic volumes of mostly solid bulk and inbound flows, but within a dense and tertiary environment, relatively poorer than average and more peripheral in the network. The combination of solid bulk and tertiary sector may relate to the importance of construction activities and urban waste. The seventh cluster (*metropolitan gateway*) is similar to the second by its specialization in containers, general cargo, density, and degree centrality, but its profile is much more influenced by GDP (a much richer region), tertiary activities, and domestic outbound traffic, with less unemployment, less developed hub functions, and a higher concentration of traffic and lower population within the host countries. Because port regions in this cluster have high degree centrality (or many links) but a limited hub function (or in a relatively secondary position in the maritime network), their negative score for the industry sector and highly negative score for bulky traffic underline needless supply chain advantages. Finally, the last cluster (*periphery*), with 13 regions, has a very low traffic share (1.1 percent) and specializes in general cargo and the primary sector. The combination of low population density, low GDP, and lower degree centrality and lower hub function suggests a region with logistical and socio-economic difficulties. In contrast to the second and third clusters, or hub clusters, periphery regions are far away from maritime trunk lines.

Port-region specialization and the maritime network

The share and dominant commodity type of vessel traffic among the clusters are presented in Figure 16.3. Each line corresponds to the sum of (weighted) vessel flows between each cluster and others, while the specialization of each link (crossing) is highlighted by grayscale based on a coefficient calculated by rows and columns. For instance, 25.1 percent of flows of industrial centres connect value-added city-hubs, and this link is mostly made of containers, whereas 40.8 percent of flows of value-added city-hubs connect industrial centres, mostly based on liquid bulks. In other words, this figure shows the degree of vessel traffic dependences for each link between regions of each cluster. The specialization coefficient differs on the same link depending on which cluster is the reference for the total. Unsurprisingly, the two clusters specialized in container traffic connect each other and other clusters mostly through container flows, while container flows do not occur on any pair of other clusters. They also have a high degree centrality (but middle and negative hub function) and density, and tertiary region, or urbanized (less industrialized) profile. Dependence and specialization linkages can vary depending on the chosen perspective. All clusters are linked to agri-bulk hubs with varying degrees of dependence but dominantly based on solid bulks, albeit conversely, while agri-bulk hubs depend for 60 percent of their traffic upon industrial centres, again based on solid bulks. The rest of their flows with other clusters are more specialized in other commodities. Thus, there is a spatial division of economic activities among port regions that is well apparent when looking at the nature of maritime flows connecting them. Although this analysis does not take into account the flows between port regions and inland regions through land-based transport, it is already able to capture a noticeable part (if not the backbone) of the value chains for this part of the Pacific Rim area.

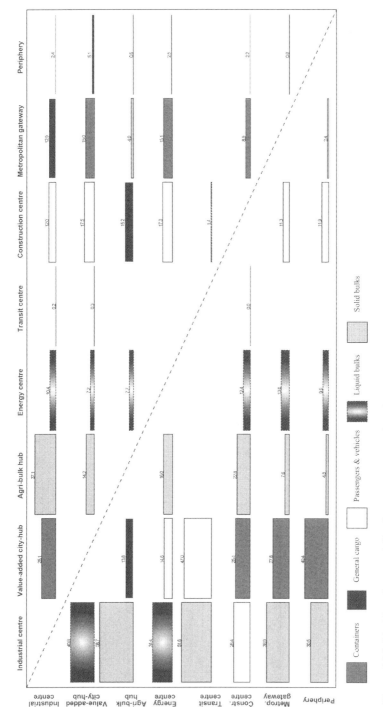

Figure 16.3 Maritime flow specialization among port region clusters.

Lastly, the analysis proposes a simplification of the graph to highlight the dominant structure of the maritime network (Figure 16.4), based on the "nodal region" methodology proposed by Nystuen and Dacey (1961). Based on weighted vessel traffic in the multigraph (or multiplex graph), only the largest flow (or vessel traffic) link of each region to another region has been kept, with its commodity type and shipping direction, thus making a weighted and directed tree graph while splitting the network into three connected components, or strings of links. The largest component has a line or corridor structure centralized on a few large hubs, such as Gyeongnam (Korea), Kanagawa (Japan), California, Shanghai, Beijing/Tianjin, and Western Australia. All these hubs have a different nature, so one may assume the existence of a polycentric, multifunctional system. Two other smaller components are made of Queensland and New South Wales centralizing mainly Japanese regions by means of solid bulk and general cargo flows on the one hand, and of Maharashtra (India) and Selangor (Malaysia), connecting mainly South Asian regions through container and general cargo flows.

The largest component is geographically diverse in terms of port region clusters and nodal commodity flows. It conveys major flows from two distribution or consolidation sources (Gyeongnam and Western Australia) towards one sink, composed of Chinese port regions (Shanghai and Beijing/Tianjin metropolitan gateways) alongside a number of other secondary sources in terms of traffic volume. Even though this analysis only focuses on the Pacific Rim area, California stands out as the largest traffic region to which multiple commodity flows of various natures converge, mostly containers. California is also the gateway for inland freight movements in North America (see Ducruet and Itoh, 2015). While the right-hand side of the figure (south, mainly Australia) is made of bulk chains, the left-hand side (mainly Japan and South Korea) is composed of light industry chains. Although directionality only applies to vessel movements, not trade import or export, it helps in understanding how major production regions of raw materials (e.g. grain, coal, minerals, and ores) are focal nodes for redistribution towards consumption regions and intermediate regions between them.

One very important outcome of this analysis is that the network centrality of port regions is much influenced by the local socio-economic environment (see also Appendix 16.2). For instance, the cluster of agri-bulk hubs is the only case where regions can have low GDP, high degree centrality, and lower population density, due to the specific case of (solid) bulk traffic that employs relatively lower-skilled workforce and less advanced technologies for production and shipment, and also fewer industries or services, with less connectivity function for industries. Most of the time, strong hub functions and high degree centrality (i.e. many maritime links) go along with a higher GDP than the national average. Although this may be in some way counterintuitive due to the limited developmental impact of transhipment hub ports, it still validates a number of ideas about the positive externalities provided by (dynamic) cities to ports (Hall and Jacobs, 2012).

In the maritime network, the so-called industrial centres as well as the agri-bulk hubs are essential for feeding the more urbanized port regions concentrating populations and services along the main trunk line. Important subsystems also

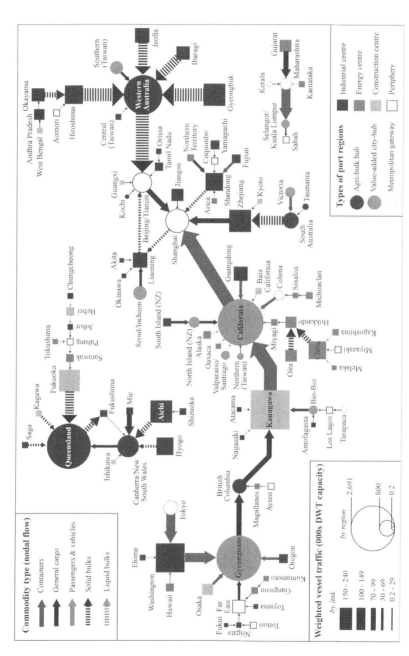

Figure 16.4 Nodal maritime flows among Asia–Pacific port regions.

appear, such as among Chinese provinces in the northern part of the country (Shanghai, Beijing, Shandong, Liaoning, Zhejiang, Jiangsu), while Guangdong, the factory of the world, is more strongly connected with California, the main gateway to China's largest customer of finished products. International and domestic logistics intermingle due to complex distribution circuits such as coal shipping, notably since China shifted from being the world's main exporter to being its main importer, using coastal shipping internally (Wang and Ducruet, 2014). Still, the largest regional economies are much connected with each other along the trunk line, proving the influence of hierarchy and market size on network configuration. As a complement, most of the secondary linkages are dominantly in proximity, i.e. within specific sub-regions of the Pacific Rim: Yellow Sea (Korea–China), Japan (coastal shipping), China (domestic river transport), East Sea (Korea–Japan–Russia), etc. The role of multifunctional distribution platforms such as Busan (Gyeongnam region), is of course one main explanation, beyond shortsea linkages. Although Hong Kong and Singapore, two dominant East Asian hubs, are excluded from this study due to the absence of district-level socio-economic data, such evidence well depicts the emergence of Asian hubs in a context of intensifying trans-Pacific trade (Robinson, 1998).

Conclusion

The analysis of the socio-economic determinants of port and maritime traffic across the Pacific Rim region is fruitful in many ways. First, it confirms that the intensity, specialization, and spatial distribution of maritime flows are far from being random or disconnected from the local environment where such flows are handled. Such evidence confirms previous empirical investigation based on worldwide port traffic statistics (Ducruet and Itoh, 2015), despite the fact that land-based (or hinterland) flows are not included per se in vessel movement data. As such, tertiary regions tend to concentrate container flows, and regions specialized in the primary sector concentrate solid bulk traffic. One particularity of the Asia–Pacific area is the higher centrality of industrial regions in the maritime network, due to the export-led profile of many Asian economies for manufacturing, as part of a global horizontal division of supply chains, especially in Northeast Asia, including Taiwan. Another peculiarity is the hub function of certain regions specialized in raw (solid) materials traffic as they distribute natural resources worldwide in a context of growing regional and global demands, especially in Australia. Still, one commonality is that on average, larger and more value-added traffic concentrates at larger, richer, and more urbanized regions, a trend which appears to be more evident when weighting traffic figures to lower the rather artificial importance of bulk traffic, because maritime transport for high value-added goods achieves efficient vessel schedules and frequencies.

Policy orientations can be addressed based on this research. In line with Hall and Jacobs (2012), our results point to the need to motivate maritime transport actors (and beyond, transport and value chain actors) to cultivate a certain embedding with the local level beyond their logistical needs and short-term network configurations. They should be aware that their activity contributes to and benefits from localized socio-economic structures. In turn, such actors may wish to further participate in the related territorial debates when it comes to promoting efficient urban and regional planning. It is the role of the local players (the so-called port community and beyond) to open the door to fruitful discussions with the ocean carriers in order to ensure their mid- or long-term development and sustainable position in maritime networks. As already suggested by Ducruet and Itoh (2015), there is a subtle equilibrium at stake between port-region match and mismatch when it comes to the local embedding of commodity flows. Large urban agglomerations and service centres are, at the same time, important markets dictating the origin and destination of major flows and logistical constraints to the fluid transit of such flows due to land use tensions for port operations. In parallel, certain commodities are more embedded than others in the local port-industrial complex, and a strong port-industry relationship may cause either growth or decline alongside price and geopolitical fluctuations at the international level. Lastly, this new identification of the spatial division of port region specialization within certain maritime circuits can lead to new policies for interregional cooperation to avoid the growth of inequalities in a context of excessive regional and port competition, especially in Asia.

Further research shall address in more depth the linkages between cargo types and economic activities performed by localities based on more disaggregated figures of regional employment, based on six rather than on three categories. But this will require more thorough investigation into the statistical sources available in each country. Another important possible refinement will be to complement the measurement of maritime flows by adding more exhaustive movements to reach a higher representativeness of the yearly total. At present, this study has captured only a very small portion of annual vessel movements, so that it remains hindered by possible seasonality bias and trade fluctuations. One potential remedy would be to offer a more dynamic view on the way regional economies and maritime flows have co-evolved on a middle and longer-term, possibly going back to the early 1980s as long as vessel types and capacities are reported uniformly by the data source. Expanding the study to other regions of the world such as Europe and Africa (as well as the Atlantic Ocean and the Mediterranean and Black Sea as a whole) would certainly help to verify whether the Pacific Rim trend is emblematic of a more universal one in terms of the ties that bind regional development and maritime transport.

Acknowledgements

The research leading to these results has received funding from the European Research Council under the European Union's Seventh Framework Programme (FP/2007-2013)/ERC Grant Agreement n. [313847] "World Seastems." In addition, the research was supported by JSPS KAKENHI Grant Number 24730259, Japan.

Appendix 16.1 Main results of the principal components analysis

Sum of Explained Variance

	F1	F2	F3	F4	F5	F6	F7
Eigenvalues	3.286	1.906	1.647	1.511	1.347	1.266	1.075
Variance (%)	19.329	11.212	9.690	8.890	7.926	7.450	6.322
% cumulated	19.329	30.540	40.231	49.121	57.047	64.497	70.819

Components

Indicators	F1	F2	F3	F4	F5	F6	F7
P_DWT%	0.723	0.247	−0.200	0.263	0.293	0.037	0.040
P_Containers	0.688	−0.076	−0.079	−0.108	−0.011	−0.063	0.197
P_General	−0.009	−0.179	0.157	−0.354	0.606	0.346	−0.512
P_Liquid	−0.032	−0.578	0.348	0.492	0.043	−0.094	0.264
P_Passenger	−0.105	−0.275	−0.559	−0.145	−0.084	0.131	0.519
P_Solid	−0.387	0.726	−0.038	0.042	−0.413	−0.199	−0.210
P_Domestic	−0.167	−0.418	0.160	0.577	0.122	−0.213	−0.234
P_Inbound	−0.054	−0.253	0.457	0.169	−0.457	0.263	−0.060
P_Degree	0.658	0.197	0.101	0.338	0.052	−0.247	−0.037
P_Inv_CC	0.136	0.413	−0.164	0.461	−0.073	−0.028	−0.106
R_Primary	−0.697	0.110	−0.204	0.256	0.259	0.024	−0.016
R_Secondary	0.325	0.246	0.704	−0.244	0.049	−0.075	0.256
R_Tertiary	0.235	−0.464	−0.525	0.071	−0.320	0.017	−0.352
R_Pop (%)	0.594	0.208	−0.186	0.273	0.228	0.416	0.094
R_Density	0.590	−0.211	0.042	−0.242	−0.450	0.138	−0.159
R_Unemp	0.157	0.148	0.128	0.232	−0.237	0.623	−0.141
R_GDPpc	0.522	−0.154	−0.071	−0.185	0.024	−0.559	−0.274

Appendix 16.2 Main results of the non-hierarchical clustering

Cluster/ indicator	C1 Industrial centre	C2 Value-added city-hub	C3 Agri-bulk hub	C4 Energy centre	C5 Transit centre	C6 Construction centre	C7 Metropolitan gateway	C8 Periphery
R_Primary	-0.113	-0.778	0.419	0.464	0.655	-0.259	-1.247	0.708
R_Secondary	0.749	0.273	-0.433	-0.544	-1.955	-0.054	-0.563	-0.286
R_Tertiary	-0.777	0.201	-0.041	0.344	1.174	0.332	1.918	-0.311
P_DWT%	0.006	1.839	1.065	-0.387	-0.622	-0.660	0.517	-0.432
P_Containers	0.103	1.158	-0.066	-0.376	0.433	-0.250	1.019	-0.717
P_General	-0.230	0.334	-0.960	-0.232	-1.462	-0.370	0.340	2.073
P_Liquid	-0.031	-0.088	-0.745	1.074	-0.241	-0.458	-0.369	-0.582
P_Passenger	-0.156	0.136	-0.452	0.046	4.246	-0.051	-0.179	-0.301
P_Solid	0.191	-1.026	1.479	-0.372	-1.131	0.784	-0.581	-0.423
P_Domestic	-0.301	-0.401	-0.070	1.123	-1.520	-0.430	0.263	-0.095
P_Inbound	-0.160	-0.317	-0.496	0.378	-0.954	0.735	-0.430	-0.371
P_Degree	0.152	1.114	0.957	-0.104	-1.958	-0.423	0.776	-0.965
P_Inv_CC	-0.087	0.554	1.580	-0.026	-0.965	-0.015	-0.222	-0.607
R_Pop (%)	-0.155	1.993	0.898	-0.409	0.080	-0.382	-0.243	-0.106
R_Density	-0.230	0.616	-0.397	-0.365	-0.168	0.648	1.455	-0.575
R_Unemp	-0.322	0.872	0.534	-0.200	-0.670	0.602	-0.803	0.075
R_GDPpc	0.042	0.114	-0.131	-0.090	-1.242	-0.313	2.329	-0.477
Distribution of port regions and vessel traffic								
No. regions (share for total)	38 (30.6%)	10 (8.1%)	7 (5.6%)	25 (20.2%)	3 (2.4%)	19 (15.3%)	7 (5.6%)	13 (10.5%)
Traffic share	36.8%	18.0%	17.4%	10.3%	0.0%	7.5%	8.5%	1.1%

Notes

1 Percentage of actual closed triplets (or triangles) in the maximum possible number of closed triplets (or triangles) for each port and its neighbours.
2 Port tonnage statistics in metric tons were obtained from various international and national organizations for the year 2009.
3 This table shows the weighted impact values of each indicator calculated by cluster centres and the components' scores from PCA in each cluster.

References

Beyers W.B., Fowler C.S. (2012) Economic structure, technological change and location theory: the evolution of models explaining the link between cities and flows. In: Hall P.V. and Hesse M. (Eds), *Cities, Regions and Flows*. London: Routledge, pp. 23–41.
Boschma R., Frenken K. (2011a) The emerging empirics of evolutionary economic geography. *Journal of Economic Geography*, 11(2): 295–307.
Boschma R., Frenken K. (2011b) Technological relatedness, related variety and economic geography. In: Cooke P., Asheim B., Boschma R., Martin R., Swartz D., Tödtling F. (Eds), *Handbook on Regional Innovation and Growth*, Cheltenham and Northampton: Edward Elgar, pp. 187–97.
Bottasso A., Conti M., Ferrari C., Merk O., Tei A. (2013) The impact of port throughput on local employment: evidence from a panel of European regions. *Transport Policy*, 27: 32–38.
Charlier J. (1994) Sur le concept de tonnages pondérés en économie portuaire. *Les Cahiers Scientifiques du Transport*, 29: 75–84.
Cheung S.M.S., Yip T.L. (2011) Port city factors and port production: analysis of Chinese ports. *Transportation Journal*, 50(2): 162–75.
Dawkins C.J. (2003) Regional development theory: conceptual foundations, classic works, and recent developments. *Journal of Planning Literature*, 18(2): 131–72.
Decker E.H., Elliott S., Smith F.A., Blake D.R., Rowland S. (2000) Energy and material flow through the urban system. *Energy and the Environment*, 25: 685–740.
Deng P., Lu S., Xiao H. (2013) Evaluation of the relevance measure between ports and regional economy using structural equation modeling. *Transport Policy*, 27: 123–33.
Derudder B., Witlox F. (2010) *Commodity Chains and World Cities*. Wiley-Blackwell.
Dicken P. (2001) Chains and networks, territories and scales: Towards a relational framework for analysing the global economy. *Global Networks*, 1: 99–123.
Doi M., Tiwari P., Itoh H. (2001) A computable general equilibrium analysis of efficiency improvements at Japanese ports. *Review of Urban and Regional Development Studies*, 13(3): 187–206.
Ducruet C. (2009) Port regions and globalisation. In: Notteboom T.E., Ducruet C., De Langen P.W. (Eds), *Ports in Proximity: Competition and Cooperation among Adjacent Seaports*. Aldershot: Ashgate, pp. 41–53.
Ducruet C. (2013) Network diversity and maritime flows. *Journal of Transport Geography*, 30: 77–88.
Ducruet C., Lugo I. (2013) Structure and dynamics of transportation networks: models, concepts, and applications. In: Rodrigue J.P., Notteboom T.E., Shaw J. (Eds), *The SAGE Handbook of Transport Studies*, SAGE Publications Ltd., pp. 347–64.
Ducruet C., Itoh H. (2015) Regions and material flows: investigating the regional branching and industry relatedness of port traffic in a global perspective. *Journal of Economic Geography*, doi: 10.1093/jeg/lbv010.
Ducruet C., Koster H.R.A., Van der Beek D.J. (2010) Commodity variety and seaport performance. *Regional Studies*, 44(9): 1221–40.

Ducruet C., Itoh H., Joly O. (2015) Ports and the local embedding of commodity flows. *Papers in Regional Science*, doi: 10.1111/pirs.12083

Fujita M., Mori T. (1996) The role of ports in the making of major cities: self-agglomeration and hub-effect. *Journal of Development Economics*, 49(1): 93–120.

Fujita M., Krugman P., Venables A.J. (1999) *The Spatial Economy: Cities, Regions and International Trade*. Cambridge and London: MIT Press.

Graham S. (1997) Telecommunications and the future of cities: debunking the myths. *Cities*, 14(1): 21–9.

Guerrero D. (2014) Deep-sea hinterlands: some empirical evidence of the spatial impact of containerization. *Journal of Transport Geography*, 35: 84–94.

Guerrero D., Proulhac L. (2014) Freight flows and urban hierarchy. *Research in Transportation Business and Management*, 11: 105–15.

Hall P.V., Jacobs W. (2012) Why are maritime ports (still) urban and why should policy-makers care? *Maritime Policy and Management*, 39(2): 89–206.

Harrigan J. (2004) Specialization and the volume of trade: do the data obey the laws? In: Choi E.K., Harrigan J. (Eds), *Handbook of International Trade*, Oxford: Wiley-Blackwell.

Itoh H. (2013) Market area analysis of port in Japan: an application of fuzzy clustering. *Proceedings of the 2013 International Association of Maritime Economists Conference (IAME)*, Marseilles, 3–5 July.

Kawakami T., Doi M. (2004) Port capital formation and economic development in Japan: A vector autoregression approach. *Papers in Regional Science*, 83: 723–32.

Lee S.W., Song D.W., Ducruet C. (2008) A tale of Asia's world ports: the spatial evolution in global hub port cities. *Geoforum*, 39(2): 372–85.

Leslie D., Reimer S. (1999) Spatializing commodity chains. *Progress in Human Geography*, 23: 401–20.

Löfgren H., Robinson S. (1999) *Spatial Networks in Multi-region Computable General Equilibrium Models*. Trade and Macroeconomics Division Research Paper No. 35, International Food Policy Research Institute, Washington DC.

McCann P., Shefer D. (2004) Location, agglomeration and infrastructure. *Papers in Regional Science*, 83(1): 177–93.

Merk O., Manshanden W.J.J., Dröes M.I. (2013) Inter-regional spillovers of seaports: the case of Northwest Europe. *International Journal of Transport Economics*, 40(3): 401–17.

Neffke F., Henning M., Boschma R. (2011) How do regions diversify over time? Industry relatedness and the development of new growth paths in regions. *Economic Geography*, 87(3): 237–65.

Nystuen J.D., Dacey M.F. (1961) A graph theoretical interpretation of nodal regions. *Papers in Regional Science*, 7(1): 29–42.

Rimmer P.J. (2014) *Asian-Pacific Rim Logistics. Global Context and Local Policies*. Cheltenham and Northampton: Edward Elgar.

Robinson R. (1998) Asian hub/feeder nets: The dynamics of restructuring. *Maritime Policy and Management*, 25(1): 21–40.

Scott A.J., Storper M. (2003) Regions, globalisation, development. *Regional Studies*, 37(6–7): 579–593.

Song L., Van Geenhuizen M. (2014) Port infrastructure investment and regional economic growth in China: panel evidence in port regions and provinces. *Transport Policy*, 36: 173–83.

Tabuchi T., Thisse J.F. (2002) *Regional Specialization and Transport Costs*. Discussion Paper. London: CEPR.

UNCTAD (2008) *Review of Maritime Transport*. Geneva: United Nations.

Wang C., Ducruet C. (2014) Transport corridors and regional balance in China: the case of coal trade and logistics. *Journal of Transport Geography*, 40: 3–16.

17 Explaining international trade flows with shipping-based distances

*David Guerrero, Claude Grasland,
César Ducruet*

Despite the strong reliance of world trade on maritime transport,[1] little has been done to investigate their actual interdependencies. The usefulness of maritime transport to "take the pulse of world trade and movement" (Ullman, 1949) has somewhat faded, while scholars interested in shipping and ports have focused increasingly on operational aspects rather than on broader socio-economic linkages (Ng and Ducruet, 2014). Many reports on world trade and the economy simply ignore maritime transport while focusing primarily on air transport, which is believed to have largely contributed to the shrinking of distances (Nelson, 2008).[2] Air transport is also more often associated with the vitality, image, and future of regions and urban growth, whereas ports and shipping have lost their initial socio-economic importance for localities (Jacobs *et al.*, 2010).

This chapter, however, wishes to go further into measuring the maritime dimension of trade flows. Existing analyses practically do not take into account the underlying physical (transport) architecture by which such flows are made possible (see also Hall and Hesse, 2012). In particular, studies using spatial interaction models remain very abstract, as they use crow's flight distances to explain trade flows among country pairs (McCallum, 1995; Feenstra *et al.*, 2001). This is somewhat unrealistic, given that information technologies and telecommunications complement and facilitate rather than replace purely physical flows of goods along the transport and logistics chain, which includes many detours and overcomes the friction of space in a very specific way (Hesse and Rodrigue, 2004). We believe that results from the application of the gravity model to world trade flows can noticeably improve if we include more practical logistics distances. In particular, maritime transport does not follow an infrastructure of track and therefore belongs to the class of non-planar spatial networks based on the design of observed flows (Ducruet and Lugo, 2013). Thus, the sole nautical distance between two countries cannot account for the true "maritime distance" even though it may include aspects of speed and size of vessels. Instead, maritime transport in this chapter is understood as the functional link between two countries based on operational aspects or observed flows. Although the observed maritime flows are in some way part of the broader trade flows, specific network configurations and logistical arrangements made by ocean carriers make them rather specific and not only a "part of the whole." The maritime network architecture is thus considered in this chapter as a facilitator rather than as a sole component of international trade. Our main hypothesis is that on average, country pairs well connected by such network services will be favored in terms of trade. Liner shipping connectivity is thus seen in this chapter as a trade facilitator against distance friction.

The remainder of this chapter is as follows. The next section offers a wider literature review on the links between trade and maritime transport to strengthen the background and originality of our approach and main hypothesis. Then, we go further into the methodological aspects of a global analysis using shipping networks as distance parameters into the gravity model destined to explain trade flows among world countries. Afterwards, we present the main findings of the study, and this is followed by a discussion and conclusion on the main lessons learned.

World trade and global maritime transport

Patterns of global maritime flows

Overall, the role of maritime transport is to overcome separation by sea among trading partners. The absence of a track infrastructure allows great flexibility in designing maritime routes which are, in turn, constrained by physical (the shape of coastlines, climatic conditions, tidal ranges), political (forbidden waters for certain fleet nationalities, trade embargoes, customs regulations), and technical (quality of port services, accessibility of port terminals, overall port costs) factors. Especially in liner shipping, the architecture of container flows is also shaped to a large extent by the specific network configurations of ocean carriers. Thus, container shipping is a trade-off between shippers' needs (call frequency, accessibility, transit time, reliability) to connect markets and carriers' imperatives (ship routing, size, number of strings, geographic coverage) to deploy their services to meet demand (Notteboom, 2006). Fast increases in vessel speed, size, and frequency as well as congestion bottlenecks in traditional port cities made it necessary for shipping lines to rationalize their services by reducing the number of port calls and concentrating them at a few large transhipment hubs located such that they optimized transport and limited deviation from the trunk line followed by mother vessels (Zohil and Prijon, 1999). A global equatorial beltway or circumterrestrial route has thus emerged combining bundling services (round-the-world, pendulum) and transhipment services (hub-and-spokes, relay-interlining) within and between the connected regions (Ducruet and Notteboom, 2012a).

A number of empirical analyses of global maritime flows were proposed in recent years, mostly to describe the topological structure of the network, without direct connection to trade flows. Some scholars have applied several measures from complex networks research to verify the scale-free and small-world dimensions of the global maritime network, mostly for container shipping flows (Deng *et al.*, 2009; Hu and Zhu, 2009) as well as other fleet types (Kaluza *et al.*, 2010; Ducruet, 2013). This work confirmed that as a scale-free network, the global shipping network is composed of a few large nodes having many connections to other nodes, and a majority of small nodes with only a few links. This was also confirmed by applying more classic methods such as single linkage analysis revealing dominant hub ports and their affiliated nodal regions (Wang and Wang, 2011) and statistical measures showing the growing concentration of container traffic among world ports since the early 1970s (Ducruet and Notteboom, 2012b). Other work has searched for interdependencies with airline networks (Parshani *et al.*, 2010). While all these studies have defined the network based on ports as nodes and vessel movements (or schedules) as links between them, other scholars have also focused on large regions as nodes (Joly, 1999; Li *et al.*, 2015).

Such works could have shed new empirical light on both carrier and trade factors in shaping global maritime flows. On the one hand, carrier factors fostered the emergence of intermediate hubs ensuring intra- and interregional shipping connectivity (see also Frémont, 2007; Rodrigue and Notteboom, 2010). Among those hubs, some were also hinterland gateways enjoying land-based centrality, such as Rotterdam and Hamburg, while others were mostly defined by their intermediacy, such as Singapore and Gioia Tauro (Ng, 2006). On the other hand, the geographic coverage of maritime flows also revealed their high concentration on shorter (kilometric) distances, preferential linkages among neighbouring ports, and noticeable regional shifts such as most of African traffic being increasingly polarized by Asia, and a decreasing role of Europe in global maritime flows (see also Ducruet *et al.*, 2014). Despite its initial specification in relation with global trade flows, the model proposed by Tavasszy *et al.* (2011) on multimodal networks and flows was mostly designed to address the likely impacts of different scenarios on the level and distribution of port container throughputs. For instance, they calculated that a new polar cap shortcut or a better developed Europe–Asia railway land-bridge would not provoke enormous shifts of container flows from routes going through Suez. While their results proved to be accurate and realistic, they did not further link their model with trade flows.

Trade and shipping interdependencies

The interdependencies at stake between trade and shipping have been researched by a number of scholars in recent years, from various perspectives. For instance, it has been demonstrated that coastal economies are favored compared with landlocked countries due to the role of transportation gateways (Behrens *et al.*, 2006), to such an extent that landlocked countries assume 50 percent more transport costs than coastal countries (Limao and Venables, 2001). The influence of port infrastructure quality and efficiency on shipping costs was also underlined by Clark *et al.*, 2004 and Haddad *et al.* (2010). Perhaps the most relevant approach to the current chapter is the one by Bernhofen *et al.* (2013) on the effects of the container revolution on world trade. Using time series data for 1962–1990, the authors particularly underlined the stronger effect of container adoption (port and railway) on trade growth compared with the effects of trade liberalization, mostly for north–north trade. While such results confirm the importance of (container) shipping for world trade, the role of developing countries and notably the export-led newly industrialized countries of Asia remained little discussed.

The reason why analyses of shipping and of trade remain apart is mostly practical. Trade statistics by transport mode do not exist, while shipping statistics refer to tonnage rather than to the value of the goods carried by ships and handled at port terminals. Such differences in data units are aggravated by differences in the respective definitions of flows. Unlike trade statistics, shipping and port statistics often include transhipment, i.e. transit trade between origin and destination, thus complicating their direct comparison. Another aspect is that tonnage data rarely mentions the origins and destinations of flows. On a world level, the International Road Transport Union (IRU) ceased to publish country-level tonnage figures after 1996, which could then be complemented by the yearbooks of the United Nations.[3] But the most striking change in data availability is the disappearance of the Maritime Transport Study published by the United Nations as *Commodity Trade (by Sea) Statistics*[4] until the 1980s. It was, to our knowledge, used in only one research paper in the whole academic literature (van den Bremen and de Jong, 1986) for describing world patterns of maritime trade flows. Yet, the authors used the information to measure and map the amount of flows per region and per commodity rather than focusing on flows between regions of the world. Finally, indicators available on a country basis, such as the Liner Shipping Connectivity Index (LSCI), can be considered as a "proxy of the accessibility to global trade" and "jointly considered as a measure of connectivity to maritime shipping and as a measure of trade facilitation" (Rodrigue *et al.*, 2013). However, such indicators are not related with trade itself and remain bound to transport and logistics performance measurements.

Data and methodology

In this work a spatial interaction model is used as a tool to measure the influence of the frequency of containerized shipping services on trade. Instead of focusing on shipping as flows, as in the aforementioned literature on global maritime networks, it considers shipping services as a functional distance among countries of the world.

Data on international trade

Unfortunately for researchers in maritime transportation, an exhaustive large-scale world database of freight flows in tonnes is not available. Empirical evidence on international freight flows in tonnes can be gathered only from national databases (such as customs), which are not comprehensive on a worldwide basis. For these reasons, we have decided to make use of *Chelem*, a single database of international trade in constant dollars, created by the French research centre in international economics (CEPII). We know that it is an imperfect proxy of freight flows since these are sensitive to fluctuations in market prices as well as changes in interest and exchange rates. The impact of these fluctuations is partially offset by providing segmented results of the model by types of cargo.[5] Data on distances between country capitals used in the spatial interaction model has also been obtained from *Chelem*.

This work is focused on containerized shipping, which operates on a fixed geographic itinerary and publicly advertised sailing schedule. In general, containerized transport mainly consists of manufactured goods, usually of high value. Since in our trade database there is no specification on the type of packaging, we have created a *containerizable* category with the cargo categories that seem most likely to be carried in containers. Obviously, there is no firm rule one way or the other on this issue, and one type of cargo can be either containerized or not depending on many different parameters such as the size of the shipment or the handling tools available at seaports. For example, cereals that can be either transported in containers or in bulk ships are considered non-containerizable since most volumes are conveyed in bulk carriers. Steel coils, which are sometimes differently packed and conveyed in specific ships, are however considered as containerizable. Another shortcoming of international trade databases is their lack

Coastal countries included in this study

Inland and coastal countries not included in this study

Figure 17.1 Countries included in this study.

of specification of the mode of transport. Even if most trade in value is conveyed by ships (70 percent according to UNCTAD, 2013), a substantial part of it is also conveyed by ground transport and plane. In this study, the impact of non-maritime modes seems to have been reduced by the structure of the sample, which consists exclusively of countries with access to maritime networks (Figure 17.1).

Data on shipping services

Shipping services have been calculated using the *Lloyd's List* database about the movements of ships in 1996 and 2006. The latter are based on the number of weekly opportunities to send cargo between two ports on the same ship. The opportunities have been aggregated at the level of countries to match with the data on trade flows. Unfortunately, the data does not take into account the indirect opportunities to link two ports. Therefore the accessibility of regions usually served by feeder services via transhipment hubs (Africa, Oceania, and South America) is underestimated. However, it could be argued that in most industries there is a preference for direct maritime connections, generally considered more reliable and faster than indirect ones (Woxenius, 2012). The impact of transit time in trade is potentially high. But it could vary from one service to another, even if we consider the same couple of ports (see Table 17.1). This variability is linked both to the itinerary (through canals or not) and the number of scales of the service. The use of average transit time (roughly correlated with distance) has not been tested, since it is difficult to estimate and does not seem to provide relevant information to the model.

Finally, the two measures used to explain the geographical distribution of international trade (distance and frequency of containerized services) reflect different but complementary dimensions of contemporary systems of production. These

Table 17.1 Weekly direct services between Le Havre and Hong Kong (January 2014)

Day of the week (dep)	Departure time	Shipping Company	Transit time (days)	Day of the week (arriv)
MON	10h10	Hanjin	34	SUN
MON	14h30	UASC/CMA CGM	41	SUN
TUE	12h55	APL/OOCL	27	MON
TUE	13h00	UASC/CMA CGM	42	TUE
WED	10h25	Hapag Lloyd	27	TUE
WED	14h30	UASC	48	TUE
THU	19h00	Cosco/Hanjin	39	MON
FRI	08h25	Maersk	37	SUN
FRI	20h20	NYK Line	27	THU
SAT	20h40	CSCL	36	SUN
SUN	12h50	OOCL/NYK	30	TUE
SUN	17h15	Maersk	35	SUN

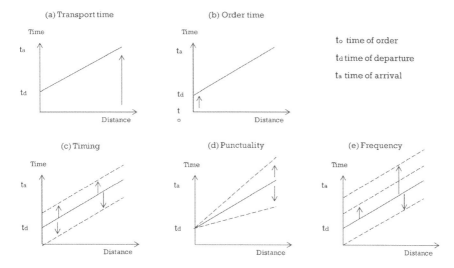

Figure 17.2 Temporal elements in production networks (Woxenius, 2006).

dimensions have been analysed by empirical work about the extension of automotive production networks (Woxenius, 2006) that considers five different temporal elements (Figure 17.2). Between them only transport time (a) and order time (b) are linked with speed, and by extension with geographical distance. The other time elements (timing, punctuality, and frequency) seem to be much more related to the regularity and reliability of transport services, and then more or less directly linked with the frequency of transport services. So, traditional spatial interaction models explain trade only by taking into account the two first temporal elements (order time and transport time) but completely neglect the three last ones. By using the frequency of containerized shipping services, this chapter aims to shed some light on the other temporal elements that remain largely unknown.

Methodology

Spatial interaction models are employed to evaluate the impact of distance and the frequency of shipping services on trace for different types of cargo. They provide an explanation of the spatial pattern of trade flows between countries in terms of value. After testing different kinds of models (see Appendix 17.3), the spatial interaction models selected are those that provide the highest explanatory power. They are formulated as follows:

$$Fij = Ai \cdot Oi \cdot Bj \cdot Dj \cdot dij_1^{\alpha} \tag{17.1}$$

$$Fij = Ai \cdot Oi \cdot Bj \cdot Dj \cdot dij_1^{\alpha} \cdot dij_2^{\gamma} \tag{17.2}$$

where Oi is the total value of exports of the country called i; Dj is the total value of imports of the country called j (see Table 17.1); dij is the separation (Euclidean distance/frequency of shipping services) between i and j; α is the decay parameter associated with distance (dij_1); γ is the elasticity associated with the frequency of shipping services (dij_2); and $Ai\cdot$ and $Bj\cdot$ are the balancing factors ensuring that the origin i and destination j constraints are satisfied. When a country is exporting, it is referred to as "i" and when a country is importing, it is referred to as "j".

The choice of measure of distance influences the results of the spatial interaction model. The Euclidean distance between capitals has been selected because it seems to be more consistent with the situation of most of the countries analysed, where more than one port handles international trade. Moreover, the explanatory power of the model is slightly higher when the distance between capitals is used, as compared to the distance between centroids.

The data used is a matrix of freight flows between countries (Table 17.2). The value of r_1^2 is the part of the total variance explained by the model. It is a measure of the goodness of fit of the model to explain the spatial distribution of flows between the countries. A r_1^2 of 100 percent would indicate that the regression line perfectly fits the data. This means that the spatial distribution of flows between countries can be perfectly predicted by the total exports of the country i, the total imports of country j, and the distance separating both. A second parameter r_2^2 is calculated as a measure of variance specifically

Table 17.2 Matrix of origin–destination of flows between coastal countries

To From	Country 1	Country 2	Country ...	Country j	Exports
Country 1	0	I12	I1...	I1j	Exp Country 1
Country 2	I21	0	0	I2j	Exp Country 2
Country ...	I...1	I...2	0	I...j	Exp Country ...
Country i	Ii1	Ii2	Ii...	0	Exp Country j
Imports	Imp Country 1	Imp Country 2	...	Imp Country j	

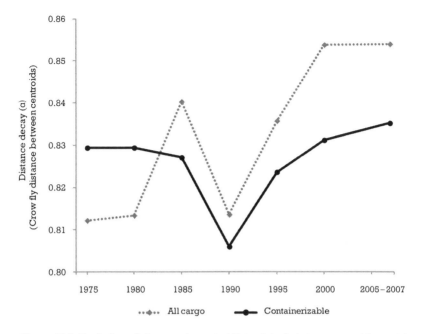

Figure 17.3 Evolution of distance decay in bilateral trade between coastal countries (1975–2007).

Table 17.3 Results of a spatial interaction model using crow's flight distance

2006, *crow's flight distance*	α	r_1^2	r_2^2
All cargo	−0.86	89%	69%
Containerizable	−0.84	89%	68%

explained by the distance. A third parameter r_3^2 measures the specific explanatory power of shipping services. A Poisson regression has been used to fit the spatial doubly constrained model (Fotheringham and O'Kelly, 1989; D'Aubigny *et al.*, 2000).

Results

Long-term evolution of trade (1975–2010): the impact of economic regionalization

Table 17.3 shows the results of the spatial interaction model of trade flows between coastal countries in 2006, distinguishing containerizable cargo. The model, exclusively based on traffic and distance (see Equation 17.1) explains 89 percent of the geographical distribution of all flows but only half of those of container-izable cargo. Alone, the distance between countries plays an important role in the model, explaining two-thirds (69 percent) of the geographical distribution of all trade but only 21 percent of the containerized flows. Obviously distance plays a negative role in trade either or not containerizable. The average value of distance-decay parameter (α) varies between 0.84 and 0.86 (flows in dollars, including petroleum products), which means that a 10 percent increase in distance lowers trade by about 8.5 percent. Although trade between coastal countries is strongly distance-constrained, it is less than if we include inland countries, for which the average distance-decay parameter is slightly higher (Disdier and Head, 2008). This difference could be due to the lack of direct access to the sea of inland countries that would imply difficulties to reach distant markets.

Analysis of long series of data provides insight into the evolving influence of distance between coastal countries. Over the last three decades the distance decay has gone up (+0.03 for all cargo, +0.01 for containerized) although with periods of ups and downs. Considering that the differences in the trends of containerized and all cargo before 1985 are probably due to the rise of the price of oil after the (oil) crises in 1973 and 1979, periods of decline (1975–1990) and ascent (1990–2007) can be identified. The decline of the influence of distance in 1975–1990 seems to be linked both to the fulfilment of the main waves of containerization (Guerrero and Rodrigue, 2014) and the removal of protectionist measures, especially in the emerging economies (Krugman, 1995). The recovery and rise of the effect of distance since 1990 should be interpreted in a broader trend since the 1950s (Head and Mayer, 2010). According to Disdier and Head (2008) three explanations can be provided to explain the long-term rise of distance-decay since the aftermath of the Second World War. The first is that technological advances such as email and the Internet may have been smaller or less ubiquitous than certain works would suggest (see, for example, Cairncross, 2001). Second, as suggested above, the influence of time on trade seems to be increasing (Hummels, 2001; Woxenius, 2006). Third, changes in the composition of trade might be biased towards goods with high distance costs (Berthelon and Freund, 2008). Another explanation of this shift would be that falling transport costs (mainly derived from containerization) push firms to trade more sophisticated goods with higher transaction costs and this would contribute to maintain distance-decay high (Duranton and Storper, 2006).

Medium-term evolution of trade (1996–2006): looking at the impact of maritime services on trade

To test the influence of the frequency of maritime transport on trade, the number of weekly shipping services has been introduced in the model. Traffic, distance, and shipping services account together for 91 percent (r_3^2) of the geographic distribution of trade flows. If we eliminate mass and distance factors, the contribution of shipping services to the model is statistically significant but is globally low ($r_3^2 = 1.4$ percent). Obviously, the effect of the frequency of containerized services is a positive one ($\gamma = 0.10$ in 2006), which means that an increase of 10 percent in the number of weekly shipping services implies a rise in trade of about 1 percent. Therefore, greater opportunities to ship cargo from one country to another might lead to increasing opportunities for profitable trade. However, it seems that the effect of the frequency of shipping services in trade has decreased between 1996 ($\gamma = 0.14$) and 2006 ($\gamma = 0.10$). This would result from the generalization of containerized services that are today more ubiquitous than in the past, implying less spatial differentiation between trade routes. Moreover, the further development of hubbing and transhipment in containerized networks since the 1990s would have increased the relative importance of indirect connections compared to direct ones, which are those we have used.

The significance of shipping services in explaining trade between coastal countries varies considerably between industries (Table 17.4). These differences mean that the needs of frequent containerized services are not equal for all industries, depending on factors such stock levels and inventory management strategies. When isolated from distance and traffic, the explanatory power of shipping services for paper and pulp ($r_3^2 = 2.0$ percent), building materials ($r_3^2 = 1.9$ percent), and machines, equipment, and arms ($r_3^2 = 1.8$ percent), is as much as four times higher than those of food and beverages ($r_3^2 = 0.4$ percent), vehicle components and engines ($r_3^2 = 0.5$ percent), and precision instruments ($r_3^2 = 0.6$ percent). These

Table 17.4 Results of a spatial interaction model using shipping services as distance measurement

	1996					2006				
	α	γ	r_1^2	r_2^2	r_3^2	α	γ	r_1^2	r_2^2	r_3^2
Electronics	−.48	.14	89%	52%	2.1%	−.62	.09	87%	52%	1.1%
Textile	−.86	.12	84%	56%	1.3%	−.94	.08	86%	55%	.8%
Food and beverages	−.96	.10	84%	61%	.8%	−.99	.06	83%	61%	.4%
Vehicle components and engines	−.92	.12	87%	68%	.9%	−.97	.07	89%	69%	.5%
Paper and pulp	−1.01	.16	88%	75%	1.7%	−1.00	.15	87%	72%	2.0%
Building materials	−1.04	.14	88%	73%	1.1%	−1.00	.15	87%	71%	1.9%
Plastic and miscellaneous articles	−.83	.17	88%	70%	1.9%	−.91	.12	89%	71%	1.4%
Chemicals and pharmaceuticals	−.72	.12	88%	63%	1.7%	−.73	.08	86%	54%	1.2%
Metallic structures and hardware	−.88	.17	89%	72%	1.9%	−.90	.10	89%	69%	1.3%
Machines, equipment and arms	−.66	.14	89%	69%	2.5%	−.70	.09	89%	67%	1.8%
Precision instruments	−.55	.15	91%	60%	2.5%	−.61	.06	89%	53%	.6%
Wood and furniture	−1.01	.20	90%	73%	2.1%	−1.08	.12	90%	70%	1.5%
Containerizable cargo	−.73	.14	90%	71%	1.8%	−.78	.10	91%	73%	1.4%

results are surprising. On the one hand sectors like textiles, electronics, and precision instruments, known as highly dependent on time-to-market, are not well explained by shipping services. On the other, flows generated by more traditional sectors like paper manufacturing or construction are much better explained by the frequency of transport services. One partial explanation would be the importance of other means of transport conveying the international trade generated by these sectors: air transport for long distances and ground transport for short ones. A comparison of these results with those of 1996 provides some further explanation. The explanatory power of shipping services was considerably higher for electronics ($r_3^2 = 2.1$ percent) and for precision instruments ($r_3^2 = 2.5$ percent). The shrinkage of the explanatory power of shipping services for these sectors means that they rely less on the frequency of transport services than in the past. Another possible explanation is that strategies of cost reduction in transport, implying less frequent shipments, have grown in importance within these sectors.

All industries are not equally sensitive to the frequency of containerized services (Table 17.3). The most sensitive ones are also those for which its explanatory power is the highest: paper and pulp and building materials with elasticity values (γ) of 0.15. The high influence of the frequency of shipping services in these sectors can be due to the relatively important volumes that they generate, leading to high storage costs. The less sensitive ones are food and beverages, precision instruments, and vehicle components and engines $\gamma = 0.6$–0.7. These differences mean that variations in the frequency of shipping services have unequal effects on the flows generated by different activities. It should be noted that the differences of activities with regard to shipping services sensitivity remain roughly unchanged between 1996 and 2006. The impact of shipping services has considerably decreased between 1996 and 2006 for most industries (in 2006, $\gamma = 0.17$). The decrease has been particularly dramatic for trade flows generated by wood and furniture, plastic objects, and metallic structures and hardware.

According to the model, the distance and frequency of shipping services thus explain to a large extent the spatial variation of international trade flows. However, this type of analysis naturally raises the question of deviations from the predictions. Table 17.5 shows the differences between the observed and expected (as of the model) distributions of flows. The left column shows trade routes with larger flows than expected (underestimations), the right column outlines those with smaller flows than expected (overestimations). In order to make the results more easily understandable, deviations between countries have been aggregated at the level of regions.

A substantial number of underestimations take place between neighbouring countries within the same region. Therefore, European (31 percent), Asian (9 percent) and North American (7 percent) internal trade accounts for almost one-half the underestimations of the model. In the case of Europe and North America, this can be explained by the intense ground transportation flows between neighboring countries within the same economic region (for example, between the United

Table 17.5 Deviations of a spatial interaction model using shipping services as distance measurement

Main underestimations, by region		Main overestimations, by region	
Intra-Europe	31%	North Atlantic	25%
North Pacific	17%	Intra-Europe	21%
Asia–Europe	10%	Intra-Asia	18%
Intra-Asia	9%	Asia–Europe	11%
Intra-North America	7%	South America–North America	4%
Intra-South America	2%	Russia → Europe	2%
Others	24%	Others	20%

Main underestimations, by country				Main overestimations, by country			
CHN → USA	8%	CHN → CAN	1%	DEU → USA	4%	MYS → SGP	1%
MEX → USA	4%	CHN → NLD	1%	CHN → KOR	3%	DNK → DEU	1%
USA → MEX	3%	ESP → FRA	1%	CHN → TWN	3%	GBR → FRA	1%
TWN → CHN	2%	DEU → ITA	1%	ITA → USA	2%	GBR → BEL	1%
JPN → TWN	2%	ESP → PRT	1%	KOR → JPN	2%	FRA → NLD	1%
USA → JPN	2%	DEU → ESP	1%	FRA → GBR	2%	BRA → USA	1%
MYS → USA	2%	DEU → FRA	1%	USA → ESP	2%	DEU → DNK	1%
ITA → FRA	1%	FRA → ITA	1%	FRA → USA	2%	BEL → GBR	1%
BEL → DEU	1%	NLD → DEU	1%	ESP → USA	2%	USA → FRA	1%
DEU → BEL	1%	BEL → ITA	1%	CHN → JPN	2%	GBR → NLD	1%
GBR → IRL	1%	CHN → GBR	1%	USA → ITA	1%	NLD → FRA	1%
USA → KOR	1%	NLD → ITA	1%	USA → DEU	1%	CHN → THA	1%
FRA → ESP	1%	CHN → DEU	1%	NLD → USA	1%	DEU → NOR	1%
JPN → THA	1%	FRA → DEU	1%	SWE → DEU	1%	TWN → JPN	1%
CAN → USA	1%	*Others*	56%	BEL → USA	1%	*Others*	60%

States and Mexico in NAFTA, or between France and Italy inside the EU). In the case of Asia, the reasons are more complex: specific political relationships between Taiwan and China, and strong economic partnerships between Japan, Taiwan, and Thailand. Other important underestimations of the model are the flows between Asian countries and the rest of the world, especially with North American countries (17 percent) and European ones (10 percent). This trade, which takes place over very long distances and with very large ships (in order to achieve economies of scale), is logically underestimated since the model only takes into account the frequency of shipping services. Moreover, a substantial share of the trade between North America and Asian countries is transhipped by foreign ports such as Singapore for Malaysia and Busan (South Korea) and Kaohsiung (Taiwan) for Japan.

Surprisingly, a substantial share of overestimations of the model can be found again in the trade within the same regions. Intra-European and intra-Asian trades account together for 40 percent of the overestimations of the model. The reason for this is quite simple, since most of these overestimations take place in trade with countries with large shipping hubs that concentrate maritime connections without being the point of origin or destination of goods. As explained above, the international trade of Asian countries such as Malaysia and Japan is largely transhipped in foreign countries such Singapore, South Korea, and Taiwan. In Europe, the trade between Germany and most Scandinavian countries is overestimated since the port of Hamburg is their main transhipment hub. Russian ports also rely on western-European hubs such as Hamburg and Rotterdam to convey their international trade. Other important overestimations of the model are found in long-distance routes: North Atlantic and Asia–Europe account for 25 percent and 11 percent of the total, respectively. Most of these overestimations are found in countries with large shipping hubs such as Italy (Gioia Tauro), Spain (Algeciras), the Netherlands (Rotterdam), and Germany (Hamburg).

Finally, most of the deviations to the model are explained by the strategies pursued by shipping companies in terms of hub location and allocation of ships of different sizes. The hub-and-spokes networks tend to concentrate supply in a small number of seaports. The choice of a seaport as a hub by a particular shipping company is essentially determined by its more or less favorable location in relation to the demand of its hinterland and to its position in the global maritime network. It is important to avoid making excessive detours. This means that seaports that do not necessarily have a deep hinterland (such as Algeciras or Gioia Tauro) but that are located near the main shipping routes will be favoured in terms of opportunities to trade and will be overestimated by the model. On the other hand, the long distance trade of countries that rely on foreign hubs to convey their trade, such as Japan or Malaysia, will be underestimated by the model. Since shippers usually prefer to use direct connections, this deficit could eventually have a negative impact on the trade of these countries.

Discussion and conclusion

The results provided by the spatial interaction model suggest several things. First, both distance and shipping services are important variables in explaining the geographical pattern of trade flows between coastal countries. The influence of shipping services on trade is important but less than that of distance. This means that containerized cargo remain strongly distance-constrained, despite the diminution of transport costs and the increase in frequency. Contrary to what one might expect, the influence of shipping services on trade has slightly decreased between 1996 and 2006. This trend affects all types of flows, no matter the industry. The achievement of containerization and increased hubbing by shipping lines has helped to encourage this phenomenon. The shipping-services-based model as proposed does not explain an important proportion of the variance in the dataset. There are probably some variables, other than volume and distance, which have some effect on spatial structure of flows between countries. However, the simultaneous inclusion of distance and shipping services in a single model might help increase its explanatory power.

Our conclusions are valid only for a sample of coastal areas where African countries are largely underrepresented. More empirical research is necessary to make further generalization. African countries are particularly reliant on their maritime trade, even if the type of goods exported seems to be less sensitive to sophisticated time elements like frequency. Moreover, the hinterlands of large seaports like Antwerp or Rotterdam go far beyond the national borders of Belgium and the Netherlands (Guerrero, 2014). Other ports, like Singapore or Marsaxlokk mainly act as transhipment hubs for the trade of other countries. So the frequency of shipping services to and from these countries can hardly explain their much weaker trade volumes. One important implication of this work is that the model has also quantified the elasticity values of shipping services for different types of cargo. This is an important finding, as it provides empirical support for visualizing scenarios with regard to the impact of reducing or increasing shipping frequencies. This result could be useful for maritime companies in planning the distribution of their capacities and also for public policy to supporting certain maritime links in order to develop external trade and reduce land transport bottlenecks.

The last year of observation in this study is 2006. The increase of containerized capacities since then has considerably impacted the number of services offered in the main shipping lines, using fewer and larger ships. Moreover, reconfigurations in liner services since the financial crisis of 2008 have resulted in cargo consolidation in larger ports, leading to a global reduction of the number of direct calls and further development of feeder services to secondary ports. This will probably result in a reduction of the explanatory power of the model. It is, however, not entirely clear at this point to what extent these trends will affect how shipping services are interrelated with international trade.

Appendix 17.1 List of countries included in this study

Albania, Algeria, Argentina, Australia, Bangladesh, Belgium, Brazil, Brunei Darussalam, Bulgaria, Cameroon, Canada, Sri Lanka, Chile, China, Taiwan, Province of China, Colombia, Croatia, Denmark, Ecuador, Estonia, Finland, France, Gabon, Germany, Greece, Iceland, India, Indonesia, Ireland, Israel, Italy, Ivory Coast, Japan, Kenya, Korea, Republic of, Latvia, Libya, Lithuania, Malaysia, Mexico, Morocco, Netherlands, New Zealand, Nigeria, Norway, Pakistan, Peru, Philippines, Poland, Portugal, Russian Federation, Saudi Arabia, Singapore, Viet Nam, Slovenia, South Africa, Spain, Sweden, Thailand, Tunisia, Turkey, Ukraine, Egypt, United Kingdom, United States, Uruguay, Bolivarian Republic of Venezuela.

Appendix 17.2 Families of cargo included in this study based on Chelem categories

Containerizable: All types of cargo except

FT	Cars and cycles
FU	Commercial Vehicles
FV	Ships
FW	Aeronautics
HA	Iron ores
HB	Non ferrous ores
HC	Unprocessed minerals
IA	Coals
IB	Crude oil
IC	Natural gas
IG	Coke
IH	Refined petroleum
II	Electricity
JA	Cereals
JB	Other edible agricultural
JC	Non-edible agricultural
NA	Jewellery, works of art
NB	Non-monetary gold

Vehicle components and engines

FS	Vehicles components
FC	Engines, turbines and pumps

Paper and pulp

EC	Paper and pulp
ED	Printing

Building materials

BA	Cement
BB	Ceramics
BC	Glass

Metallic structures and miscellaneous hardware

FA	Large metallic structures
FB	Miscellaneous hardware

Precision instruments

FI	Precision instruments
FJ	Watch and clockmaking
FK	Optics

Electronics

FL	Electronic components
FM	Consumer electronics
FN	Telecommunications
FO	Computer equipment

Textile

DA	Yarns, fabrics
DB	Clothing
DC	Knitwear
DD	Carpets
DE	Leather

Food and beverages

KA	Cereal products
KB	Fats
KC	Meat
KD	Preserved meat/fish
KE	Preserved fruits
KF	Sugar
KH	Beverages

Plastic and miscellaneous manuf. articles

EE	Toys and Miscellaneous mnf.
GG	Plastics
GH	Plastic articles
GI	Rubber articles

Chemicals and pharmaceuticals

GA	Basic inorganic chemicals
GB	Fertilizers
GC	Basic organic chemicals
GF	Pharmaceuticals

Machines, equipment, and arms

FD	Agricultural equipment
FE	Machine tools
FF	Construction equipment
FG	Specialized machines
FH	Arms and weaponery

Wood and furniture

EA	Wood articles
EB	Furniture

Appendix 17.3 Results of various spatial interaction models

Containerizable cargo	1996					2006				
	α	γ	r_1^2	r_2^2	r_3^2	α	γ	r_1^2	r_2^2	r_3^2
$F_{ij} = A_i \cdot O_i \cdot B_j \cdot D_j \cdot dij_1^{\alpha} \cdot dij_2^{\gamma}$	−.73	.14	90%	71%	1.8%	−.78	.10	91%	73%	1.4%
$F_{ij} = A_i \cdot O_i \cdot B_j \cdot D_j \cdot dij_1^{\alpha} \cdot \gamma \cdot dij_2$	.46	.00	82%	49%	1.0%	−.94	.00	91%	72%	.3%
$F_{ij} = A_i \cdot O_i \cdot B_j \cdot D_j \cdot \alpha \cdot dij_1 \cdot \gamma \cdot dij_2$	.00	.00	83%	51%	.9%	.00	.00	85%	56%	.0%
$F_{ij} = A_i \cdot O_i \cdot B_j \cdot D_j \cdot \alpha \cdot dij_1 \cdot dij_2^{\gamma}$	.00	.28	86%	58%	7.9%	.00	.20	88%	62%	6.3%
$F_{ij} = A_i \cdot O_i \cdot B_j \cdot D_j \cdot dij_1^{\alpha}$	−.88	N/A	89%	69%	N/A	−.90	N/A	91%	71%	N/A
$F_{ij} = A_i \cdot O_i \cdot B_j \cdot D_j \cdot dij_2^{\gamma}$	N/A	.51	82%	48%	N/A	N/A	.43	83%	47%	N/A
$F_{ij} = A_i \cdot O_i \cdot B_j \cdot D_j \cdot \alpha \cdot dij_1$	.00	N/A	83%	50%	N/A	.00	N/A	85%	56%	N/A
$F_{ij} = A_i \cdot O_i \cdot B_j \cdot D_j \cdot \gamma \cdot dij_2$	N/A	.00	72%	20%	N/A	N/A	.00	72%	15%	N/A

Notes

1 It is estimated that more than 90 percent of world trade volumes are carried by sea transport.
2 Interestingly in this report, the analysis of "global urban accessibility" does not even include air transport linkages but rather, maritime flows alongside other elements.
3 Related publications are: *World Transport Data* (IRU, 1996), *Statistical Yearbook* (United Nations, 2000), and *Review of Maritime Transport* (UNCTAD, 2001).
4 Coastal countries included in this study are specified in Appendix 17.1.
5 The content of the ten cargo families considered in this work is specified in Appendix 17.2.

References

Behrens K., Gaigné C., Ottaviano G.I.P., Thisse J.F. (2006) Is remoteness a locational disadvantage? *Journal of Economic Geography*, 6: 347–68.

Bernhofen D.M., El-Sahli Z., Kneller R. (2013) *Estimating the Effects of the Container Revolution on World Trade*. Lund University Working Paper 2013:4, Department of Economics, School of Economics and Management.

Berthelon M., Freund C. (2008) On the conservation of distance in international trade. *Journal of International Economics*, 75(2): 310–20.

Cairncross, F. (2001) *The Death of Distance: How the Communications Revolution is Changing our Lives*. Boston: Harvard Business Press.

Clark X., Dollar D., Micco A. (2004) Port efficiency, maritime transport costs, and bilateral trade. *Journal of Development Economics*, 75(2): 417–50.

D'Aubigny G., Calzada C., Grasland C., Robert D., Viho G., Vincent, J. M. (2000). Approche poissonnienne des modéles d'interaction spatiale. Cybergéo, 126. https://cybergeo.revues.org/4357. [Accessed July 2015.]

Deng W.B., Long G., Wei L., Xu C. (2009) Worldwide marine transportation network: Efficiency and container throughput. *Chinese Physics Letters*, 26(11): 118901.

Disdier A.C., Head, K. (2008) The puzzling persistence of the distance effect on bilateral trade. *The Review of Economics and Statistics*, 90(1): 37–48.

Ducruet C., Notteboom T.E. (2012a) Developing liner service networks in container shipping. In: Song D.W., Panayides P. (Eds), *Maritime Logistics: A Complete Guide to Effective Shipping and Port*.

Ducruet C., Notteboom T.E. (2012b) The worldwide maritime network of container shipping: spatial structure and regional dynamics. *Global Networks*, 12(3): 395–423; *Management*. London: Kogan Page, pp. 77–100.

Ducruet C. (2013) Network diversity and maritime flows. *Journal of Transport Geography*, 30: 77–88.

Ducruet C., Lugo I. (2013) Cities and transport networks in shipping and logistics research. *Asian Journal of Shipping and Logistics*, 29(2): 149–70.

Ducruet C., Joly O., Le Cam M. (2014) Europe in global maritime flows: gateways, forelands, and subnetworks. In: Pain K., Van Hamme G. (Eds), *Changing Urban and Regional Relations in a Globalizing World. Europe as a Global Macro-Region*, Cheltenham: Edward Elgar, pp. 164–80.

Duranton G., Storper M. (2006) Agglomeration and growth: a dialogue between economists and geographers. *Journal of Economic Geography*, 6(1): 1–7.

Feenstra R.C., Markusen J.R., Rose, A.K. (2001) Using the gravity equation to differentiate among alternative theories of trade. *Canadian Journal of Economics*, 34(2): 430–47.

Fotheringham A., O'Kelly M.E. (1989) *Spatial Interaction Models: Formulations and Applications (Vol. 5)*. Dordrecht: Kluwer Academic Pub.

Frémont A. (2007) Global maritime networks: The case of Maersk. *Journal of Transport Geography*, 15(6): 431–42.

Guerrero D. (2014) Deep-sea hinterlands: some empirical evidence of the spatial impact of containerization. *Journal of Transport Geography*, 35: 84–94.

Guerrero D., Rodrigue J.P. (2014) The waves of containerization: shifts in global maritime transportation. *Journal of Transport Geography*, 35: 151–64.

Hall P.V., Hesse M. (2012) *Cities, Regions and Flows*. London and New York: Routledge.

Haddad E.A., Hewings G.J.D., Perobelli F.S., dos Santos R.A.C. (2010) Regional effects of port infrastructure: A spatial CGE application to Brazil. *International Regional Science Review*, 33(3): 239–63.

Head K., Mayer, T. (2010) Gravity, market potential and economic development. *Journal of Economic Geography*, 11(2): 281–94.

Hesse M., Rodrigue J.P. (2004) The transport geography of logistics and freight distribution. *Journal of Transport Geography*, 12(3): 171–84.

Hu Y., Zhu D. (2009) Empirical analysis of the worldwide maritime transportation network. *Physica A*, 388(10): 2061–71.

Hummels D. (2001) Time as a trade barrier, Research Report, Purdue University. http://www.krannert.purdue.edu/faculty/hummelsd/research/time3b.pdf [accessed April 2015].

IRU (1996) *World Transport Data*. Geneva: International Road Transport Union.

Jacobs W., Ducruet C., De Langen P.W. (2010) Integrating world cities into production networks: The case of port cities. *Global Networks*, 10(1): 92–113.

Joly O. (1999) *La structuration des réseaux de circulation maritime*. Unpublished PhD Dissertation in Territorial Planning, Le Havre University, CIRTAI.

Kaluza P., Kölzsch A., Gastner M.T., Blasius, B. (2010) The complex network of global cargo ship movements. *Journal of the Royal Society Interface*, 7(48): 1093–103.

Krugman P. (1995) Growing world trade: causes and consequences. *Brookings Papers on Economic Activity*, 26: 327–77.

Li Z., Xu M., Shi Y. (2015) Centrality in global shipping network basing on worldwide shipping areas. *Geojournal*, 80(1): 47–60.

Limao N., Venables A.J. (2001) Infrastructure, geographical disadvantage, transport costs, and trade. *The World Bank Economic Review*, 15(3): 451–79.

McCallum J. (1995) National borders matter: Canada–US regional trade patterns. *The American Economic Review*, 85(3): 615–23.

Nelson A. (2008) *Travel Time to Major Cties: A Global Map of Accessibility.* Global Environment Monitoring Unit, Joint Research Centre of the European Commission, Ispra Italy. https://ec.europa.eu/jrc/en/scientific-tool/global-environmental-monitoring-map-showing-travel-time-major-cities [accessed July 2015].

Ng A.K.Y. (2006) Assessing the attractiveness of ports in the North European container transshipment market: an agenda for future research in port competition. *Maritime Economics and Logistics*, 8(3): 234–50.

Ng A.K.Y., Ducruet C. (2014) The changing tides of port geography (1950–2012). *Progress in Human Geography*, 38(6): 785–823.

Notteboom T.E. (2006) The time factor in liner shipping services. *Maritime Economics and Logistics*, 8(1): 19–39.

Parshani R., Rozenblat C., Ietri D., Ducruet C., Havlin S. (2010) Inter-similarity between coupled networks. *Europhysics Letters*, 92: 68002.

Rodrigue J.P., Notteboom T.E. (2010) Foreland-based regionalization: Integrating inter-mediate hubs with port hinterlands. *Research in Transportation Economics*, 27(1): 19–29.

Rodrigue J.P., Comtois C., Slack B. (2013) *The Geography of Transport Systems.* New York: Routledge.

Tavasszy L., Minderhoud M., Perrin J.F., Notteboom T.E. (2011) A strategic network choice model for global container flows: Specification, estimation and application. *Journal of Transport Geography*, 19(6): 1163–72.

Ullman E.L. (1949) Mapping the world's ocean trade: a research proposal. *The Professional Geographer*, 1(2): 19–22.

UNCTAD (2001) *Review of Maritime Transport.* Geneva: United Nations.

UNCTAD (2013) *Review of Maritime Transport.* Geneva: United Nations.

United Nations (2000) *Statistical Yearbook.* New York: Department of Economic and Social Affairs, Statistics Division.

van den Bremen W.J., de Jong B. (1986) The aggregate spatial patterns of maritime transport at world scale: a macro-scale approach in transport geography. *Geojournal*, 12(3): 289–303.

Wang C., Wang J. (2011) Spatial pattern of the global shipping network and its hub-and-spoke system. *Research in Transportation Economics*, 32(1): 54–63.

Woxenius J. (2006) Temporal elements in the spatial extension of production networks. *Growth and Change*, 37(4): 526–49.

Woxenius J. (2012) Directness as a key performance indicator for freight transport chains. *Research in Transportation Economics*, 36(1): 63–72.

Zohil J., Prijon M. (1999) The MED rule: the interdependence of container throughput and transhipment volumes in the Mediterranean ports. *Maritime Policy and Management*, 26: 175–93.

18 Interplay between maritime and land modes in a system of cities

Igor Lugo

Maritime and land transportation modes play a vital role in the growth of urban places and the distribution of resources. In particular, port terminals and road infrastructures connect urban areas in different scales, from local to global regions, because they share common characteristics in order to avoid geographical discontinuities (Rodrigue, 2013). However, modeling spatial networks and analyzing their statistical attributes is not trivial because there is little agreement among disciplines on a common framework. The economic and transport geography subfields exemplify this situation, and they have implicitly or explicitly analyzed geospatial configurations (Henderson and Thisse, 2004; Batty, 2013). The new economic geography, such as the work of Krugman (1996), offers an approach to model theoretical systems of cities, but its application has been narrowed by managing big spatial data. On the other hand, spatial networks have applied this complex data and generated interesting models but have missed explanations of social mechanisms behind real-world geographical patterns (Barthelemy, 2011). Therefore, we propose a novel application where economic geography ideas are translated to a spatial network based on ports, roads, and urban data.

This study aims to address the following questions: How important are port locations in a system of cities connected by road networks? And is the distance between ports and cities a key factor to describe economies of agglomerations? To answer these questions, we used spatial network models and geoprocessing tools based on the theoretical approach of city systems (Krugman, 1996; Fujita *et al.*, 1999; Batty, 2005). We generated a geometric graph where ports and cities were connected by road infrastructures to show the interplay between maritime, land, and urban systems. We used geospatial data from Mexico and selected the road network topology as a basic structure to add ports and cities along a specific set of nodes (Lugo, 2012; Okabe and Sugihara, 2012). Furthermore, we computed shortest paths along route sections between ports and cities and generated two types of null models to identify and compare spatial and statistical characteristics (NetworkX, 2014; Bradde *et al.*, 2010; Ruzzenenti *et al.*, 2012). We believe that the route distance is an accurate measure of the transport cost concept and it explains the location of significant urban agglomerations. Our method offers a generic approach to model the relationship between large-scale transport and urban systems.

The first section of this chapter will present the materials and methods, the second section will display results, and the last section offers conclusions, significance, limitations, and future directions of the research.

Materials

Open spatial data increases every year, along with geographic information systems (GIS) technology. However, some databases are noisy, and they have to be processed before modelling any spatial network. To solve this limitation, we used official geospatial data from Mexico related to vector models of road lines, port points, and urban polygons (INEGI, 2015a, b, c). Because they are geometric objects, it was possible to process and translate them to a network that presented the identical spatial attributes as original vector data.

Economic geography and spatial networks

An interdisciplinary method offers flexible ways for modelling complex spatial networks. Economic geography and spatial networks share similar questions about human spatial patterns, but their approaches use different ideas and models. To decrease this gap, we generated a spatial network or a graph using geographic data of ports, roads, and cities. We generated two types of null models and applied complex network methods to test implications and to analyse port terminals in a system of cities.

Economic geography has developed key ideas related to model systems of cities (Henderson, 1974; Abdel-Rahman, 2004). In particular, the "racetrack" model is one of the most important contributions; it describes a circular graph where cities are associated with nodes located evenly along the circumference and edges are connections based on the distance between a pair of cities (Turing, 1952; Krugman, 1996; Fujita *et al.*, 1999). This formulation tested the effects of local spatial autocorrelations in the growth and organization of cities. Therefore, the presence of skewed distributions of urban population was related to a growth process based on the interplay between centripetal and centrifugal forces (Fujita and Thisse, 2002; Batty, 2005; Pumain, 2006). However, empirical applications of this model have been limited because of the complex topology of geospatial data. They introduce asymmetries and multiple equilibriums in the system. For example, vector maps exhibit geometric shapes ranging from simple points to complex polygons. The spatial networks approach models systems based on complex data (Bavaud and Merger, 2009; Barthelemy, 2011). It provides sources for creating local or large-scale spatial structures that present singular geographic patterns. In particular, transport geography has represented modes as spatial graphs where nodes are terminals or crossing roads, and edges are routes or physical connections (Clark and Holton, 1991). However, this approach is insufficient to explain intricate geographic patterns based on social theories. Responding to these limitations, we united ideas from both fields using common spatial elements to model a geometric graph.

We defined a system of ports and cities as a pool of geometric sets of objects explicitly and spatially interrelated to each other. Ports and cities are collections of spatial objects (points) representing terminals and urban attributes, for example points associated with the entrance/exit of different resources into/from a country or urban location. Connections among objects are sets of spatial objects (lines) related to transport infrastructures, for example route sections. To apply this formulation, we selected the road network topology as the main structure to port and city data in some vertices because roads are distributed across landscapes and connect places and regions. Vertices then represent locations that not only show intersections in road lines but also contain information of ports and city objects. The resulting graph is a two-dimensional geometry without crossing edges, known as a planar network (Jungnickel, 1999). Furthermore, we generated two classes of null models for comparing and testing this graph, and we computed network measures to analyze the importance of port locations and their spatial relationship to cities. Finally, we identified the type of continuous distribution associated with port–city route distances and used the two-sample Kolmogorov–Smirnov (KS) test of goodness-of-fit to compare them (Massey, 1951; Hartigan and Hartigan, 1985).

The process for generating planar networks was divided into two parts: working on the empirical spatial network and working with spatial null models. The former used geospatial data and translated them to a graph in which ports and cities were connected by the road infrastructure. We used three layers: point data of ports, cities, and road sections. The first layer represented port locations, the second layer showed centroids of the main urban polygons (56 metropolitan areas) (Secretaría de Desarrollo Social *et al.*, 2005), and the third layer displayed a pair of coordinates related to the start/end of a single road section. To identify port and city proximities to closer points in road sections, we applied the distance matrix tool. Each layer of ports and cities was compared to points in road lines to compute the distance to the nearest target point. Subsequently, we translated this data to a graph where each node corresponded to the location of points in road lines, and edges were connections between a pair of such points. Ports and cities were associated with a single set of nodes, and each edge was weighted by its distance. Finally, we identified the most important connected component in the graph to compute the shortest path measure based on the route factor (Levinson and El-Geneidy, 2007). Each port location computed its distance to all cities. Therefore, this process generated an empirical, weighted, and undirected planar network.

In addition, we used two spatial null models to compare efficient and costly structures to our empirical data. They were a Delaunay triangulation (Tri) and a minimum spanning tree (MST). Each represents variations in planar graphs in which the addition of an extra edge produces a non-planar structure, and they depend on geometric constraints (Barthelemy, 2011; Bradde *et al.*, 2010, Ruzzenenti *et al.*, 2012). Therefore, we generated them based on random points distributed uniformly on the plane constrained by the administrative boundaries of Mexico. Next, we produced artificial triangulations and filtered out lines that intersected water objects. To identify port and city points in these triangulations, we applied the same process explained in the paragraph above. In addition, we constructed the MST applying Kruskal's algorithm, which identified a subgraph with the minimum sum of edge weights (Kruskal, 1956). Finally, we computed the shortest path measure for each model to get route distances between ports and cities.

Results

Maritime and land modes are constrained by different types of surfaces that directly affect the spatial relationship between ports and cities. However, road infrastructures connect almost all land locations. To understand the importance of ports and their possible effects on cities in the road network, we compared our empirical and null models.

Ports and cities connected by road networks were modeled as a planar spatial network. After applying the process for generating an empirical network, we obtained a graph with 537,748 nodes and 540,220 edges. Based on these edges, and increasing their number at least 8 percent, we produced the Tri and the MST models. The reason for this was to compare the location of route paths instead of replicating their geometrical shapes. Therefore, these models are approximately similar to the number of edges in empirical data. The Tri started with 200,000 nodes and 599,965 edges. After geoprocessing and getting the first connected component, we counted 196,992 nodes and 584,334 edges. This process deleted 1.5 percent of the nodes and 2.6 percent of the edges of the original triangulation. In addition, the MST, which was based on an independent random triangulation, started with 200,000 nodes and 599,963 edges. After geoprocessing the data

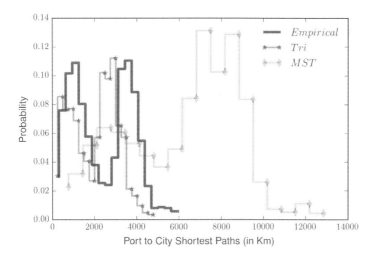

Figure 18.1 Probability density function of shortest paths between ports and cities.

The multimodality test, Hartigans' dip statistical test, showed the following results: Empirical ($D = 0.0663$, p-value $= 2.2 \times 10^{-16}$), Tri ($D = 0.0386$, p-value $= 2.2 \times 10^{-16}$), and MST ($D = 0.0182$, p-value $= 0.0014$). All rejected the hypothesis of unimodality.

and finding the first connected component, it showed 197,027 nodes and 197,026 edges. The process deleted 1.4 percent of the nodes and 32.8 percent of the edges of the initial topology.

Turning now to statistically compare and describe these structures, we show the territory divided into two regions with different spatial logistics related to route distances between ports and cities (Figure 18.1). The probability density function (PDF) of each data is best described by a bimodal distribution. Each represents a mixture model that depends on the port locations. The first peak is related to close distances between ports in almost the entire territory, except Baja California and cities. This data represents strong road connections because ports reach most of the cities. On the other hand, the second mode displayed long distances between ports in the peninsula and cities. This data characterizes weak preferences of using roads because ports are far away from most of the cities. Therefore, the geography matters to connect locations by the distance route factor. It suggests that port terminals affect cities' ability to distribute resources, which influences levels of economies of agglomerations, for example increasing the population size and clusters of companies.

In addition, empirical distances between ports and cities display an interesting efficient attribute (Figure 18.2). The cumulative density function (CDF) of empirical data shows close but insignificant behaviour related to the Tri model. We inferred that redundant routes increased the connectivity between ports and cities

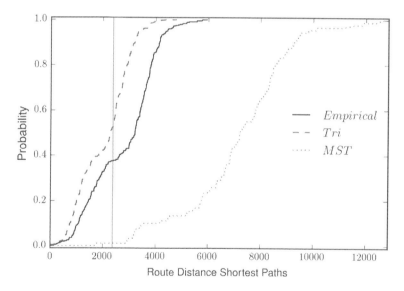

Figure 18.2 Comparison between cumulative distribute function of shortest paths.

The KS test of goodness-of-fit rejected similarities between empirical and null models: Empirical vs Tri ($D = 0.2694$, p-value $= 2.2 \times 10^{-16}$), Empirical vs MST ($D = 0.6518$, p-value $= 2.2 \times 10^{-16}$), and Tri vs MST ($D = 0.7167$, p-value $= 2.2 \times 10^{-16}$). The vertical line represents the mean value of empirical data.

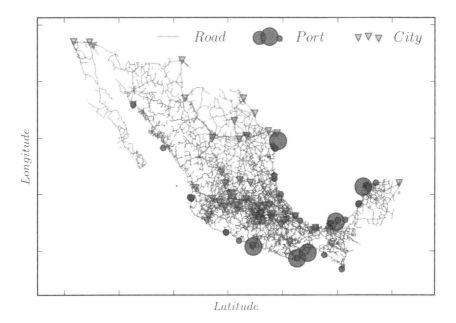

Figure 18.3 Ports connected to all cities in the road network.

The most important ports are connected with the 56 metropolitan areas.

and enhanced the maintenance cost of each road section. However, this is only true for ports related to the first mode, which is displayed by the vertical line. In addition, the figure showed CDFs of empirical data and MST far from each other, meaning that the former is costly but presents high levels of connectivity to any pair of locations on land.

Finally, such an efficient attribute in the empirical data identified the most important ports connected to all the metropolitan areas in the road network (Figure 18.3). Port symbols with big sizes represent a complete connection to cities. This spatial relationship implies that some ports are fundamental transport terminals for cities because they distribute resources and affect local and regional urban growth.

Discussion

The empirical findings of this study provide a better understanding of the interplay between maritime and land transport modes in a system of cities. The inclusion of ports in a spatial system of cities connected by road networks complements economic geography applications to the complex networks approach. In particular, the resultant planar graph displays significant geometric attributes to define and model a system of spatial objects. Such attributes help to identify valuable port locations based on their route distance to cities without extra information, for example statistical freight data. These results suggest that port locations are significant nodes in the spatial network because they affect transport logistics to cities. Furthermore, the route distance measure between ports and cities could explain the intensity of economies of agglomeration because if a port is well connected to a set of cities, they will receive the benefits of efficient resource distribution. In the case of Mexico, these findings indicate that the road network is the most efficient transport mode for connecting ports and cities and distributing resources, although they show increasing maintenance costs per route section.

Limitations of this study are related to processing spatial data and generating spatial null models. Spatial data increase their structure to collect information. However, it is not easy to decide which of those are significant to model and to analyze large-scale systems. A natural response is to identify a social theory that suggests which variables and relationships among them can explain mechanisms to produce complex geospatial patterns. Unfortunately, this choice can be time-consuming if a scientist is not familiar with such theories. Spatial null models depend on two main components: the first is the size of the empirical network, which affects the topology of such models because they depend on the number of nodes or edges, and the second is the type of spatial network to model. Planar graphs are restrictive because of their geometry, which affects how nodes are connected to edges. Therefore, generating these models is not a direct process. Researchers need to build different types of structures and test them with empirical data based on economic theories.

Finally, further work needs to be done to validate the impact of ports in a system of cities connected by road networks, in particular to develop applications based on the economic geography approach that describes structural properties in such a system. Furthermore, we need to produce complex network measures to analyse different spatial networks. It is time to apply an interdisciplinary approach that not only describes spatial systems but also identifies economic or social mechanisms behind complex spatial patterns.

Acknowledgment

I would like to thank UNAM for the supercomputing resources and services provided by DGTIC (project number SC15-1-S-46).

References

Abdel-Rahman H.M. (2004) Theories of systems of cities. In: Henderson J.V., Thisse J.F. (Eds), *Handbook of Regional and Urban Economics*, Vol. 4, pp. 2063–3073.
Barthelemy M. (2011) Spatial Networks. *Physics Reports*, 499: 1–101.
Batty M. (2005) *Cities and Complexity: Understanding Cities with Cellular Automata, Agent-based Models, and Fractals*. Cambridge: MIT Press.
Batty M. (2013) *The New Science of Cities*. Cambridge: MIT Press
Bavaud F., Merger C. (2009) *Handbook of Theoretical and Quantitative Geography*, Lausanne: University of Lausanne.
Bradde S., Caccioli F., Dall'Asta L., Bianconi G. (2010) Critical fluctuations in spatial complex networks, *Phys. Rev. Lett.*, 104: 218701.
Clark J., Holton D.A. (1991) *A First Look at Graph Theory*. World Scientific.

Fujita M., Thisse J.F. (2002) *Economies of Agglomeration*. Cambridge: Cambridge University Press.

Fujita M., Krugman P., Venables A.J. (1999) *The Spatial Economy: Cities, Regions and International Trade*. Cambridge & London: MIT Press.

Hartigan J.A., Hartigan P.M. (1985) The dip test of unimodality. *Ann. Statist.*, 13(1): 70–84.

Henderson J.V. (1974) The sizes and types of cities. *American Economic Review*, 64: 640–56.

Henderson J.V., Thisse J.F. (2004) *Handbook of Regional and Urban Economics*. Amsterdam: Elsevier B.V.

Instituto Nacional de Estadística y Geografía (INEGI) (2015a) Marco Geoestadístico Nacional. Available online at: http://www.inegi.org.mx/geo/contenidos/geoestadistica/m_geoestadistico.aspx [accessed 25 March 2015].

Instituto Nacional de Estadística y Geografía (INEGI) (2015b) Productos, Red Nacional de Caminos. Available online at: http://www3.inegi.org.mx/sistemas/productos/ [accessed 25 March 2015].

Instituto Nacional de Estadística y Geografía (INEGI) (2015c) Topografía. Available online at: http://www.inegi.org.mx/geo/contenidos/topografia/topografia_1m.aspx [accessed 20 March 2015].

Jungnickel D. (1999) Graph, networks and algorithms. In: Cohen A.M. et al. (Eds), *Algorithm and Computation in Mathematics*, Heidelberg: Springer Verlag.

Krugman P. (1996) *The Self-organizing Economy*. Oxford: Wiley-Blackwell.

Kruskal J.B. (1956) On the shortest spanning subtree of a graph and the traveling salesman problem. *Proceedings of the American Mathematical Society*, 7(1): 48–50.

Levinson D., El-Geneidy A. (2007) The minimum circuity frontier and the journey to work. *Regional Science and Urban Economics*, 39: 732–8.

Lugo I. (2012) Spatial externalities approach to modelling the preferential attachment process in urban systems. In: Gilbert T., Kirkilionis M., Nicolis G. (Eds), *Proceedings of the European Conference on Complex Systems 2012*, Springer Proceedings in Complexity.

Massey F.J. (1951) The Kolmogorov–Smirnov test for goodness of fit. *Journal of the American Statistical Association*, 46(253): 68–78.

NetworkX (2014) Documentation, shortest paths length. Available online at: http://networkx.github.io/documentation/latest/reference/algorithms.shortest_paths.html [accessed 20 March 2015].

Okabe A., Sugihara K. (2012) *Spatial Analysis along Networks: Statistical and Computational Methods*. Chichester: John Wiley & Sons Ltd.

Pumain D. (2006) Alternative explanations of hierarchical differentiation in urban systems. In: Pumain D. (Ed), *Hierarchy in Natural and Social Sciences*, Springer Methodos Series 3, Dordrecht: Springer, pp. 169–222.

Rodrigue J.P. (2013) *The Geography of Transport Systems*. Third Edition, New York: Routledge.

Ruzzenenti F., Picciolo F., Basosi R., Garlaschelli D. (2012) Spatial effects in real networks: measures, null models, and applications. *Physical Review E*, 86: 066110.

Secretaria de Desarrollo Social, Consejo Nacional de Población, and INEGI (2005) Delimitación de las zonas metropolitanas de México, primera edición.

Turing A.M. (1952) The chemical basis of morphogenesis. *Philosophical Transactions of the Royal Society B*, 237: 37–72.

19 The regionalization of maritime networks

Evidence from a comparative analysis of maritime basins

Nora Mareï, César Ducruet

Throughout the maritime literature, most studies of port systems are focused on the national level or on a single port through a case study. This classic approach should be revisited in the context of international trade reorganization, given the evolution of shipping and cargo handling technologies (the spread of containerization) and changes in the economic environment itself (role of multinational firms, declining role of states, consolidation of transnational custom unions, etc.). The regional perspective is increasingly being questioned by geographers, economists, and political scientists alike. The role of transport (by sea, land, or air) remains little explored in this context.

One crucial question explored in this chapter is the relevance of the "region" in port and maritime geography. Does the concept of "maritime region" provide a valid framework for the analysis of ports and maritime networks? How is it or should it be defined? How can a better understanding of the regional dimension contribute to existing port and maritime studies? In the vast related literature (see Ng and Ducruet, 2014), port regionalization is better defined from a continental perspective (Notteboom and Rodrigue, 2005) of multimodal corridor development (Monios and Wilsmeier, 2012) and traffic concentration (Notteboom, 1997). Many case studies, too numerous to be cited, have contributed to the understanding of maritime regions at various scales, such as on deltas, straits, corridors, ranges, seaboards, basins, seas, and oceans, but often without a clear definition of the concept of maritime region itself. Monios and Wilsmeier (2012) recognize that regionalization in maritime geography has not been defined adequately and that the question remains open-ended, and they insist on the role of "collective action" in reaching a better understanding of port regionalization in an "inland" perspective.

Notteboom (2012) underlined the development of transhipment relay and interlining activities at ports along the "equatorial round-the-world route," thereby forming dedicated regions based on intermediary hubs (see also Rodrigue and Notteboom, 2010). Several seas are required passages on that road: the Mediterranean, the Caribbean, and the China Seas. These basins have all been strongly affected by the spread of containerization that caused a new "maritime order" (Vigarié, 1990) or a new "spatial cycle" (Rodrigue *et al.*, 1997) and modified over the long-run the spatial design of regional networks. Yet, regional evolutions that are influenced by global strategies differ from one region to the other due to specific development pathways (Jacobs and Notteboom, 2011), so that these basins remain heterogeneous in their organization (maritime range, isolated or integrated hub-and-spokes system, dispersed or polarized networks). Similar trends can, however, be observed and analysed in this "global-regional" context and encourage us to think about the internal dimension of flows in each region.

Other conceptual advances, never really linked with the aforementioned works, came from the field of area studies where the analysis of maritime basins was presented as a useful complement to the more dominant continental approaches in world history and "metageography" (Bentley, 1999; Lewis and Wigen, 1999; Grataloup, 2007). The maritime region was thus seen as a contact zone between different coastal societies through various linkages made possible mostly via sea transport. One main idea is that the actual contours and internal configurations of maritime regions are not necessarily determined by the physical layout of coastlines; they may fluctuate over time and have, in turn, strong influence over future developments.

The rest of the chapter is organized as follows. The next section goes through classical and recent definitions of the concept of "region" in geography and social sciences in general, before embarking on more empirical studies of regions in transport and mobility studies as well as in the specific area of port and maritime studies. Based on such a background, we propose an analysis of the evolution of maritime links within the Mediterranean basin and two other regions, namely the Caribbean basin and East Asia, based on container flows over the last 30 years (1996–2011). The last section discusses the results in light of current territorial factors underlying the observed evolutions.

Regions, flows, and maritime areas

We first propose going back to the concept of region as one major spatial entity or category to describe the shift from a purely physical approach to a more functional, or relational, approach. In such a context, the region and its construction processes (regionalization and regional integration) are more and more seen as multiple and multiscalar. It is perhaps where port and maritime studies have the most to learn, although regional forms of organization have long been identified but in more implicit ways.

From physical/administrative regions to functional/relational regions

One classic approach to the concept of region has been limited to the administrative criterion, i.e. the subnational entity designed for territorial management, such as the 22 French régions, the 17 Spanish comunidades autónomas, or the 16 German Länders. Another classic approach can be found in the works of de la Blache (1903) where the region is categorized as urban, agricultural, nodal, or in decline, also at the subnational level. Later, and for other geographers, the region owed its existence to perception and cognition based on the daily practice of space (Frémont, 1976). French researchers also developed the idea of polarized and peripheral regions depending on the ability of urban centres and industrial activities to facilitate the emergence of growth poles (Perroux, 1991), a view that has become essential in the development of the new economic geography (NEG) in recent decades. This long tradition of seeing the region as a subnational entity (see also Claval, 1968) through numerous monographs tended to decline in the late twentieth century, notably with the renewed approaches of Veltz (1996) and Sassen (1991) about the dematerialization of the world economy. Yet, some recent works have proposed adapting the classic framework to larger spatial scales somewhere between local and global (Beckouche, 2008; Girault, 2009; Richard, 2010), while early geographers such as Vidal de la Blache were recently revisited in their ability to define a global economic structure (Arrault, 2008).

The macro-regional level is thus clearly part of the "new regionalism" (Hettne and Söderbaum, 1998) where the region is extroverted and whose limits remain fuzzy. Some authors even insisted on the "rescaling" of the region (Jones and Paasi, 2013) and its necessary geographical connectedness (Amin, 2004). The most comprehensive view of the region was proposed by Hettne and Söderbaum (2000) for whom the region is a dynamic regionalization process "in the making" made of both top-down and bottom-up factors. They proposed the notion of "regionness" to describe the emergence of the region as an evolutionary process.

Regions and flows

The material dimension of the more relational region has been the focus of numerous works, both theoretical and in the more empirical field of transport and mobility studies. For instance, the study entitled *Area Studies: Regional Worlds* a White Paper produced for the Ford Foundation in 1997 and quoted by Lewis and Wigen (1999) recalled earlier studies of the "world system" whereby different regions of the world economy are linked with each other through certain dominant nodes (Wallerstein, 1979; Braudel, 1985) and/or through complex, multiscalar relations (Dollfus *et al.*, 1999; Dicken *et al.*, 2001).

Indeed, economic globalization that is supposed to transgress nation-states and allow the emergence of "winner regions" (Benko and Lipietz, 1992), "global cities" (Sassen, 1991), and "global city-regions" (Scott, 2001) greatly influenced territorial structures. Through accelerated mobility, territories are more and more hierarchically organized, internally and externally, as regions become, according to Ohmae (1996), "natural operational units of the contemporary world economy," modelled by capital flows, comparative advantage, and the productivity of territories. The relational analysis of territories based on pioneering works on nodal regions (Rochefort, 1960; Nystuen and Dacey, 1961) and telecommunication flows among cities found fertile ground in transport and mobility studies such as on airline flows (see Ducruet and Lugo, 2013). Analyses at the world level did not omit the importance of proximity in the design and regionalization of flows. However, the link between world regionalization and flows remains little studied, except from the point of view of monetary unions or trade agreements (Balassa, 1961; Snyder and Kick, 1979; Beauguitte, 2013) or simply based on country data (Didelon *et al.*, 2008). Other studies have focused on trade or migration flows to seek regional and hierarchical tendencies (Massey *et al.*, 1993; Tarrius, 2007; Richard and Zanin, 2009), often arguing that regionalization processes are strong components underlying world patterns.

Maritime regions

Throughout port and maritime geography, Vigarié (1964) and Charlier (1996) have pioneered the analysis of transnational maritime ranges (Northern Range, Benelux port system) based on the idea of similar development paths caused by shared hinterlands, shipping services, and regional integration. But, as mentioned above, most studies of port systems remained bound to the national level. A look at the 399 papers listed by Ng and Ducruet (2014) in their review of port geography confirms that 48 percent of this corpus focused upon a single port through a case study, 22 percent on country-level studies, 10.3 percent were subnational studies, 13.5 percent were transnational studies, and less than 1 percent concerned the level of entire basins, while the world level only occupied 5.5 percent of all papers. Such a state of affairs clearly explains the lack of consensus upon the appropriate concepts used in port and maritime studies, such as range, system, region, etc. (Ducruet, 2009). Empirical studies should be classified according to four types of approaches, (which are not exhaustive):

- **Port development within a given region**: mostly reviews of port development projects, this approach offers useful evidence about the homogeneity or heterogeneity of certain areas of the world in terms of the pace, scale, and governance of such developments, notably at the level of large regions such as the Mediterranean (Ridolfi, 1999; Marcadon, 2002; Mareï, 2012), the Caribbean (McCalla *et al.*, 2005; Vergé-Dépré, 2006), and the Baltic (Serry, 2006);
- **Port traffic concentration studies**: based on statistical measures such as the Gini coefficient or the HHI index, these studies quantitatively test the applicability of port system evolutionary models on certain areas such as Europe as a whole (Notteboom, 1997);
- **Geographical distribution of maritime linkages**: since Rimmer's (1967) critique of port system evolutionary models for their ignorance of maritime linkages among ports, a number of scholars have analyzed the pattern of such linkages in various contexts and under different methodologies, from simple cartography to graph theory and complex network research. They particularly highlighted the hierarchical structure of flows and the role of certain hubs in ensuring connectivity, as seen in the Caribbean (Veenstra *et al.*, 2005; Wilmsmeier and Hoffmann, 2008), the Mediterranean (Cisic *et al.*, 2007), East Asia (Ducruet *et al.*, 2011; Lam, 2011), the Atlantic (Ducruet *et al.*, 2010) and at world level (Ducruet, 2013); or Wilmsmeier and Notteboom (2011) for a comparison between the west coast of South America and Northern Europe;

- **Emergence and resilience of regional trends in global flows**: this approach looks not only at the hierarchical structure of global flows but also at the existence of tightly connected groups of ports as well as the geographic dimension of this connectivity (Kaluza *et al.*, 2010; Ducruet and Notteboom, 2012; Gonzalez Laxe *et al.*, 2012). For instance, while proximity or short-distance links carry the biggest proportion of inter-port traffic at the world level, Ducruet and Notteboom (2012) also identified a large nodal region expanding from East Asia across Africa, the Mediterranean basin, and the Pacific Ocean. The cohesiveness of "Europe" as a functional entity in global maritime flows was also examined through a multivariate analysis of global maritime flows (Ducruet *et al.*, 2014).

Overall, the concept of region remains little explored in port and maritime geography, despite the strategic role of basins, deltas, and straits in global shipping, as delineations are often taken for granted based on physical geography (e.g. Yangtze River Delta, Gulf of Guinea). Yet, basins are made of several coasts that are not necessarily continuous (unlike closed seas, e.g. Black Sea), thereby implying a neighbourhood relationship between distinct subsystems. The concept of "maritime region" thus appears as a useful one for the study of how connected and integrated such heterogeneous areas are (cf. Lewis and Wigen, 1999). So it is necessary to differentiate the port region, group of ports in proximity within a given geographical area (Ducruet, 2009), and the maritime region, which we define as a functional area in which the mutual interactions and links between the mosaic of territories and scales are analyzed.

In this context, we undertake an empirical analysis of maritime flows in distinct areas in order to elucidate how network structures are being shaped in various contexts and how they can be compared. This would contribute to both maritime studies and regionalization studies.

The comparative analysis of maritime regions

Interestingly, the "Mediterranean" concept has been applied already to the Caribbean basin and to East Asia to highlight certain similarities in terms of coastal and maritime organization (Gipouloux, 2009; Allix, 1933) and in terms of logistics patterns, such as their concentration of transhipment activities at intermediate hubs (Notteboom, 2012) despite differences in absolute traffic volumes (Figure 19.1). It is thus a challenge to compare these three maritime regions and how their respective connectivity has evolved in 1996–2011, a period characterized by a boom in container trade. The method has been to compute vessel movement data into three origin–destination matrices where local and transit flows of containers are mixed, from one major source, *Lloyd's List*, a world leader in shipping intelligence. We wish to verify whether the three regions have gone through similar development paths in terms of network topology and flow patterns, and if there is convergence or divergence. Recent qualitative analyses described the Caribbean basin as a dispersed system (McCalla *et al.*, 2005; Vergé-Dépré, 2006)

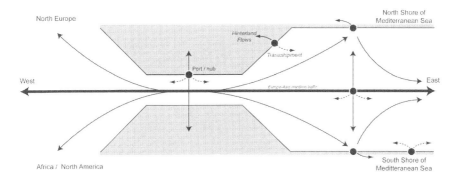

Figure 19.1 A spatial model of the Mediterranean basin.

Source: own elaboration based on *Containerisation International.*

whereas East Asia was becoming an integrated range with the de-concentration of the port system and the reinforcement of local economies. The Mediterranean case would appear as an intermediate situation, between dispersion/fragmentation and integration.

The Mediterranean basin remains a very heterogeneous area that is not yet structured as a coherent maritime range; there is scattered development of southern and eastern subparts and concentration of flows in northwestern ports (Gouvernal *et al.*, 2005). As such, the Mediterranean basin is currently designed by one major east–west axis and secondary north–south linkages (Figure 19.2). The so-called "MED rule" refers to the strong relationship between transhipment volumes and distance to main trunk routes (Zohil and Prijon, 1999).

Graph properties of regional maritime networks

A series of network indices has been calculated for each regional graph: network size (number of ports and links among them), density (or beta index: average number of links per port), completeness (or gamma index: proportion of observed links in the maximum possible number of links), clustering (or average clustering coefficient: proportion of closed triangles in the maximum possible number of closed triangles around ports), eccentricity (average number of stops between all pairs of ports), diameter (length of the longest of the shortest paths), and path length (average length of the shortest paths). These are complementary classic measures used in graph theory and complex networks to reveal how (transport) networks are internally structured (Ducruet and Lugo, 2013).

The study of the three specific basins shows that density (links per port) is growing, and the Mediterranean basin records the higher values (Table 19.1). Completeness is often the highest for the Mediterranean except in 2011, when it decreased in the Mediterranean and East Asia but increased in the Caribbean. This may suggest that although the growth rate of links always surpasses that of ports, many of the latter remain poorly connected or connected via larger ones

Figure 19.2 Container port throughput in 2009.

Source: Mareï (2012).

Table 19.1 Graph properties of regional maritime networks, 1996–2011

Region	Year	No. Links	No. Ports	Density	Completeness	Clustering	Eccentricity	Diameter	APL
Mediterranean basin	1996	221	51	4.333	0.173	0.401	0.593	5	2.189
	2006	373	73	5.110	0.142	0.506	0.623	5	2.347
	2011	640	100	6.400	0.129	0.532	0.696	5	2.284
Caribbean basin	1996	158	52	3.038	0.119	0.462	0.745	7	2.624
	2006	193	55	3.509	0.130	0.531	0.597	5	2.368
	2011	263	63	4.175	0.135	0.432	0.681	6	2.348
East Asia	1996	416	109	3.817	0.071	0.617	0.528	5	2.413
	2006	861	182	4.731	0.052	0.541	0.635	6	2.560
	2011	1234	216	5.713	0.053	0.554	0.686	6	2.597

Source: own elaboration based on data from *Lloyd's List Intelligence*.

such as hub ports (cf. growing density). However, such a trend is visible only in East Asia, where decreasing clustering underlines a stronger hub position of certain ports, whereas it has increased in the Mediterranean but from lower levels. The Mediterranean was more centralized around major ports (cf. highest densities) but this tendency has diminished, probably because of growing intra-regional linkages (motorways of the sea, Marco Polo European programme) especially between Spain, Italy, Turkey, and Greece, and to the modernization and emergence of new container ports along the southern coasts (e.g. Tangier-Med in Morocco, Port Saïd in Egypt), which in the end counterbalance the network effects of increased transhipment via container hubs. Another explanation is that the multiplication of hub ports lowers the hierarchical configuration of the network by offering more alternatives to shipping lines instead of concentrating their calls at one main hub. Whatever the main cause, transhipment via hub ports or coastal trade, the growing eccentricity of the Mediterranean and East Asian networks confirms that on average, the internal connectivity of these basins is improving.

Two other topological measures allow us to discuss the efficiency of the network: diameter and average path length (APL). The Caribbean basin is the only one to witness a lowering APL over the period, while it has continuously increased in East Asia and stabilized in the Mediterranean. Yet the latter region remains easier to circulate through, given its comparatively lower diameter and APL.

Interestingly, these changes occur despite the implementation of hub-and-spokes systems, which by definition make the network more efficient. The establishment of a hub-and-spokes system (around a few hubs) replacing port-to-port organization allows for easier access across the network via the main hubs, as seen in the Caribbean case. On the contrary, the proliferation of such systems may also complicate circulation from the perspective of the spokes, which become less connected (and sometimes simply disconnected) except indirectly through hubs. In that sense, parts of the networks may have become less connected than in the past because of the hub-and-spokes strategy. The efficiency brought by hub-and-spokes systems, in fact, mostly benefits the carrier and the hub but implies a drastic reorganization of the way other ports are connected in the network. The idea of a phased development of the role of hubs in the network is found in the work of Ducruet (2008) and Wilsmeier and Notteboom (2011) on the evolutionary patterns of liner shipping network configuration. The latter study even proposes that "the hub sees its functional position undermined" in the final phase characterized by the maturity of overseas markets and the development of secondary networks.

Nodal hierarchies of regional maritime networks

The analysis of the three (container) networks by the graph simplification method of single linkage analysis allows us to go deeper into the internal organization of maritime regions. Removing all links of each port except the largest one with another port reveals which ports dominate others and whether regional networks are split into subgroups or "connected components." The size of links among ports is defined by the sum of all vessel capacities having circulated during one

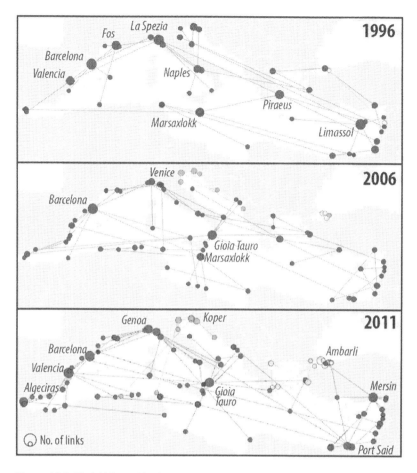

Figure 19.3 Nodal hierarchies in the Mediterranean basin, 1996–2011.
Source: own elaboration based on *Lloyd's List*.

month of navigation. In Figures 19.3 and 19.4, ports are differentiated by circle size, which expresses the number of remaining links after simplification (see also Table 19.3 for a ranking), and by colour, which provides an indication about the belonged connected component. For instance, the Caribbean is strongly defined by the shrinking influence of Houston, the emergence of local dynamics in 2006, and centralization around major hub ports in 2011 (e.g. Colon, Port Everglades, Kingston, Freeport). In the Mediterranean, one can observe that the hubs along the east–west trunk line (i.e. Algeciras, Marsaxlokk, Port Saïd) function apart from the rest of the basin. This state of affairs disappears in subsequent years, which would mean that such hub ports have been better integrated into the local and regional maritime system. Subregional interdependencies appear as well in parallel, such as local clusters of ports in the Adriatic, as well as around Turkish ports and the

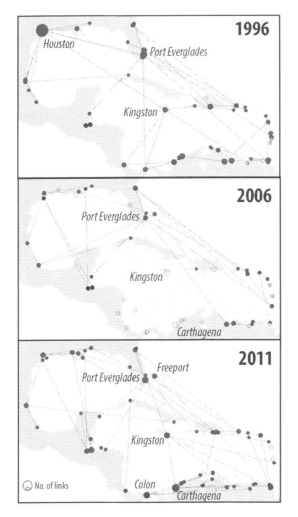

Figure 19.4 Nodal hierarchies in the Caribbean basin, 1996–2011.

Source: own elaboration based on *Lloyd's List*.

Strait of Gibraltar in 2011. The emergence of local port clusters is by no means revelatory of how host countries have improved their economic development and maritime connectivity in recent years. The growing position of Gioia Tauro is also clearly visible, at the expense of formerly well positioned ports such as Piraeus and Limassol, which do not play a crucial role in the later period.

The multiplication of Asian hubs is visible as the region goes through a growing north–south differentiation based on proximity linkages and optimal location factors (Figure 19.5). Japanese ports have much declined over time in terms of

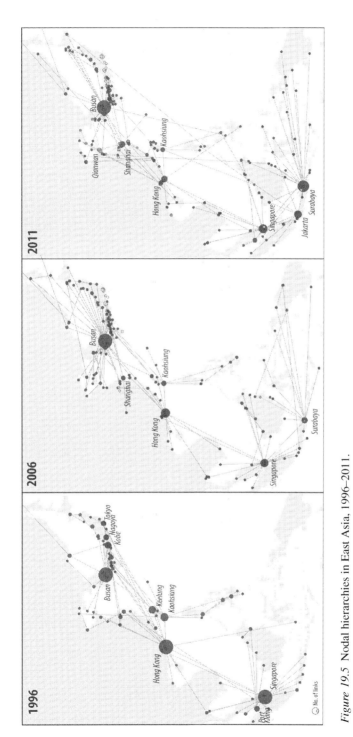

Figure 19.5 Nodal hierarchies in East Asia, 1996–2011.

Source: own elaboration based on *Lloyd's List*.

centrality, thereby favouring the South Korean hub of Busan, while in the south-eastern part of the network, Surabaya and, later on, Jakarta gain grounds on the transhipment market to connect secondary ports of Indonesia (domestic hubs). While Singapore managed to maintain its position in the network, largely due to rather aggressive port development policies reinforcing transit trade in competition with Malaysia, Hong Kong has gradually lost ground with regard to its integration into mainland China's Pearl River Delta and the more relaxed policy towards Taiwan: since 2008, vessels are allowed to connect directly between Taiwanese and main Chinese ports without transhipping through Hong Kong. Mainland Chinese ports, however, have not yet become more central in the East Asian network despite their absolute growth in container throughputs, mostly due to their domestic role for shipping.

The intermingling of multiple scales and functions

One last crucial step in the analysis of maritime regions is the distinction between two scales of circulation: intra- versus extra-regional. Each vessel has been coded according to the geographical scope of its movements, i.e. within the region exclusively, or connecting the region with other regions. Such an approach allowed measuring four main types of traffic by region, by year, over links, and among ports (Table 19.2): extra-regional, intra-regional, exclusive, and mixed. Exclusive traffic refers to the presence of only intra- or extra-regional traffic at one link or port, while mixed traffic is the opposite, i.e. certain links and ports handled both intra- and extra-regional. This approach to maritime networks is fruitful because it provides essential evidences about the intermingling of different scales of flows within maritime regions.

In terms of links among ports, one striking difference between the three regions is that although East Asia exhibits a much higher share of intra-regional links in total traffic, most of its extra-regional traffic is mixed with intra-regional traffic, i.e. occurring on the same links. The same applies to its intra-regional links, which also have a higher proportion of mixed traffic. Such evidence suggest that East Asia is much more integrated than the two other regions because the different scales of maritime circulation are overlapped in space, whereas for the Mediterranean and the Caribbean, intra-regional and extra-regional flows tend to follow different tracks. Yet the two latter regions have in common a growing proportion of mixed traffic over time, as seen with the 20 percent increase of the share of mixed traffics in total extra-regional traffic. However, their intra-regional traffic remains balanced between exclusive and mixed in a somewhat stable way. Another important difference between East Asia and the other regions is the high share of intra-regional traffic in total exclusive traffic, as well as the high share of mixed traffic in total traffic: this tendency is the inverse in the Mediterranean and the Caribbean.

In terms of traffic distribution among ports, the three regions have in common a very high proportion of extra-regional traffic that is mixed. This means that extra-regional traffic everywhere is performed by ports that also handle intra-regional

Table 19.2 Traffic distribution by region and type of circulation, 1996–2011

Region	Mediterranean			Caribbean			East Asia		
Year	1996	2006	2011	1996	2006	2011	1996	2006	2011
Traffic shares on links (% DWT)									
Extra, *of which*	89.6	75.7	78.9	67.4	77.1	60.0	59.2	59.9	50.6
exclusive	71.7	54.8	49.4	73.4	52.6	52.7	6.5	10.4	7.4
mixed	28.3	45.2	50.6	26.6	47.4	47.3	93.5	89.6	92.6
Intra, *of which*	10.4	24.3	21.1	32.6	22.9	40.0	40.8	40.1	49.4
exclusive	48.8	51.5	47.4	58.7	52.2	55.2	41.7	41.9	37.3
mixed	51.2	48.5	52.6	41.3	47.8	44.8	58.3	58.1	62.7
Exclusive, *of which*	69.3	54.0	49.0	68.6	52.5	53.7	20.8	23.0	22.2
extra-	92.7	76.8	79.5	72.2	77.3	58.9	18.3	26.9	17.0
intra-	7.3	23.2	20.5	27.8	22.7	41.1	81.7	73.1	83.0
Mixed, *of which*	30.7	46.0	51.0	31.4	47.5	46.3	79.2	77.0	77.8
extra-	82.6	74.3	78.2	57.1	77.0	61.3	70.0	69.7	60.2
intra-	17.4	25.7	21.8	42.9	23.0	38.7	30.0	30.3	39.8
Traffic shares on ports (% DWT)									
Extra, *of which*	89.6	75.7	78.9	67.4	77.1	59.5	59.2	59.9	50.6
exclusive	13.9	0.2	1.3	14.5	5.0	1.4	0.3	0.1	0.0
mixed	86.1	99.8	98.7	85.5	95.0	98.6	99.7	99.9	100.0
Intra, *of which*	10.4	24.3	21.1	32.6	22.9	40.5	40.8	40.1	49.4
exclusive	2.8	3.9	2.3	14.3	12.7	4.4	14.1	10.3	8.2
mixed	97.2	96.1	97.7	85.7	87.3	95.6	85.9	89.7	91.8
Exclusive, *of which*	12.8	1.1	1.5	14.4	6.7	2.6	5.9	4.2	4.1
extra-	97.7	14.7	67.9	67.8	57.1	31.6	3.0	0.8	0.3
intra-	2.3	85.3	32.1	32.2	42.9	68.4	97.0	99.2	99.7
Mixed, *of which*	87.2	98.9	98.5	85.6	93.3	97.4	94.1	95.8	95.9
extra-	88.4	76.3	79.0	67.4	78.6	60.2	62.8	62.4	52.7
intra-	11.6	23.7	21.0	32.6	21.4	39.8	37.2	37.6	47.3

Source: own elaboration based on data from *Lloyd's List Intelligence*.

Note: *Deadweight tonnage (DWT).*

traffic, and this tendency has increased over time. This share remains the highest for East Asia, where only a handful of ports perform exclusively extra-regional traffic. In parallel, the share of port traffic being exclusively intra- or extra-regional has diminished over time. But East Asia remains strikingly different by the very high share of intra-regional traffics in total exclusive port traffic, which is the opposite for the Mediterranean (except in 2006) and the Caribbean. Even though the share of exclusive traffic remains low everywhere, it is more the outcome of intra-regional traffic in East Asia. Another sign of change that is specific to certain regions is the growing share of intra-regional traffic in total mixed traffic, especially in East Asia.

Overall, the Mediterranean basin is the most extroverted region, because extra-regional flows dominate not only total flows but also exclusive and mixed flows. It means that this region is well inserted into global maritime circulation, but this occurs at the expense of internal linkages, which remain secondary. Such a situation and evolution is produced by the combination of two factors: the increasing importance of intermediate hubs, and the limited trade and logistical integration between the different Mediterranean economies. In comparison, the Caribbean basin appears to have a more balanced profile between global and local integration, while East Asia has the most advanced character, with intra-regional traffic having a high share in general and an increasing connexion with extra-regional traffic over the same links and ports. One important explanation is that Mediterranean hubs greatly differ from their Asian and Caribbean counterparts because they are spatially and functionally disconnected from their hinterland. Ports such as Gioia Tauro, Algeciras, Taranto, Marsaxlokk, and Cagliari mostly serve the interests of

Table 19.3 Top ten dominant ports by maritime region, 1996–2011

	No. dominant links			Intra-regional traffic (% DWT)		
	1996	*2006*	*2011*	*1996*	*2006*	*2011*
Mediterranean						
Barcelona	5	10	8	4.8	12.2	8.7
Valencia	4	4	8	2.7	12.4	8.4
Gioia Tauro	1	8	7	52.5	25.5	14.5
Mersin	2	2	7	47.0	51.3	27.6
Algeciras	2	4	6	0.0	16.0	12.0
Ambarli	0	3	6	–	–	–
Genoa	2	5	6	2.3	5.4	6.3
Damietta	1	2	5	9.2	7.7	9.7
La Spezia	5	3	5	2.8	12.5	6.5
Alexandria (EGY)	2	1	4	2.5	43.4	18.4
Caribbean						
Cartagena (COL)	3	6	8	11.8	12.4	42.4
Coco Solo	1	1	6	48.6	61.4	29.0
Port Everglades	4	4	6	42.0	18.3	32.1
Kingston (JAM)	3	6	5	46.0	26.1	35.8
Puerto Cortes	2	3	5	86.7	52.1	70.6
Freeport (BHS)	0	3	4	–	6.3	13.9
Houston	9	3	4	1.4	13.1	23.2
Point Lisas	2	1	4	100.0	24.9	62.2
Santo Tomas de Castilla	2	2	4	100.0	22.4	67.9
Altamira	2	2	3	0.0	7.9	22.7
East Asia						
Busan	16	35	29	28.3	38.5	47.5
Surabaya	1	11	22	100.0	93.3	98.9
Singapore	16	17	16	42.5	31.7	37.4
Jakarta	1	2	13	100.0	82.9	95.4
Hong Kong	16	20	10	29.9	28.0	38.6
Shanghai	3	7	9	47.0	31.8	34.1
Kaohsiung	8	9	6	28.8	28.7	41.6
Port Klang	5	2	6	34.4	35.1	32.4
Qianwan	0	0	6	–	–	–
Tanoura	0	0	6	–	–	–

Source: own elaboration based on data from *Lloyd's List Intelligence.*

shipping lines and port operators, located relatively far from the main regional markets but close to the liner trunk route. One difficulty, however, is the inability to untangle "hub-feeder effects" and "short-sea effects" in the distribution and evolution of intra-regional flows. Yet, the fact that in all three regions, the share of mixed versus exclusive traffic has increased is in itself a good indicator of a growing convergence between local and global scales of maritime circulation. The fact that intra-regional and extra-regional linkages and traffic have increasingly occurred over same links and ports confirms that the different scales have gradually been adjusted to each other across space. In that perspective, maritime networks can be analyzed through their level of "branching" between different levels of activity.

This difficulty can be tackled by looking at the share of intra-regional traffic at the dominant ports for each region (Table 19.3). Some ports specialized in transhipment activities have a higher share of intra-regional traffic due to the high frequency of vessel calls induced by the hub-feeder system, such as Busan and Gioia Tauro. Yet, the trajectory of those two ports is opposed, as Gioia Tauro is increasingly extra-regional while Busan reinforces its local traffic. This can be explained by the reinforcement of interlining versus hub-and-spokes transhipment at Gioia Tauro, while Busan maintained its position as a hub for western Japan and northern China. Traditional gateways tend to have a rather limited share of intra-regional traffic (e.g. Barcelona, Valencia), but some of them witnessed a continuous increase due to their growing dependence upon transhipment hubs through which long-distance trades are getting rerouted (e.g. Genoa, Houston). High shares of intra-regional traffic also occur at ports trading mostly within the region without being hubs (e.g. Mersin) or developing hub functions while being at the same time under the dominance of a larger hub, such as Surabaya and Jakarta being national hubs polarized by Singapore. Many factors thus influence port evolution, such as the scale and scope of trading flows and the nature of competition.

Discussion and conclusion

This chapter has provided an original comparative analysis of three major maritime regions, namely the Mediterranean basin, the Caribbean basin, and East Asia. The focus on vessel movements as a way of verifying the topological and functional consistency of maritime regions had various outcomes at different levels. One main result is that major hub ports are not disconnected from more local dynamics of trade exchanges within each region. Thus, it helps us to rethink what exactly is the role of these intermediate hubs and their integration into regional flows. In addition, the growth of transhipment hubs is only partly visible due to the parallel multiplication of links that do not use these hubs, either through local trade linkages or more long-distance ones, but deeper verification of the underlying logics of flows would necessitate further research and scrutiny of the original data. Another factor to take into account when comparing different maritime regions is their overall throughput volume of containers, which in some way influences the emergence or not of intermediate hubs. In the Mediterranean basin, which was at centre stage in this study, new centralities appear over time, with the growth of Turkish ports and the steady role of Gibraltar (including Tangier-Med) sometimes replacing former ones such as those of Greece or Cyprus.

The new Moroccan port of Tangier-Med is emblematic of such a local-global tension within the basin. Competing with Algeciras to capture new transhipment flows the new port has attracted major terminal operators (e.g. APM Terminal, Maersk, CMA-CGM, and PSA) and looks forward to expanding its capacity to 8 million TEUs when Tangier-Med II is completed. As suggested in the various analyses, such a project goes beyond sole transhipments as it also consists in developing many economic zones while promoting new regional planning in the Tangier-Tetouan region of Morocco. The main objective is thus to attract foreign investment (e.g. Renault in 2012 in the Meloussa free-trade zone) and to support regional economic development as well as transport system modernization (Mareï, 2013). Other examples include the modernization of other ports in the region, such as in the Maghreb (Algeria) but also Egypt and Turkey, often through ambitious port reforms and foreign intervention (e.g. DP World in Algeria). Other shipping markets are also represented besides containers, such as roll-on/roll-off (ro-ro) and oil products, in a context where the regional economy should grow by 18 percent in future years (AGAM, 2013; Lloyd's Marine Intelligence Unit, 2008). Yet, the regional integration process remains limited, since only 2.3 percent of Europe's foreign direct investments focus on the southern Mediterranean economies, compared with about 20 percent when it comes to US or Japan investments towards their southern counterparts (Telle, 2009). The extent to which maritime flows and networks constitute a component, a constraint, or an engine for further regional integration in the Mediterranean basin and elsewhere remains to be seen. However, the approach proposed by the analysis of two scales of circulation (intra- versus extra-regional) is particularly significant because it shows how the different scales of maritime circulation overlap in space. This information is useful for assessing regional integration: the share of mixed traffic is thus a good indicator of the convergence between local and global dynamics.

By revealing how scales overlap through regionalization and maritimization, our study reviewed theoretical research on scales that opens up new possibilities for regional analysis. The macro-regional scale, that of the maritime basins, enables us to identify processes of local, global, and regional origins and thus to grasp the multiscalar complexity of our study object. The approach in terms of flows and networks is very useful in this regard. It allows to focus on interactions among places and to support the idea of the new regionalism that helps us to understand the transformation of the global space.

In this context, the analysis of a maritime basin as a singular geographical object in the sense that it is maritime and terrestrial, transnational and transcontinental, and that it forms at the same time a junction point and a limit, has a dual contribution. For port and maritime geography, network analysis of a maritime region contributes to the revival of a discipline where the port is primarily studied in its terrestrial environment (regional or national hinterland) but less from the perspective of the maritime links connecting regional neighbours or the rest of the world. For regional geography, the study of these basins provides an interesting example of heterogeneous regions, outside institutional territories and driven by internal and external exchange. The network approach allows us to highlight the internal dynamics likely to contribute to a process of regional economic integration.

Acknowledgements

The research leading to these results has received funding from the European Research Council under the European Union's Seventh Framework Programme (FP/2007-2013)/ERC Grant Agreement n. [313847] "World Seastems." The authors also would like to thank Olaf Merk (OECD-ITF) for his support on data collection.

References

Agence d'urbanisme de l'agglomération marseillaise (AGAM). 2013. *Atlas des villes portuaires du sud et de l'Est de La Méditerranée*, http://www.agam.org/fr/agence/actions-en-reseaux/international.html

Allix A. (1933) La Méditerranée. In: Quillet A. (Ed), *Géographie Universelle*, pp. 511–530.

Amin A. (2004) Regions unbound: towards a new politics of place. *Geografiska Annaler Series B*, 86(1): 33–44.

Arrault J.B. (2008) Une géographie inattendue: le système mondial vu par Paul Vidal de La Blache. *L'Espace Géographique*, 37(1): 75–88.

Balassa B. (1961) *The Theory of Economic Integration. Homewood, Illinois:* Richard Irwin.

Beauguitte L. (2013) Les votes de l'Assemblée générale de l'ONU de 1985 à nos jours. Pistes (carto)graphiques. *Mappemonde*, 97 (online).

Beckouche P. (2008) *Les Régions Nord-Sud*. Paris: Belin.

Benko G., Lipietz A. (1992) *Les Régions qui Gagnent: Districts et Réseaux: les Nouveaux Paradigmes de La Géographie Economique*. Paris: Presses Universitaires de France.

Bentley J. (1999) Seas and ocean basins as frameworks of historical interaction. *Geographical Review*, 89(2): 215–224.

Braudel F. (1985) *Civilization and Capitalism*. New York: Harper and Row.

Charlier J. (1996) The Benelux seaport system. *Tijdschrift voor Economische en Sociale Geografie*, 87: 310–321.

Cisic D., Komadina P., Hlaca B. (2007) Network analysis applied to Mediterranean liner transport system. Paper presented at the International Association of Maritime Economists Conference, Athens, Greece, July 4–6.

Claval P. (1968) *Régions, Nations, Grands Espaces. Géographie Générale des Ensembles Territoriaux*. Paris: Marie-Thérèse Génin.

de La Blache P. (1903) Tableau Géographique de La France. Paris: Hachette.

Dicken P., Kelly P.F., Olds K., Yeung H.W.C. (2001) Chains and networks, territories and scales: Towards a relational framework for analysing the global economy. *Global Networks*, 1(2): 89–112.

Didelon C., Grasland C., Richard Y. (2008) *Atlas de l'Europe dans le Monde*. Paris: La Documentation française.

Dollfus O., Grataloup C. and Lévy J., 1999. Trois ou quatre choses que La mondialisation dit à La géographie. *L'Espace Géographique*, 1: 1–11.

Ducruet C. (2008) Hub dependence in constrained economies: The case of North Korea. *Maritime Policy and Management*, 35(4): 74–88.

Ducruet C. (2009) Port regions and globalisation, In: Notteboom T.E., Ducruet C. and De Langen P.W. (Eds), *Ports in Proximity: Competition and Cooperation among Adjacent Seaports*, Aldershot: Ashgate, pp. 41–53.

Ducruet C. (2013) Network diversity and maritime flows. *Journal of Transport Geography*, 30: 77–88.

Ducruet C., Notteboom T.E. (2012) The worldwide maritime network of container shipping: Spatial structure and regional dynamics. *Global Networks*, 12(3): 395–423.

Ducruet C., Lugo I. (2013) Cities and transport networks in shipping and logistics research. *Asian Journal of Shipping and Logistics*, 29(2): 149–170.

Ducruet C., Rozenblat C., Zaidi F. (2010) Ports in multi-level maritime networks: Evidence from the Atlantic (1996-2006). *Journal of Transport Geography*, 18(4): 508–518.

Ducruet C., Lee S.W., Ng A.K.Y. (2011) Port competition and network polarization at the East Asian maritime corridor. *Territoire en Mouvement*, 10: 60–74.

Ducruet C., Joly O., Le Cam M. (2014) Europe in global maritime flows: Gateways, forelands, and subnetworks. In: Pain K., Van Hamme G. (Eds), *Changing Urban and Regional Relations in a Globalizing World. Europe as a Global Macro-Region*, Edward Elgar, pp. 164–180.

Frémont A. (1976) *La Région, Espace Vécu*. Paris: PUF.

Gipouloux F. (2009) *La Méditerranée Asiatique. Villes portuaires et Réseaux Marchands en Chine, au Japon et en Asie du Sud-Est, XVIe – XXIe siècle*. Paris: CNRS.

Girault C. (2009) *Intégrations en Amérique du Sud*. Paris: Presses de La Sorbonne Nouvelle.

Gonzalez Laxe F., Freire Seoane M.J., Montes C.P. (2012) Maritime degree, centrality and vulnerability: Port hierarchies and emerging areas in containerized transport (2008–2010). *Journal of Transport Geography*, 24: 33–44.

Gouvernal E., Debrie J., Slack B. (2005) Dynamics of change in the port system of the western Mediterranean. *Maritime Policy and Management*, 32(2): 107–121.

Grataloup C. (2007) *Géohistoire de La mondialisation. Le temps long du monde*. Paris: Armand Colin.

Hettne B., Söderbaum F. (1998) The New Regionalism approach. *Politeia*, 17(3): 6–22.

Hettne B., Söderbaum F. (2000) Theorizing the rize of regionness. *New Political Economy*, 5(3): 457–474.

Jacobs W., Notteboom T.E. (2011) An evolutionary perspective on regional port systems: The role of windows of opportunity in shaping seaport competition. *Environment and Planning A*, 43(7): 1674–1692.

Jones M., Paasi A. (2013) Guest editorial: Regional world(s): Advancing the geography of regions. *Regional Studies*, 47: 1–5.

Kaluza P., Kölzsch A., Gastner M.T., Blasius, B. (2010) The complex network of global cargo ship movements. *Journal of the Royal Society Interface*, 7(48): 1093–1103.

Lam J.S.L. (2011) Patterns of maritime supply chains: Slot capacity analysis. *Journal of Transport Geography*, 19(2): 366–374.

Lewis M.W., Wigen K. (1999) A maritime response to the crisis in area studies. *Geographical Review*, 89(2): 161–168.

Lloyd's Marine Intelligence Unit (2008) étude des flux du transport maritime en mer Méditerranée. REMPEC: http://www.euromedtransport.eu/Fr/image.php?id=2492

Marcadon J. (2002) Géographie portuaire de l'espace euro-méditerranéen. *Méditerranée*, 98(1): 55–66.

Mareï N. (2012) *Le détroit de Gibraltar, Porte du Monde, Frontière de l'Europe. Analyse et Perspectives de Territorialité d'un Espace de Transit*. PhD dissertation in geography, Université de Nantes.

Mareï N. (2013) Le détroit de Gibraltar, des réseaux mondiaux aux enjeux locaux de développement. *Geotransports*, 1–2: 205–220.

Massey D., Arango J., Hugo G., Kouaouci A., Pellegrino A., Taylor E. (1993) Theories of international migration: A review and appraisal. *Population and Development Review*, 19(3): 431–466.

McCalla R.J., Slack B., Comtois C. (2005) The Caribbean basin: Adjusting to global trends in containerization. *Maritime Policy and Management*, 32(3): 245–261.

Monios J., Wilsmeier G. (2012) Giving a direction to port regionalisation. *Transportation Research Part A*, 46(10): 1551–1561.

Ng A.K.Y., Ducruet C. (2014) The changing tides of port geography (1950–2012). *Progress in Human Geography*, 38(6): 785–823.

Notteboom T.E. (1997) Concentration and load centre development in the European container port system. *Journal of Transport Geography*, 5(2): 99–115.

Notteboom T.E. (2012) Towards a new intermediate hub region in container shipping? Relay and interlining via the Cape route vs. the Suez route. *Journal of Transport Geography*, 22: 164–178.

Notteboom T.E., Rodrigue J.P. (2005) Port regionalization: Towards a new phase in port development. *Maritime Policy and Management*, 32(3): 297–313.

Nystuen J.D., Dacey M.F. (1961) A graph theoretical interpretation of nodal regions. Papers in Regional Science 7(1): 29–42.

Ohmae K. (1996) *De l'Etat-nation aux Etats-régions*. Paris: Dunod.

Perroux F. (1991) *L'économie du XXe siècle*. Grenoble: Presses Universitaires de Grenoble.

Richard Y. (2010) *L'Union Européenne et ses Voisins Orientaux. Contribution à l'étude des Intégrations Régionales dans le Monde*. Habilitation à Diriger des Recherches, Université Paris 1 Panthéon-Sorbonne.

Richard Y., Zanin C. (2009) L'Europe dans La régionalisation de l'espace mondial. *Géocarrefour*, 84(3): 137–149.

Ridolfi G. (1999) Containerisation in the Mediterranean: Between global ocean routeways and feeder services. *Geojournal*, 48(1): 29–34.

Rimmer P.J. (1967) The search for spatial regularities in the development of Australian seaports 1861–1961/2. *Geografiska Annaler*, 49B: 42–54.

Rochefort M. (1960) *L'organisation Urbaine de l'Alsace*. Paris: Les Belles Lettres.

Rodrigue J.P., Comtois C., Slack B. (1997) Transportation and spatial cycles: Evidence from maritime systems. *Journal of Transport Geography*, 5(2): 87–98.

Rodrigue J.P., Notteboom T.E. (2010) Foreland-based regionalization: Integrating intermediate hubs with port hinterlands. *Research in Transportation Economics*, 27(1): 19–29.

Sassen S. (1991) *The Global City, New York, London, Tokyo*. Princeton: Princeton University Press.

Scott A.J. (2001) *Global City-Regions: Trends, Theory, Policy*. Oxford University Press.

Serry A. (2006) *La Réorganisation Portuaire de La Baltique Orientale: l'émergence d'une Nouvelle Région en Europe*. PhD dissertation in geography, Université du Havre.

Snyder D., Kick E.L. (1979) Structural position in the world system and economic growth, 1955–1970: A multiple-network analysis of transnational interactions. *American Journal of Sociology*, 84: 1096–1126.

Tarrius A. (2007) *La Remontée des Sud: Afghans et Marocains en Europe méridionale*. Editions de l'Aube.

Telle S. (2009) L'Union pour La Méditerranée: un héritage contrasté mais une continuité indispensable. *Outre-Terre*, 23(3): 19–29.

Veenstra A.W., Mulder H.M., Sels R.A. (2005) Analysing container flows in the Caribbean. *Journal of Transport Geography*, 13(4): 295–305.

Veltz P. (1996) *Mondialisation, Villes et Territoires, l'Economie d'Archipel*. Paris: Presses Universitaires de France.

Vergé-Dépré C.R. (2006) Les nouvelles hiérarchies du système portuaire dans le Bassin Caraïbe. *Etudes Caribéennes* (online).

Vigarié A. (1964) *Les Grands Ports de Commerce de La Seine au Rhin, leur Evolution devant l'Industrialisation des Arrière-pays.* Paris: SABRI.

Vigarié A. (1990) *Economie Maritime et Géostratégique des Océans.* Caen: Paradigme.

Wallerstein I. (1979) *The Capitalist World Economy.* Cambridge University Press.

Wilmsmeier G., Hoffmann J. (2008) Liner shipping connectivity and port infrastructure as determinants of freight rates in the Caribbean. *Maritime Economics and Logistics,* 10: 130–151.

Wilmsmeier G., Notteboom T.E. (2011) Determinants of liner shipping network configuration: A two-region comparison. *Geojournal,* 76(3): 213–228.

Zohil J., Prijon M. (1999) The MED rule: The interdependence of container throughput and transhipment volumes in the Mediterranean ports. *Maritime Policy and Management,* 26: 175–193.

20 Co-evolutionary dynamics of ports and cities in the global maritime network, 1950–90

César Ducruet, Sylvain Cuyala,
Ali El Hosni,
Zuzanna Kosowska-Stamirowska

Port cities and maritime networks

Models and trends of port-city evolution

Much has been said about the evolution of port cities, from the perspectives of planners, architects, sociologists, economists, historians, and geographers alike, especially in terms of changing urban landscape, port morphology, and other inter-actions between port and city. Although the definition of the port city concept itself has remained blurred (Ducruet, 2011), most studies converged around the idea that large cities will ultimately get rid of their port activity so as to diversify their economy, prevent their citizens from environmental degradation, be more creative and knowledge-based. Various forms of waterfront redevelopment strategies have emerged since the 1950s to value the city's maritime culture and atmosphere for other uses than cargo handling operations and related industries. At the same time, transport chain actors, of which the port was one, increasingly saw the city as a constraint to infrastructure expansion, which was required to encourage growth and improved fluidity/movement of traffic. As a result, modern terminals were often developed outside the city's jurisdiction, where suitable and sufficient land was available, together with better accessibility both by sea and by land.

Port geography contributed to depict these trends by providing spatial models of port-city evolution organized around successive phases, as well as numerous port impact studies and in-depth investigation of particular ports and port cities (Ng *et al.*, 2014). The Anyport model of James Bird (1963) provided a generalization of the spatial shift of modern port terminals from the upstream city towards down-stream deep-sea locations as a response to urban growth and port growth. Brian Hoyle (1989) later modelled the evolution of the port-city interface to explain how cities and ports grew increasingly apart due to technological change in port and shipping operations, favouring the rise of "placeless ports" and new urban chal-lenges in a postmodern society (Norcliffe *et al.*, 1996). Historians as well proposed a stage approach to port city diversification (Murphey, 1989).

Nevertheless, because cities remain more than ever essential consumption and production centres, there remains a debate on whether such a physical and func-tional separation process is truly universal (Lee *et al.*, 2008) due to its regional diversity and varying intensity. Geographers also contributed to the debate by discussing the fundamentally urban dimension of commodity chains and the integration versus disintegration dynamics taking place in and around port cities (Hesse, 2010, 2013). Other scholars motivated policy-makers to maintain the benefits of port-city proximity due to the positive externalities provided by cities to ports (Hall and Jacobs, 2012), which was recently illustrated by the creation of new container terminals in the vicinity of certain global cities in order to reduce trucking to and from distant terminals, such as London, Taipei, Tokyo, and Yokohama. Such examples seem to question the validity of classic port-city evolutionary models.

Measuring port-city interdependence on a larger scale

Most of the time, empirical investigations of port-city evolution remained focused on specific places and projects, at the level of the urban waterfront. As already discussed by Ducruet and Itoh (2015), there are very scarce large-scale analyses of port-region and port-city interdependences (see also Chapter 16 by Ducruet and Itoh on port regions and material flows). Numerous analyses looked at the changing economic impact of ports on their local economy based on a variety of disaggregated data but in turn, these studies remained impossible to compare to one another and over time given the diversity of sources and methods to measure spillovers, related employment, and value added. Looking at the geographical determinants of the port and maritime industries, several works concluded to a stronger influence of urban size (often measured by the number of inhabitants) than port size (as measured by total tonnage or containerized cargo volume) on the distribution of port and maritime services in Australia (O'Connor, 1987, 1989), Canada (Slack, 1989), and at the world scale (Jacobs *et al.*, 2010). Such results suggested that while physical cargo handling operations are more and more performed outside large cities, the latter keep concentrating more "white-collar" office-based activities such as brokers, insurers, and traders. More dynamic analyses came to the similar conclusion that the correlation between port and city was no longer relevant, given the lack of a significant statistical correlation between port traffic growth and urban population growth in France (Steck, 1995) and the decline of the linear correlation between port traffic volume and urban population in India (Kidwai, 1989). A more systematic, global measurement of the relationship between port and urban development was proposed by Ducruet and Lee (2006) over the period 1970–2005. It also confirmed the decreasing correlation between traffic and population, but was solely based on container throughput volumes.

Another drawback of the port-city literature is the rarity of a network approach. Jacobs *et al.* (2010) did provide a classification of port cities based on their situation in the global network of maritime advanced provider services and their port throughput, but it remained rather static and did not address the distribution of physical flows among port cities. More likely in geography and elsewhere are studies of cities in abstract models of urban interaction where actual flows are absent, or in other types of networks such as airlines, roads and railways, but no study has ever been done about the urban dimension of maritime networks (Ducruet and Lugo, 2013; Ducruet and Beauguitte, 2014). Graph-theoretical and statistical methods were used to explain, for instance, the accessibility and centrality of cities and regions in airline networks by their population and gross domestic product (Choi *et al.*, 2006; Neal, 2011; Wang *et al.*, 2011; Dobruszkes *et al.*, 2011). For other transport modes, Cattan (1995) analyzed barrier effects in air and rail flows among European cities, and Guerrero and Proulhac (2014) revealed distinct relationships between the urban hierarchy and the spatial distribution of the respective export volumes of wholesalers and manufacturing companies in France. One aspect of maritime centrality for cities was explored, however, when investigating the respective role of maritime and airline networks in the combined air–sea centrality of cities, but without taking into account other urban data (Ducruet *et al.*, 2011). The same applies to other types of inter-city linkages, which were analysed regardless of other urban attributes, such as those of multinational firms in various sectors (Rozenblat, 2010; Taylor, 2012), with the exception of Jacobs *et al.* (2011) showing the limited influence of container port traffic on the amount of maritime advanced producer services in world cities.

Reconciling port cities and maritime networks

This chapter proposes to remedy the aforementioned lack of a global and dynamic view by an analysis of combined maritime traffic and urban population data. This is the first-ever analysis of maritime flows in relation to cities based on rigourous harmonization and manipulation of multiple historical data sources. It aims to measure the influence of urban demographic size on the distribution of global maritime flows, as a means to re-explore the existing literature on ports and cities. It also engages in a wider debate on whether urban development had become increasingly virtual, to such extent that material flows (and their related infrastructures) are increasingly disconnected from human settlements and planning/development priorities (Hall and Hesse, 2012). It gives paramount importance to the definition of the port city itself as a spatial unit, considering not only the locality of the port, but also the extended urban environment at a city-region (or urban area) level, which is more of a morphological nature and has the advantage of being comparable over time and across space. Another innovation compared with previous work is the application of a graph-theoretical framework thanks to the extraction of vessel movement data from the *Lloyd's List* corpus, in particular the *Lloyd's Shipping Index* providing information on the last known movement of each vessel recorded. For the first time, not only traffic and population weights are considered when statistically measuring port-city relationships, but also effective maritime linkages between port cities, here by the cumulated number of vessel calls.

Such a global and dynamic approach will test the extent to which the global maritime network is centralized by larger cities, and how has the correlation between maritime traffic and urban population evolved over time. This research has, therefore, wider implications than for the sole port-city issue. The topological features of spatial networks have rarely been confronted to the socio-characteristics of its nodes (Ducruet and Beauguitte, 2014). Providing a demographic weight to ports thus allows testing numerous ideas about the dependence of maritime networks upon a hierarchy of urban places rather than considering nodes only as ports or terminals. Because it is often the case that several ports belong to the same morphological urban area, the analysis is more compact and aggregated and thus may shed new light about port-city evolution in the last decades. For practical reason of data availability, and because the research is still in progress, the proposed analysis is limited to the period 1950–90. One main hypothesis is based on the literature on port cities and maritime networks: the initially strong link between maritime flows and urban development has gradually declined. Yet, such a hypothesis might be questioned thanks to a renewed methodological framework where port cities and maritime flows are observed in a radically different way than in the past.

Data and methodology

First of all, this research was motivated by the availability of demographic data in the *Geopolis* database, which provides the number of inhabitants in urban areas based on morphological criteria over the period 1950–90 (Moriconi-Ebrard, 1994). It was preferred to other possible sources, such as the United Nations, as *Geopolis* rests on a more robust definition of the city. It includes cities having at least 100,000 inhabitants in 1990. This database was completed by *Populstat* for the rest of the period (Lahmeyer, 2006) to zoom on specific port cities at the end of the chapter. Both databases have the advantage to be historical and to consider urban areas rather than sole administrative boundaries.

With reference to Figure 20.1, each port or terminal was associated to the nearest urban centre taking into account urbanization patterns, physical proximity, road accessibility, and urban system layout. This manual method was preferred to any automatic matching in a Geographical Information System (GIS) to avoid putting together cross-border locations belonging to radically different socio-economic contexts. More precisely, two levels of urban activity have been distinguished, city

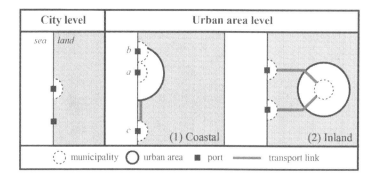

Figure 20.1 Methodology for port-city matching.

Source: own realization.

and urban area. The city level is the municipality where the port is located, i.e. the smallest administrative area that is often the eponym of the port itself, but not in all cases. The urban area level is the agglomeration or urban morphological area, with two possibilities: the urban area to which the city belongs, or a more distant, inland urban area that connects by road the city, the latter being the maritime outlet of the former. Two or more cities may be included in the same urban area, such as Tokyo and Yokohama that are administratively distinct cities but belong to the same morphological entity. The same methodology applied to coastal and river port cities. A third type occurred, that is the combination of coastal and inland, especially in the case of the urban area of Santos (Brazil) being the gateway of the urban area of Sao Paulo, i.e. two urban areas next to each other.

As a result, it was possible to aggregate many ports and terminals altogether that in fact serve the same city, and gain in spatial coherence. For instance, we calculated that London port itself accounted for about 85–90 percent of the urban area's total vessels calls between 1890 and 1965, but it rapidly dropped since then, reaching 26 percent in 2008, with the gradual shift of terminals and traffic to deep-sea terminals along the Thames and up to Felixstowe (Figure 20.2). Although the two curves went through similar evolutions over the whole period, the gap has widened following the shift of modern terminals towards suburban, deep-sea locations outside of the urban core. This is a typical example that confirms the accuracy of the Anyport model (Bird, 1963) in which such a trend was observed around the same period. Notably, Felixstowe set up Britain's first container terminal in 1967

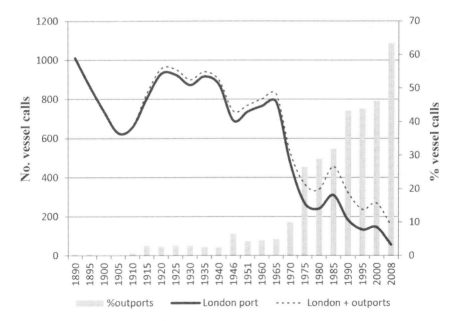

Figure 20.2 London's maritime traffic at port and urban area level, 1890–2008.

Source: own realization.

Table 20.1 Characteristics of the port-urban database, 1950–90

	Year							
	1951	*1960*	*1965*	*1970*	*1975*	*1980*	*1985*	*1990*
No. urban areas	442	490	498	498	511	523	550	547
World share (%)								
No. ports	50.9	42.5	46.8	51.7	54.6	57.1	59.3	62.8
Urban population	52.9	51.5	50.9	50.4	48.5	47.1	46.8	46.7
No. vessel calls	81.9	81.3	82.2	82.5	81.4	80.6	78.1	78.1
Average population (000s inhab.)								
Port cities	418	538	616	687	765	847	932	1014
Non-port cities	141	167	189	221	251	297	340	382

and at the same time, between 1960 and 1980, the London Docklands were gradually closed and the port activity relocated to Tilbury, Thamesport, and Felixstowe. This long-term view is currently in progress when it comes to the whole sample of ports worldwide. Port activity corresponds to the number of vessel calls calculated from the *Lloyd's Shipping Index*.

Because the population data was available only every decade, it was decided to calculate the year-on-year average for the intermediate years of 1965, 1975, and 1985, to better see a trend in the association between population and traffic. As a result and considering only the urban-area level, the global port-urban database concentrates a noticeable proportion of world ports and population, with about 500 urban areas considered for this time period (Table 20.1). The share of ports included in urban areas has increased, but the share of population and vessel calls has decreased, which is mainly due to the exclusion of smaller cities by *Geopolis*. Nevertheless, this sample is very representative of global maritime activity, as it remains around 80 percent of total vessel calls over time. This is already in itself an indication that maritime traffic is more likely to concentrate in larger cities. In addition, the urban areas exerting maritime trade have always been three times larger on average than other cities in terms of demographic size. Although such evidence is insufficient to conclude mutual port-city growth effects, it confirms the observation that port cities enjoyed stronger dynamics due to their direct access to international trade networks (Dogan, 1988).

The changing correlation between traffic and population

One possible way to further check the respective influence of urban size and maritime traffic distribution is to look at the linear correlation among them and at the changing share of city size classes (quantiles) (Table 20.2). Despite certain fluctuations, maritime traffic is distributed hierarchically as its share increases along with population. The distribution among the six classes is relatively stable over time. Noticeable changes can be highlighted, however. For instance, the largest

Table 20.2 City sizes and traffic distribution, 1950–90

Quantiles	Year							
	1951	*1960*	*1965*	*1970*	*1975*	*1980*	*1985*	*1990*
Share of world vessel calls (%)								
6	59.4	59.4	56.9	56.8	56.9	49.2	49.7	49.7
5	18.9	15.5	18.7	18.6	15.4	22.4	20.8	20.2
4	8.3	10.6	10.8	10.1	11.3	11.7	10.1	11.1
3	6.4	7.3	6.2	6.9	8.2	7.8	8.5	8.1
2	4.1	3.8	4.6	4.6	5.6	5.2	6.3	5.6
1	2.8	3.4	2.7	2.9	2.6	3.7	4.7	5.3
Total	100.0	100.0	100.0	100.0	100.0	100.0	100.0	100.0
Correlation (Pearson)								
Coastal urban areas	0.521	0.485	0.404	0.408	0.326	0.315	0.338	0.288
Coastal & inland urban areas	0.559	0.581	0.535	0.572	0.511	0.467	0.498	0.437
Traffic concentration								
Gini coefficient	0.724	0.710	0.704	0.696	0.712	0.697	0.684	0.684
Herfindahl index	0.012	0.011	0.010	0.009	0.011	0.010	0.009	0.011

cities regularly dominate world traffic but their share has dropped from 59.4 to 49.7 percent between 1951 and 1990, while the share of the smallest cities has almost doubled, from 2.8 to 5.3 percent. In fact, traffic gradually shifted from the largest cities towards smaller ones, as each class gained around 2 percent over the period. This shift largely explains the decreasing concentration of maritime traffic among cities, as seen with the Gini coefficient (0.724 to 0.684) and the Herfindahl index, but the latter has been more stable than the first.

One very important result is the decreasing linear correlation between traffic and population. The linear function was in all cases the best fit between the two variables. Interestingly, the correlation coefficients obtained for port urban areas (i.e. the port city itself) are always lower than when including non-port urban areas (i.e. distant cities served by the port). Indeed, numerous inland cities are the true engines of port activity, despite road distance between port and city, and taking into account such an important aspect has been beneficial to the results.[1] Another result is that the correlation has somewhat stabilized, creating a widening gap with the one obtained based on coastal urban areas only. This directly relates to the "hinterland effect" by which ports situated in minor coastal cities may have handle traffic volumes far beyond the needs of their host city, so that considering the nearby inland urban area as the city of reference improved the coherence of the results. While the correlation coefficient for coastal cities dropped by half, the one based on coastal and inland cities lost only one point.

Urban centrality in the global maritime network

The relationship between centrality and demography

Another important dimension of the research is the influence of demographic size on the centrality of cities in worldwide maritime flows. Commonly accepted measures of node centrality were calculated and compared (Table 20.3) so as to reveal their possible link with demographic size. Overall, all indicators exhibited a declining correlation with urban population, especially since 1960. Betweenness centrality, which corresponds to the number of occurrences of nodes on shortest paths in the entire graph, had the highest correlation in 1951, superseded by degree centrality, a more local measure (i.e. number of adjacent neighbours), since 1960. Eccentricity always had a lower correlation, while the clustering coefficient is negatively correlated and remains around −0.2. This negative score means that despite its low significance, the ability of nodes to be stars in the network (i.e. lower scores correspond to hubs with poorly connected neighbours) is more likely to apply to larger cities.

The latter evidence is confirmed when looking at the average clustering coefficient by classes of urban size (quantiles). While for all cities the clustering coefficient has regularly decreased, suggesting a general evolution of the network towards a hub-and-spokes or "scale-free" structure, the largest cities always score the lowest, as they tend to be the hubs for multiple, poorly connected and smaller cities. With a few exceptions, the average clustering coefficient increases from one class to another as population increases, which suggests that as cities get smaller, their ability to centralize maritime flows decreases. Yet, the gap between

Table 20.3 City sizes and network measures, 1950–90

Quantiles	Year				
	1951	*1960*	*1970*	*1980*	*1990*
Average clustering coefficient*					
6	0.434	0.417	0.413	0.371	0.361
5	0.532	0.539	0.457	0.398	0.377
4	0.584	0.567	0.493	0.476	0.422
3	0.580	0.562	0.547	0.488	0.512
2	0.627	0.587	0.543	0.500	0.476
1	0.756	0.663	0.676	0.560	0.515
All	0.542	0.542	0.534	0.487	0.465
Correlation					
Clustering coefficient*	−0.231	−0.251	−0.255	−0.202	−0.210
Degree centrality	0.462	0.521	0.469	0.465	0.423
Betweenness centrality*	0.507	0.494	0.449	0.452	0.344
Eccentricity*	0.312	0.356	0.325	0.312	0.232
Rich-club coefficient	5.597	5.959	5.166	4.974	4.843

Note: Zero values are excluded for variables marked with *.

Table 20.4 Maritime flows and urban homophily, 1950–90

Quantiles	Year				
	1951	*1960*	*1970*	*1980*	*1990*
Intra-class (%)					
6	67.5	63.8	50.3	44.4	45.3
5	15.2	13.5	16.9	20.4	17.5
4	11.9	12.5	12.6	11.0	12.3
3	5.0	9.1	6.0	7.7	8.7
2	3.8	3.5	3.1	4.5	5.8
1	2.2	4.5	2.9	3.3	5.5
All	48.0	43.9	39.0	34.7	37.8
Inter-class (%)					
Opposed (1/6)	0.9	7.6	10.1	12.5	13.8
Adjacent	22.5	19.7	21.4	22.1	20.6
All	52.0	56.1	61.0	65.3	62.2

the average clustering coefficient of the smallest and the largest cities has narrowed over time, from 0.32 to 0.15, which means that the probability for hub functions to concentrate at larger cities has become somewhat more blurred than in the earlier decades. Lastly, the rich-club coefficient that divides the link density (or completeness) among larger cities by the link density among all cities shows that larger cities tended to be around five times better connected with each other. Thus, the urban hierarchy certainly influences, at least partly, the spatial distribution of the global maritime network, notwithstanding important changes. Yet, it is also important to address how hierarchically connected are cities of various size in the network.

The analysis of priority linkages is a useful method to further understand the influence of urban hierarchies on the distribution of maritime flows. At the level of city size classes (Table 20.4), the share of vessel calls distributed between urban areas of similar size (intra-class) always remained lower than for the flows between other cities, and it has even decreased over time, from 48 percent in 1951 to about 38 percent in 1990. In comparison, the share of flows between adjacent classes oscillated around 20 percent of inter-class flows, while flows between demographically opposed cities (i.e. largest to/from smallest) increased from 0.9 percent to 13.8 percent. Overall, largest cities connect primarily with each other, as the two top classes (5 and 6) have a combined share of 82.7 percent of total intra-class flows in 1951, but this share dropped to 62.8 percent in 1990. Such elements motivate the reference to the declining clustering coefficient on the level of the entire network, as one may conclude to the growing centralization of network flows, especially around larger cities, which become more connected to smaller ones due their increasing role as intermediary hubs in the network.

Additional evidence was obtained from the analysis of network assortativity (Table 20.5). As defined by Newman (2002), assortativity (or assortative mixing)

Table 20.5 Evolution of network assortativity, 1950–90

Urban weight	Population (raw)		Population (log)	
Links weight	unweighted	weighted	unweighted	weighted
1951	−0.0297	0.0406	−0.0183	0.0974
p	0.0053	9.98E-10	0.0865	5.88E-49
1960	−0.0425	0.0029	−0.0420	0.0773
p	5.18E-06	0.6119	6.50E-06	7.39E-40
1970	−0.0278	0.0414	−0.0274	0.0814
p	0.0011	4.35E-14	0.0013	8.36E-50
1980	−0.0126	0.1024	−0.0108	0.1394
p	0.1601	4.57E-65	0.2310	1.81E-119
1990	−0.0117	0.1177	0.0041	0.2032
p	0.1587	9.08E-111	0.6215	0.0

is measured by the Pearson correlation coefficient of degree between pairs of linked nodes. It indicates whether nodes of similar (or dissimilar) size preferentially connect to each other in a network. Urban area population was preferred to degree in this chapter to elucidate whether city size plays a role in the distribution of maritime flows. Assortativity was calculated with the Python NetworkX package based on real population numbers and their logarithm, and on binary or weighted city-to-city matrix. Results were insignificant when considering binary linkages (presence or absence of a link). Taking into account weighted edges provided a positive and growing assortativity of the network, especially between 1970 and 1990, and this was even truer with logs for urban population. Despite the growing centralization of maritime flows by larger cities (towards smaller cities) and just like scale-free networks in general, large hubs strongly connect each other while multiplying links towards smaller nodes.

Cities in nodal maritime regions

Priority linkages may also be mapped based on the nodal region algorithm (or single linkage analysis) by which only the largest flow link of each node is kept in the graph (see also Appendices 20-1 and 20-2 for an overview of the ranking and geographic distribution of vessel calls and urban population). Such a method helps revealing which nodes centralize flows in a tree graph and eventually the hidden subsystems composing the network. In this analysis, urban area population is taken as the referent metric to map nodes (Figure 20.3), while nodal regions are positioned using a GEM-Frick visualization algorithm in the TULIP software to put major nodes and components at the centre of the figure and less important ones at its periphery. One first observation is that the number of large connected components has decreased from seven in 1951 to two or three in 1990, which underlines both the growing integration of global trade (Feenstra, 1999), and centralization of the global maritime network around fewer pivotal hubs. The latter being an illustration of the declining clustering coefficient observed in Table 20.3.

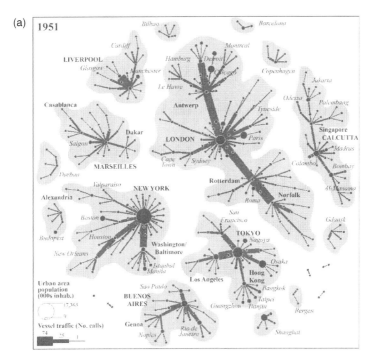

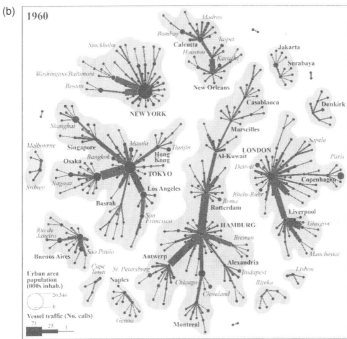

Figure 20.3 Urban centrality and nodal regions in the global maritime network, 1951–90. *(Continued)*

Source: own realization based on data from *Geopolis* and *Lloyd's Shipping Index*.

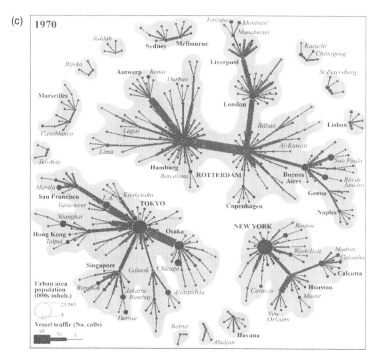

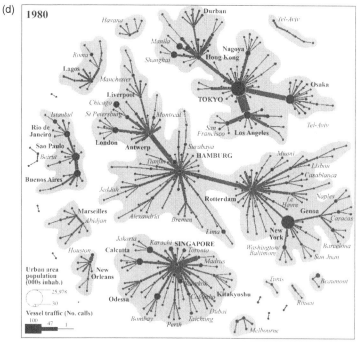

Figure 20.3 (Continued)

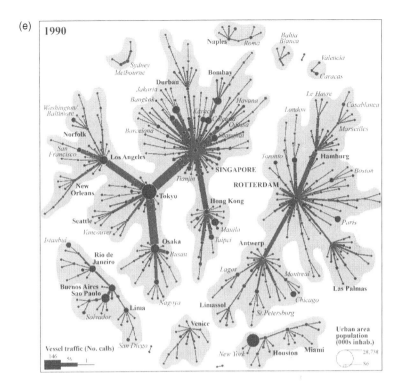

Figure 20.3

A second observation is that the geographic dimension of the components has fundamentally changed through a reinforced regionalization of maritime flows. The hubs of these components tend to gradually restrict their dominance towards geographically close port cities, whereas in the beginning of the period, it was often the case that port cities from different, distant continents were included in the same subgraph. This brings concrete evidence about the shift from a colonial, centre-periphery system to a more polycentric one based on intra-regional freight distribution where the logistical factor had become prominent.

The extent to which larger cities always dominate smaller cities can be discussed based on this analysis. In 1951, the central hubs of the three largest components are also the world's largest port cities, namely London, Tokyo, and New York. It is not a coincidence that exactly these three nodes are titled "global cities" by Sassen (1991) in the title of her masterpiece on the matter, although her essay did not pay much attention to the port and maritime function of these cities per se. These major maritime nodes dominate a large number of other ones through the principle of transitivity, not only in their close vicinity but also through long-distance trade exchanges, such as London directly or indirectly centralizing flows connecting Europe with Africa, Australia, and the Americas.

However, the demographic size of certain port cities is not always reflected by an equivalent position in the maritime network. Some port cities have simply faced trade decline despite their demographic growth, such as Mumbai and Calcutta, following the demise of the British Empire and the 1947 independence, and Buenos Aires, facing internal political tensions that gradually eroded its previous prosperity. The large, global city of Paris (France) being a river port 250 kilometres from the coast has always appeared as a terminal node. This is also the case of the Great Lakes cities, such as Chicago, Toronto, and Detroit, whose maritime accessibility is hampered by the necessary passage through the St. Lawrence Seaway before reaching international sea routes. Conversely, port cities, such as Kuwait City or Basrah, in 1960 enjoyed a strong nodal position regardless of their smaller urban size mostly due to the boom of oil business in the Middle East. But the most impressive example of this gap is the outstanding centrality of Antwerp and Rotterdam in the European component, especially since 1970, despite a relatively minor urban dimension compared with other world port cities, as they became Europe's largest gateways and still occupy this role nowadays, together with Hamburg, the latter being three times larger by its population. The same phenomenon occurred in Asia, where Singapore and Hong Kong, which are still large cities, gradually became the major hub ports for a number of even larger cities such as Bangkok, Jakarta, Shanghai, and Karachi. The latter ports became constrained by urban growth as shipping lines centralized their networks upon a few, strategically located transhipment nodes. London and New York have become minor ports in the network by 1990, despite their urban size and the volume of their traffic, due to the reorientation of major trunk lines towards external hub ports in North Europe and the Caribbean, respectively. With the exception of Tokyo, Osaka, Sao Paulo, and Los Angeles, most of the largest cities have become somewhat peripheral in the maritime network of 1990.

Another reason is the influence of political events and transitions, as seen with the isolation of the Barcelona, Bilbao, and Shanghai components in 1951, their respective governments having imposed trade barriers with the outside world at the time (i.e. during the regimes of Franco and Mao). However, Shanghai integrated the larger Tokyo component through Singapore in 1960 and Hong Kong in 1970. Perhaps, the isolation of the Alexandria (Egypt) component can be explained by the imminent revolution of 1952. Other examples include the Kiel–Murmansk dyad in 1960 in a context of the Cold War, and the Tel-Aviv–Haifa (Israel) component in 1970 and 1980 that did not include neighbouring ports until becoming part of the larger Venice component in 1980. This is also the case for Beirut–Lattakia in 1970 and 1980 before and during the civil war, and of Havana (Cuba) connecting principally Cuban ports, Rostock (East Germany), and Varna (Bulgaria) in 1970 also reflecting upon the Cold War era. In 1980, Havana still stands apart but has one connexion with Vigo in Spain, and although it integrated the larger Singapore component in 1990, it was through Odessa (Ukraine) as part of the USSR trading system.

Another observed factor is the persistence of specialized long-distance linkages such as those based on maintained colonial ties, as seen with the Dunkirk component in 1951 comprising Le Havre, Brest, Bordeaux together with colonial ports (Madagascar, Vietnam, Benin, Congo, and Senegal) and the Lisbon component in 1951, 1960, and 1970 including Porto, Angolese, and Guinea-Bissau ports. To some extent, the Marseilles component that remains isolated until 1990 may be placed in this category, since it has a relatively smaller size than the largest components and mostly includes French and African ports, reflecting upon the somewhat independent French trading system. Lastly, the isolation of certain smaller components from the larger ones may also be caused by coastal morphology and geographic proximity. It is the case of the North Adriatic component of Rijeka–Trieste–Venice in 1960, of the Southern African component Cape Town–Durban in 1951 and 1960. The Sydney–Melbourne component has always been apart from 1951 to 1990. Numerous other intra-European components fall in this category based on specialized intra-regional trades.

Port-urban trajectories

This research can potentially shed more light on the long-term evolution of port cities. The selection of a few examples is a first step in such a direction. The analysis benefited from the inclusion of additional urban data drawn from the *Populstat* database, still at the level of urban areas rather than the sole administrative unit. Comparing urban population and maritime traffic, Figure 20.4 shows that the number of vessel calls and inhabitants of London underwent various trends over the period: opposite growth (1890–1905), parallel growth (1905–20), opposite growth (1920–40), and reverse growth (1965–2008), the latter being defined by both traffic and population decline. As mentioned in the methodological section, there has

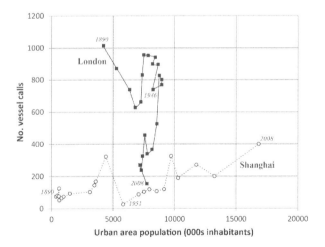

Figure 20.4 Port-urban trajectory of London and Shanghai, 1890–2008.

Source: own elaboration.

Appendix 20.1 Top 30 urban areas by the number of vessel calls, 1950–90

Rank	1951		1960		1970		1980		1990	
1	London	799	Hamburg	889	Rotterdam	941	Rotterdam	1,130	Singapore	1,718
2	Rotterdam	741	London	863	Hamburg	918	Singapore	993	Rotterdam	1,114
3	New York	698	Rotterdam	851	Tokyo	905	Hamburg	872	Tokyo	989
4	Antwerp	633	New York	718	London	586	Tokyo	839	Antwerp	758
5	Hampton Rds	520	Tokyo	599	New York	585	Antwerp	772	Hamburg	644
6	Liverpool	517	Antwerp	597	Antwerp	582	New Orleans	748	Hong Kong	602
7	Hamburg	380	Liverpool	488	Osaka	555	Osaka	458	Osaka	593
8	Tokyo	379	Osaka	399	Singapore	445	New York	414	New Orleans	578
9	Baltimore	348	New Orleans	372	New Orleans	426	Jeddah	384	Los Angeles	456
10	Buenos Aires	338	Buenos Aires	351	Liverpool	390	Los Angeles	371	Houston	312
11	Calcutta	275	Houston	339	Houston	357	Hong Kong	362	Las Palmas	301
12	Portland	272	Hampton Rds	335	Hampton Rds	357	London	357	Bangkok	285
13	Houston	262	Kuwait City	327	Genoa	335	Houston	335	Odessa	284
14	Amsterdam	257	Genoa	319	Hong Kong	311	Lagos	311	Vancouver	277
15	New Orleans	246	Calcutta	301	Vancouver	286	Marseille	286	London	273
16	Al-Kuwayt	235	Baltimore	278	Buenos Aires	276	Gdansk	276	Kaohsiung	268

Appendix 20.1

Rank	1951		1960		1970		1980		1990	
17	Marseille	234	Bremen	277	San Francisco	276	Alexandria	293	Nagoya	263
18	Los Angeles	229	Amsterdam	276	Marseille	274	Buenos Aires	292	Marseille	262
19	Genoa	229	Singapore	270	Gdansk	272	Vancouver	290	Constanta	252
20	Le Havre	201	Montreal	267	Los Angeles	252	Bremen	276	Durban	242
21	Glasgow	199	Vancouver	245	Cape Town	251	Basrah	275	New York	236
22	Tyneside	197	Los Angeles	239	Durban	250	Constanta	253	Mumbai	226
23	Montreal	191	Copenhagen	224	Lisbon	244	Lisbon	252	Hampton Rds	226
24	San Francisco	189	Glasgow	222	Kuwait City	239	Las Palmas	243	Pusan	210
25	Copenhagen	188	Hong Kong	216	Calcutta	233	Mumbai	235	Gdansk	206
26	Hull	185	Portland	210	Bremen	230	Hampton Rds	234	Le Havre	204
27	Bremen	184	San Francisco	199	Las Palmas	225	Genoa	231	Jeddah	197
28	Seattle	179	Gdansk	198	Portland	212	Odessa	224	San Francisco	188
29	Singapore	170	Hull	194	Kitakyushu	212	Le Havre	218	Shanghai	188
30	Sydney	168	Marseille	184	Baltimore	206	Durban	214	Alexandria	185

Note: The following short names for urban areas are in parentheses: Norfolk/Portsmouth VA (Hampton Roads), Megalopolis Central (New York), Los Angeles/Riverside/Oxnard (Los Angeles), Megalopolis South (Washington/Baltimore), Liverpool/Birkenhead (Liverpool).

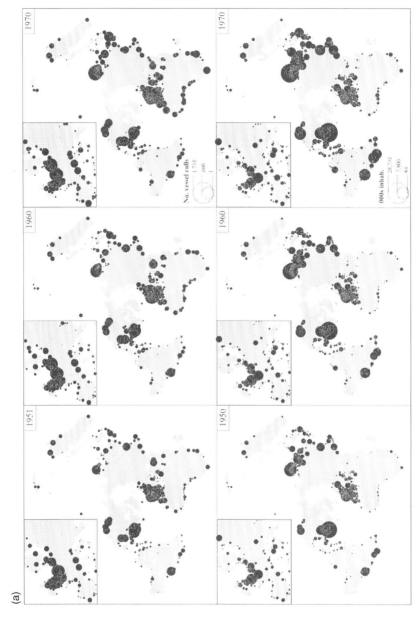

Appendix 20.2 World distribution of vessel calls and population by urban area, 1950–90.

(b)

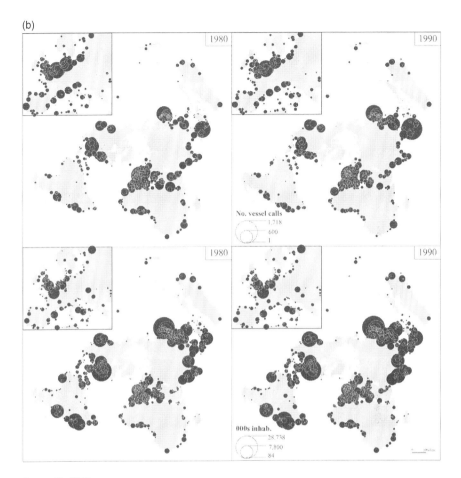

Appendix 20.2

been a rapid traffic shift towards modern terminals situated outside the urban core, alongside drastic waterfront redevelopments in the Dockland area. Nevertheless, welcoming ever-bigger ships had led to a decreasing number of port calls, due to increasing ship size, while a large proportion of UK traffic became rerouted via Benelux ports and notably Rotterdam, as seen in Figure 20.3. Such factors can explain at least partly London's traffic evolution. But at the same time, London's population has also shrunk over time, in similar ways than traffic, although the two evolutions may not be directly interdependent. Population stagnation or decline in large Western cities is a general phenomenon that is caused by wider demographic trends such as ageing and urban sprawl.

In the case of Shanghai, the determination coefficient over the whole period remains moderately significant (45 percent), but it is much higher when splitting the period in two, namely 1890–1946 (76 percent) and 1951–2008 (73 percent). In 1949, a major political change occurred, namely the proclamation of the People's Republic of China, causing a drastic traffic decline, which recovered in accordance with the urban system. Contrary to the general belief that China as a whole was closed to international trade under the Mao rule, port activity resumed rather rapidly in the 1960s, while the spatial distribution of maritime traffic again overlapped the urban hierarchy of coastal port cities. This was also demonstrated by Wang and Ducruet (2013) in their analysis of Chinese port tonnage over the period 1868–2010, which was based on customs and ministry data, the conclusion being that there was a strong resilience of the port system to political disturbances. The direct impact of China's official opening to foreign investment and international trade in 1978, known as the Open Door Policy led by Deng Xiaoping, is clearly illustrated by rapid traffic growth between 1975 and 1980. Urban population, fed by massive internal migration from rural areas, has grown steadily since then, backed by ongoing industrialization (Wang and Ducruet, 2012).

Conclusion

The link between port and city had often been analyzed at the intra-urban level in previous research, where the separation process, both physical and functional, had been most visible. Expanding the analysis at the urban area level for the period 1950–90, through a systematic quantitative approach of hundreds of port cities, allowed the confirmation of a growing disarticulation between the global urban hierarchy and the global maritime network. Yet, the magnitude of urban development remains an essential factor to explain maritime traffic distribution across the globe, notwithstanding the rise of less-urbanized hub ports and the influence of other factors such as site constraints, political contexts, and the changing pattern of trade routes. This first-ever dynamic and global analysis of combined maritime and urban data from a network perspective could, at least, fill this gap in the related urban and transport literature, which was still very much monographic or focused on other types of networks.

Further research shall concentrate on refining the statistical approach to port-city evolution, by applying more sophisticated tests on maritime and urban time series data, especially to check the direction of their mutual influence, and the possible regional logic behind such an influence. This will necessitate to fully exploiting the potential of the *Populstat* database for all cities, which goes back to the nineteenth century and extends the time coverage up to the 2000s. Including more many smaller cities and urban areas will inevitably improve the results in terms of global port-city correlation, traffic distribution, and evolution. The analysis of port-urban trajectories should be expanded so as to check whether comparable trends can be extracted and compared. In particular, certain properties such as assortativity or clustering may translate subsequent industrial and regional changes, such as the emergence of hub-and-spokes systems in liner shipping and the prolonged Asian growth.

Acknowledgements

The research leading to these results has received funding from the European Research Council under the European Union's Seventh Framework Programme (FP/2007-2013)/ERC Grant Agreement n. [313847] "World Seastems."

Note

1 The synthesis provided by the OECD (2014) on port-city development included a figure showing the relationship between inland cities and coastal ports, distinguishing amongst independent metropolis (large port city far away from an inland core), short-range corridor (coastal and inland cities belong to the same morphological area), long-range corridor (port city under the shadow of the inland city within a 200 km radius), and dependent satellite (large inland city near a minor port city). The four possible types of spatial configuration were discussed in terms of self-agglomeration or lock-in effects based on the model of Fujita and Mori (1996) about the development of port cities.

References

Bird J. (1963) *The Major Seaports of the United Kingdom*. London: Hutchinson.
Cattan N. (1995) Barrier effects: the case of air and rail flows. *International Political Science Review* 16(3): 237–48.
Choi J.H., Barnett J.A., Chon B.S. (2006) Comparing world city networks: a network analysis of Internet backbone and air transport intercity linkages. *Global Networks* 6(1): 81–99.
Dobruszkes F., Lennert M., Van Hamme G. (2011) An analysis of the determinants of air traffic volume for European metropolitan areas. *Journal of Transport Geography* 19(4): 755–62.
Dogan M. (1988) Giant cities as maritime gateways. In: Dogan M., Kasarda J.D. (Eds), *The Metropolis Era: A World of Giant Cities*, London : Sage Publications, pp. 30–55.
Ducruet C. (2011) The port city in multidisciplinary analysis. In: Alemany J., Brutomesso R. (Eds), *The Port City of the XXIth Century: New Challenges in the Relationship between Port and City*, Venice: RETE Association & International Centre for Cities on Water, pp. 32–48.
Ducruet C., Beauguitte L. (2014) Network science and spatial science: review and outcomes of a complex relationship. *Networks and Spatial Economics*, 14(3–4): 297–316.
Ducruet C., Itoh H. (2015) Regions and material flows: Investigating the regional branching and industry relatedness of port traffic in a global perspective. *Journal of Economic Geography* (forthcoming).
Ducruet C., Lee S.W. (2006) Frontline soldiers of globalisation: port-city evolution and regional competition. *Geojournal* 67(2): 107–22.
Ducruet C., Lugo I. (2013) Cities and transport networks in shipping and logistics research. *Asian Journal of Shipping and Logistics*, 29(2): 149–170.
Ducruet C., Lee S.W., Ng A.K.Y. (2011a) Port competition and network polarization at the East Asian maritime corridor. *Territoire en Mouvement*, 10: 60–74.
Feenstra R.C. (1999) Integration of trade and disintegration of production in the global economy. *The Journal of Economic Perspectives*, 12(4): 31–50.
Fujita M., Mori T. (1996) The role of ports in the making of major cities: Self-agglomeration and hub-effect. *Journal of Development Economics*, 49(1): 93–120.
Guerrero D., Proulhac L. (2014) Freight flows and urban hierarchy. *Research in Transportation Business and Management* 11: 105–15.
Hall P.V., Hesse M. (2012) *Cities, Regions and Flows*. Abingdon: Routledge.

Hall P.V., Jacobs W. (2012) Why are maritime ports (still) urban, and why should policy makers care? *Maritime Policy and Management* 39(2): 189–206.

Hesse M. (2010) Cities, material flows and the geography of spatial interaction: urban places in the system of chains. *Global Networks*, 10(1): 75–91.

Hesse M. (2013) Cities and flows: re-asserting a relationship as fundamental as it is delicate. *Journal of Transport Geography*, 29: 33–42.

Hoyle B.S. (1989) The port-city interface: trends, problems, and examples. *Geoforum* 20(4): 429–35.

Jacobs W., Ducruet C., De Langen P.W. (2010) Integrating world cities into production networks: the case of port cities. *Global Networks* 10(1): 92–113.

Jacobs W., Hall P.V., Koster H.R.A. (2011) The location and global network structure of maritime advanced producer services. *Urban Studies* 48(13): 2749–69.

Kidwai A.H. (1989) Port cities in a national system of ports and cities: a geographical analysis of India in the 20th century. In: Broeze F. (Ed), *Brides of the Sea: Port Cities of Asia from the 16th–20th Centuries*, Honolulu: University of Hawaii Press, pp. 207–22.

Lahmeyer J. (2006) Population statistics. Growth of the population per country in a historical perspective, including their administrative divisions and principal towns. An online resource available at www.populstat.info [accessed 7 June 2015].

Lee S.W., Song D.W., Ducruet C. (2008) A tale of Asia's world ports: the spatial evolution in global hub port cities. *Geoforum* 39: 372–85.

Moriconi-Ebrard F. (1994) *Geopolis: Pour Comparer les Villes du Monde*. Paris: Anthropos.

Murphey R. (1989) On the evolution of the port city. In: Broeze F. (Ed), *Brides of the Sea: Port Cities of Asia from the 16th–20th Centuries*, Honolulu: University of Hawaii Press, pp. 223–45.

Neal Z.P. (2011) The causal relationship between employment and business networks in US cities. *Journal of Urban Affairs* 33(2): 167–84.

Newman M.E.J. (2002) Assortative mixing in networks. *Physical Review Letters*, 89: 208701.

Ng A.K.Y., Ducruet C., Jacobs W., Monios J., Notteboom T.E., Rodrigue J.P., Slack B., Tam K.C., Wilmsmeier G. (2014) Port geography at the crossroads with human geography: Between flows and spaces. *Journal of Transport Geography*, 41: 84–96.

Norcliffe G., Bassett K., Hoare T. (1996) The emergence of postmodernism on the urban waterfront: geographical perspectives on changing relationships. *Journal of Transport Geography*, 4(2): 123–34.

O'Connor K. (1987) The location of services involved with international trade. *Environment and Planning A*, 19(5): 687–700.

O'Connor K. (1989) Australian ports, metropolitan areas and trade-related services. *Australian Geographer*, 20(2): 167–72.

OECD (2014) *The Competitiveness of Global Port-Cities*. Paris: OECD Publishing.

Rozenblat C. (2010) Opening the black box of agglomeration economies for measuring cities' competitiveness through international firm networks. *Urban Studies*, 47(13): 2841–65.

Sassen S. (1991) *The Global City: New York, London, Tokyo*. Princeton: Princeton University Press.

Slack B. (1989) Port services, ports and the urban hierarchy. *Tijdschrift voor Economische en Sociale Geografie*, 80(4): 236–43.

Steck B. (1995) Les villes portuaires dans le réseau urbain français. *Proceedings of the Colloquium Vivre et Habiter La Ville Portuaire*, 12–14 October 1994, Paris, Rouen, Le Havre: Plan Construction et Architecture, pp. 101–11.

Taylor P.J. (2012) The challenge facing world city network analysis. *Globalisation and World Cities Research Bulletin*, 409. Available online at www.lboro.ac. uk/gawc/rb/rb409.html [accessed 7 June 2015].

Wang C., Ducruet C. (2012) New port development and global city making: emergence of the Shanghai–Yangshan multilayered gateway-hub. *Journal of Transport Geography*, 25: 58–69.

Wang C., Ducruet C. (2013) Regional resilience and spatial cycles: long-term evolution of the Chinese port system (221BC–2010AD). *Tijdschrift voor Economische en Sociale Geografie*, 104(5): 524–38.

Wang J., Mo H., Wang F., Jin F. (2011) Exploring the network structure and nodal centrality of China's air transport network: a complex network approach. *Journal of Transport Geography* 19(4): 712–721.

Afterword

This book reminds us that it may be altogether too easy to take the notion of maritime networks, or port systems or maritime systems for granted; rather, it demonstrates that the academic literature points to an exceptional richness of alternative perspectives and a depth of analysis and research that are worthy of more serious analysis. It is easy to be fascinated by accounts in the text of Venice's maritime trade in the middle ages; or of the archaeological records of inter-island links in the Aegean Sea; but the challenge in understanding contemporary network structures and dynamics is real and important. The book is a comprehensive handbook for researchers, teachers, policy makers and those with maritime interests of one sort or another.

On a personal note I have been surprised but also delighted to acknowledge the significance attributed to my earlier PhD thesis – and in so doing appreciate the editor's considerable forensic skills as well as his insights into thinking about the explanatory frameworks that emerged almost a half-century ago.

In this brief afterword I take the view that our understanding of maritime networks has been something of a moving target – phased in its timing and adjusting from local and proximate networks to dynamic, rapidly transforming global and globally-aligned supply chains in a relatively short time span. Clearly, the increasing reach of rapidly metamorphosing container shipping alliances – with increasing ship sizes, higher levels of operational efficiency and rapid deployment and re-deployment patterns (and their equally rapid adjustments in ancillary (and feeder networks) – have become centre-stage in macro-spatial and macro-analytical perspectives. This perspective is, of course, somewhat focused; it is essentially a strategic framework and strategic planning – which we tend to do rather badly – is up-front. But it may be worth a short note here to suggest that this particular view of maritime networks is only one view of many if we conceptualise maritime networks in a rigorous though somewhat broader framework. Consider, then, that maritime networks (though variously defined) are usefully conceptualised as *artefacts* – simply, devices or contrivances. Alternately, they may be usefully seen as *constructs* – in a fabrication of separate objects, a new thing having a definite shape and adopted for a desired purpose. By convention, the researcher defines it as fit-for-purpose, as a framework within which to demonstrate a particular notion of reality. This framework allows, I think, for a rich – though necessarily rigorously analytical framework – for maritime networks. It enables a view of the way in which the artefact or construct modifies or changes or transforms through time and to that extent is useful in this context.

In the following discussion I reflect on 'the moves in a moving target' over the last 50 years or so as I have been involved in them – though often, I suspect, not appreciating the subtleties of change or indeed the broader paradigm shifts taking place. It is, therefore, a somewhat idiosyncratic view; others may see the changes differently.

Conceptual frames in a moving target; maritime networks over 50 years

It was my exceptional privilege, as a young and enthusiastic graduate researcher, to meet and talk with James Bird when he visited the University of New England in Australia in the late 1960s. From the University of London, he had just completed his major study on the port of London – and though I knew little about the port this seemed a fascinating, way to deal with the geography of a port. In later work, his *Anyport* model clarified how ports grew and how they competed – but his work set in place a morphological perspective of ports arranged along a linear coastline and obviously important hinterland links. Others underscored the importance of landside linkages; and Peter Rimmer, looking at New Zealand's ports, underlined the critical importance in that setting of shipping services and linkages. Somewhat later, the sometimes tedious debate about forelands and hinterlands at least underlined the notion that port growth was probably related to foreland as much as to hinterland dynamics.

Frame 1: Here was the default setting for ports and maritime nets in the 1960s and the thinking influenced considerable research effort.

For me, a graduate fellowship at the University of British Columbia in the late 1960s provided an exceptional opportunity to pursue ideas about how ports grew – at least, how they grew and competed in the Pacific northwest. In this particular context the ports, and the shipping serving them, seemed not to fit linear coastlines and hinterlands appeared less complex in their linkages. Observation suggested that ports might grow and compete because they were locked into shipping networks – into topological rather than topographical networks that might be seen as existing in dimensionless space. A graph theoretic framework – and connectivity, connectedness, Markovian theory describing movement and the structuring of space in a regional science perspective seemed to offer new insights into port growth and competition. Clearly, the network was dominated by the port of Vancouver and growth spinoffs were critical.

> Frame 2: Ports as points in aspatial maritime networks conceptualised an alternative construct of maritime networks that could reveal underlying spatial structures and drivers of port growth and competition.

In the event, the PhD research at the University of British Columbia was focused not only on local network linkages and the dominance of the port of Vancouver but also on a much wider and more strategic issue that was being driven by the emerging pressures of containerisation. Particularly, the port of Vancouver was locked into the question of whether or not the new trans-Pacific container services from Hong Kong and Singapore would focus on Canadian exports and imports onto the port of Vancouver or onto Montreal and US ports via the Panama canal.

> Frame 3: The emergent reality was that port networks at one scale were embedded in networks at a different scale; and the dynamics of port growth and competition became at once more complex, more global and in due course were impacted by a constantly adjusting shipping industry and the way it conducted its business.

In due course PhD studies at the University of British Columbia concluded; and for me an invitation to join the new Port Research Team at UNCTAD in Geneva and an opportunity to use the earlier research to support a simulation and optimisation model aimed at improving port efficiency was too enticing a 'post-doctoral' experience to forego. The new paradigm was 'port efficiency' – in any or most of its meanings – but certainly including operational, cost, pricing and investment efficiency; and, given a simulation framework, the critical message of the interdependence of system actions and reactions.

> Frame 4: The 'efficiency bubble' had begun – and though not attributable only to Geneva, shipping lines had much to gain from efficient ports and nets.

Over a decade, global and regional containerisation continued apace and posed severe problems for developed and developing countries. I was fortunate in being involved in directing the Port Development Program for UNESCAP in Bangkok over a period of five years. The 'efficiency bubble' was alive and well – but efficiency lost its sharp edge of operational and mechanical efficiency and managers and others began to see the need for a much more inclusive view of efficiency.

Fast forward now to the turn of the century and to 2015. Maritime and port networks still exist and ports grow and compete – but are there not fundamental processes forcing a new conceptual framework yet again? There are; for over the last decade 'the maritime sector has increasingly been considered a part of a wider international logistics industry that supports, contributes to, and represents an integral element of, global supply chains' (Cullinane, 2010: 1). Clearly this offers a more macroscopic perspective and suggests that the competitive position of ports is under threat without a careful analysis and understanding of this wider context. Further, the insight that ports are embedded in often complex matrices of supply chains suggest that decision makers will need to 'understand the architecture and dynamics of port-linked supply chains in order to adequately define the functionality of the port' (Cullinane, 2010: 1). In effect, 'the emergence of new value pools in globalising supply chains requires new thinking about port development strategies' (Cullinane, 2010: 2).

Frame 5: Ports are elements in value-driven chains; and 'it is the chain…that delivers value to the customer and the customer's customer' (Robinson, 2002). Effective value analysis embedded in effective business models with high levels of business process integration in the chain will underlie the new maritime networks. These are big steps requiring much deeper understanding of business strategy, of chain structuring, architecture and dynamics, of strategic management and planning (Robinson, 2010).

Ross Robinson
Victoria University

References

Cullinane, K. (2010) *International Handbook of Maritime Business*, Cheltenham: Edward Elgar.

Robinson, R. (2002) Ports as elements in value-driven chain systems: the new paradigm, *Maritime Policy and Management*, 29(3), 241–55.

Robinson, R. (2010) Business models supply chain efficiency and port efficiency: new strategic imperatives. In: Cullinane, K., *International Handbook of Maritime Business*, Cheltenham: Edward Elgar, pp. 13–37.

Index